PANDORA'S BOX OPENED

D1596481

Pandora's Box Opened

An Examination and Defense of
Historical-Critical Method and
Its Master Practitioners

Roy A. Harrisville

WILLIAM B. EERDMANS PUBLISHING COMPANY
GRAND RAPIDS, MICHIGAN / CAMBRIDGE, U.K.

Published 2014 by

Wm. B. Eerdmans Publishing Co.

2140 Oak Industrial Drive N.E., Grand Rapids, Michigan 49505 /

P.O. Box 163, Cambridge CB3 9PU U.K.

Printed in the United States of America

20 19 18 17 16 15 14   7 6 5 4 3 2 1

Library of Congress Cataloging-in-Publication Data

Harrisville, Roy A.

Pandora's box opened: an examination and defense of historical-critical method
and its master practitioners / Roy Harrisville.

pages   cm

Includes bibliographical references and index.

ISBN 978-0-8028-6980-7 (pbk.: alk. paper)

1. Bible — Hermeneutics.

2. Bible — Criticism, interpretation, etc.

I. Title.

BS476.H285   2014

220.6'7 — dc23

2014003478

www.eerdmans.com

Contents

Preface

For many, the critical method as applied to Bible interpretation has released a host of threats to Christian faith and confession. It is no secret that the method was first given birth by those who were hostile to the Bible's authority or were anxious to demonstrate its inability to function as sole criterion of faith and morals. For others, the critical method has proved to be a failure, due principally to the assumption that diachronic, linear research could master any and all of the questions and problems attendant on interpretation. It is no secret that many who used the method did so in the expectation that it would guarantee a status equal to that of other scientific disciplines. Still others believed that the method, shorn of its unwarranted arrogance, could be harnessed in service to the gospel, thus rendering it a reliable resource for Bible interpretation and proclamation of the Good News.

Apart from a glance at ancient "thumbnail history" and the precritical Reformation period, four chapters of this book are devoted to the emergence and use of the critical method. In these chapters no attempt has been made to separate critics who believed use of the method diminished biblical authority from those who believed it enhanced it. The result is a congeries, a "Duke's mixture" of interpreters. More, since not everyone undertaking an interpretation of the Bible makes specific reference to the method underlying it, restriction to those who have done so has necessarily resulted in a company of strange bed-fellows. Bengel and Flacius, Spinoza and Baumgarten, Semler and Ewald are hardly twins. Books and articles written on many of the scholars and interpreters listed here omit their attitude toward the Bible or its interpretation. For this reason the appearance of some and the absence of others may strike the reader as odd. More yet, some of the selection has been purely subjective, due to interest in this or that personage, to the effect that the only thing each cluster of researchers and scholars share is the period, and roughly the period, in which they lived. The impression to be left with the reader is that use of the method and its users comprises a "Pandora's Box," containing all the methodological vagaries of the generations, and when opened bringing "a myriad other pains," though, as per the ancient myth, one item, that of hope, remains:

> Only [Hope] remained there in the unbreakable home under the mouth of the storage jar, and did not fly out; for before that could happen [Pandora] closed the lid of the storage jar, by the plans of the aegis-holder, the cloud-gatherer, Zeus.[1]

Commencing with Jonathan Edwards in the eighteenth century and leading up to the various university divinity schools in the twentieth, American attention to critical method appears slim when matched against European preoccupation with it. One reason is that Americans came late to use of the method. If not the first, certainly Moses Stuart of Yale was among the first to publicize the method as used in Europe. But there were other reasons for the minimal attention given to the critical method in this country. For some, until Stuart's time at least, criticism European-style smacked of the "sere remains of foreign harvests." Later, for others, such as Shailer Mathews of Chicago, use of the historical-critical method was a thing to be jettisoned, a baggage that only impeded movement. In any case, American reading of the Bible assumed another form. The so-called pragmatic approach, that is, pitching a method of whatever sort to instruction and preaching, had the upper hand, a use decried by more than one across the Atlantic. To cite just one:

> When exegesis from the outset is oriented to the furthering of proclamation, it can easily lead to prior interests giving too short shrift to the total content of the New Testament. . . . The principal, programmatic mixture of exegesis and proclamation is perilous. One best avoids this danger when one preserves the independence of Bible research.[2]

---

1. Hesiod, *Works and Days,* trans. Glenn W. Most, Loeb Classical Library (Cambridge, Mass.: Harvard University Press, 2006), pp. 95, 96-99.

2. Edvin Larsson, "Notwendigkeit und Grenze der historisch-kritischen Methode," in *Schrift und Auslegung,* ed. Heinrich Kraft (Erlangen: Martin Luther Verlag, 1987), p. 116.

A page or two later, the same author wrote that "exegesis as a theological discipline, as an area of research may not be involved in the work of actualization."[3] The "principal, programmatic mixture" was an American phenomenon. For this reason, among Americans involved in Bible interpretation, only a few such as Henry Joel Cadbury of Harvard, Frank Porter of Yale, and Otto Piper of Princeton, devoted space to methodology. In any case, whether this or the other side of the Atlantic, the particular theological persuasion of a given scholar or critic is given attention here only insofar as it is reflected in that scholar's use of historical method. This should help to explain the lesser space given to American scholarship.

Following a summing up of the various uses of the critical method on the part of its advocates, attention is given the malaise come over the method, a condition that persists to this moment. "Ten thousand times ten thousand" are the voices that challenge or dismiss the historical-critical method. The synchronic is thrown against the diachronic, orality against textuality, the text against authorial intent, the intra-textual against the referential, reader-response against text autonomy, feminist against patriarchal interpretation, and so on and on. The critical method brought with it a certain uniformity and order. It was as if the community of scholars held membership in a communion in which the liturgy was the same wherever one worshiped. The language, if not shared by all, the assumptions, if not held by all, were nonetheless known and familiar to all. One could step into the method and feel at home. In a sense, the entire affair was a kind of microcosm of the Middle Ages, in which a single conceptuality reigned and facilitated communicating ideas without having to clear the air of alien assumptions. "Everything [was] in its place, and [there was] a place for everything." Now, that "mainline denomination," that uniform and ordered method of interpretation, has all the aspects of a battlefield strewn with its dead.

It may be small comfort to a Hegel or a Baur that there is not a man alive or dead who is or ever has been capable of getting at the "big picture," that the scholar must be content with the sight of smaller chains of cause and effect, tinier continua. The alleged demise of the method may give considerable comfort to someone persuaded of its evils due to the presuppositions to which it has allegedly been shackled. But comfort small or great, the historical question will not down, it will not go away, so that despite the now glaringly obvious limitations of the method the researcher must somehow, in some way, give it attention.

3. Larsson, "Notwendigkeit und Grenze der historisch-kritischen Methode," p. 124.

The last, eleventh chapter, is devoted to commending the method, now downsized, shorn of its arrogance. However well or poorly stated, the conviction expressed is that despite the evils its opening has visited on biblical interpretation, in Pandora's box there is still a hope remaining. True enough, it is slight, not enough to guarantee to the one who entertains it a place equal to the other "higher" disciplines, but sufficient to suggest in a methodological way God's having entered into time.

This book has grown from lectures given at Luther Seminary in the spring of 2007, a series arranged for by Kari Bostrom, Luther assistant archivist. To her and the students enrolled in that seminar I owe the stimulus for this attempt. The book is dedicated to Otto A. Piper of blessed memory, Princeton Seminary's Helen P. Manson Professor of New Testament and Exegesis, my doctor-father, who nursed me through my New Testament studies, read every line of my dissertation before its completion, opened his home to me and my new wife, assuaged my grief at the death of my father, directed me to my first parish, planned my postdoctoral research at Tübingen University, correspondence with whom I allowed to lag in callow, selfish youth. Finally, I want to acknowledge my debt to Associate Managing Editor Jennifer Hoffman of the Eerdmans Publishing Co., who kept constant watch over the gestating of this creature, and to Wm. B. Eerdmans, Jr., for allowing it to live.

ROY A. HARRISVILLE

CHAPTER ONE

Ancient Thumbnail History

Hermes and Homer

Before the Old and New Testaments were written, text interpretation had enjoyed a long life. It may all have begun with the Greeks, who were repelled by the all-too human antics of the Olympian gods in Homer's epics and ventured to rehabilitate them by way of allegory. The observation that by this method the Greeks were deliberately reading something into Homer is incorrect. For them the *Iliad* and *Odyssey* were a universally recognized authority that contained but one truth. Homer himself had given license to allegorizing when he transformed Hermes, god of life, symbolized by the phallus capping those old stone heaps *(herma)* that resisted the plow, into a glorious youth who carried messages to humans from the gods above. In this guise the god appears, for example, in Plato's *Symposium*:

> "And what is that, Diotima?" "A great spirit, Socrates: for the whole of the spiritual is between divine and mortal." "Possessing what power?" I asked. "Interpreting and transporting human things to the gods and divine things to men; entreaties and sacrifices from below, and ordinances and requitals from above: being midway between, it makes each to supplement the other, so that the whole is combined in one. Through it are conveyed all divination and priest-craft concerning sacrifice and ritual and incantations, and all soothsaying and sorcery."[1]

1. Plato, *Symposium,* 202E, trans. W. R. M. Lamb, Loeb Classical Library (Cambridge, Mass.: Harvard University Press, 1961), p. 179.

It was this Hermes, scrubbed and cleaned, who would give his name to the practice of interpretation *(hermeneuein),*[2] and with whom the apostle Paul would be identified by the citizens of Lystra in Acts.

> In Lystra there was a man sitting who could not use his feet and had never walked. . . . And Paul, looking at him intently and seeing that he had faith to be healed, said in a loud voice, "Stand upright on your feet." And the man sprang up and began to walk. When the crowds saw what Paul had done, they shouted in the Lycaonian language, "The gods have come down to us in human form!" Barnabas they called Zeus, and Paul they called Hermes, because he was the chief speaker. (Acts 14:8-12)

Before Christ, when syncretism was in vogue, Hermes had been fused with the Egyptian Thoth, "scribe of the gods" or "lord of divine words," celebrated for bringing humans their trustiest weapon or *eruma,*[3] the *logos,* word of speech and understanding. In a hodgepodge of oriental and Greek religious literature called the *Hermetica* appears "Thrice-Greatest Hermes," whose cult persisted into the post-Christian era and gave the nascent Christian community a considerable run for its money.

Although Plato nursed considerable distaste for Homer's stories of the gods and their allegorical interpretation, for many Greeks the "reading" of Homer went beyond allegorization. For the philosophically minded, metaphysical insights lay beneath whatever allegory disclosed. Note, for example, Aristotle's interpretation of the *Iliad's* story of Zeus's summons of the gods to a tug of war in support of his theory of the Unmoved Mover:

> Must there, then, or must there not, be something immovable and at rest outside that which is moved and forming no part of it? And must

---

2. See, for example, Plato's reference in *Ion* to the poet as the *hermeneus* of the gods, whose task is "to proclaim," "to expound," or "to interpret," as well as use of the verb *hermeneuein* to denote explanation in 1 Cor. 12:10, 30; 14:5, 13, 26-28. In Luke 24:27 (the Emmaus event), the term with a prepositional prefix added means "to expound the scripture." See Plato, *Ion,* 534C, trans. W. R. M. Lamb, Loeb Classical Library (Cambridge, Mass.: Harvard University Press, 1962), p. 423.

3. In terms of etymology, there are only short steps from *herma* (stone heaps) to the *eruma* (humans' trustiest weapon, i.e., the *logos*), to *Hermes* (messenger of the gods), to *hermeneuein* (to proclaim, to expound, to interpret), and the *Hermetica.*

this be true also of the universe? For it would perhaps seem strange if the origin of motion were inside. And so to those who hold this view Homer's words would seem appropriate.

> Nay, ye could never pull down to the earth from the summit of
>   heaven
> Zeus, the highest of all, no, not if ye toiled to the utmost.
> Come, ye gods and ye goddesses all, set your hands to the
>   hawsers.[4]

Halakhah and Haggadah

In Jesus' time and forever after on every Sabbath in every Jewish synagogue one of fifty-four sections of the Tanakh (Torah, Prophets, and Writings) would be read, analogous to the present lectionary practice of the liturgical denominations. Present Jewish scholarship dates the Tanakh's earliest portions to 500 B.C., and its first five books together with the prophets as constituting a "canon" in 200 B.C. Difficulty emerged when the Torah, regarded by the Jews as revealed by God to Moses on Sinai, thus as holy and unassailable, no longer corresponded to the altered conditions of Jewish life. At this point the Mishnah arose with its dual appeal to the God-given Torah and to oral tradition, likewise revealed at Sinai and given by Moses to the elders of Israel. The latter tradition gave rise to two embattled parties, Pharisees and Sadducees, the former accepting the oral tradition and the latter adhering to the Torah alone.

Since this dual tradition required application to contemporary Jewish life, a system of exposition and interpretation emerged called Midrash, from a Hebrew verb meaning "to investigate," "to expound," or "to interpret." The first of this type to emerge was the Midrash Halakhah, originating in about 200 B.C. and ultimately (exclusively) taken up into the Mishnah. In it all the laws and regulations of the Torah were treated, forming the basis for Jewish religion. The second, later type comprised the Midrash Haggadah, an exposition of biblical narrative by means of stories and legends. The Old Testament pseudepigraphical book of Jubilees, authored ca. 150 B.C., contains halakhic material such as in its rules respecting Sabbath observance:

---

4. Aristotle, "Movement of Animals," trans. E. S. Forster, *Aristotle,* Loeb Classical Library (Cambridge, Mass.: Harvard University Press, 1961), p. 453.

Let the man who does anything on it die. Every man who will profane this day, who will lie with his wife, and whoever will discuss a
matter that he will do on it so that he might make on it a journey for
any buying or selling, and whoever draws water on it, which was not
prepared for him on the sixth day, and whoever lifts up anything that
he will carry to take out of his tent or from his house, let him die.
(Jubilees 50:6-9)[5]

Jubilees also contains haggadic material such as in its portrait of Abram
as an amateur astrologer, able to heed God's command to count the stars:

And in the sixth week, in [the] fifth year, Abram sat up during the night
on the first of the seventh month, so that he might observe the stars
from evening until daybreak so that he might see what the nature of
the year would be with respect to rain. (Jubilees 12:16)[6]

In the so-called rabbinic period beginning with Jerusalem's destruction, the rules of Torah interpretation were combined in a few catalogues
that later came to be expanded. According to tradition, the earliest cat-
alogue includes the seven rules of Rabbi Hillel (110 B.C.-A.D. 10), one of
the two famous teachers in Judaism during the reign of Herod (37-4 B.C.),
the other being his adversary Rabbi Shammai (50 B.C.-A.D. 30). The aim
of Hillel's seven rules was to regulate appeal from one biblical text to the
other, and to ensure that nothing would be added or taken away from the
requirements laid down in the Torah. In the Tannaitic period interpretation was practical and non-allegorical. Only in a later period, that of
the Zohar (thirteenth century A.D.) was there an attempt to uncover the
mysteries beneath the letter. One of the most well-known of Hillel's rules
is the *qal-wachomer,* or in its more familiar Latin form, the *a minore ad
maius,* "from the easy to the hard." The rule reads that a particular conclusion of lighter weight may be applied to a heavier one. A primer on Jewish
religious literature furnishes the following illustration:

A man may not burden the ass of his enemy in such a way that he collapses under the load.

5. *The Old Testament Pseudepigrapha,* ed. James H. Charlesworth, vol. 2 (New York:
Doubleday & Co., 1985), p. 142.
6. Charlesworth, ed., *The Old Testament Pseudepigrapha,* vol. 2, p. 81.

In application of the *qal-wachomer* this means that no one may ever load the ass of his friend.[7] Overall, the rabbis' major interest was legal. They were at home in the letter of the Old Testament, viewed the oral law on a par with the written word, and turned from the oral to the written in order to confirm their views. Their view of scripture was atomistic: every verse, phrase, word could stand by itself as an independent oracle. To the rabbis' skill as jurists was added their imaginative powers as haggadists and preachers. This dialectic method, appropriate to the jurist and casuist concerned with Halakhah, together with an unrestrained fancy in haggadic exposition hindered genuinely historical interpretation of the Old Testament.[8]

Alexandria and Antioch

After the apostles had left the scene, two schools of Bible interpretation emerged, the one from the center of Greek thought in Egyptian Alexandria, the other in the early Christian stronghold of Syrian Antioch. The most celebrated representative of the Alexandrian school was Origen (ca. A.D. 185-254), author of the *Hexapla,* or sixfold Bible, with its translations of the Old Testament in Hebrew, a Greek transliteration of the Hebrew, the Septuagint, and three other Greek translations. Origen's best-known work is entitled *Peri archōn* (Latin: *De principiis*), usually translated in English as *First Principles.* Whatever "principles" Origen may have had in mind, of the Christian faith, of a philosophy of religion, of "principalities and powers," or of the "beginnings" of the universe,[9] the book may be the first to deal with biblical interpretation in any systematic fashion. Taking his cue from Paul's words in 2 Corinthians 3:15-17 and 5:16,[10] Origen likened the Bible to the body, soul, and spirit. To the body corresponded its

---

7. Rosetta C. Musaph-Andriesse, *Von der Tora bis zur Kabbala* (Göttingen: Vandenhoeck & Ruprecht, 1986), p. 30.

8. Frederick C. Grant, *An Introduction to New Testament Thought* (New York: Abingdon-Cokesbury, 1950), pp. 82-84.

9. See Henri de Lubac's introduction to the Torchbook edition of *Origen on First Principles,* trans. G. W. Butterworth (New York: Harper and Row, 1966), p. liii.

10. "To this very day whenever Moses is read, a veil lies over their [the people of Israel's] minds; but when one turns to the Lord, the veil is removed. Now the Lord is the Spirit, and where the Spirit is, there is freedom. . . . From now on, therefore, we regard no one from a human point of view; even though we once knew Christ from a human point of view, we know him no longer in that way."

literal sense, available to those nonetheless unable to perceive the mystery of what had become flesh; to the soul corresponded its psychic meaning, a middle stage from the fleshly understanding toward the spiritual; and to the spirit corresponded its spiritual meaning, comprehended "among the perfect."[11]

Origen's exposition of Proverbs 22:20-21 yields an oft-cited example of his method:

> "Do thou," it says, "portray these things to thyself in counsel and knowledge, so that thou mayest answer words of truth to those who question thee." Each one must therefore portray the meaning of the divine writings in a threefold way upon his own soul; that is, so that the simple may be edified by what we may call the flesh of the scripture, this name being given to the obvious interpretation; while the man who has made some progress may be edified by its soul, as it were; and the man who is perfect and like those mentioned by the apostle ... may be edified by the spiritual law, which has "a shadow of the good things to come."[12]

Many have insisted that Origen regarded only the third or spiritual sense as God's Word and authoritative, thus demeaning the literal sense. But if his reflections on the Bible are to be construed in parallel with what he had to say about the Lord's Supper and the church, then he cannot be seen as dismissing the literal sense but as holding to it as somehow taken up into the spiritual, as "sacramental." For if it is true that Origen held to the incarnation as his one great "principle," the inference may be legitimately drawn that, however inchoate or undeveloped the idea, he viewed the Bible in analogy to the two natures of Christ, the Word enfleshed in the historical, the literal.[13]

The Antiochene School, tracing its origins to a martyred priest named Lucian (d. 312), was celebrated for its rejection of Alexandrian exegesis and concentration on grammatical-historical interpretation. Chief among its members, which included Diodorus of Tarsus (d. ca. 392) and John Chrystostom (A.D. 347-407), was Theodore of Mopsuestia (A.D. 350-

---

11. See *Origen on First Principles*, book 4, chapter 2, 4, pp. 275-76.

12. *Origen on First Principles*, p. 276.

13. See Markus Barth, "Vom Geheimnis der Bibel," *Theologische Existenz Heute*, n.s. 100 (München: Chr. Kaiser Verlag, 1962), pp. 13-15.

428). Representing a feel for the peculiarity of the biblical language and an insistence on interpreting scripture from out of itself, Theodore's commentaries represent the highpoint of Antiochene exegesis. The difference between the Alexandrian appetite for allegory and the Antiochene distaste for it, that is, where not intended by scripture itself, may be illustrated by a comparison of Origen's and Theodore's expositions of Psalm 72, long regarded as a prophecy of Christ and his kingdom.

Origen writes as follows on verses 1, 2, 9, and 11. Verse 1: "Give the king your justice, O God, and your righteousness to a king's son." "Christ is the king, Son of God the king. For this reason he reigns until all his enemies are subjected to him. Then he will hand the kingdom over to God and the Father." Verse 2: "May he judge your people with righteousness, and your poor with justice." "Not all the poor are of God, but those who for standing by Jesus are declared blessed by him." Verse 9: "May his foes bow down before him, and his enemies lick the dust. May the kings of Tarshish and of the isles render him tribute." "I think this indicates the difference with those who come to Christ." Verse 11: "all nations give him service." "If all the nations serve him, certainly even those who make war will serve [him]. And if this is so, assuredly every rational nature will serve Christ. This is what was said by Paul, that 'to him every knee shall bow.' "[14]

Commenting on verses 5 and 17, Theodore writes:

> The word "before" does not refer to time, as some supposed; for how will it have any relation to the word "to endure"? For the (LXX) text says "he will endure as long as the sun and before the moon, in generations of generations." . . . Verse 17 shows that the word "before" (LXX: "before the sun his name will endure") does not refer to time, so that it may be supposed to apply to Christ, as some thought. For if the word "before" refers to time and to what existed earlier, how will what refers to future things remain? For this reason then it says his [Solomon's] name is glorious, no less than the sun and the moon. And evidence for this is that as long as the sun and moon remain he will remain and be remembered by all men, and is glorious in wisdom, in glory, in honor.[15]

14. Origen, *Commentariis in Psalmos, Origenis Opera Omnia,* Patrologia Graeca, ed. J.-P. Migne, vol. 12 (Paris, 1862; reprint, Turnholt: Typographi Brepols Editores Pontificii), pp. 1522-24.

15. Theodore of Mopsuestia, *Expositio in Psalmos, Theodori Mopsuesteni Episcopi,* Patrologia Graeca, vol. 66 (Paris, 1864; reprint, Turnholt: Typographi Brepols Editores Pontificii), pp. 690-93.

At the conclusion of his study of Theodore,[16] Rudolf Bultmann wrote:

> Where does the historical interest begin to stir that we note at such a height in Theodore? Where and how does it begin to develop? Clearly, only when we can understand these questions have we fully come to know the nature and significance of Theodore's exegesis. For the present, we are not in a position to do so. Still, we may perhaps say one thing, its import of course, intended as a question: from the nature of Christianity as a historical religion that draws the best part of its power from the past, and from the fact that the content of this past was given in a book — does it not seem necessarily to follow that historical exegesis had to arise at some time or other?[17]

Bultmann added that such historical understanding could only emerge in the midst of conflict. And so it did. At the Council of Constantinople in A.D. 553, 125 years after Theodore's death, his writings were condemned, and he himself consigned to hell. The principal reason for that action could not have been his plain, matter-of-fact reading of the biblical text. It had to have been his "alien commitment" to a Platonic notion of the Word of God as totally removed from the world, for which reason he had to assign equality with the Father to Christ's divine rather than his human nature.

Cassian and Augustine

For what may have been the first time in the history of interpretation, John Cassian (ca. A.D. 360-432), contemporary of Augustine and founder of the first cloisters in Gaul, introduced the fourfold sense of scripture. The largest of Cassian's works, *The Conferences,* comprise twenty-four elongated versions of conversations divided into three major parts, all purporting to record dialogues held in the Egyptian desert at various times and places. The conferences are attributed to fifteen abbots. The nineteenth conference deals with scripture interpretation and is entitled "The First

---

16. The study consisted of a postdoctoral dissertation *(Habilitationsschrift)* that qualified Bultmann to supervise doctoral candidates and to teach. Rudolf Bultmann, *Die Exegese des Thodor von Mopsuestia* (Stuttgart: Kohlhammer, 1984).

17. Bultmann, *Die Exegese des Thodor von Mopsuestia,* p. 191.

Conference of Abbot Nesteros: On Spiritual Knowledge." According to the Anchorite Nesteros (d. 185?), biblical understanding like practical knowledge is twofold. It has to do with historical interpretation *(praktikē)* and spiritual understanding *(theōtikē),* the former dealing simply with historical fact and the latter with the deeper meanings of the text. These deeper meanings, or "spiritual senses," in turn divide into three — allegory, anagogy, and tropology. Accordingly, Nesteros states:

> History embraces the knowledge of past and visible things, which is repeated by the apostle thus: "It is written that Abraham had two sons, one from a slave and the other from a free woman. The one from the slave was born according to the flesh, but the one from the free woman by promise." Then things that follow belong to allegory, however, because what really occurred is said to have prefigured the form of another mystery. "For these," it says, "are two covenants, one from Mount Sinai, begetting unto slavery, which is Hagar." But anagogy, which mounts from spiritual mysteries to certain more sublime and sacred heavenly secrets, is added by the apostle Paul: "But the Jerusalem from above, which is our mother, is free." Tropology is moral explanation pertaining to correction of life and to practical instruction, as if we understood these same two covenants as πρακτικη [*praktikē*] and as theoretical discipline.[18]

In book 1 of his *De doctrina Christiana,* the first systematically arranged theory of Bible interpretation, Augustine (A.D. 354-430), bishop of Hippo, North Africa, distinguished between the "things" that were to be used and the "things" that were to be enjoyed. The "things" to be enjoyed were the "double love" of God and neighbor, and the "things" to be used were the scriptures, which make known the commandment to love. Thus, as the celebrated church father wrote in book 3, the entire aim of scripture is to promote love *(caritas)* and condemn lust *(cupiditas)*:

> But scripture enjoins nothing but love, and censures nothing but lust.[19]

---

18. John Cassian, *The Conferences,* trans. and annot. Boniface Ramsey, O.P., Ancient Christian Writers, no. 57 (New York: Paulist, 1997), pp. 509-10.

19. Augustine, *De doctrina Christiana,* trans. R. P. H. Green (Oxford: Clarendon, 1995), p. 149.

According to Augustine, where this aim is not apparent in the letter, one must seek it beneath the veil of the letter. Moreover, this lack or ambiguity was of use. It served "to exercise the intellect so that the truth may come to the reader in a pleasant and memorable way."[20]

In the third book of *De doctrina Christiana,* Augustine deals at length with the problem of ambiguity. Where the punctuation or articulation of a passage is involved, the interpreter is to consult the rule of faith as perceived by the plainer passages together with the church's authority. If one or more readings meet that requirement, the context is to be consulted. If the problem still cannot be resolved, any punctuation or articulation following one or the other of the readings will suffice. Augustine writes:

> As far as the books of Holy Scripture are concerned, it is very unusual, and very difficult, to find cases of ambiguity which cannot be resolved either by the particular details of the context . . . or by a comparison of Latin translations or an inspection of the original language.[21]

Respecting the ambiguity of metaphor, Augustine is equally sanguine. He states first that "one must take care not to interpret a figurative expression literally," reflecting a kind of "spiritual slavery" that interprets signs as things. Fortunately, among the Jews such slavery proved to be an advantage since it resulted in their being drawn to worship the one God.[22] Augustine then devotes considerable space to warning against treating the metaphorical as literal, concluding that anything that cannot be related to good morals or the true faith is to be taken figuratively. The ambiguous passage should thus be read until its interpretation can be connected with that "double love" of God and neighbor.[23] Writing that the interpreter must take care not to apply to our time what the Old Testament may not regard as evil by its standards, Augustine concludes that all or nearly all of the deeds recorded there are to be interpreted figuratively as well as literally.[24] He goes on to discuss the interpretation of terms involving several, even contrary meanings, as well as terms that signify two or more ideas. In this case, he writes,

20. D. W. Robertson, "The Doctrine of Charity in Mediaeval Literary Gardens: A Topical Approach through Symbolism and Allegory," *Speculum* 24, no. 2 (January 1951): 24.
21. Augustine, *De doctrina Christiana,* p. 141.
22. Augustine, *De doctrina Christiana,* p. 143.
23. Augustine, *De doctrina Christiana,* p. 157.
24. Augustine, *De doctrina Christiana,* p. 165.

the person examining the divine utterances must of course do his best to arrive at the intention of the writer through whom the Holy Spirit produced that part of scripture.[25]

If, however, the equivocal meaning cannot be verified by unequivocal biblical support, then it must be arrived at "by a process of reasoning."[26]

Obviously, Augustine was touching on problems that would preoccupy modern Bible interpretation. On the one hand, he devotes space to the practice of criticism proper, to the questions of punctuation, articulation, context, historicity, authorial intent, and the like. On the other, he gives space to conjecture, a "dangerous" practice,[27] but permissible if "beyond dispute." For example, in his work on Genesis,[28] he approves the habit of some who do not interpret the stages of the world's creation in chapter 1 as a real progression in time, but as a mere progression in the narrative. He himself suggests that "evening" would be "for all things, as it were, the *terminus ad quem* of their complete and perfect establishment," while "morning" would represent "their starting line."[29] In chapter 27 of *On Genesis* entitled "The ordinary days of the week are quite unlike the seven days of Genesis," Augustine writes:

> let us suppose that these seven days, which in their stead constitute the week that whirls times and seasons along by its constant recurrence, in which one day is the whole circuit of the sun from sunrise to sunrise — that these seven represent those first seven in some fashion, though we must be in no doubt that they are not at all like them, but very, very dissimilar.[30]

This latitude in Augustine's interpretation of Genesis in harmony with natural knowledge would set a precedent for later "accommodation" of the biblical narrative to the natural or scientific. Finally, Augustine did not restrict figurative or allegorical interpretation merely to texts whose literal sense appeared unclear or ambiguous, that is, simply to texts that could not

---

25. Augustine, *De doctrina Christiana,* p. 169.
26. Augustine, *De doctrina Christiana,* p. 171.
27. Augustine, *De doctrina Christiana,* p. 171.
28. Augustine, *On Genesis,* trans. Edmund Hill and Matthew O'Connell, The Works of Saint Augustine, vol. 13 (New York: New City, 2002).
29. Augustine, *On Genesis,* p. 241.
30. Augustine, *On Genesis,* p. 267.

be related to good morals or true faith. He reveled in allegory, and clearly set the pattern for subsequent interpretation that began with the letter of the text, then turned to its sense or obvious meaning, and finally, and above all, to its "sentence," that is, to whatever in the text yielded allegorical or tropological sense. Commenting on Adam and Eve's hiding themselves "among the trees of the garden" (Gen. 3:8) after eating the forbidden fruit, Augustine asks:

> Who are the ones who hide themselves from the sight of God, but those who have turned their backs on him and are beginning to love what is their very own? You see, they already had a covering for their falsehood, and anyone who utters falsehood is speaking from what is his own (Jn 8:44). And that is why they are said to have hidden themselves at the tree which was in the middle of paradise, that is, at themselves, ranged as they were in the middle of things, below God and above bodies.[31]

Hugh of St. Victor (ca. 1096-1141) would associate the tree with Babylon. Peter Lombard (1096-1164) would identify it as the end of a journey toward which one was moved by *cupiditas*. In one way or another, in dependence on Augustine, the changes would be rung on that tree from St. Victor to Lombard to Bonaventure (1221-74) to Gerard of Liege (12th cent.), to the *Glossa ordinaria*, to the venerable Bede (ca. 672-735), and St. Bernard (1090-1153), and even to the Grendel episode in Beowulf. As has been demonstrated, in the Middle Ages, the position of the trees from which Adam and Eve could or could not eat would give rise to "an enormous complex of associations."[32]

To sum up,[33] for generations the Bible would be thought of as having a "cortex" and a "nucleus," terms that took on popularity in literary and theological circles during the Middle Ages. The interpreter's task was thus to strip away the cortex to reveal the nucleus, or "sentence." This was the goal toward which all interpretation was directed. Thus the Bible's ambiguity was not viewed as an evil, but as an advantage. First, determining its inner meaning required an exercise of the mind that discouraged sloth and

---

31. Augustine, *On Genesis,* p. 87.

32. See Robertson, "The Doctrine of Charity in Mediaeval Literary Gardens," pp. 26-34.

33. In dependence on D. W. Robertson, "Historical Criticism," in *English Institute Essays,* ed. A. S. Downer (Princeton, N.J.: Princeton University Press, 1950), pp. 11-14.

contempt for the text. Second, arrival at the nucleus gave the pleasure of discovery. Third, truths of faith expressed too openly spelled casting pearls before swine or enabling fools to recite the text without understanding. Contemporary discussion of medieval literature, preoccupied with the "letter" and the "sense," would have been unsatisfactory to the medieval reader.

CHAPTER TWO

The Reformation Era

Martin Luther

Martin Luther's (1483-1546) approach to Bible interpretation did not emerge full blown overnight. His dependence on medieval exegesis is easily established. What distinguished Luther's interpretation from that of his forerunners was the use to which he put what he inherited.

Luther owed a great debt to Augustine, to William of Occam (1285-1349), and to Lefevre d'Etaples (Faber Stapulensis [1455-1536]), whom he quotes or of whom he indicates awareness 242 times in his glosses on Romans. From Augustine Luther learned that the letter is dead until made alive by the Spirit. From Augustine he also learned to draw the distinction between letter and spirit. Where Luther exceeded his teacher was in his sounder sense of the historical. Occam's influence on Luther was threefold — in his emphasis on the authority of the scriptures, his conviction that human reason cannot attain to sure knowledge of the realities of faith, and his emphasis on the absolute power of God. The obstacle set by Occam to Luther's understanding was his accent on the capabilities of the human will, an emphasis that plunged Luther into a profound distress of conscience and compelled him to follow the way of self-perfection to the verge of despair. The vehemence of his attacks on the scholastics, particularly in his lectures on Romans, is to be seen against this background. The scholastics and their patron Aristotle had caused Luther intense suffering through their over-evaluation of the human's capacity for goodness and their intellectualizing of revelation and faith. From Faber Luther learned that the literal sense of the Bible is the sense intended by the Spirit, the true author of the Bible. More, in his *Quincuplex Psalterium,* Faber had construed the literal sense in a twofold way, that is, as a congruence of the literal and the spiritual, a sense that Luther came to call the "tropological." But Luther's understanding of letter and spirit was radically different from that of Faber. Underlying Faber's distinction was a mystical and neo-Platonic notion of faith, that is, as a presupposition for understanding, a *notitia* or *assensus,* an observing, a taking note, a giving assent, thus an attitude to be adopted. As a result, spiritual understanding and faith were separated; the believer could prepare himself or herself by way of humility and works of love for the additional gift of understanding given by the Spirit. For Luther there was no separation. Understanding was given in faith. To Augustine, Occam, and Faber could be added Nicolaus of Lyra (1270-1349); Paul of Burgos (1351-1436); Matthew Thoring, minister of the Minorite Province of Saxony; Johann Reuchlin (1455-1522); and Desiderius Erasmus Roterodamus (1466/1469-1536) — the first for his so-called *postilla,* marginal notes and commentaries on biblical texts;[1] the second for his *additiones,* additions to Lyra's postils; the third for his *replicis,* or defenses; Reuchlin for his *rudimenta,* aids in the study of Hebrew; and Erasmus for his 1516 edition of the Greek New Testament. As early as 1509 Luther began to study Hebrew with the help of Reuchlin's aids, though he still maintained loyalty to the Vulgate. Not until 1516, in the course of his lectures on Romans, did he recognize the weight of the original. It was then that he began to use the Greek Testament of Erasmus.

Luther also stood in the ancient tradition of the *lectio continua,* that is, in the tradition of the use of biblical materials for congregational worship. He held almost exclusively to the ancient church pericopal system, according to which texts from the Gospels and epistles were assigned the Sundays of the so-called Church Year. By this means more than half of the essential material of the Gospels was offered, and in a well-balanced selection. But since these texts were measured for their preaching value, the ancient epistle selections did not always meet Luther's criteria, and were exchanged for texts of his own choosing.

As to method, initially Luther's interpretation was comparable to twelfth-century attempts, to the so-called *Quadriga,* or fourfold method of interpretation, the traditional formulation of which read: "litera gesta docet; quid credas allegoria; moralis, quid agas; sed quid speres, anagoge"

---

1. Of Lyra Luther said, "if Lyra had not plucked the lyre, Luther would not have danced" ("si Lyra non lyrasset Lutherus non salt asset"); see Frederick C. Grant, *An Introduction to New Testament Thought* (New York: Abingdon-Cokesbury, 1950), p. 50.

("the letter teaches concerning the actual events; allegory [teaches] what you believe; the moral how you are to behave; and the anagogic what you hope for"). Again, the method underwent a new articulation by way of the "tropological" sense according to which the biblical texts were interpreted in the light of the revelation in Christ. To this new articulation Johann von Staupitz (1460-1524), vicar-general of the Augustinian Order, abbot at the Erfurt monastery, and Luther's confessor, paved the way. Meditation on the crucified Christ lay at the heart of Staupitz's devotional exercise, and through his personal influence became the key to Luther's understanding of the gospel. Convinced that the weakness of traditional exegesis was its failure to relate everything to Christ, from the *Dictata super Psalterium* on, Luther altered the *Quadriga* from a mechanical scheme to a Christological and soteriological principle. Like the medieval exegetes, Luther also made use of symbolic and typological exposition, and only gradually renounced allegory. Again, the Christological principle was used as a standard to keep the uncontrolled use of these methods in check.[2]

Luther seldom devoted space to outlining his interpretive method. In the 1520 defense of his articles against the papal bull, he wrote:

> I do not wish to put myself forward as more learned than all, but only that scripture rule, nor that it be interpreted by my spirit or that of any other man, but I want it to be understood by itself and its spirit.[3]

In his 1525 commentary on Deuteronomy he wrote:

> Such is the way of the whole of Scripture: it wants to be interpreted by a comparison of passages from everywhere, and understood under its own direction. The safest of all methods for discerning the meaning of Scripture is to work for it by drawing together and scrutinizing passages.[4]

---

2. For a discussion of Luther's dependence on earlier attempts at interpretation I have drawn liberally from Warren A. Quanbeck, "The Hermeneutical Principles of Luther's Early Exegesis" (Ph.D. diss., Princeton Theological Seminary, 1948); see also *Theologische Realenzyklopädie*, ed. Gerhard Müller (Berlin: Walter de Gruyter, 1999), vol. 30, pp. 481-82, 529-30.

3. *Dr. Martin Luthers Werke, Assertio omnium articulorum M. Lutheri per bullam Leonis X. novissimam damnatorum, 1520,* in *Weimar Ausgabe* (hereafter referred to as *WA*) (Weimar: Hermann Böhlaus Nachfolger, 1883-1993), 7, 98.40-99.2.

4. *Lectures on Deuteronomy,* in *Luther's Works* (hereafter referred to as *LW*), ed. Jaroslav Pelikan (St. Louis: Concordia, 1955-86), vol. 9, p. 21.

In his 1530 *Open Letter on Translating,* Luther responded to those who objected to his insertion of the term *solum* or *allein* in his translation of Romans 3:21-22a.[5] First, he simply stated that he would have it so, citing a passage from Juvenal's satire on a hen-pecking wife,[6] obviously not averse to assuming the role. Next, conceding that the term does not appear in either the Greek or the Latin text, he argued that the German tongue required it in order to render the phrase clearer and more complete, a tongue learned only from the mother in the home, children on the street, and the fellow in the market. Insisting that wherever a passage is crucial he kept tenaciously to the original, he added that here the context, particularly Paul's argument respecting Abraham in Romans 4, necessitated the addition. Then, Luther appealed to the expository tradition, stating that Ambrose, Augustine, and many others before him had stated that faith alone makes one righteous. Finally, he argued that the condition of his readers demanded the insertion.[7]

Any real clarity respecting Luther's approach to Bible interpretation can only be had by consulting his exegetical works. First of all, in his interpretation of the various biblical books the Reformer repeatedly insisted on the text's autonomy, signaled in the so-called exclusive particle, *sola scriptura,* "scripture alone." The particle spelled reaction to the claim that any subjectivity, bias, or prejudice in interpretation could be transcended by a magisterium, a papal office, or the collective "spirit" of the like-minded. Scripture alone would guarantee correct interpretation. But by itself alone *sola scriptura* was no more than a reaction, a defense.

Thus, "scripture alone" needed supplementing in an understanding of scripture as "its own interpreter," in Luther's words, as *sui ipsius interpres.* This assumed a radically different interpretive model, for it established scripture as authoritative over the hearer. No independent or privileged status was assigned the interpreter, whether as individual or collective. In fact, the roles of text and interpreter were reversed: the text, not the exegete, assumed the role of interpreter; the text exegeted the exegete.

In order for the text to speak, to be heard, the subjectivity of the

5. "But now, apart from law, the righteousness of God has been disclosed, and is attested by the law and the prophets, the righteousness of God through faith in Jesus Christ for all who believe."

6. "Sic volo, sic iubeo, sit pro ratione voluntas": "I want it, I command it, what I want is reason enough." Martin Luther, "Sendbrief von Dolmetschen," *WA* 30/II, 635.

7. *WA* 30/II, 642-43.

individual or collective, or as Luther put it, "one's own spirit," "one's own perception" *(spiritus proprius, sensus proprius),* had to be transcended. Above all, Roman Catholic tradition, in a struggle with which Luther's interpretive method achieved its maturity, was itself a classic case of subjectivity, of the *sensus proprius.* With its concern for authority, its setting of an authoritative office between text and hearer-reader, it introduced a foreign and legalistic element into the relation, as a consequence of which church order, church law, and political action displaced proclamation. But Luther saw the claims of the individual spiritualist, or "enthusiast" *(der Schwärmer),* as of the same sort. The enthusiast demanded recognition, instilled obedience among his mass of clients and adherents in order to gain a semblance of objectivity. Both pope and spiritualist, then, pretending to be scripture interpreters or organs of revelation so as to exercise their authority, introduced a criterion into scripture interpretation foreign to the concern of scripture. Both illustrated the general human penchant toward the subjective; neither could avoid the danger of the *spiritus proprius* or *sensus proprius.* Nor could construing scripture as authority in a purely formal way, apart from pope or enthusiast, guarantee against subjectivism. In fact, the understanding of scripture in a purely abstract way could be more inhumane than the principle of tradition or enthusiasm because it handed the individual over to the Bible as law, whereas with tradition or enthusiasm the individual could still know he or she was connected with the fellowship of the church or of the spirit. If tradition did not exist to call attention to itself, if the "and" in "scripture and tradition" was not a plus sign that elevated tradition to the same level as scripture, or in practice above it, it might help to resist that penchant toward subjectivity, might help to clear the way.

According to Luther, the way needed clearing for the *scopus,* the "goal," the "bull's eye," for what the text, and not the author, had to say. Luther defined the goal as follows:

> This is the true test by which to judge all books, when we see whether or not they inculcate Christ. For all the scriptures show us Christ, Romans 3 . . . and St. Paul will know nothing but Christ, 1 Corinthians 2. . . . Whatever does not teach Christ is not yet apostolic, even though St. Peter or St. Paul does the teaching. Again, whatever preaches Christ would be apostolic, even if Judas, Annas, Pilate, and Herod were doing it.[8]

8. *LW* 35, p. 396.

Thus, not the doctrine of justification, but Christ himself was *scopus.* From out of this Christological center Luther developed the bases of his exposition, and whatever multiple senses he used bent them in its service. More, Luther contended that this goal expressed the hearer's most genuine concern, the relation to God effected by Christ.

This *scopus,* then, gave scripture its authority, or better, since scripture's intention was what is now called "orality," that is, since it intended further to be heard, from that hearing it derived its authority. The text intended to speak, intended to be heard, for which reason hearing took precedence over thinking since through hearing the word of scripture did its work, that is, created faith. The scriptures, thus, were not normative in any formal way. Their authority consisted in that ability to create faith. For this reason the interpreter was not to transfer the spirit of the text into his or her own, but quite the reverse, was to transfer his or her spirit into that of the text. "And note," Luther wrote, "that the strength of scripture is this, that it is not changed into him who studies it, but that it transforms its lover into itself and its strengths." When the *spiritus proprius* was surrendered, scripture was changed from a system of objects and ideas into an oral word by which its content as saving event came into its own.

After all, then, it was the *usus,* the use to which interpretation is put, which engaged Luther's attention. Use was the category of the existential relation to the text. For example, one needed to know not only the story of the resurrection, but also its use and fruit,[9] and unless the exegete had first experienced the power of scripture as the bearer of Christ, he or she could not teach others.[10] This concept allowed Luther to address the questions of scripture interpretation in freedom and in obligation. In his dissertation on the hermeneutical principles of Luther's early exegesis, Warren Quanbeck summarized Luther's understanding of the purpose of interpretation. First, he viewed the Bible as a living book, speaking to the needs of the present day. Second, he conceived the message of the Bible as personal, addressed to individuals and demanding a personal response. Third, he regarded the purpose of the Bible as practical, intent on the edification of the church of God and the destruction of error and falsehood.[11]

9. "Non satis est historiam resurrectionis scire, sed etiam usum et fructum": *WA* 17/I, 86,31–87,20.

10. "Quia nisi quis primo in sacreto cordis a Deo doceatur, perverse in publice docet alios": *WA* 4, 282, 27; 4, 21, 344; 4, 79, 33.

11. Quanbeck, "The Hermeneutical Principles of Luther's Early Exegesis," p. 85.

John Calvin

John Calvin's (1509-64) contribution to biblical interpretation involved two stages. His *Institutes of the Christian Religion* represented stage 1, and his commentaries on the Old and New Testaments stage 2. The *Institutes* were thus not to be read apart from the commentaries, nor the commentaries to be separated from the *Institutes*. It is from both, then, that we get a look-see into Calvin's interpretive principles.

Calvin's commentaries covered every book of the Old and New Testaments with the exception of Revelation. Back of this prodigious outlay was the conviction that all of scripture comprised a covenant document of the one, single covenant of grace. But this peculiar emphasis on the idea of covenant did not blind Calvin to the differences between the two Testaments. In the Old Testament God had rendered his revelation palatable by way of earthly benefits, whereas in the New he renounced that meaner type of exercise. The Old yielded only a picture or a shadow rather than a body since it did not yet contain the whole truth. The Old was literal, bringing death, whereas the New is spiritual, an instrument of life. Or again, the Old Testament yielded a picture of things that decline and disappear with time, but the New Testament enjoys a powerful and enduring solidity. Finally, according to Calvin the Old Testament was a Testament of servitude, intended to beget fear in souls, whereas the New Testament is a Testament of freedom, intended to raise them to trust and certainty. A fifth possible difference lay in the restriction of God's grace to Israel until the advent of Christ.[12] Despite these differences, Calvin's emphasis on the one covenant of grace embracing both Testaments rendered him hostile to "those fanatics who vaunt that the Old Testament is abolished, and that it belongs not in any degree to Christians; for with what front can they turn away Christians from those things which, as Paul testifies, have been appointed by God for their salvation!"[13]

According to Calvin, what gave to this "covenant document of grace" its authority was not a "canon" given once for all on the authority of the church. To assume that scripture was of importance only on the suffrage of the church was a "most pernicious error." "What," he wrote,

12. The sources are on p. 376 in Franz Lau, *Der Glaube der Reformatoren* (Bremen: C. Schunemann, 1964).

13. John Calvin, *Commentaries on the Epistle of Paul the Apostle to the Romans*, trans. John Owen (Grand Rapids: Baker, 1979), p. 517.

"is to become of miserable consciences in quest of some solid assurance of eternal life, if all the promises with regard to it have no better support than man's judgment?"[14] Further, belief denoted something more than the mind's obedient submission to the church. "Faith," wrote Calvin, "does not consist in ignorance but in knowledge. . . . We do not arrive at salvation either by being ready to take what the Church has prescribed to be true, or assign to it the sphere of research and knowledge."[15] In fact, since the Christian church was first founded on the writings of the prophets and apostles, their doctrine was sanctioned antecedently to the church, and without it the church would never have existed.[16] Calvin agreed that the consent of the church was not without weight. It was of no small consequence that so many ages concurred in obedience to it. In fact, it was no small proof of its authority that scripture was sealed with the blood of so many witnesses.[17] But in the last analysis none of this could guarantee its authority.

This attitude toward ecclesiastical authority was reflected in Calvin's use of the "fathers" in Bible interpretation. For example, his intent to follow wherever the text leads moves him to write of Augustine: "What Augustine says is true . . . but it is not relevant to this passage." "This is a godly observation, but has nothing to do with Paul's meaning."[18] Or, in what has turned out to be the *locus classicus* of Calvin's judgment on allegory, he writes of Origen's exegesis of Galatians 4:22-24 that it twists scripture this way and that; it infers the literal sense is too lowly and mean, that beneath the rind of the letter lie hidden deeper mysteries that can be extracted only by inventing allegories. "I acknowledge," he writes, "that Scripture is the most rich and inexhaustible fount of all wisdom; but I deny that its fertility consists in the varied meanings which anyone may fasten to it at his pleasure."[19] To the complaint of a professor of Greek at Wittenberg that he had reproached and reviled the translation and interpretation of the books of Moses by Luther, "that greatest of men," Calvin reacted vigorously to what he regarded as an attack on the interpreter's freedom:

14. John Calvin, *Institutes of the Christian Religion,* trans. Henry Beveridge (Grand Rapids: Eerdmans, 1953), I, VII, 1, pp. 68-69.

15. See Lau, *Der Glaube der Reformatoren,* p. 426.

16. Calvin, *Institutes,* I, VII, 2, p. 69.

17. Calvin, *Institutes,* I, VIII, 12-13, p. 82.

18. T. H. L. Parker, *Calvin's New Testament Commentaries* (Grand Rapids: Eerdmans, 1971), p. 80.

19. Parker, *Calvin's New Testament Commentaries,* pp. 63-64.

If each interpreter is not permitted in individual places in Scripture to put forward what he thinks, into what sort of slavery shall we not sink back? No, if I am not allowed anywhere to dissent from Luther's judgment, it would be absurd and ridiculous to take up the office of interpreting.[20]

Most of Calvin's critical comments, however, were "cloaked in the decent anonymity of *alii* and *quidam:* 'some say . . . ,' 'the opinion of some, that.'" Clearly, it was Calvin's habit to keep his witnesses masked.[21]

If, then, neither the consent of the church nor its being sealed with "the blood of so many witnesses" guaranteed to scripture its authority, then that authority had to be derived from a higher source: "the inward testimony of the Spirit."[22] This testimony gave to scripture, with all its "contemptible meanness of words," a power beyond the rhetorician's art, vindicated its truth in opposition to every doubt, and rendered it sufficient unto itself.[23] Only when its certainty was founded on that inward persuasion of the Spirit could it suffice to give a saving knowledge of God.[24]

So it was to the *text* of scripture that the Spirit attached the testimony. For this reason Calvin's commentaries are full of philological observations about Greek terms, about the Hebrew idioms lying back of the Greek expressions, about particles, copulas, and the like, and for this reason he engages in textual criticism, at times to the point of trivializing. Clearly, in all of this allegory had no place.[25] For "certain giddy men" of his own generation who tried to pry the Spirit from the text he reserved his bitterest invective:

I wish they would tell me what spirit it is whose inspiration raises them to such a sublime height that they dare despise the doctrine of Scripture as mean and childish. . . . [Isaiah] shows that, under the reign of Christ, the true and full felicity of the new Church will consist in their being ruled not less by the Word than by the Spirit of God. Hence

20. Parker, *Calvin's New Testament Commentaries*, p. 86.
21. Parker, *Calvin's New Testament Commentaries*, p. 86.
22. Calvin, *Institutes*, I, VII, 4, p. 72.
23. Calvin, *Institutes*, I, VIII, 1, p. 75.
24. Calvin, *Institutes*, I, VIII, 13, p. 83.
25. Tord Larsson, *God in the Fourth Gospel: A Hermeneutical Study of the History of Interpretations* (Stockholm: Almqvist & Wicksell, 2001), pp. 92-94.

we infer that these miscreants are guilty of fearful sacrilege in tearing asunder what the prophet joins in indissoluble union.[26]

"What an infatuation of the devil," he writes, "to fancy that Scripture, which conducts the sons of God to the final goal, is of transient and temporary use."[27]

As to how or in what manner the scripture came to be, Calvin was adamant. Commenting on 2 Timothy 3:16,[28] he wrote that the authors of scripture were "organs of the Holy Spirit," uttering only what they had been commissioned to declare, and thus did not deliver a doctrine according to men's will and pleasure, but "dictated by the Holy Spirit." "The Scripture," he wrote, "has nothing belonging to man mixed with it."[29] The full authority the biblical writings should enjoy among believers demanded the belief that they came from heaven "as directly as if God had been heard giving utterance to them."[30] Later, in Protestant orthodoxy, this view of the Bible's inspiration would assume hardened form in the assertion that the Holy Spirit moved the authors of scripture to write *(impulsus ad scribendum), and* furnished them with the fitting word *(suggestio verbi)* and the fitting content *(suggestio rerum).* But if the later verbal inspiration theory of orthodoxy refused to acknowledge errors in the Bible, this was not true of Calvin. For example, commenting on the reference in Matthew 27:9 to the chief priests' purchase of a potter's field with Judas's thirty pieces of silver as fulfilling the prophecy of Jeremiah, Calvin wrote, "The passage itself plainly shows that the name of Jeremiah has been put down by mistake, instead of Zechariah. . . . [I]n Jeremiah we find nothing of this sort, nor any thing that even approaches to it." Or again, regarding the reference in Acts 7:16 to Joseph's burial at Shechem in a tomb bought by Abraham from the sons of Hamor, Calvin writes of the manifest mistake in the mention of Abraham. In fact, Abraham had bought a double cave from Ephron the Hittite in which to bury his wife Sarah. "Wherefore," Calvin concluded, "this place must be mended."[31] It may be that the most difficult problem

---

26. Calvin, *Institutes,* I, IX, 1, p. 84.

27. Calvin, *Institutes,* I, IX, 1, p. 85.

28. "All scripture is inspired by God and is useful for teaching, for reproof, for correction, and for training in righteousness."

29. John Calvin, *Commentaries on the Epistles to Timothy, Titus, and Philemon,* trans. John Owen (Grand Rapids: Baker, 1979), p. 249.

30. Calvin, *Institutes,* I, VII, 1, p. 68.

31. John Calvin, *Commentary on a Harmony of the Evangelists,* trans. William Pringle

in all of Calvin's theology is his concept of scripture as the Word of God, "dictated" by the Spirit to his "amanuenses," but also as a human production, at times incorrect respecting matters of fact.[32]

Always eager to explicate what the text of scripture had to say rather than the method by which he came to understand what it had to say, Calvin spent little time outlining his method of interpretation. One thing is sure: he believed his paramount task was to get at the mind of the author. He assumed that the author was able to give expression to his thought, and that the expositor was able to understand it. There could thus be no separation between the author's thought and his language; the text, the everlasting text, was the spot at which the interpreter encountered the author. In the preface to his commentary on Romans, Calvin reminisces with an old friend respecting the interpretation of scripture. "We two were agreed," he wrote, "that the interpreter's chief virtue consists of clear brevity." "At the same time," he adds, "I know that this view is not accepted by all . . . but I am not able to be dissuaded from the love of brevity."[33] And this brevity was to serve getting at the mind of the author, the interpreter's "sole task."[34] What detracted from the commentaries of other Reformation interpreters such as Philipp Melanchthon (1497-1560), Heinrich Bullinger (1504-75), and Martin Bucer (1491-1551) was that Melanchthon's method led to an arbitrary choice of topics, whereas Bullinger's and Bucer's was excessively erudite. *Perspicua brevitas,* "clear brevity," was the way by which Calvin was to fulfill his "office" of uncovering the mind of the author. Of this, he was absolutely convinced.

One, if not the only, presupposition guiding Calvin's interpretation was that just as God could not reveal himself in his absolute majesty but came within reach of human perception in Jesus Christ, so the biblical text accommodated itself to given times and circumstances. As noted above, in the *Institutes* he distinguished the Old from the New Testament as making

---

(Grand Rapids: Baker, 1979), vol. 3, p. 272; *Commentary on the Acts of the Apostles,* ed. Henry Beveridge (Grand Rapids: Baker, 1979), vol. 1, p. 265.

32. Parker, *Calvin's New Testament Commentaries,* p. 56.

33. Joannis Calvini, *Opera exegetica,* vol. XIII, *Commentarius in Epistolam Pauli ad Romanos,* ed. T. H. L. Parker and D. C. Parker (Geneva: Librairie Droz, 1999), p. 3: "Sentiebat enim uterque nostrum, praecipuam interpretis virtutem in perspicua brevitate esse positam . . . Quanquam autem scio sententiam hanc non apud omnes receptam esse . . . ego tamen dimoveri non possum ab amore compendii."

34. "unicum illius officium, mentem scriptoris, quem explicandum sumpsit, patefacere," in Calvini, *Opera exegetica,* vol. XIII.

the heavenly inheritance "evident and in a certain sense palatable" by way of "earthly benefits."[35] In his concluding statements on John 21:25[36] Calvin writes:

> If, turning his eyes toward that splendor, the evangelist in astonishment exclaims that not even the whole world can contain everything told, who should be surprised? For there is less to be found fault with if he uses well-worn and received figures to commend the excellence of the works of Christ. For we know that God accommodates himself to the ordinary mode of speaking because of our ignorance, that for the time being he lisps, as it were.[37]

A principal interpreter of Calvin and editor of his works writes that for Calvin the revelation of God in scripture was direct and indirect, direct in that it is God who speaks to humans, and indirect in that God speaks in a way alien to himself. To the writer also, he adds, God speaks in this alien manner.[38] The choice of the word "alien" is not a happy one since for Calvin what is human, thus "palatable" or "alien," unerringly communicates what is dictated by the Spirit. The author himself adds that "if the expositor reveals the mind of the writer, he is revealing the mind of the Spirit."[39] Once more we are confronted with that dialectic in Calvin's understanding of scripture as the Word of God and an altogether human word.

Thomas Müntzer

Thomas Müntzer is the most celebrated representative of the so-called left wing of the Reformation, hailed by Erich Honecker (1912-94), onetime

---

35. Lau, *Der Glaube der Reformatoren,* p. 417.

36. "There are also many other things that Jesus did; if every one of them were written down, I suppose that the world itself could not contain the books that would be written."

37. Joannis Calvini, *Opera exegetica,* vol. XI/2, *In Evangelium Secundum Johannem Commentarius pars altera,* ed. Helmut Feld (Geneva: Librairie Droz, 1998, p. 318: "In eum si Euangelista oculos coniiciens attonitus exclamat, iustam narrationem ne a toto quidem mundo capi posse, quis miretur? Deinde minime reprehendendus est, si trita receptaque figura ad commendandam operum Christi excellentiam utitur. Scimus enim, ut se ad communem loquendi modum accommodet Deus ruditatis nostrae causa, imo interdum quodammodo balbutiat."

38. Parker, *Calvin's New Testament Commentaries,* p. 58.

39. Parker, *Calvin's New Testament Commentaries,* p. 59.

head of the German Democratic Republic, as "a revolutionary who is one of the best our people has produced." An educated monk, born ca. 1490, Müntzer was won for the Reformation and in 1520 recommended by Luther to serve as pastor at Zwickau. Dismissed from Zwickau in 1521 for polarizing the populace, he left for Bohemia, from which he also had to flee. In 1523 he gained a position as preacher in the little city of Allstedt in Electoral Saxony. Here, in a sermon preached on the occasion of a visit by two princes, he first made public his revolutionary plans. When the princes turned a deaf ear, principally due to a warning from Luther, Müntzer's preaching took on a demagogic cast, and he was forced to leave Allstedt in 1524 for the imperial city of Mühlhausen, where he founded the "eternal covenant of God." Later, at Nürnberg, he published his "Highly Occasioned Defense and Reply to the Spiritless, Soft-Living Flesh at Wittenberg," a riposte to Luther's polemic.[40] In 1524 he joined the peasants in the Upper Rhine resistance. Returning to Mühlhausen and the pastorate of St. Marien in 1525, he came to the aid of the rebels at Eichsfeld and Frankenhausen. When the revolt was crushed at Frankenhausen in May 1525, Müntzer was taken prisoner, tortured, and beheaded, and his head was impaled on a stake.

Müntzer's biblical work was restricted to the translation of fifty-nine texts for use in his liturgical works, the "German Church Office" and the "German-Evangelical Mass."[41] The long-held assumption that his emphasis on the activity of the Spirit led to a marginalizing of scripture has been challenged.[42] For example, in his exposition of the parable of the tares in Matthew 13, he enunciates the principle that "the divine art must be attested to from the Holy Bible in strict comparison of all the terms clearly described in both Testaments."[43] The assumption that when Müntzer resorts to the biblical text, it is principally to the text of the Old Testament,[44] has also been challenged. For example, the impetus for striking at his oppo-

---

40. "Hoch-verursachte Schutzrede und Antwort wider das geistlose sanftlebende Fleisch zu Wittenberg."

41. *Deutsches Kirchenamt* and *Deutsch-evangelische Messe.*

42. See Rolf Dismer, "Geschichte, Glaube, Revolution, zur Schriftauslegung Thomas Müntzers" (Ph.D. diss., University of Hamburg, April 1974).

43. T. Müntzer, *Schriften und Briefe, Kritische Gesamtausgabe,* ed. Günther Franz, Quelle und Forschungen zur Reformationsgeschichte, no. 33 (Gütersloh, 1968), p. 228, 20-23, quoted in Dismer, "Geschichte, Glaube, Revolution," p. 94.

44. See Walter Elliger, "Müntzer und das Alte Testament," in *Wort und Geschichte, Festschrift für K. Elliger zum 70 Geburtstag,* Alten Orient und Altes Testament, Veröffentlichungen zur Kultur und Geschichte des Alten Orients und des Alten Testaments, no. 18 (Kevelaer-Neukirchen-Vluyn, 1973).

nents derives from his reading of the Pauline and Johannine literature.[45] It is thus not scripture itself that draws his fire but scripture as "stolen" by the "scribes and Pharisees," that is, by the Wittenbergers who have left the direct path of the Reformation and teach a "whitewashed faith"[46] consisting in holding certain propositions drawn from scripture to be true. Further, because scripture exercises a twofold function, to kill and to make alive, the Lutherans refuse to take its killing function seriously and read out of it merely a justification of the status quo.[47]

None of the tools and methods used throughout the history of exegesis are alien to Müntzer. First of all, he accents the necessity of scholarship. When, for example, he rebukes the "scribes," it has nothing to do with their scholarly acumen, but their dull expository technique, or, as in the case of infant baptism, with their inability to draw clear evidence from the Bible.[48] As regards his methodology, to a large extent typology controls Müntzer's exegesis; he construes biblical persons and reports as figures and figurations, for example, in his references to the Lutherans as "scribes" or "Pharisees." Nor is he stranger to allegory, as is clear from his exposition of the second and third chapters of the Fourth Gospel, where water throughout is understood as "movement."[49] And, just as for Luther so also for Müntzer the so-called tropological, or moral, comprises scripture's primary sense.[50] One distinctive methodological difference between Müntzer and his contemporaries is his idea of context. By "context" he means nothing less than the entire scripture. The innumerable Bible references, as well as the bulging marginal notes, intended to support his assertions, to deepen what the text itself says, or to furnish arguments not cited in the text, make clear the role that association plays in Müntzer's method.

As to the ancient exegetical tradition, Müntzer is aware of it, but with the exception of the biblical figures, he names only Hegesippus, early church chronicler (ca. 110-180), and Eusebius, the "father of church

45. See Dismer, "Geschichte, Glaube, Revolution," p. 200.

46. The term Müntzer uses is *getichter Glaube;* see Dismer, "Geschichte, Glaube, Revolution," p. 79.

47. See Müntzer, *Schriften und Briefe,* p. 218, 17-21, quoted in Dismer, "Geschichte, Glaube, Revolution," pp. 208, 210.

48. In his *"Protestation,"* of 1521, Müntzer begs "all the persnickety scholars" to show him "where it stands in the holy letters" that Jesus and the apostles baptized children; see Dismer, "Geschichte, Glaube, Revolution," pp. 76-77.

49. See Dismer, "Geschichte, Glaube, Revolution," pp. 217-18.

50. See Dismer, "Geschichte, Glaube, Revolution," p. 211.

history" (ca. 263-339). As one scholar writes, "[he] does not consciously oppose the exegetical tradition. He knows it, but does not oppose it. He sweeps it from the table."[51] With respect to contemporary interpretation, and particularly that of Luther, Müntzer's "Office" and "Mass" reflect greater or lesser dependence on the Reformer's translations of the Psalms and the New Testament, a dependence Müntzer does not regard as lessening his own worth. To get at the meaning of the original text behind the Vulgate, Müntzer, like Luther, will often exercise astonishing freedom from the literal text of his exemplar, thus setting himself off from the entire pre-Lutheran tradition of German Bible translation. In his *Propositiones* of 1521-22, Müntzer attempts to show that Johannes Sylvius Egranus (d. 1535), a Zwickau preacher and alleged Erasmian humanist, believes that the meaning of scripture may be grasped by the understanding alone, without the cooperation of the Holy Spirit. If such was Egranus's position, here also Müntzer is in agreement with Luther respecting the activity of the Spirit as giving sense to and deriving sense from the Bible.[52] But despite his agreement with Luther that the "mystery" is a matter of meaning and not the mere arrangement of words, Müntzer's work reflects a different perspective toward the Word of God.

First of all, Müntzer distinguishes the Word of God recorded in the Bible from the Word of God still to be heard here and now. If, he contends, God spoke only once and then disappeared into thin air, the Bible could hardly be God's Word since only the living God can attest to scripture.[53] Müntzer then distinguishes an "external" from an "internal" Word of God. The Word to which genuine faith adheres is not "a hundred thousand miles" away, but "springs up from the recess of the heart."[54] The "external" Word, or the "Word of God in the letter," is the bread that must be broken by the preacher if it is not to remain a "poor letter."[55] In the *Prager Manifest* of 1521 Müntzer addresses a circle of "humanists" that embraces a strict biblicism, thus for whom scripture in its literal sense is the norm for a faith and life independent of Rome. Such "scripture belief," Müntzer

---

51. Dismer, "Geschichte, Glaube, Revolution," pp. 103-4, 106.

52. See Walter Elliger, *Thomas Müntzer, Leben und Werk,* 9th ed. (Göttingen: Vandenhoeck & Ruprecht, 1976), pp. 159-60.

53. See Dismer, "Geschichte, Glaube, Revolution," p. 219.

54. Müntzer, *Schriften und Briefe,* p. 237, 5ff., quoted in Dismer, "Geschichte, Glaube, Revolution," p. 226.

55. Müntzer, *Schriften und Briefe,* pp. 492f., quoted in Dismer, "Geschichte, Glaube, Revolution," p. 228.

states, is the wrong path on which Rome through its spiritless priests has led Christianity into error. God, Müntzer insists, intends to speak with persons now. He does not intend to write as he once did in scripture, but will write the true scripture with his living finger. Only an inner appropriation of that scripture directly spoken into the heart by the living God can bring certainty of salvation. The church is in decline because it ignores this truly Christian faith, and imagines it can escape with appeal to the written word. But, Müntzer declares, whoever relies on the mere letter has been abandoned by God. The precondition for the reception of this illumination is purification through suffering. "Yes," Müntzer declares,

> it is a right apostolic, patriarchal and prophetic Spirit, to wait for visions and get them with painful distress. So it is no wonder that Brother Fattened Pig and Brother Easy Life (i.e., Martin Luther) rejects it.[56]

This "painful distress" is indispensable, it is salutary. It "empties" the feelings and prepares for reception of the Spirit. In fact, there can be no faith, no reception of the Spirit, without it.

> No more than the field may bear all kinds of grain without the plowshare, no more may one say he is a Christian who does not experience beforehand through his cross expectancy of God's work and word. . . . Even if you gobbled up the Bible, it does not help; you must endure the sharp plowshare.[57]

For Müntzer the "scripture" that is directly spoken into the heart involves dreams and visions, the one a revelation in sleep, the other in the waking state. Contrary to Luther's accusation that he drags his dreams into scripture, Müntzer is not interested in dream interpretation but in the dream as a means of communication, just as the Bible itself attests. In fact, it is scripture as witness to the activity of the Spirit in the past that verifies the manifestations of the Spirit in the present. Scripture thus exercises

56. "Auslegung des zweiten Kapitels Daniels, das Propheten, gepredigt auf dem Schloss zu Allstedt vor den tätigen teuren Herzögen und Vorstehern zu Sachsen durch Thomas Müntzer, Diener des Wort Gottes"; quoted in Franz Lau, *Der Linke Flügel der Reformation, Klassiker des Protestantismus,* ed. Heinold Fast (Bremen: Carl Schünemann, 1962), p. 286.

57. Müntzer, *Schriften und Briefe,* p. 218, 5-11, and p. 233, 29, p. 234, 4, quoted in Dismer, "Geschichte, Glaube, Revolution," pp. 101-2.

control, a control needed to prevent extreme subjectivity by testing the event of the vision itself. "The elect," Müntzer says,

> must have regard for the vision's effect, that it does not arise by human doing but flows simply according to God's immovable will, and take special care that not one tiny portion is lacking of what he has seen.[58]

Clearly, Müntzer is aware of the danger of self-deception, of the hindrance to allowing God alone to speak.

The connection that Müntzer makes between Bible and "Word of God" is made between "Spirit" and scripture. In almost all the instances in which he refers to the Spirit, he reinforces it with sentences from the Bible: "Every half-sentence, every statement about the Spirit of Christ follows the biblical foundation, confirmation, or source."[59] The Spirit also works as a corrective, not of scripture, but of "stolen scripture." Since it is the Spirit who is present in the "internal" Word of God, that is, who effects oral communication with God, or who "speaks into the heart," the battle with the Wittenbergers is not only over interpretation, but also over one's relation to the living, speaking God.[60] Indeed, God's voice may be heard "without all the books,"[61] but such is not a condition. The "scribes" themselves give testimony to the "external" Word as unable to give assurance of faith. For this reason one must be emancipated from them and their "obscenities." The alternative to Spirit, then, is not scripture, but "flesh." Over the analysis of Müntzer's work to this point a warning needs sounding. As the scholar most preoccupied with Müntzer's Bible interpretation until now has stated, the "contradictions" or "simultaneously diverging ideas" in Müntzer's thought cannot be reconciled by a theory in which everything meshes nicely. Until now, his understanding of scripture has been too little clarified to serve as the basis for any wide-ranging conclusions.[62]

Finally, according to Müntzer existence of the "scribes," the "groat-guzzling Lutherans with their besmeared mercy," is proof we are living in the end-time.[63] Thus, Jesus' word in the parable of the tares, "let both

58. Quoted in Dismer, "Geschichte, Glaube, Revolution," p. 284.

59. See Dismer, "Geschichte, Glaube, Revolution," p. 230.

60. See Dismer, "Geschichte, Glaube, Revolution," p. 233.

61. Müntzer, *Schriften und Briefe*, p. 278, 30-36, quoted in Dismer, "Geschichte, Glaube, Revolution," p. 234.

62. See Dismer, "Geschichte, Glaube, Revolution," pp. 227, 232.

63. See Dismer, "Geschichte, Glaube, Revolution," p. 108.

[tares and wheat] grow together until the harvest," no longer applies. It is harvest time. In the *Prager Manifest,* Müntzer, conscious of himself as called, if not to bring in the end, then, at least, to introduce it, thunders:

> The end-time is here. So God himself has sent *(gemit)* me into his harvest. I have sharpened my sickle, for my thoughts are aflame for the truth, and my lips, skin, hands, hair, soul, body, and life curse the unbelieving.[64]

Failure of the Allstedt "experiment" may have helped to raise that consciousness, and to the point that whatever in scripture might sanction the status quo in view of the parousia's delay is now contested, fractured, and interpreted in a revolutionary way. At any rate, to unsheathe the sword and strike is the counsel Müntzer takes from Paul.[65] In the Fürstenpredigt, his sermon to the princes at Allstedt in 1524, Müntzer deals with Nebuchadnezzar's dream of the decline of the world powers in Daniel 2, and announces the breaking in of the final phase of world history, the age of the Spirit. In that age Bible and scribe will be marginalized, the will of God will be made known in visions and dreams, and at its realization the princes can undertake their signal task, led by the prophet Müntzer, the "new Daniel."[66] Assuming the mantle of prophet and revolutionary, Müntzer delivers his summons:

> No longer let evildoers live who estrange us from God, for a godless man has no right to live when he hinders believers. In Exodus 22:1 God says: "You shall not let the evildoers live." St. Paul has the same in mind when he says of the rulers' sword that it is given for vengeance on the evil and for protection of the faithful (Rom. 13:4). God is your protection and will teach you to fight his enemies (Ps. 18:35). He will prepare your hands for battle and preserve you.[67]

---

64. Müntzer, *Schriften und Briefe,* p. 504, 10-11, quoted in Dismer, "Geschichte, Glaube, Revolution," p. 99.

65. See 1 Corinthians 5:13b: "Drive out the wicked person from among you," and Romans 13:4: "The authority does not bear the sword in vain! It is the servant of God to execute wrath on the wrongdoer."

66. At this time Müntzer had already organized a secret Bund to serve as the picked troops for his revolutionary plans.

67. Thomas Müntzer, "Auslegung des zweiten Kapitels Daniels," in Lau, *Der Linke Flügel der Reformation,* p. 292.

The Wittenbergers, ignorant as to whether they should instruct the elect and the godless respecting their condition, despise the coming church in which knowledge of the Lord will appear in full measure. Once more, Müntzer appeals to the Danielic vision:

> The kingship and dominion and the greatness of the kingdoms under the whole heaven shall be given to the people of the holy ones of the Most High; their kingdom shall be an everlasting kingdom, and all dominions shall serve and obey them. (Dan. 7:27)

CHAPTER THREE

Orthodoxy and Pietism

Matthias Flacius Illyricus

Matthias Flacius (Vlacich, Latinized: Flacius) Illyricus was born in 1520 in Labin (Italian: Albona), Croatia. While studying the *Humaniora,* or humane sciences, in Venice he came under the influence of the evangelical propaganda widely disseminated there. As a result, ca. 1539 Flacius left Croatia and made his way toward Germany. Arriving in Basel he met with the Reformation scholar Simon Grynaeus (1493-1541), schoolmate of Philipp Melanchthon (1497-1560) and successor of Desiderius Erasmus (1466?-1536). There, the Erasmian-Zwinglian climate plunged him into deep despair to the point that "at the margin of suicide under the darkness of God's wrath he wore himself out between a melancholy lassitude and a raging hatred of God."[1] After a stay in Tübingen, where he was befriended by Johann Camerarius (1500-1574), another Reformation scholar and intimate of Melanchthon, in 1541 he arrived in Wittenberg, where he was welcomed by Melanchthon and came under the influence of the aging Luther. In 1545, now an unmistakable pupil of Melanchthon and candidate for the title of Luther's successor, Flacius married and established his household in Wittenberg. Embroiled in dispute due largely to his position on what later came to be called total depravity, Flacius left Wittenberg for Magdeburg in 1549, left Magdeburg for Jena in 1557, left Jena in 1562 for Regensburg, and left Regensburg for Antwerp in 1566. Driven by war from Antwerp in 1567 Flacius moved to Frankfurt, where

---

1. Jörg Baur, "Flacius — Radikale Theologie," *Zeitschrift für Theologie und Kirche* 72 (1975): 367-68.

he was opposed by the authorities, and left for Strasbourg. Ordered to leave Strasbourg by the city authorities in 1573, Flacius sought asylum in Frankfurt, where he died in 1575.

If Bible interpretation as we have come to know it began with Protestantism, Matthias Flacius Illyricus, one of the greatest and most embattled scholars of his time, was its initiator. The occasion for his concentration was furnished by the Council of Trent. At its April 8, 1546, session, the Council had hurled a decree respecting the Vulgate and its interpretation against the Protestant principle of scripture:

> If anyone, however, should not accept the said books as sacred and canonical, entire with all their parts, as they were wont to be read in the Catholic Church, and as they are contained in the Old Latin Vulgate edition, and if both knowingly and deliberately he should condemn the aforesaid traditions let him be anathema.[2]

At bottom, the attack of Trent contained two elements. The first accented the absence among current interpreters of linguistic talent enjoyed by such ancient fathers as Origen and Jerome. The second emphasized the insufficiency of scripture and the need for the authority of tradition. Flacius made easy work of the first, and gave all his energy in responding to the second. If, he argued, scripture is not understood, it is not because of its unintelligibility but because of improper language study applied to it and the false methods used for its interpretation. To correct the error and apply the remedy Flacius produced his so-called Golden Key, the *Clavis scripturae sacrae* ("Key to the Holy Scripture") of 1567, and thus founded the discipline of hermeneutics. With its grasp of patristic literature together with its interpretive methods and rules, the *Clavis* would outrun its successors and determine the discipline of interpretation for years to come.

The first part of the *Clavis* is a concordance, a cluster of articles dealing in lexical fashion with the biblical language, described by Flacius as his "book of Hebraisms" since it examines the terms of both Testaments on the basis of their Hebrew background. In his preface to the work Flacius indicates what he intends with it, makes clear his understanding of why and how the Bible came to be, and explains how it is to be interpreted. First of all, he is concerned that the students of theology find and possess

---

2. *The Sources of Catholic Dogma*, trans. Roy J. Deferrari (St. Louis: B. Herder, 1957), para. 784.

the most certain truth from Holy Scripture and its proven proclamation. As to why the Bible came to be he writes that God spoke with the human race through patriarchs and, prophets, through his own Son, and finally through the apostles. But since God wanted to come to the aid of our weakness and oppose all deceivers, he took care that his will should be clearly and unequivocally fixed in writing. The how of the Bible's existence Flacius describes as by dictation of the Holy Spirit. For this reason it is an indivisible unity, the sole source of salvation and of divine truth, its meaning not to be gotten from the fathers, but solely through comparison of one passage with another. For this reason, philosophical principles may not be superimposed on it, such as the scholastics had done with Aristotle, to the point of altering the biblical definitions. Flacius refuses to say anything more of the Bible's inspiration. He will not describe the biblical authors as amanuenses, as did Johann Gerhard (1582-1637) a generation later, or call them "live and writing pens" *(calami viventes et scribentes)* as did the Huguenot scholar Andre Rivet (1595-1650). God speaks through the scripture, writes Flacius, and the biblical writers' function as instruments of the Spirit involves no loss of human personality. As to the way in which the Bible should be interpreted the Croatian scholar takes a decidedly Christological approach: only the Lamb of God can open the scripture, hence the title of his work, "The Key," an obvious reference to Revelation 5:1-5.

The second part of the *Clavis* is composed of seven tracts that deal with the rules (sixty) necessary to a knowledge of Holy Scripture, with a discussion of problems involved in interpretation; observations on grammar, figures, and style; a summarizing of older works on interpretation; three lectures held during Flacius's teaching career; and polemics against Trent. Sandwiched in among them is the notorious tract in which Flacius proposes a theory of sin as of the essence of human existence. As Wilhelm Dilthey (1833-1911), Berlin historian-philosopher and interpreter of Schleiermacher, wrote, the *Clavis* reflects two elements of different origin and historical significance. The first stems from the depth of religious experience in the Protestant world; the second, from the humanistic tradition and its striving to arrive at a clear understanding of written works.[3]

From the first tract entitled *De ratione cognoscendi Sacras Literas,*

---

3. Wilhelm Dilthey, *Die Hermeneutik vor Schleiermacher,* quoted in *Seminar: Philosophische Hermeneutik,* ed. Hans-Georg Gadamer and Gottfried Boehm (Frankfurt: Suhrkamp am Main, 1976), pp. 17-18.

freely translated "How One Should Read the Sacred Scriptures," the following rules give Flacius's principal concerns. Where the meaning of the
text is clear, rules 9 through 12 apply. First, keep in mind the point of view,
purpose, or intention of the passage or work. Second, strive to have the
entire argument in hand. Third, determine the layout and organization of
the entire work. Finally, index the entire piece. Where the text or passage
is obscure, rules 20 to 24 apply. Examine the viewpoint and genre of the
entire corpus. After determining the genre, investigate the parts or sub-
parts of the work. Nothing that is reasonable lacks a certain viewpoint or
arrangement of parts that agree with each other or with the entire piece.
Once more pay attention to the rules having to do with the genre of the
passage. Determine its relation to all the other genres of scripture, as well
as their influence on people's lives and behavior. Apply the "Lydian stone"[4]
of logical rules to determine whether the emphasis is on grammar, rhetoric, or dialectic. Where dialectic is concerned, weigh matters of organization, definition, division, and type of argumentation. Finally, rule 25:
"There is no little profit when you put what was written into your own
words, as though, after performing your dissection . . . you were outlining
the skeleton . . . so as to take up only those sentences which are, as it were,
the basis for the whole."[5]

Flacius furnishes illustrations of the various rules to be observed.
For example, in indicating the need for noting the viewpoint or the various parts of a writing he refers to the anointing of Jesus' feet in Luke
7:47: "[The woman's] sins, which were many, have been forgiven; hence
she has shown great love." The question as to whether forgiveness of the
woman's sins is the cause or effect of her love is answered when one observes whether Christ is instructing his critic in causes and effects as a
teacher would a pupil, or whether he is refuting his critic's false opinion.
The particle translated "hence" denotes a forgiveness already occurred,
thus a refutation of the critic's opinion. Again, the passage in John 6:52
("How can this man give us his flesh to eat?") can be easily understood
when its goal is kept in mind. The enemies of Christ are not interested in
inquiring how they should use his body, for benefit or for teaching, but
rather in trapping him in an obvious lie. Or again, when the words of the

4. A touchstone of jasper used in Asia Minor to determine the types and properties
of minerals.
5. Matthias Flacius Illyricus, "Anweisungen, wie man die Heilige Schrift lesen soll,
die wir nach unserem Urteil gesammelt oder ausgedacht haben," in *Seminar: Philosophische
Hermeneutik*, pp. 44-48.

Lord's Supper are distinguished respecting their essence and result, it is clear that they do not merely furnish allusions and silhouettes or report dreams, but establish a testament and corroborate a covenant.

Interlaced with these reflections on interpretation are Flacius's attacks on Roman Catholic expositors and on such Reformation figures as Georg Major (1502-74), Philipp Melanchthon, Justus Menius (1449-1558), Andreas Osiander (1514-1604), and Caspar Schwenckfeld (1489-1561). The first is attacked for his notion of a specifically Christian morality, the second for his penchant for compromise, the third for his resistance to the unabridged character of the universal priesthood of believers, the fourth for his ontological premises leading to the deification of the Christian, and the last for his spiritualism — all these in, with, and under the rules and prescriptions contained in both parts of the *Clavis.* Obviously, Flacius could not resist tilting against a host of his contemporaries. It may have been Flacius whom Melanchthon first had in mind when on his death bed he prayed to be free of the *rabies theologorum,* the "rage of the theologians." Nor was Flacius invulnerable to attack. In its very first article on sin, the Lutheran *Formula of Concord* of 1577 raises him to a kind of enduring life with its rejection of his view of sin as of the essence of human existence. The notion that even in the movement of faith the believer remained the *imago Satanae* or *diaboli* would resurface in existentialist theology, albeit translated to read that whether apart from or in faith the "structures of existence" remained the same.[6]

Scholars have noted Flacius's dependence on the ancients and moderns of his time. Dilthey notes that he drew from most of the fourth book of Augustine's *De doctrina Christiana,* and that aid came to him from rhetoric, particularly as shaped by Melanchthon. Lauri Haikola writes that Flacius proceeded from Aristotelian thought according to which every existent thing is seen from four viewpoints, that of the efficient, final, formal, or material cause. Rudolf Keller states that Flacius not only took up biblical terms, but also terms at home in church or theological language. He adds that Erasmus and the Strasburg Reformer Martin Bucer (1491-1551) had already taught that the Bible had to be understood from the perspective of the incarnation, in other words, that only the "Lamb" had the "Key." Most significantly, Keller detects an unmistakable connection between the *Clavis* and the work of the Reformed Marburg theologian Andreas Hyperius

---

6. See *Kerygma and History,* ed. Carl E. Braaten and Roy A. Harrisville (Nashville: Abingdon, 1962), p. 223.

(1511-64), indicating that Flacius regarded the "philological-rhetorical rules of interpretation belonging to humanistic hermeneutics as confessionally neutral."[7]

The relevance of Flacius's work to contemporary Bible interpretation is at least fourfold. First, he applies the rules of philological interpretation against the arbitrary dogmatic use of isolated passages, making use of concepts that describe the larger unities of meaning and text such as point of view, purpose, intention, argument, layout, organization, and the like. Second, despite his notion of Hebrew as "the mother of all languages," thus his setting the New as well as the Old Testament under the rubric of "Hebraisms," Flacius's insistence on the intimate relation between the two Testaments would be shared by exponents of the twentieth-century biblical theology movement. Third, his emphasis on biblical knowledge as needing integration in personal life, explicit in his summons to the use of the "Key," or Christological approach, squares with current calls to abandon abstraction in favor of accommodation to the matter at hand. Fourth, and finally, Dilthey's judgment that in the end a method that set out to explain each passage from the whole of scripture came close to the very thing it attacked in the Catholics, namely, the dismemberment and destruction of the whole of scripture, has Flacius at least to thank for raising the issue of the need for a valid connection between the interpretive and dogmatic tasks.[8]

Johann Albrecht Bengel

Johann Albrecht Bengel, the most influential of the eighteenth-century Württemberg pietists, celebrated for his New Testament textual criticism, his contribution to exegesis, and his chiliast theory, was born in Winnenden, Baden-Württemberg (southwest Germany), in June 1687. As a pastor's son he came in contact with radical pietism. From 1703 to 1706 he studied theology at Tübingen, in his day devoted largely to Bible interpreta-

---

7. Dilthey, *Die Hermeneutik vor Schleiermacher,* pp. 13-14; Lauri Haikola, *Gesetz und Evangelium bei Matthias Flacius Illyricus* (Lund: C. W. K. Gleerup, 1952), pp. 13-16; Rudolf Keller, *Der Schlüssel zur Schrift: Die Lehre vom Wort Gottes bei Matthias Flacius Illyricus, Arbeiten zur Geschichte und Theologie des Luthertums,* vol. 5 (Hanover: Lutherisches Verlagshaus, Neue Folge, 1984), pp. 123, 134, 148, 160.

8. Dilthey, *Die Hermeneutik vor Schleiermacher,* quoted in *Seminar: Philosophische Hermeneutik,* p. 18.

tion, corresponding to the influence of Philipp Jakob Spener (1635-1705) of Berlin, the so-called father of pietism, and August Hermann Francke (1663-1727) of the University of Halle, founded under the influence of his friend, Spener. Among his teachers at Tübingen, Bengel was drawn to the piety of Christoph Reuchlin (1660-1707), but also studied with Johann Wolfgang Jäger (1647-1720), who led him to distance himself from radical pietism and mysticism. After a time as tutor and vicar, he went on a student trip to Halle, where he spent three months, and became acquainted with Francke's *pedagogium,* established to prepare teachers for his and other schools. Bengel had great respect for Francke, whose works had contributed to his religious formation as a youth. He was affected by the Halle theologian's emphasis on "conversion," that is, a decided and intensive turning and concentration toward God, though he did not appropriate Francke's strict conversion practice. On the return trip to Tübingen, Bengel came in contact with Johann Christian Lange (1669-1756), and Johann Heinrich May (1688-1732) at Giessen, whose numbers symbolism and salvation-historical *(heilsgeschichtliche)* theology would leave their stamp on Bengel's research. Bengel never achieved university professor status, but spent his life as preceptor, probst (provost), and prelate at schools in the Baden-Württemberg area. For twenty-eight years, Bengel was one of the instructors at the evangelical cloister school at Denkendorf near Esslingen, his chief task being the preparation of future Württemberg theologians for university study.[9]

Bengel's work with the manuscript tradition of the New Testament is well known. In face of variant readings he introduced the axiom that "the difficult is better than the easy reading" ("proclivi lectioni praestat ardua"). Further, he arranged the manuscripts into historically-geographically circumscribed text families or recensions, a practice persisting until the end of the last century. As a result Bengel broke the back of what had served since the Reformation as the "received text" *(Textus Receptus),* uncritical allegiance to which he described as "worthy of boys."

On the other hand, the occasion for his text-critical work and its underlying apologetic are rarely if ever noted. Simply put, Bengel's students were

9. See "Die Zeit Johann Albrecht Bengels und seiner Schüler," in *Geschichte des Pietismus: Der Pietismus im aschtzehnten Jahrhundert,* ed. Martin Brecht and Klaus Deppermann (Göttingen: Vandenhoeck & Ruprecht, 1993-2004), vol. 2, pp. 251-52; and Martin Brecht, "Bengel," in *Theologische Realenzyklopädie,* ed. Gerhard Krause and Gerhard Müller (Berlin: Walter de Gruyter, 1980), vol. 5, pp. 583-84.

troubled[10] by the number of variants in the biblical texts. In Bengel's day, the manuscript tradition was in sufficient quantity and sufficiently diffuse to challenge the conviction that the biblical word was undivided and unambiguous. If the Bible was the Word of God, how could it reflect such ambiguity? The question furnished the occasion for the philologically trained Bengel to set himself to the task of arriving at a stable result through a critical edition. Concern for his students lay at the heart of the project. More, that stability which Bengel hoped to achieve with his editions of the New Testament text (first appearing in 1734) was to reflect the undivided and unambiguous nature of the Word of God itself. In the first paragraph of his preface to the *Gnomon,* an explanation of the New Testament designed to accompany the edition of the Greek text, and first published in 1742, Bengel wrote:

> It is because they contain God's words and are the Lord's Book, that they are called *"Holy Scripture."* . . . The scriptures, therefore, of the Old and New Testaments, form a most Reliable and precious *system* of Divine testimonies. For not Only are the various writings, when considered separately, Worthy of God, but they together exhibit one complete and Harmonious body, unimpaired by excess or defects.[11]

If Bengel's textual research was to eliminate confusion resulting from a divided and ambiguous text, the *Gnomon* was to respond to "the abundant discrepancies of opinion" in the church.[12] As its title reads, it was to serve as "a pointer to the New Testament in which from the original power of the words there is indicated the simplicity, depth, connection, and salutariness of the heavenly meanings." Scripture and church enjoyed a reciprocal relationship. When the one flourished, so did the other; when the one became languid or morbid, so did the other. Bengel believed he was called to address the current morbidity through his commentary, not out of any "prior confidence," but "under divine guidance" and "by little and little."[13]

Bengel wrote most extensively of the principles guiding his work in

---

10. One commentator describes them as suffering inner attack *(Anfechtungen);* see "Die Bedeutung der Bibel im deutschen Pietismus: 1. Die Bibel im Pietismus des 17. und 18. Jahrhunderts," in *Glaubenswelt und Lebenswelten: Geschichte des Pietismus,* ed. Hartmut Lehmann (Göttingen: Vandenhoeck & Ruprecht, 2004), p. 108.

11. *John Albert Bengel's Gnomon of the New Testament,* a new translation by Charlton T. Lewis and Marvin R. Vincent (Philadelphia: Perkinpine & Higgins, 1860), para. I, p. xii.

12. *John Albert Bengel's Gnomon,* para. V, p. xiii.

13. *John Albert Bengel's Gnomon,* para. VI, p. xiv.

the preface to the *Gnomon.* After devoting considerable space to the text-critical problem of distinguishing "the clearly genuine words of the Sacred Text from those which various readings render doubtful," he proceeded to the requirements of a proper interpretation of the biblical word. First, he referred to the exact knowledge of the Truth, the systematic arrangement of subject, the precise expression of meaning, and the genuine strength of feeling exhibited by the biblical authors, adding that "in the Works of God, even to the smallest plant, there is the most entire symmetry . . . the most finished harmony, even to a letter." It was thus the special office of every interpretation to "exhibit adequately the force and significance of the words which the text contains, so as to express everything which the author intended." Further, in order precisely to weigh the force of the words, it was essential to observe the Hebraisms that tinged the Greek of the New Testament since the "entire perpetual spirit of the language of the New Testament" was a distinct Hebraizing. Next, writing that the sacred writings have a disposition or character of their own, Bengel insisted that the interpreter should pay "due regard" to the biblical writer's "feelings," that is, to the "affect" the writer intended to evoke. Admittedly, this requirement could be fulfilled only by those who were "endued with spiritual experience." Adding that he did not think it necessary to add practical application of the principles, that whoever submits to the working of the Divine Love in the Truth imbibes from the Divine Words everything profitable for salvation, "without labor and without stimulus," Bengel concluded that in his day the "nefarious contempt of Holy Scripture" had reached its climax, to the point that those who fed on the scripture were considered to be grovelers or fools. But despite all, those who approved "the best things" were to preserve the Heavenly Deposit that God "has bestowed upon us not in vain."[14]

Bengel's biblical interpretation reflects three major characteristics. The first is an apocalyptic view tied to a numbers symbolism set within a salvation-historical *(heilsgeschichtliche)* context. This view exercised a radical effect on Bengel's understanding of the Bible, particularly on his interpretation of the book of Revelation. In fact, Bengel confessed to being a chiliast and appealed expressly to Spener, according to whom the Last Day would not directly follow the unmasking of the antichrist as Reformation doctrine taught and as Luther supposed.[15] Preoccupation with apocalyptic

---

14. *John Albert Bengel's Gnomon,* para. VI, pp. xxiii-xxxii.
15. See "Geschichte, Gegenwart, Zukunft: 6. Johann Albrecht Bengel und seine Nachwirkungen," in *Glaubenswelt und Lebenswelten,* p. 33.

began with an exegetical discovery, later interpreted by Bengel as worked by God, during sermon preparation for the second Sunday in Advent of 1724. The discovery was that the "number of the beast" in Revelation 13:18 was to be interpreted as years and related to the medieval history of the popes.[16] Since 666, the number of the beast, was the number of the antichrist, and since the end of the antichrist and the beginning of the events of the end belonged together, the rule of the antichrist began roughly with Gregory VII (1020/1025-85), who committed "the hideous innovation" of assigning the name of pope in the exalted sense to the one bishop at Rome.[17] From this point on Bengel developed his salvation-historical theology, arranging the entire biblical chronology from the beginning of the world to its end. In his *Erklärten Offenbarung Johannis* of 1740, and in the *Sechzig erbaulichen Reden über die Offenbarung Johannis* of 1747, he drew a two-millennium view, a differentiation until then unknown. In Revelation 20:1-7, wrote Bengel, the reference is not to a single period of a thousand years, but to two thousand-year periods, the one following the other. The first thousand years, the breaking in of which was dated June 18, 1836, would be denoted by the binding of Satan, after which Satan would be briefly let loose, leading to wars and temptations on earth. After another depotentiation the second thousand years would commence, marked by the lordship of Christ and concluding with the Last Judgment and the creation of the new heavens and earth. The first millennium, wrote Bengel, would see a "spiritual change." Jerusalem would be a "showplace of very great things." This change in the spiritual realm would be reflected in a change within the individual and social conditions of life on earth. If preoccupation with apocalyptic as such reflected the influence of Spener, at this point that influence had dissipated. The strictly spiritual character of Spener's chiliasm had been exchanged for a social-political utopia.[18] Overall, the task

16. Brecht, "Bengel," p. 587.

17. Johann Albrecht Bengel, *Gnomon oder Zeiger des Neuen Testaments,* ed. C. F. Werner (Ludwigsburg: Druck und Verlag von Ferd. Riehm, 1860), vol. 2, p. 763. The English translation of 1860 contains only a small portion of Bengel's commentary on the Apocalypse, and the translation of 1893 omits his commentary altogether. The editor of the 1893 edition writes that "time has so thoroughly exposed the fallacy of his calculations of times and seasons, that the publishers and editors of this translation thought the wisest course would be to suppress that part of his work almost entirely." "Note to the Apocalypse," in *Gnomon of the New Testament by John Albert Bengel,* ed. W. L. Blackley and James Hawes, with an introduction by Revere F. Weidner (Chicago: Revell, 1893), p. v.

18. "Geschichte, Gegenwart, Zukunft: 6. Johann Albrecht Bengel und seine Nachwirkungen," pp. 34-35.

was labor consuming, and required harmonizing all the data of the Apocalypse with the initial beginning and relating all previous church history to the revelation of events about to take place. Thus, if preoccupation with apocalyptic reflected the influence of Spener, at least in its initial stages, the baroque numerology, the fascination with numbers and their symbolism, had Johann Heinrich May for a father. All of it, however, was pressed into the service of a salvation-history scheme leading from creation to the end of the world. And, if one never spoke of "history" in the singular before the second half of the eighteenth century, but always of "histories," and if it was Bengel's scheme that needed the collective, then it may have been Bengel, if not Hamann before him, who helped give it birth.[19]

A second characteristic of Bengel's biblical interpretation was his assumption that the biblical utterances and the course of history corroborate one another. This mutual legitimation served a dual apologetic interest: the truth of scripture was secured by historical facts, and in history itself God's reign is revealed. For example, in the gnomon on Revelation 13:18, by comparing ancient Greek and Roman authors (Plato, Xenophon, Polybius, Dio Cassius, Quintus Curtius Rufus, and Pliny the Younger), ancient Christian writers (Irenaeus, Orosius, the disciple of Augustine, and Hesychius), and sixteenth- and seventeenth-century Protestant and Roman Catholic writers (the Scot John Napeir, inventor of logarithms; John Lightfoot, the great English Protestant divine; Rupert, abbot of Tuitien; and Campegius Vitringa [1659-1722], Dutch Protestant, disciple of Jan Cocceius, celebrated for his "federal theology," ancestor of the salvation-historical or *heilsgeschichtliche* scheme),[20] Bengel brings the reader, step by step, to the identification of the beast in terms of papal history, culminating in Gregory VII.[21]

On one occasion Bengel developed a theory from a single biblical passage. Perhaps he was much too meticulous a philologist to allow this one instance to be described as reflective of his work, but it deserves attention because of the space given it in the *Gnomon*. On Hebrews 12:24 Bengel wrote that the blood of Christ is viewed here "insofar as it is in heaven," that "we call the state of the shed blood that lingering of the blood outside the body." During the three days Jesus was among the dead his

---

19. See Oswald Bayer, *Zeitgenosse im Widerspruch: Johann Georg Hamann als radikaler Aufklärer* (Munich: Piper Verlag, 1988), p. 151.

20. On his student trip to Halle, Bengel was introduced to the *Anacrisis ad Apocalypsin* of Campegius Vitringa.

21. These references appear only in the original, *D. Joh. Alberti Bengelii, Gnomon Novi Testamenti,* 3rd ed. (Stuttgart: Sumtibus J. F. Steinkopf, 1860 [1773]), pp. 1095-1105.

body remained undecayed without the blood, and the blood without the body. All the more, after he overcame death, the body and blood remain undecayed. Now, when Christ entered into the Holy Place through his own blood, he bore his own blood sundered from the body. It was precisely at the time of his ascension that Christ had his blood separated from his body. Jesus himself is in heaven, wrote Bengel, and so is his body; but his blood is also in heaven, for which reason it is no longer in his body. Further on, commenting on Hebrews 13:12, Bengel wrote that here also the blood of Jesus is considered apart from his body. That is, the shed blood, the price of eternal redemption offered to God, is offered without being returned to the Redeemer's body. The resurrection and glorified body of Jesus Christ do not annul the condition of the shed blood. On the contrary, the life in glory has no need for a circulation of the blood; it is totally from God. Thus, at the death of Christ, his blood was removed from his body. In other words, the blood of Christ, separated from his body, continues on in heaven and within the liturgy described in Hebrews is the medium of atonement. The atonement is thus not a historical act on the cross but a present event in heaven, in which faith experiences a purifying sprinkling with the blood of Christ.[22] As his interpreters state, in this "realistic" view of the atonement lay the strength of Bengel's conception. But it could not last, not even among pietists. What did remain was respect for his attempt to master the problem of the contemporizing of the atonement.[23]

Finally, Bengel's conviction that for the one open to the Spirit of scripture nothing is small and unimportant, that one seeks by a most exact comprehension of what is said in its most tender shade of meaning to glean from it what it says, may reflect an "historically anxious type" of interpretation, a "legalistically hanging on to the letters of the Bible," a "laboriously nit-picking for a pious purpose," but for all that still reflected a gift for grammatical-philological-rhetorical observation.[24] As for Bengel's chronology, or better, his numbers symbolism, it was too liable of a thousand and one throws of the dice to be fixed within a salvation-historical scheme.[25] As his *Gnomon* on Romans 11:32 and 1 Corinthians 15:26 makes clear, and as at least implied in his earliest works on the Apocalypse, this scheme allowed for a *Wiederbringung*, for the reconciliation of all to salva-

22. Bengel, *Gnomon oder Zeiger des Neuen Testaments,* vol. 2, pp. 617-22.

23. "Die Zeit Johann Albrecht Bengels und seiner Schüler," p. 256.

24. See Emanuel Hirsch, *Geschichte der neueren evangelischen Theologie,* vol. 3 (Gütersloh: C. Bertelsmann, 1951), p. 183.

25. "Die Zeit Johann Albrecht Bengels und seiner Schüler," p. 256.

tion, a view he could not publicly affirm and only managed to harmonize with Lutheran teaching by way of an artifice, after the example of Spener.[26]

With its weaknesses and its strengths the *Gnomon* of 1742 represents the end and highpoint of exposition in the era of pietism. It underwent new editions and translations in German and English in the eighteenth and nineteenth centuries, its edifying passages referred to in such works as the *Explanatory Notes upon the New Testament* by John Wesley (1703-91),[27] and left its traces among the spiritual descendants of Spener and Francke in the twentieth century.[28] One year before his death at Stuttgart in 1752, Bengel received an honorary doctorate from Tübingen University, where he had once hoped to be called to a chair.

26. "Die Zeit Johann Albrecht Bengels und seiner Schüler," p. 185.

27. In his preface Wesley wrote, "no sooner was I acquainted with that great light of the Christian world . . . Bengelius, than I entirely changed my design, being thoroughly convinced it might be of more service to the cause of religion, were I barely to translate his *Gnomon Novi Testamenti,* than to write many volumes upon it. Many of his excellent notes I have therefore translated; many more I have abridged. . . . Those various readings, likewise, which he has showed to have a vast majority of ancient copies and translations on their side, I have without scruple incorporated with the text; which, after his manner, I have divided all along . . . according to the matter it contains. . . . And even this is such a help, in many places, as one who has not tried it can scarcely conceive." *Explanatory Notes upon the New Testament* (London: Epworth, reprinted 1958), pp. 7-8.

28. Brecht writes that from the end of the eighteenth century on, Bengel's apocalyptic expectations took on new actuality, and that one of its consequences was emigration in the East and later also to Palestine; see Brecht, "Bengel," p. 589.

CHAPTER FOUR

The Enlightenment

Used to denote a specific epoch in human intellectual history, the term "Enlightenment" is a catchall. The term may have first had to do with a meteorological event and meant "to illumine," "to brighten," then came to be used metaphorically for the intellectual sphere. Exactly when the "Enlightenment" as an intellectual period began is a matter of debate, but there are some clues respecting its origins. One has to do with the Thirty Years' War. This conflict, which began between Protestants and Catholics, ended in 1648 with a political-secular peace treaty that suspended questions of truth and in the face of a plural Christianity tried to arrive at trans-confessional ethical norms. It thus may well have been Christians of every stripe who accented the ideals and qualities later embodied by English deists and German *Aufklärer,* who thus created the atmosphere "when manners were beginning to be polished, toleration became fashionable, and pulpits filled with Latitudinarians, Arminians, and rational Catholics."[1] As to its extent, as good a guess as any is that having begun in the last half of the seventeenth century, the "Enlightenment" gave way to the "modern period" at the end of the eighteenth century.

The factors that occasioned the Enlightenment were many and varied. One was growing exhaustion over the theological controversies that had led to the religious wars of the period preceding. Another was the expansion of the political, economic, and intellectual horizon. Still another was the marked advance in the natural sciences, leading to growing confidence in human reason and the secularization of the state.

---

1. Peter Gay, *The Enlightenment, an Interpretation,* vol. 1: *The Rise of Modern Paganism* (New York: W. W. Norton, 1966), p. 325.

More than a philosophy or ideology, "Enlightenment" denoted a stance, a perspective, a critical freedom, expressed in the maxim "dare to think on your own!" The maxim was Immanuel Kant's (1724-1804), contained in a tiny essay entitled "What Is Enlightenment?" the first lines of which read:

> Enlightenment is one's exit from a self-incurred immaturity. Immaturity is the inability to think on one's own without another's control. This immaturity is self-incurred when it is not caused by a lack of intelligence, but of resolution and the courage to think on one's own without another's control. Sapere aude! Dare to think on your own! is thus the watchword of the Enlightenment.[2]

Whatever nuance one gave the stance, criticism was a leading idea, its postulate the autonomy of human reason, issuing in the demand for the right to question everything. From this perspective and its postulate resulted what Peter Gay, a leading student of the Enlightenment, described as the period's three principles: relativism, according to which no single set of convictions could have absolute validity; eclecticism, according to which no system possesses the whole truth, thus fulfilling Kant's maxim; and toleration, the political counterpart of the two.[3] Anthropocentrism was another leading idea. That is, the period was marked by a preoccupation with the individual self suggestive of Protagoras's ancient maxim: "Man is the measure of all things." More, it was sparked by the idea of progress and human perfectibility that birthed a dynamic extending to the political, social, ethical, and religious spheres.

Convinced of the autonomy of human reason as well as of the principal intelligibility of the world, the Enlightenment led to explaining everything in terms of immanence, and thus to the secularization of thought. This had to spell emancipation from the revealed doctrine of the church. On the continent, the prevailing concept assumed classical expression in the axiom of Gotthold Ephraim Lessing (1729-81): "The accidental truths of history cannot prove the necessary truths of reason." "This is the loathsome wide ditch," Lessing wrote, "across which I cannot get, however

2. Immanuel Kant, "Beantwortung der Frage: Was Ist Aufklärung?" in *Immanuel Kant Werke in Sechs Bänden,* ed. Wilhelm Weischedel, vol. 6: *Schriften zur Anthropologie: Geschichtsphilosophie, Politik und Pädagogik* (Frankfurt am Main: Insel Verlag, 1964), p. 53.
3. Gay, *The Enlightenment,* p. 163.

often and earnestly I have attempted to leap over it."[4] In his "Education of the Human Race" (1774, 1778), Lessing argued that historical revelation could only be a pedagogical shortcut in humankind's long and painful process toward the "necessary truths of reason," truths that could have been discovered apart from revelation. The Bible, Jesus, had nothing new to say, at least, nothing humans could not have discovered on their own, sooner or later. Accordingly, the Enlightenment tackled the difficult fact that the Bible so poorly coincides with the timeless truths of reason by using the concepts of development and accommodation. The idea of development assumed that the perfect clarity of the religion of reason could be attained only at the end of a long progression from the darkness of superstition and mysticism. Religions, including Christianity, were nothing but stages along this path. The idea of accommodation could help connect reverence for Jesus with the criticism of his teaching. God could only make himself understood by accommodating himself to the thought-forms and conditions of the various ages involved. Historical criticism was thus the means by which these truths of reason could be wrung from the Bible and brought into the clear light of day. When Lessing was finally refused entrée to the media of his day due to his radical views, he took to the stage. In the "drama of toleration" entitled *Nathan the Wise* (1779), with the "Ring Parable" at its heart, he depicted true belief as independent of any so-called positive structure or doctrinal system, and thus gave a head start to the idea of religion as a private affair.

With respect to the Bible, Enlightenment critics proceeded to dismantle the proofs from prophecy and the miracle narratives. They engaged in what one author has called an "in part frivolously exaggerated" attack on the morals of biblical personalities and events,[5] and distilled ethical-moral teachings from the Bible to which reason could give assent. At the conclusion of his essay on "The End of All Things," Kant wrote:

> Should Christianity ever reach the point where it ceases to be amiable
> (which of course, could happen, if it were armed with peremptory

---

4. Gotthold Ephraim Lessing, *Gesammelte Werke,* ed. Paul Rilla, vol. 8 (Berlin: Aufbau Verlag, 1956), p. 14.

5. See Albrecht Beutel, "Aufklärung," in *Religion in Geschichte und Gegenwart,* 4th ed. (Tübingen: J. C. B. Mohr, 1998-2007), vol. 1, p. 943; see also Beutel's discussion of the concept of the Enlightenment as an element of historical structure, as the designation of an epoch, its presuppositions, its literature, and as an epoch in historical and ecclesiastical history, pp. 929-34, 938, 942-47.

authority rather than its gentle spirit): then, because there is no neutrality in matters of morality (still less a coalition of opposing principles), antipathy and opposition to it would have to be men's dominant attitude toward it; and the Anti-Christ, who, by the way, is taken to be the forerunner of the last day, would begin his however brief rule (founded presumably on fear and selfishness). But then, since Christianity would be destined to be the universal world religion, but to be such would not be smiled on by fate, the end of all things would take place as regards morality.[6]

To repeat, if it was "largely these Christians" who created the atmosphere into which the *philosophes,* or Enlightenment thinkers, were born, then the Reformation played its part. It had reduced everything to the "text," to the word of the Bible as the sole normative document of Christian faith. It had individualized religion, emphasized the uniqueness and freedom of the individual conscience, and brought about the reform of education such individualization required. As for pietism, that outgrowth of an orthodoxy that ended in a "rigid, obtuse, authoritarian clerical hierarchy more interested in the minutiae of observance and quibbles on dogma than the great tenets of faith,"[7] its affinities to the Enlightenment were unmistakable. It too turned away from polemic, and aimed at religious, moral, and social progress, at the ethicizing of what was Christian. It too was preoccupied with the religious subject, with the "I."

Baruch Spinoza

Among Enlightenment figures preoccupied with matters of religion the Dutch thinker Baruch (Benedict) Spinoza was preeminent. Born in Amsterdam in 1632, the child of Jewish Portuguese émigrés, Spinoza was engaged in his father's business for seventeen years. In 1656 he was excommunicated from the Jewish community for heretical opinions, moved to Rijnsburg, and was employed there as a lens grinder. At Rijnsburg he penned his first philosophical pieces and began work on the *Ethics.* In 1663 he settled at Voorburg, and two years later occupied himself with the *Theological-Political Treatise.* Though the treatise was published anon-

6. Immanuel Kant, "Das Ende Aller Dinge," in *Immanuel Kant Werke,* vol. 6, p. 190.
7. Gay, *The Enlightenment,* p. 328.

ymously in 1670, Spinoza was known and vilified as its author. Residing in The Hague from 1670, in 1673 he rejected a call to a chair at the University of Heidelberg. Two years later he completed the *Ethics,* but failed to publish it. Toward the end of his life Spinoza began work on another political treatise, returning to a lifelong concern. The treatise remained unfinished. Spinoza died at the age of forty-five; his works were published posthumously by friends.

Spinoza assumed a central position in the conflict of his century over the relation between reason and religion. Since he believed religious division led to tyranny and oppression, he saw his task as stripping the Bible of any usefulness to the philosophical rationalists and theological dogmatists who lent that division support. Securing religious and intellectual liberty and questioning biblical authority, at least as represented by Spinoza's contemporaries, were thus two sides of the same coin. The questioning of biblical authority led to Spinoza's invention of the "historical method." That he intended to use this method to reduce biblical authority to irrelevance, and that the language he used in its employ was calculated to "tranquilize unwary readers and camouflage his own subversive purpose"[8] seems too artful an estimate. At any rate, of the two fronts at which Spinoza aimed his fire, the one insisted that the Bible had to be suited to reason, and the other that reason had to be suited to the Bible.

To the first category Spinoza assigned the Jewish medieval philosopher Maimonides (1138-1204), "first among the Pharisees to openly maintain that Scripture must be made to conform with reason."[9] Summarizing the philosopher's method he wrote, "if in its literal sense [a passage] is found to be contrary to reason, then however clear the passage may appear, he maintains that it must be interpreted in a different way." If, for example, Maimonides were persuaded that the Genesis creation story represented the idea of the eternity of the world, an interpretation would be demanded to remove the idea since "belief that the world is eternal . . . destroys the very foundations of the Law." Conversely, Spinoza added, "if he had been convinced on rational grounds that the world is eternal, he would not have hesitated to distort and explain away Scripture until it appeared to teach the same doctrine."[10]

8. See J. Samuel Preus, *Spinoza and the Irrelevance of Biblical Authority* (Cambridge: Cambridge University Press, 2001), p. 13, n. 39.

9. Baruch Spinoza, *Theological-Political Treatise* (Gebhardt edition), trans. Samuel Shirley (Indianapolis: Hackett, 2001), p. 165.

10. Spinoza, *Theological-Political Treatise,* pp. 100-101.

To the second category Spinoza assigned the theologians, represented by a certain Rabbi Jehuda Alpakar who to avoid Maimonides' error had fallen prey to its opposite by maintaining that reason should be ancillary and completely subservient to the Bible.[11] "I ask," Spinoza writes,

> who can give mental acceptance to something against which his reason rebels? For what else is mental denial but reason's rebellion? I am utterly astonished that men can bring themselves to make reason, the greatest of all gifts and a light divine, subservient to letters that are dead, and may have been corrupted by human malice; that it should be considered no crime to denigrate the mind, the true handwriting of God's word, declaring it to be corrupt, blind and lost, whereas it is considered to be a heinous crime to entertain such thoughts of the letter, a mere shadow of God's word.[12]

Of philosophers who connived at the perspective of the theologians Spinoza stated that they never would have taught anything more than the speculations of the Aristotelians or Platonists to whom they adapted the scripture so as to avoid the appearance of being heathen. Not content with sharing the delusions of the Greeks, they sought to represent the prophets as sharing the same delusions, all of which showed that they did not even glimpse the divine nature of scripture, and the more they admired its mysteries the more clearly their attitude was that of servility rather than belief.[13]

Spinoza's solution to the problem was to separate reason and religion, each with its own domain, totally independent of the other, unable to make any claim on the other, to be suited to or to do anything against the other. The one was the realm of truth and wisdom, the other that of devotion and obedience. The one embraced a rational knowledge of God that observed his nature in and for itself and the other a revealed knowledge, a divine gift not needed for science. The goal of the one was truth, that of the other obedience and piety. Summarizing his extended discussion of the prophets in the *Treatise,* Spinoza stated that they could mediate no knowledge of natural or spiritual things, for which reason one was obliged to believe only what made up the purpose and core of their revelation, that

11. Spinoza, *Theological-Political Treatise,* p. 166.
12. Spinoza, *Theological-Political Treatise,* p. 167.
13. Spinoza, *Theological-Political Treatise,* p. 5.

is, the summons to righteousness and love of neighbor.[14] Further, the one, the rational knowledge of God, was possible only for a few, whereas the other, obedience, could be performed by all. Finally, the one had for its basis universal concepts derived from nature and the other a history and language derived from scripture and revelation.

Since, according to Spinoza, history and language attached to revelation, truth, wisdom, or God could not be mediated through words. They could not because, for one thing, words were nothing but external signs, consequently not identifiable with "the eternal word" written in the heart. Spinoza wrote,

> Those who look upon the Bible, in its present form, as a message for mankind sent down by God from heaven, will doubtless cry out that I have committed the sin against the Holy Spirit in maintaining that the Word of God is faulty, mutilated, adulterated and inconsistent, that we possess it only in fragmentary form, and that the original of God's covenant with the Jews has perished. However, I am confident that reflection will at once put an end to their outcry; for not only reason itself, but the assertions of the prophets and the Apostles clearly proclaim that God's eternal Word and covenant and true religion are divinely inscribed in men's hearts — that is, in men's minds — and that this is the true handwriting of God which he has sealed with his own seal, this seal being the idea of himself, the image of his own divinity, as it were.[15]

For another thing, truth, wisdom, or God could not be mediated through words because their definition depended on their use. It was their use that determined their sanctity. "If," Spinoza wrote, "they are so arranged that readers are moved to devotion, then these words will be sacred. . . . But if these words at a later time fall into disuse . . . then both words and book will be without value and without sanctity."[16]

According to Spinoza, this radical separation of reason and religion, of philosophy and biblical interpretation, the former a "divine gift," a "natural light," a "revealed word of God," a "simple grasp of the divine Spirit,"

14. The statement that according to Spinoza all that could be honestly gleaned from the Bible was charity is too restrictive; see Michael Legaspi, *The Death of Scripture and the Rise of Biblical Studies* (Oxford: Oxford University Press, 2010), p. 24.

15. Spinoza, *Theological-Political Treatise*, p. 145.

16. Spinoza, *Theological-Political Treatise*, p. 146.

and the latter embedded in history and language, was determined by the "divine gift," by reason itself. As for the biblical texts, any truth content in the philosophical sense was excluded. At issue in those texts was not truth but "sense" or "meaning." "The point at issue," Spinoza insisted, "is merely the meaning of the texts, not their truth." "I would go further," he continued,

> in seeking the meaning of Scripture we should take every precaution against the undue influence, not only of our own prejudices, but of our faculty of reason insofar as that is based on the principles of natural cognition. In order to avoid confusion between true meaning and truth of fact, the former must be sought simply from linguistic usage, or from a process of reasoning that looks to no other basis than Scripture.[17]

But if the *Treatise* was not cunningly devised to trap the unwary,[18] its acknowledgment of reason as the court of appeal that directed biblical interpretation to "sense," not "truth," however calculated to separate, perhaps even to demote, was not intended to denigrate or eliminate faith or religion. In fact, the two unrelated and independent "domains" enjoyed material agreement, given the difference in matters of form. In fact, they had to agree since the purpose and core of the revelation was coincident with the rational knowledge of God. They had to agree unless those few capable of that rational knowledge possessed something the others could never enjoy — a notion Spinoza would have rejected. For this reason an obligatory nature attached to the biblical utterances, at least respecting their purpose and core. Spinoza wrote,

> The domain of reason . . . does not extend so far as to enable us to conclude that men can achieve blessedness simply through obedience without understanding, whereas this alone is the message of theology, which commands only obedience and neither seeks nor is able to oppose reason.[19]

17. Spinoza, *Theological-Political Treatise,* pp. 88-89. In the opinion of one scholar, this accent on the "sense" of the speech, and not its truth, is the place in Spinoza's system where the concept of "sense" as per current definition begins its career. See Rainer Piepmeier, "Baruch de Spinoza: Vernunftanspruch und Hermeneutik," in *Klassiker der Hermeneutik,* ed. Ulrich Nassen (Paderborn: Ferdinand Schöningh, 1982), p. 31.

18. See Preus, *Spinoza and the Irrelevance of Biblical Authority,* p. 13, n. 39.

19. Spinoza, *Theological-Political Treatise,* p. 169.

By this construal, theology, religion, faith was a necessity:

> I maintain absolutely that this fundamental dogma of theology [i.e., that men may be saved simply by obedience] cannot be investigated by the natural light of reason, or at least that nobody has been successful in proving it, and that therefore it was essential that there should be revelation.[20]

Since, according to Spinoza, religion belonged to a sphere totally apart from and independent of reason, then, however reason might direct, religion deserved respect as a domain reason could not absorb. Then it followed that the biblical tradition required a hermeneutic all its own. Of the tradition itself Spinoza reckoned there was little to doubt its conscientious transmission. Stating that the "Divine Law" as taught by scripture had reached us uncorrupted, he added that other matters beyond doubt were the "chief historical narratives," the "chief facts of the Life of Christ" and his passion. "It is therefore impossible to believe," he added, "that, without the connivance of a large part of mankind — which is quite inconceivable — later generations handed down a version of the main outlines of these events different from what they had received."[21] "So," Spinoza concluded,

> any alterations or faults can have occurred only with respect to minor matters, such as a few details in history or prophecy designed to foster people's devotion, or in a few miracles so as to perplex philosophers, or in speculative matters after schismatics had begun the practice of introducing these into religion in order that each of them might buttress his own fictions by misusing divine authority.[22]

Naturally, distinctions had to be drawn. Whoever accepted everything in the Bible as "the universal and absolute teaching about God" was bound to confuse popular opinion with divine doctrine, to proclaim as divine teaching the figments and arbitrary opinions of men, and to abuse scriptural authority.[23] Since the Bible taught things that could not be derived

---

20. Spinoza, *Theological-Political Treatise,* pp. 169-70.
21. Spinoza, *Theological-Political Treatise,* p. 152.
22. Spinoza, *Theological-Political Treatise,* p. 152.
23. Spinoza, *Theological-Political Treatise,* p. 158.

from the principles of "natural light," that is, since no certain knowledge could be had regarding what was reported in the Bible, those things had to be drawn from the Bible alone, just as a knowledge of nature from nature alone. In this sense, the biblical writings took on an objectivity akin to that of natural objects.[24] For this reason, Spinoza rejected Maimonides' view that the Bible's true meaning could neither result nor be taken from itself as "harmful, unprofitable and absurd" since it deprived the common people of any confidence they could have in the Bible's meaning by simply reading it.[25]

Early on, in the preface to the *Treatise,* Spinoza outlined in some length the method he would follow in reading and interpreting the biblical text:

> I deliberately resolved to examine Scripture afresh, conscientiously and freely, and to admit nothing as its teaching which I did not most clearly derive from it. With this precaution I formulated a method of interpreting the Bible, and thus equipped I began first of all to seek answers to these questions: What is prophecy? In what way did God reveal himself to the prophets? Why were these men acceptable to God? Was it because they attained rare heights in their understanding of God and Nature? Or was it only because of their piety? . . . I then went on to enquire why the Hebrews were called God's chosen people. When I realized that this was for no other reason than that God chose for them a certain territory where they might live in security and wellbeing, I was led to understand that the law revealed by God to Moses was simply the laws of the Hebrew state alone, and was therefore binding on none but the Hebrews. . . . Furthermore, to ascertain whether Scripture taught that the human intellect is naturally corrupt, I resolved to enquire whether universal religion — i.e. the divine law revealed to all mankind through the Prophets and the Apostles — differed from the teachings of the natural light of reason; and again, whether miracles contravene the order of Nature, and whether they demonstrate God's existence and providence with greater clarity

---

24. The principle that scripture had to be interpreted by scripture alone was only in a formal way reminiscent of the Reformation concept of scripture as its own interpreter ("scriptura sui ipsius interpres"); for Luther and the Reformers this concept was theologically based, but for Spinoza it was a philosophical impossibility; see Piepmeier, "Baruch de Spinoza," p. 30.

25. Spinoza, *Theological-Political Treatise,* p. 102.

and certainty than events which we understand clearly and distinctly through their prime causes.[26]

Such a method, Spinoza wrote, was no different from the method of interpreting nature, and was in complete accord with it:

> For the method of interpreting Nature consists essentially in composing a detailed study of Nature from which, as being the source of our assured data, we can deduce the definitions of the things of Nature. Now in exactly the same way the task of Scriptural interpretation requires us to make a straightforward study of Scripture, and from this, as the source of our fixed data and principles, to deduce by logical inference the meaning of the authors of Scripture.[27]

First of all, this method involved a study of the language in which the Bible was written. Second, it involved listing the statements in each book so as to have at hand all the texts on the same subject. Third, and with particular reference to the prophetical books, it meant describing the circumstances relevant to each, giving the life, character, and pursuits of each author, detailing who he was, on what occasion and at what time and for whom and in what language he wrote. The study also involved explaining how each book was first received, into whose hands it fell, how many versions it underwent, how it came to be included in the canon, and how all the books, ultimately regarded as sacred, came to be united into a single whole.

In the use of this method only "the natural light" sufficed. Difficulty in interpretation did not derive from the lack of power in that light, but from the "negligence (not to say malice) of those who failed to compile a historical study of Scripture" while it was still possible.[28] Whoever awaited a supernatural illumination to understand the meaning of a prophet or apostle was thus "sadly in need of the natural light" common to all.[29] As for the figurative or metaphorical interpretation used by the "common run of theologians" to explain whatever their natural light convinced them contravened "the divine nature," it needed jettisoning if the Bible was in-

26. Spinoza, *Theological-Political Treatise*, pp. 5-6.
27. Spinoza, *Theological-Political Treatise*, p. 87.
28. Spinoza, *Theological-Political Treatise*, p. 99.
29. Spinoza, *Theological-Political Treatise*, p. 100.

tended for the common folk as well as the learned.[30] What remained of the Bible once its purpose and core were exposed should give the interpreter no pause. "We have no reason to be unduly anxious," Spinoza wrote, "concerning the other contents of Scripture; for since for the most part they are beyond the grasp of reason and intellect, they belong to the sphere of the curious rather than the profitable."[31]

Spinoza did not balk at indicating the difficulties attaching to his method. First of all, no information was left to posterity respecting the basic principles and study of the Hebrew language. Second, the language gave rise to ambiguities that made it impossible to devise a method that could guarantee certainty respecting the meaning of a biblical passage. Among these ambiguities were the substitution of one letter for another involving the same organ of speech; the multiple meanings of conjunctions and adverbs; and verbs in the indicative mood lacking the present, imperfect, pluperfect, and future perfect tenses. Added to these ambiguities the absence of letters for vowels as well as of punctuation rendered impossible a method that could account for them all. Further difficulties included the impossibility of constructing a history of all the biblical books, and the fact that some had not been preserved in the language in which they were first written.[32] These difficulties, wrote Spinoza, were so grave that "we either do not know the true meaning of Scripture or we can do no more than make conjecture."

Ultimately, however, these difficulties could inhibit understanding "only in matters beyond normal comprehension," not in matters "open to intellectual perception, whereof we can readily form a clear conception." Obviously, those "matters" had to do with the purpose and core of the biblical tradition. Spinoza concluded his enumeration of the problems awaiting the interpreter with these words:

> Things which of their own nature are readily apprehended can never be so obscurely worded that they are not easily understood. . . . Thus we can conclude that, with the help of such a historical study of Scripture as is available to us, we can readily grasp the meanings of its moral doctrines and be certain of their true sense. For the teachings of true piety are expressed in quite ordinary language, and being directed to

30. Spinoza, *Theological-Political Treatise,* p. 157.
31. Spinoza, *Theological-Political Treatise,* p. 99.
32. See Spinoza, *Theological-Political Treatise,* pp. 94-98.

the generality of people they are therefore straightforward and easy to understand. Since true salvation and blessedness consist in true contentment of mind and we find our true peace only in what we clearly understand, it most evidently follows that we can understand the meaning of Scripture with confidence in matters relating to salvation and necessary blessedness.[33]

John Locke

John Locke (1632-1704), together with Francis Bacon (1561-1626) and Isaac Newton (1643-1727) described as "patron saints" and "pioneers" of the Enlightenment in contrast to its French propagandists and colporteurs, or cited as "the last in the long line of pagan Christians,"[34] authored a text entitled *The Reasonableness of Christianity* (1695). In it he attempted to demonstrate precisely what the title of the book suggests. Surprisingly, and to the irritation of members of the "guild," Locke did not initiate the attempt with an appeal to reason, but to the infallible authority of a divinely inspired Bible. According to Locke, scripture was a divine revelation, the written Word of God. Evidence for this major hermeneutical presupposition Locke either refused to give or regarded as unnecessary. At the same time, he acknowledged that the Bible had been written by fallible human beings, but it would be left to others to reconcile the contradictories and attempt an analogy between the divinity and humanity of the Bible and the two natures of Christ.

Part and parcel of his presupposition was Locke's insistence on a plain and intelligible gospel. Those fundamental articles of faith contained in the Bible and comprising the essence of Christian belief were equally available to all, thus not discoverable by reason. The ignorant could locate them, and the learned would find they did not contradict reason. Both would thus be indebted to a revelation transcending intellection. Locke's discussion of the entry of death by way of Adam's sin illustrates his insistence on the Bible's clarity:

This is so clear . . . and so much the current of the New Testament, that no body can deny, but that the Doctrine of the Gospel is, that

33. Spinoza, *Theological-Political Treatise*, p. 98.
34. Spinoza, *Theological-Political Treatise*, pp. 11, 321.

Death came on all Men by *Adam's* sin; only they differ about the signification of the word *Death*. For some will have it to be a state of Guilt wherein not only he, but all his Posterity was so involved, that every one descended of him deserved endless torment in Hell-fire. . . . But it seems a strange way of understanding a Law, which requires the plainest and directest words, that by *Death* should be meant Eternal Life in misery.[35]

Still and all, since the fundamental articles of faith contained in the Bible were available to all, belief had to consist of intellectual assent. The "perspicuity" of scripture and intellectual assent were thus complementary, though in the last analysis reason was to determine what was and was not divine revelation.

This description of Locke's principal hermeneutical presupposition may be too surgical. For example, in chapter XI of *Reasonableness,* he writes that "repentance is as absolute a Condition of the Covenant of Grace, as Faith; and as necessary to be performed as that."[36] He thus seemed to require something more than or in addition to intellectual assent for salvation, and by inference, for understanding or interpreting those fundamental articles forming the essence of Christian belief. But again, according to Locke, the evidence for a crucial part of the Bible's content, that is, the person and activity of Jesus, could not help but evoke rational assent. This reference to Jesus' centrality was a characteristic of Enlightenment reflection. In a section of his *Religion within the Limits of Reason Alone,* entitled "The Christian Religion as a Natural Religion," Kant writes that if Jesus cannot be regarded as the Founder of the religion written in all men's hearts, certainly as Founder of the first true church he deserves highest place. Then, to certify Jesus' authority as a "divine mission" Kant cites those teachings that accord with a "religion of reason" and concludes:

To those, therefore, who with hand in lap quite passively suppose they can await this moral possession as a heavenly gift down from

---

35. John Locke, *The Reasonableness of Christianity,* ed. John C. Higgins-Biddle (Oxford: Clarendon, 1999), p. 7. This review of Locke is in part indebted to Biddle's introduction, as well as to Arthur W. Wainwright's comments on Locke's *A Paraphrase and Notes on the Epistles of St Paul to the Galatians, 1 and 2 Corinthians, Romans, Ephesians,* 2 vols. (Oxford: Clarendon, 1987).

36. Locke, *The Reasonableness of Christianity,* p. 110.

above, [Jesus] denies all hope. Whoever makes no use of the natural disposition toward the good which lies in human nature (as a talent entrusted to it), in the slothful assurance that a higher moral influence will otherwise supply him with the moral condition and perfection he lacks, this one he threatens that even the good he might have done from his natural condition, shall not be able to support him because of this neglect.[37]

For Locke as for his contemporaries, Jesus' teaching as recorded in the Gospel narratives was the principal authority in matters of religion. But Locke went a step beyond when he attempted to prove the truth of Jesus' self-declaration that he was Messiah by referring to Jesus' miracles, to his circumlocution, or to his "plain and direct words":

The healing of the Sick, the restoring sight to the Blind by a word, the raising, and being raised from the Dead, are matters of Fact, which they can without difficulty conceive; And that he who does such things, must do them by the assistance of a Divine Power. These things lie level to the ordinariest Apprehension.[38]

Locke concluded,

that as it suits the lowest Capacities of Reasonable Creatures, so it reaches and satisfies, Nay, enlightens the highest. The most elevated Understandings cannot but submit to the Authority of this Doctrine as Divine.[39]

Here, certainly, Locke parted company with the greater number of Enlightenment thinkers, and certainly from Kant who regarded belief in miracles as a belief in knowing something by experience that could not possibly be accepted as having occurred when measured against the "objective" laws of experience.[40]

37. Immanuel Kant, "Die christliche Religion als natürliche Religion," in *Religion innerhalb der Grenzen der blossen Vernunft*, ed. Karl Vorländer, intro. Hermann Noack (Hamburg: Verlag von Felix Meiner, 1956), pp. 176, 179.

38. Locke, *The Reasonableness of Christianity*, p. 158.

39. Locke, *The Reasonableness of Christianity*, p. 159.

40. Immanuel Kant, "Allgemeine Anmerkung (von den 'Gnadenmitteln')," in *Religion innerhalb der Grenzen der blossen Vernunft*, p. 220.

From the clarity and intelligibility of a Bible available to all Locke drew the conclusion that no authority existed beyond the Bible's own designation of the fundamental articles of faith. He thus contrasted biblical authority so conceived with theological systems, and attacked the idea of the pope as an infallible interpreter. God was capable of communicating his will to humanity without such interpreters:

> A Collection of Writings designed by God for the Instruction of the illiterate bulk of Mankind in the way to Salvation; and therefore generally and in necessary points to be understood in the plain direct meaning of the words and phrases, such as they may be supposed to have had in the mouths of the Speakers, who used them according to the Language of that Time and Country wherein they lived, without such learned, Artificial, and forced senses of them, as are sought out, and Put upon them in most of the Systems of Divinity, according to the Notions, that each one has been bred up in.[41]

Hostility toward a magisterium authorized to regulate or interpret doctrine with a pope at its apex was an all-too familiar target. The Königsberger had called such a structure a fetishism bordering on paganism:

> The form of it (hierarchy) may be monarchical or aristocratic or democratic. This has to do merely with its organization. Beneath all these forms its constitution is and remains forever despotic. Where statutes of faith are part of the law that determines form, there a clergy is in power that believes it can dispense with reason and finally even with scholarship, since as sole authorized guardian and interpreter of the will of the invisible Lawgiver it has the exclusive right to superintend the requisites of faith and thus, equipped with this power, may not convince, but merely command.[42]

Locke gave legs to his presuppositions by adopting a historical, yet not always literal, method of interpretation that included categorizing the content of biblical texts, drawing comparisons between them, giving at-

---

41. Locke, *The Reasonableness of Christianity,* p. 6.
42. Immanuel Kant, "Vom Pfaffentum als einem Regiment im Afterdienst des guten Prinzips," part I, "Vom Dienst und Afterdienst unter der Herrschaft des guten Prinzips oder von Religion und Pfaffentum," in *Religion innerhalb der Grenzen der blossen Vernunft,* p. 203.

tention to their contexts, and, for a lack of better description, what might be called a distinguishing between things lesser and greater in the Bible. Accordingly, Locke distinguished four categories of the Bible's content. To the first category belonged the Genesis narrative of the forbidden fruit, a story that neither needed nor deserved a reader or interpreter. To the second belonged such profound mysteries of the scripture as the Trinity or the union of the divine and human natures of Christ, mysteries that transcended the capacity of the human mind and could not be interpreted. In the third category Locke set the things that scripture makes necessary to salvation — the moral duties, so clear and unambiguous that none could doubt them. In the fourth and final category he placed matters that in themselves and by nature are indifferent. As to comparison, Locke could describe his method overall as the comparing of texts with texts, or the reading and rereading of the Gospels and Acts. More important, he was insistent about the need to interpret texts from out of their contexts. In chapter XV of *Reasonableness,* he wrote:

> We must look into the drift of the Discourse, observe the coherence and connexion of the Parts, and see how it is consistent with itself, and other parts of Scripture; if we will conceive it right. We must not cull out, as best suits our System, here and there a Period or a Verse; as if they were all distinct and independent Aphorisms; and make these the Fundamental articles of the Christian Faith.

and again,

> Where [the interpreter] cannot put several Texts, and make them consist together; What Remedy? He must either interpret one by the other, or suspend his Opinion. He that thinks that more is, or can be required, of poor frail Man in matters of Faith, will do well to consider what absurdities he will run into.[43]

The evidence is clear that Locke spent a good part of his book attempting to prove that the Bible distinguished a few fundamental articles. Again in chapter XV, he wrote that the truths contained in the epistles were not necessary to salvation, but were for edification. Respecting the claims of theological systems he wrote,

43. Locke, *The Reasonableness of Christianity,* pp. 165, 169.

Yet every Sentence of theirs must not be taken up, and looked on as a Fundamental Article necessary to Salvation, without an explicit belief whereof, no body could be a Member of Christ's Church here, Nor be admitted into his Eternal Kingdom hereafter,

and made appeal to those who allowed for scripture's authority, but differed over the significance of its various texts.[44]

Locke was not backward about detecting errors in the Bible, no doubt the consequence of his assumption of its having been written by fallible human beings. For example, in his discussion of the term "death," he notes that some interpreters describe it as a state in which not only Adam but all his posterity was involved, so that all who descended from him deserved torment in hell. This was, wrote Locke, a strange way of understanding. Further, it implied a state of "necessary sinning, and provoking God in every Action that men do." The reason for this strange interpretation, Locke concluded, "we shall perhaps find in some mistaken places of the New Testament."[45] Clearly, Locke was nautical miles removed from five-point Calvinism.

Locke's interpretation of Romans 3:24 contained in his paraphrases of the Pauline epistles aptly illustrates his method. Beginning with the historical reference, "From Corinth, Anno Aerae Vulg 57, Neronis, 3," that is, in the fifty-seventh year of the common era, the third of Nero's reign, he gives a synopsis of the entire epistle, then proceeds to its first two sections, then finally to the third, containing chapter 3, verse 24. After commenting on the contents of the section, he quotes the text according to the Authorized (King James) Version of the so-called *Textus Receptus,* for which Robertus Stephanus (1503-59), the celebrated Parisian book printer, and Theodore Beza (1519-1605), friend of John Calvin, furnished the basis. Locke then attached to the text a complete paraphrase, and engages in a brief lexicographical study of Romans 3:24, finally devoting considerable space to a discussion of the theological consequences of assigning the verse an Anselmian interpretation:

If anyone will from the literal signification of the word in English persist in it against St Pauls declaration that it necessarily implies an equivalent price paid, I desire him to consider to whom: And that if

44. Locke, *The Reasonableness of Christianity,* p. 105, n. 1; pp. 167-71.
45. Locke, *The Reasonableness of Christianity,* p. 8.

we will strictly adhere to the metaphor it must be to those, whom the redeemed are in bondage to, and from whom we are redeemd. viz Sin and Satan. . . . Nor could the price be paid to god in strictness of justice . . . unless the same person ought, by that strict justice to have, both the thing redeemd and the price paid for its redemption. For 'tis to god we are redeemd by the death of Christ.[46]

Whether relating to his method or its presuppositions, Locke could not avoid his critics. Among them were the French biblical scholar and encyclopedist Jean Le Clerc (1657-1736); Robert Jenkin (1656-1727), Fellow and later master of St. John's College in Cambridge; the Anglican theologian Thomas Scott (1747-1821); the Methodist theologian Richard Watson (1781-1833); and the American Ezra Stiles (1727-95), president of Yale College. Le Clerc claimed Locke would have succeeded at a better interpretation if he had had a better knowledge of the biblical languages. Jenkin attacked the *Paraphrase* for its making mockery of orthodoxy; Scott spoke of it as darkening counsel "by words without knowledge"; Watson took Locke to task for "trifling" with Romans 3:24; and Styles appreciated neither the mode nor the theology of the *Paraphrase,* citing its popularity as due to its Arian and Arminian principles.[47] No doubt, despite his decision to lay aside all authorities except that of the Bible itself, the criticisms cited suggest that certain "alien commitments" influenced Locke's scripture interpretation. Neither those daring to "think on their own" nor the orthodox Christians were content with him. In his valedictory on *The Reasonableness of Christianity,* Peter Gay writes:

The book did not please the pious, who thought it scandalous that Christianity could be summed up by the Divinity of Christ, and revelation be reduced to an exalted form of reason. But it did not satisfy the philosophes either: the title of Locke's book struck them as a contradiction in terms, and, largely on Lockean grounds, they repudiated any possibility of a reasonable revelation. It was a sign of their distance from Locke that while they quoted his other writings with delight, they generally passed over his *Reasonableness of Christianity* with respectful silence.[48]

46. Locke, *A Paraphrase and Notes,* vol. 2, p. 508.
47. See Wainwright's introduction to Locke's *A Paraphrase and Notes,* pp. 59-73.
48. Gay, *The Enlightenment,* p. 321.

The Enlightenment

Christian Wolff

Between Gottfried Leibniz (1646-1716), the great polymath of the seventeenth century, and Immanuel Kant, the towering thinker of the eighteenth, stands Christian Wolff, philosopher and mathematician, born at Breslau in 1679. At his father's wish Wolff studied theology at Jena, but soon drifted toward philosophy, mathematics, and physics. In 1702 he passed the master's examination at Leipzig, and in 1703 completed his habilitation, which granted him the right to teach and in which he argued on behalf of mathematics as the essence of the scientific method. On the recommendation of Leibniz, Wolff was called to the newly founded Friedrichs University of Halle, where he added physics and philosophy to his lectures on mathematics. Wolff's advocacy of theological truths as based on the evidence of mathematical certitude drew the reproach of atheism from his pietist colleagues, among them August Hermann Francke. The dispute broke out openly in 1721 when Wolff delivered an oration praising the purity of the moral precepts of Confucius, hailing them as evidence of the power of reason to attain to moral certainty on its own. After numerous and continuous skirmishes, Wolff's enemies finally gained the ear of the king, Friedrich Wilhelm I, who in 1723 decreed that "within forty-eight hours of receiving this order [Wolff] is to leave the city of Halle and all our other royal lands, on pain of hanging." In 1740 the king died suddenly, and his successor, Frederich the Great, recalled Wolff to Halle, where his entry had all the earmarks of a triumphal procession. Wolff's influence was enormous. Until displaced by the Kantian revolution, his philosophy held almost undisputed sway in Germany. Among his honors, he was invited by Tsar Peter the Great to serve as president of the newly established Academy of Science at St. Petersburg. For decades, Kant read logic and metaphysics after the style of Wolff, and celebrated him as the discoverer of the "spirit of thoroughness." Wolff died in 1754.

In two of his principal works, _Vernünftige Gedanken_ and _Philosophia Rationalis_,[49] Wolff devotes space to the interpretation of Sacred Scripture,

49. The complete title of the first reads _Vernünftige Gedanken von den Kräften des menschlichen Verstandes und ihrem richtigen Gebrauche in Erkenntnis der Wahrheit_ (Rational Thoughts on the Powers of Human Understanding and Their Proper Employment in the Cognizing of Truth), and that of the second _Philosophia Rationalis sive Logica_ (Rational Philosophy or Logic). Both appear in the _Gesammelte Werke,_ ed. and rev. J. Ecole, J. E. Hofmann, M. Thomann, and H. W. Arndt (Hildesheim: Georg Olms Verlagsbuchhandlung, 1965), the first volume edited by Arndt (1965) and the second by Ecole (1983).

the first containing twelve brief and the second fourteen more or less extended rules or canons. At the outset of his discussion in the *Philosophia Rationalis* Wolff asserts that there is no doubt that there are propositions in Holy Scripture that are able to be searched out by reason. He thus proposes to use logic in his interpretation of the Bible, or, as he states, to indicate "how, through benefit of it, ideas joined to the subjects and predicates of propositions may be investigated, and . . . the nexus between subject and predicate arrived at."[50]

To the question why this should be so, Wolff gives a twofold answer. The first is that the Holy Spirit does not immediately waken in us awareness of the connection between the word of the scriptural text and the idea it intends to convey. Here, the intention to keep clear of any suggestion of enthusiasm is obvious. The second part of his answer, and which undoubtedly aroused the ire of his critics, is that truths that pertain to earthly things and to God can be known through the proper use of the natural powers of the understanding. Like many thinkers of the Enlightenment Wolff conceived hermeneutical knowledge in analogy to the knowledge of nature and the knowledge of nature after the fashion of mathematics. From the idea of nature as a text written with mathematical signs to that of the world as a system of signs produced by God followed the idea of universal or general hermeneutics as the science of the interpretation of these signs. In consequence the text, of whatever sort, whether pertaining to earthly things or to God, was construed as a phenomenon of nature,[51] thus perceptible through human understanding.

Wolff's argument is as follows. The Bible contains doctrines that can be classified according to whether they pertain to earthly things or to God. Clearly, human reason is able to grasp the former. Since, as is clear from Ephesians 3:10,[52] the wisdom of God can be perceived from the works of redemption, divine truths must likewise enjoy such connection with other truths as is clear from their ideas, and thus be perceptible through reason. In fact, it is the coherence of reason and revelation that justifies the use of philosophy, or, as Wolff puts it, "the laws of scientific method" in the interpretation of scripture. As he writes,

50. Wolff, *Philosophia Rationalis,* para. 968, p. 692.

51. See Luigi Cataldi Madonna, "Die Unzeitgemässe Hermeneutik Christian Wolffs," in *Unzeitgemässe Hermeneutik: Verstehung und Interpretation im Denken der Aufklärung,* ed. Axel Bühler (Frankfurt am Main: Vittorio Klostermann, 1994), pp. 31-32.

52. "So that through the church the wisdom of God in its rich variety might now be made known to the rulers and authorities in the heavenly places."

"such concord argues that reason and revelation have the same author, namely God, whom the same reckoning demonstrates to be the author of reason."[53]

As to the possible mixture of perception or understanding with faith, with belief, Wolff is sanguine respecting its avoidance. If, for example, we admit the main clause of a given sentence purely for the sake of its subordinate clauses, and those clauses are accessible to reason, then the main clause is also to be regarded as accessible to reason. On the other hand, if those clauses are not accessible to reason but require being taken on faith, then the main clause is to be so taken. In one paragraph of the *Philosophia Rationalis* Wolff goes to considerable lengths to instruct the reader that whatever contradicts what is certain a posteriori or has been demonstrated by other passages in scripture is false, and whatever agrees with either of the two is true. He then prefaces his illustration of this canon by stating that the first part of the proposition enjoys unanimous reception "since the truth revealed cannot contradict the natural [truth]."[54]

In outlining the task of the interpreter, Wolff is insistent that to every word a specific concept or idea is attached. Since, he writes, the Holy Scripture is no empty sound, a certain concept must be joined with every word: "With single words there must be single ideas."[55] To suppose there are words in the Bible with which no idea agrees would render them sounds without meaning — "which," Wolff adds, "to think of Sacred Scripture, is impious."[56] On the other hand, to imagine a multiplicity of ideas as attached to a given word would be to "cut off the divine words in enthusiasm," to which Wolff adds, "in fact not one work is evident in many words."[57] Words are thus of such a sort that they waken in us the ideas consonant or in agreement with them. This consonance occurs by authorial intent. Insisting that there is only one sense, the literal sense intended by the author, and since it is the author who furnishes the idea needed for this or that word, it is incumbent on the interpreter to offer no other idea than that joined to the word by the intention of its author. The goal of interpretation, then, is neither logical truth, that is, establishing the predicate by the subject, nor metaphysical truth, that is, interpreting the sentence in agreement with reality, but only the sense intended by the

53. Wolff, *Philosophia Rationalis,* para. 979, p. 703.
54. Wolff, *Philosophia Rationalis,* para. 976, p. 699.
55. Wolff, *Philosophia Rationalis,* para. 968, p. 692.
56. Wolff, *Philosophia Rationalis,* para. 968, p. 692.
57. Wolff, *Philosophia Rationalis,* para. 970, p. 694.

author since the author himself is his best interpreter. Arriving at this sense spells "authentic interpretation," the interpretation that enjoys undisputed eminence. Where a given text is unclear Wolff allows for deviation from the rule. He writes, "when the author connects an unclear concept with a few expressions, but the reader a clear one, and both have the same object in mind, then the reader understands the spirit of the author and explains him better."[58] The reader who replaces an unclear with a clear concept in his interpretation of the author thus makes the author's idea clearer than the author himself was able to do. To this function of making clear what is unclear Wolff reserves the term "to interpret" *(interpretari)* in contrast to the term "to understand" *(intelligere),* which denotes the more general activity of producing and receiving signs within a linguistic community. When, therefore, the speech of an author has a fixed and determinative significance, and expresses his mind with sufficient intelligibility, one need not interpret but only understand.[59]

For example, Wolff writes, when Joshua orders the sun to stand still, he has in mind a particular, single idea joined to the words he speaks. The mind of Joshua is understood when the same idea is roused in the mind of the reader. Or, when Paul calls himself the servant of Jesus Christ he has a particular idea in mind as is expressed by the words. When the same idea is roused in the reader's mind he understands the mind of the apostle. As to the identity of the author, Wolff never leaves the reader in doubt; the author is God, though, as in the instances cited above, he may refer to another, as, for example, to Paul.[60] As he writes, "either God himself must teach the idea we need for this or that word or must present to us no other idea than the one we already have."[61] According to the twelfth rule in *Vernünftige Gedanken* the interpreter cannot depend on linguistics to determine what idea is to be linked to what word. Linguistics can only indicate what ideas people had who first named an object. But if I am to know whether or not such was done rationally, I must have learned to know the object in another way in order to judge whether that original nam-

58. Wolff, *Philosophia Rationalis,* para. 929, quoted by Madonna, "Die Unzeitgemässe Hermeneutik Christian Wolffs," p. 35.

59. See Madonna, "Die Unzeitgemässe Hermeneutik Christian Wolffs," pp. 37-38.

60. Wolff, *Philosophia Rationalis,* para. 969, p. 693: "Paul calls himself the servant of Jesus Christ. When he utters these words, this may be the idea in his mind that he expresses with them. Therefore, as the reader rouses the same [idea] in his mind when he reads them he understands the mind of Paul."

61. Wolff, *Vernünftige Gedanken,* para. 4, p. 229.

ing was correct or incorrect.[62] Wolff writes that "the Spirit of God does not immediately waken in us what idea is to be attached to what word." Otherwise, it would not be necessary to translate the original text into other languages; the reader-interpreter would immediately come upon the idea. Experience, however, teaches that this does not happen. For this reason the connection between word and idea as intended or taught by God must be perceived through reason, or as Wolff puts it, "through the proper use of the natural powers of the understanding." Unless there are words in scripture with which no ideas agree — an "impious" notion according to Wolff — [63] logic is indispensable in its interpretation. Respecting his axiom that to every word a particular idea is connected and that in reading or interpreting this connection is "aroused" in the mind of the reader ("in animo legentis excitare"), Wolff almost always assigns this arousal or wakening to the Holy Spirit. But he can also write of the words themselves as having this force. For example, one paragraph of the *Philosophia Rationalis* reads: "Ideas joined to the words of Holy Scripture while reading are not immediately aroused in the mind of the reader by the Holy Spirit but by force of the words read."[64] In another, Wolff writes that the words we read must rouse in us the ideas joined with them. Since words are the signs of ideas they are unable to waken those ideas in our mind in any other way than by producing the ideas of the things signified. Words are thus the means used by the Spirit to effect the awakening in the mind of the reader — a concept reminiscent of the orthodox, Reformation understanding of scripture as a "means of grace." But it is also clear that the wakening or arousal is conceived in harmony with Wolff's idea of the consonance of reason and revelation. As he puts it, "in Holy Scripture, no definition is given a word, nor can any other idea be assumed as from God than that which now inheres in our mind, or which we may have in ourselves, when by the same work there is experienced in us that of which it speaks."[65] When, for example, Joshua commanded the sun to stand still he did not rouse in his mind any other idea than that which he normally had from observing the sun in its relation to the earth. When commanding it to stand still, he had in mind only that the sun would retain its place and not alter it. Whoever would contend that the word "to stand still" signified

62. Wolff, *Vernünftige Gedanken,* para. 12, p. 231.
63. Wolff, *Philosophia Rationalis,* para. 968, p. 692.
64. Wolff, *Philosophia Rationalis,* para. 970, p. 693.
65. Wolff, *Philosophia Rationalis,* para. 971, p. 694.

inhibiting the movement of the sun would add to the mind of Joshua what is alien to it. Likewise, when in writing to the Romans Paul calls himself the servant of Christ, he is able to supply no other idea than the Romans already possessed, that of a person obligated to expend every strength of mind and body in another's service, enjoined by another, doing nothing according to one's own decision, weighing everything by another's command, seeking nothing for oneself but laying aside everything except those things that belong to the other.

Lest the conclusion be drawn that every word of the Bible rouses the appropriate idea in the mind of the reader or interpreter, Wolff draws a distinction between words to which we are and to which we are not able to attach the corresponding ideas. To the first category he assigns what he terms "mixed" and to the second "pure articles of faith," customarily called "mysteries."

"Mixed" articles include those biblical terms that refer to spiritual change, natural corruption, and other matters connected with birth. These, Wolff writes, can be supplied with no other ideas than those the reader "intuits" in himself *(in seipso intuetur)*.[66] For example, Wolff writes, it is coherent with Holy Scripture that God should be conceived as spirit, as immaterial. Thus, to assign God the organ of sight would oppose this conception. Clearly, then, the "eye of God" cannot denote an organ of sense but rather the "intuitive cognition of things present." According to this "general significance," the visual organ and the divine attribute enjoy a certain affinity.[67] Or again, in Genesis 6:6 we read that "the Lord was sorry that he had made humankind on the earth." If, Wolff writes, you interpret "sorry" as sadness from something badly done, it contradicts the interpretation and propositions demonstrated in natural theology and in the clear words of scripture. Natural theology indicates that from eternity God saw the evil done of men, and in scripture, for example, in 1 Samuel 1:29, regret is removed from God as repugnant to him. Consequently, the interpretation of God as "sorry" after the human fashion departs from the meaning of scripture conformable to the canon that things said of God in human fashion are to be understood by things, traits, characteristics that become him.[68]

According to Wolff, where the supernatural is concerned, God makes

66. Wolff, *Philosophia Rationalis,* para. 971, p. 694.
67. Wolff, *Philosophia Rationalis,* para. 975, p. 699.
68. Wolff, *Philosophia Rationalis,* para. 976, pp. 700-701.

use of words that by nature we do not understand and which he does not explain. These are the "pure articles of faith." To such pertain such words or terms as are used of the Trinity, which do not appear in scripture but are nevertheless harmonious with it. Unable to arrive at a distinct idea that coheres with the term, the anti-Trinitarians falsely reject the Trinity. The same applies to human affairs. Wolff writes that when a hunter speaks of wild animals or an artist of an instrument you have never seen, you assume, you believe, that the hunter or artist is speaking of something clear to him. Whoever called such terms sounds without meaning would be worthy of scorn. In the last analysis, however, these arguments hold only with those who maintain the possibility of accepted ideas, that is, who assume the truth of these "pure articles" on the authority of scripture. Whoever is "destitute" of such faith *(quis fide ista destitutus)* or knows but little of the divine authority of scripture doubts such arguments or regards them as hypothetical since they transcend the sphere of reason. Consequently, when Christ speaks to Nicodemus of regeneration but gives no definition of the term, that idea is to be joined with it that only the regenerate can "intuit in himself."[69] Ultimately, as rule 7 of the *Vernünftige Gedanken* reads, "when God does not permit us to arrive at a clear idea through his Word, we must leave things as they are, and not as scoffers regard the matter as of no account."[70]

In all this discussion of interpretation as reflecting awareness of the connection of word and idea intended by the author, all of it coherent with Wolff's insistence on the coincidence of reason or the "powers of human understanding" and revelation, there is the one proviso — in the interpretation of Holy Scripture it is the regenerated person whose powers of understanding lead to cognition of the truth. Wolff writes, "clearly, the words of Holy Scripture to which the practice of Christianity pertains cannot fully be understood except by the one occupied with them."[71] Or again, "it is entirely clear that the sense of the words of Sacred Scripture cannot fully reach him who has never experienced in himself those things of which it speaks."[72] In midst of his argument that ideas joined to the words of scripture are not directly roused in the reader except by the force of the words themselves, Wolff states that such occurs if anyone "moving

69. Wolff, *Philosophia Rationalis,* para. 971, pp. 694-95.
70. Wolff, *Vernünftige Gedanken,* para. 7, p. 229.
71. Wolff, *Philosophia Rationalis,* para. 971, p. 695.
72. Wolff, *Philosophia Rationalis,* para. 971, p. 695.

his finger to the words of the original text wishes to understand them, or prays to God that their sense be made clear to him by the Holy Spirit." Even in the case of a text in the vernacular, the true sense of scripture can be drawn out as well as from the original, "serious invocation of the deity preceding."[73] Thus, whatever is intuited, roused in oneself, whatever is in possession of the reader or interpreter is there by virtue of an event that Wolff does not trouble to describe, but nevertheless alludes to with his constant references to the Spirit's activity in awakening in the reader the link between word and idea, or to the power of the word.

To sum up, according to Wolff the observance of all the hermeneutical rules spells "fairness" *(Billigkeit)*. He can refer to "fair" interpretation, and to interpreters who are "fair" or "just." More, to his mind the meaning of a text or speech given "fair" interpretation is its actual or probable meaning. Conversely, an "unfair" interpretation yields a sense that is neither actual nor probable. As has been noted, this concentration on "fairness" is not Wolff's invention. It is of early origin. Nor is Wolff's use of the term "fair" (or "even," "just," "impartial" [*aequus*]) new. What is new is the central place Wolff gives to it in his attempt to legitimize hermeneutics as a science. For if, in fact, the knowledge required for interpretation is analogous to that required for understanding nature, then just as the natural scientist must be rid of whatever negatively influences his research, so the interpreter must be *billig,* or *aequus,* must set himself, his presuppositions, and his history in the background. Wolff's insistence on "fairness" in the interpretation of human utterance has lately received considerable attention in the so-called hermeneutics of charity, the classical definition of which reads that "the more sentences we conspire to accept or reject, the better we understand the rest, whether or not we agree." In other words, to the hermeneutics of suspicion, or the understanding of interpretation as antagonistic or violent, the hermeneutics of charity offers the alternative of a complementary and harmonious interpretation.

Thus, when the reader or interpreter joins the words to the ideas consonant with them as intended by the author, precise understanding occurs and there is roused in the interpreter's mind the same idea as came to the mind of the author. Thus, by the consensus of the Holy Spirit with reason regarding "mixed articles," and by no contradiction of the "pure articles" on the part of natural truths, the enemies of Holy Scripture are the more evidently and firmly confuted, and scruples about religion are

73. Wolff, *Philosophia Rationalis*, para. 970, p. 693.

more carefully examined and from the work of redemption knowledge of the divine attributes is elicited by which one learns what is worthy of God himself, and ends in the mystery of piety.[74]

Sigmund Jacob Baumgarten

Siegmund Jacob Baumgarten was born March 14, 1706, in Wolmirstedt in the state of Saxony-Anhalt. In 1722, after the death of his father, a Berlin pastor with connections to August Hermann Francke, he went with his brothers to nearby Halle, where he began his studies, first as pupil then later as instructor at the Halle Orphanage. In 1724 he entered the Halle university, and gave instruction in the higher classes of the orphanage. In 1726 he served as inspector of the Latin School, in 1728 as adjunct preacher, and in 1732 as adjunct member of the university faculty. In 1743 he was promoted to the status of full professor of theology. Baumgarten enjoyed great success as a teacher. In 1736 his strictly scientific approach and its unmistakable reflection of the influence of the exiled Christian Wolff led to unsuccessful attempts at his expulsion from the university. Celebrated as a transition theologian between old and new Protestantism, Baumgarten distanced himself from the entire generation of Halle pietists who educated him. His dogmatics, which, according to Emanuel Hirsch, "finally conquered the German language,"[75] clearly reflects the Wolffian viewpoint of the harmony of reason and revelation. For example, against the Halle doctrine of conversion or awakening as sudden, experienced, and datable, his idea of conversion is of a slow and gradual change of mind, mediated solely through instruction. Accordingly, the preacher's task is to teach the hearers a clear, lucid concept of the divine truths and lead them to a convincing knowledge of those truths necessary to their betterment.

Along with a prodigious output in the areas of historical research, dogmatics, and the translation of English world history, Baumgarten produced texts on biblical interpretation, one of which appeared posthumously in 1769, entitled *Ausführlicher Vortrag der Biblischen Hermeneutik.*[76]

---

74. Wolff, *Philosophia Rationalis,* para. 981, pp. 705-6; see *Vernünftige Gedanken,* p. 230.

75. Emanuel Hirsch, *Geschichte der neueren evangelischen Theologie,* vol. 2 (Gütersloh: C. Bertelsmann Verlag, 1951), p. 371.

76. S. J. Baumgarten, *Ausführlicher Vortrag der Biblischen Hermeneutik* (Halle: Johann Justinus Gebauer, 1769).

The volume contains ten main pieces dealing with the meaning of Holy Scripture, the meanings of words and phrases, historical circumstances, contexts and divisions of the various passages, their purpose, the content of the truths they contain, the uses of scripture, conclusions and applications respecting its use, and, in two appendices, a review of hermeneutical tasks and practices. Baumgarten's method is relatively simple, and allows the reader quickly to arrive at his presuppositions. He first discusses general hermeneutical rules and then presents dogmatic theorems *(Lehnsätze, lemmata)* in their support.

In his "Preliminary Introduction" *(Vorläufige Einleitung)*, equal to any other section in its concentration on the interpreter, Baumgarten lists the rules or requirements to be met by the interpreter. First, the interpreter of the Bible requires a "proper understanding of Holy Scripture," that is, comprehension of the very same meaning that the author intended to teach his readers, along with the ability convincingly to examine scripture's proper meaning and to furnish sufficient evidence for it.[77] Second, the interpreter requires "readiness," a *habitus* acquired through continuous practice, enabling him to undertake the task with ease. From this second requirement Baumgarten draws several rules. This readiness is to be serviceable to all Christians for the salutary use of "the more particular revelation of God" in the Bible.[78] It is indispensable to scholars, and furthered through learning and study of the rules pertaining to it. "Of this," Baumgarten writes, "hermeneutics or the art of interpretation consists."[79] Conceding that theological hermeneutics and exegesis are the same, Baumgarten nevertheless states that the two designations are more appropriately distinguished, the one comprising the theory of the rules of interpretation, the other their actual use and application.

Next Baumgarten moves to the "collection of a few dogmatic mini-theorems" in support of his rules. The first reads that "the entire Holy Scripture is inspired by God," that is, not merely its subject matter, but the words expressing it are divinely inspired. Or again, the character of the Bible as "God breathed" *(theopneustia)* and inspired "extends to the expressions and usages of Holy Scripture as well as to the subject matter and content."[80] Not here, but elsewhere, particularly in his dogmatics, Baumgarten will draw

---

77. Baumgarten, *Ausführlicher Vortrag der Biblischen Hermeneutik*, p. 2.
78. Baumgarten, *Ausführlicher Vortrag der Biblischen Hermeneutik*, p. 2.
79. Baumgarten, *Ausführlicher Vortrag der Biblischen Hermeneutik*, p. 5.
80. Baumgarten, *Ausführlicher Vortrag der Biblischen Hermeneutik*, pp. 6-7.

a distinction between revelation and inspiration, the one accordingly of narrower circumference than the other. On this view scripture consists of truths that are "inspired" by God but not necessarily "revealed."[81]

The second theorem reads that this quality applies only to the Bible's original languages, "such as we have them now."[82] Then Baumgarten adds that this does not mean that each and every passage in each and every manuscript has remained totally without error. The third proposition reads that the intention of God with Holy Scripture is to unite people with himself in a way consonant with their "rationally free condition,"[83] that through insight into the Bible's truths and influence, its impression and effect on the will, they might be improved and united with God. The fourth reads that Holy Scripture possesses all the qualities pertaining to this origin and final goal. Among those qualities Baumgarten first lists inerrancy *(infallibilitas)*, which means not only that everything in the Bible is true, but that it possesses such evidential force respecting its truth that it can be accorded greatest confidence and certainty.[84] Next in order Baumgarten lists the Bible's overall intelligibility or perspicuity *(perspicuitas)*. Just as he adds a proviso respecting the Bible's inerrancy, so here he writes that this perspicuity is not universal *(respectu materiae seu objecti)*, but has to do with the accessibility of its main content, namely, "the basic truths of the order of salvation," and this without denying or excluding the existence of what is difficult or obscure.[85] To these characteristics Baumgarten then adds the Bible's allowing for encounter with as much as its final goal requires, and the "simple majesty" of its style. The effects of these qualities, writes Baumgarten, cannot occur without the use of one's natural reflection and observance of the general rules of exposition. In other words, one cannot arrive at the Bible's salutary effects by merely opening and reading or hearing it. Just as other writings, it demands reflection. More, this reflection must be accompanied by such impression on the will that its preeminence is felt and retained. But this "supernatural power" of the Bible is so tied to one's natural power that it cannot be reached or retained through neglect of it.[86]

81. See Lutz Danneberg, "Siegmund Jacob Baumgartens biblische Hermeneutik," in *Unzeitgemässe Hermeneutik,* ed. Axel Büler, p. 111.

82. Baumgarten, *Ausführlicher Vortrag der Biblischen Hermeneutik,* p. 7.

83. Baumgarten, *Ausführlicher Vortrag der Biblischen Hermeneutik,* p. 7.

84. Baumgarten, *Ausführlicher Vortrag der Biblischen Hermeneutik,* pp. 7-8.

85. Baumgarten, *Ausführlicher Vortrag der Biblischen Hermeneutik,* p. 8.

86. Baumgarten, *Ausführlicher Vortrag der Biblischen Hermeneutik,* p. 9.

From these mini-theorems, or *lemmata,* Baumgarten draws four more. The first is that every genuine interpretation must deal with the original languages of the Bible since its inspiration extends only to the original texts. Translations must therefore be tested against the originals. The second rule is that since the perspicuity of scripture has to do exclusively with its chief content, assigning universal intelligibility to all its parts would contradict its intent. Its perspicuity, thus, is not absolute, but ordinate, conditioned *(nicht absoluta, sondern ordinate et conditionata).* The third rule is that while the general art of exposition is indispensable for the interpretation of the Bible, a special hermeneutics *(hermeneuticam sacram)* is required according to which the scriptures flowing from divine inspiration are to be explained. The fourth and final rule is that the special rules governing Bible interpretation are in part derived from the nature of language and the use of reason, so that no one can achieve any degree of readiness for interpretation without philological knowledge, logical aptitude, and insight into the Bible, and the system of doctrine. Here Baumgarten adds that the conclusion can never be drawn with respect to mere human utterance that a certain meaning is in error, for which reason it cannot reflect the true meaning of the author, whereas such conclusion can indeed be drawn respecting Holy Scripture, given the infallibility of the author and biblical content.[87]

Well into the work's first main section, Baumgarten reprises one of the chief principles of Protestant Bible interpretation, that of the Bible as its own interpreter *(scriptura sui ipsius interpres).* "Because," he writes, "a proper understanding of Holy Scripture must not only be always derived from Scripture itself, but also because the rules of its exposition are determined by and based on it," Holy Scripture must interpret itself. This does not mean that without use of the various aids one may arrive at the true meaning of a given text by merely reading it, but that it is sufficient for determining the meaning of all those passages having to do with its main content, provided one makes sufficient use of the necessary helps. Such use has two aspects. The first is that the bases for determining exposition that derive from Holy Scripture itself are to be preferred to all others. The second is that the authentic exposition of certain passages that occur elsewhere must be seen as a basis for determining the rules of exposition. For example, Hebrews 1:7 interprets Psalm 104:4 in a fashion alien to the mere words of the psalm. Apart from their "authentic explanation" in the New

---

87. Baumgarten, *Ausführlicher Vortrag der Biblischen Hermeneutik,* pp. 10-13.

Testament, the words "you make . . . fire and flame your ministers" could be interpreted to mean that God makes use of the elements, fire among them, in creating and preserving.[88]

In the fifth main section, Baumgartner deals with the purpose or goal of the passages to be interpreted. Writing that the interpreter must be concerned with the intention of the author, he insists that such cannot be determined without insight into the meanings, historical circumstances, and various parts of a biblical utterance since these furnish the basis for indicating its final goal. The goal, according to Baumgarten, is the cause or effective force behind actions to be carried out. From this, Baumgarten adds, it can be shown that all utterances of scripture have an ultimate goal. Since many goals may attach to one and the same act, that goal for the sake of which an action would still take place without all the rest constitutes the final, ultimate goal.[89] In the opinion of Hans-Georg Gadamer (1900-2002), the most celebrated student of Martin Heidegger (1889-1976), the totality of Scripture is "overspun" with Baumgarten's preoccupation with goal or purpose.[90] In fact, his entire interpretive enterprise is tailored to reaching a given goal.

In the ninth main section Baumgarten deals with the interpreter's preparation. First, "he must arouse within himself and maintain an upright and strong desire for the right understanding of the true meaning of Holy Scripture through a vivid idea of its pressing importance and of the high obligation to it, as well as of the great danger and inexcusable culpability of the opposite." Under this heading Baumgarten includes relish for the subject matter and enlistment of all the powers of the soul, the absence of apathy or indifference toward whatever is elicited as meaning, the inculcating of motives that make for desire, and the absence of impure and sinful intentions in a zeal for fame. Second, the interpreter must set aside all prejudices, seek to make his soul free of them, so that he encounters the meaning furnished by the text itself. This means that reasons for conjecture must not be set aside under the pretext of being without prejudice, or in the avoidance of prejudice on behalf of an edifying interpretation the other extreme be embraced and the driest meaning be preferred to the more edifying. Nor, Baumgarten adds, must one entertain

---

88. Baumgarten, *Ausführlicher Vortrag der Biblischen Hermeneutik,* p. 35.

89. Baumgarten, *Ausführlicher Vortrag der Biblischen Hermeneutik,* pp. 237-40.

90. Gadamer, "Einführung," in *Seminar: Philosophische Hermeneutik,* ed. Hans-Georg Gadamer and Gottfried Boehm (Frankfurt am Main: Suhrkamp, 1976), p. 25.

inordinate trust or mistrust toward his own capability and industry. Third, the interpreter must be busy about exerting and directing all his powers and capacities toward this project, toward its frequent renewal with all "unweariedness." Finally, sufficient time must be taken in order to avoid all undue haste.[91] As he often does, Baumgarten includes an addition *(Zusatz)* by which to embroider on the earlier comment. Here he writes that the livelier the interpreter's idea that his effort is the authentic means for hearing the God who speaks in his Word, the livelier his experience of the influence of such knowledge of the true meaning of Holy Scripture "throughout his whole pilgrimage," the more proper his behavior and calmness of soul, the more respectful of the salutary effects of his labors, the easier his preparation will be. "Thus," he writes, "people who have a taste for the Bible and for whom the salutary observation of the truths contained therein is of value . . . will need less preparation than those with another condition of soul or are negatively inclined." More, earnest prayer and appeal to divine assistance not only furthers preparation but effects influence of the divine co-working, though, as Baumgarten adds, such is indirect and tied to the observance of necessary order. In fact, it would be a misuse if one should tempt God under the pretext that prayer for discovering the Bible's meaning had greater effect than the best hermeneutical aid, since on this view the content of the prayer assumes the use of means.[92]

In the same main section, Baumgarten discusses "wherein the necessary condition of an interpreter's soul must consist." Intentional and zealous desire for the truth is required. Further, the quality of "fairness" *(Billigkeit)* is to be exercised toward those whose texts are being interpreted. The divine utterances in Holy Scripture require most justice, but toward human utterances appearing by way of narrative the greatest "fairness" is required, so that the most advantageous interpretation is accepted until the opposite can be proved.[93]

The evaluation of Baumgarten, dubbed by Voltaire "the crown of German scholars," is varied. In the opinion of the historical theologian Leopold Zscharnack (1877-1955), Baumgarten was worthy of the renown of a "sober orthodoxy," and outdistanced his Halle colleagues only by his more serious scientific approach, for which reason he cannot be said to

---

91. Baumgarten, *Ausführlicher Vortrag der Biblischen Hermeneutik,* pp. 496-98.
92. Baumgarten, *Ausführlicher Vortrag der Biblischen Hermeneutik,* pp. 499-500.
93. Baumgarten, *Ausführlicher Vortrag der Biblischen Hermeneutik,* pp. 538-39.

have surrendered the positive content of Christian faith.[94] On the other hand, Baumgarten's reserving infallibility and perspicuity to "the more particular revelation of God," to the "basic truths of the order of salvation," or to the Bible's "chief content," represents a deviation from the orthodox position that assigned inerrancy not merely to the expressions, usages, and subject matter of scripture's chief content, but to scripture as such, irrespective of content. Further, by separating revelation from inspiration, restricting the former exclusively to God while assigning only the latter to the biblical authors, Baumgarten further distanced himself from orthodoxy, which refused the distinction, and thus, in the opinion of one biographer, weakened the theory of verbal inspiration by regarding mere men as "authentic" authors of the Bible.[95] Together with the restriction of inerrancy to the Bible's "chief content," this distinction allowed Baumgarten to admit to chronological, geographical, and historical errors in the Bible. That which forms the background for this allowance is the idea of accommodation.[96]

Characterizing the conflict over accommodation in the seventeenth century as a debate over whether or not the biblical ideas of nature were to be explained from accommodation *ad captum vulgi* (to capture the ordinary person) and were thus historically conditioned, Baumgarten gave precision to the question by stating "whether or not certain material expressions in scripture were used by the men of God out of condescension to people's least understanding, and whether such occurred chiefly in the description of natural things."[97] By "material" things Baumgarten meant the Bible's use of figurative or graphic expression, and by "natural" things its reference to natural events, as, for example, its use of such "optic types of speech" as the earth's standing still, or the sun's going up and down.[98] As to how these types were to be understood, Baumgarten distinguished three different postures. The first or orthodox view took the optic types literally, holding them to be true. The second rejected the orthodox doc-

94. Leopold Zscharnack, "Baumgarten, S. J.," in *Realenzyklopädie* (Leipzig: J. C. Hinrich'sche Buchhandlung, 1897), vol. 2, pp. 464-66.

95. Martin Schloemann, "Baumgarten, Siegmund Jacob," in *Religion in Geschichte und Gegenwart,* vol. 1, pp. 1180-81.

96. Danneberg, "Siegmund Jacob Baumgartens biblische Hermeneutik," p. 111; Gadamer, "Einführung," p. 25.

97. S. J. Baumgarten, *Untersuchung theologischer Streitigkeiten* (Halle: Johann Justinus Gebauer, 1764), p. 181.

98. Baumgarten, *Untersuchung theologischer Streitigkeiten,* pp. 181f., 188ff.

trine of scripture and its special idea of truth as unscientific, assuming that the biblical authors accommodated themselves to the prescientific ideas of their time. Baumgarten proposed a middle way. Together with the orthodox he refused to admit to "errors" in the Bible. Together with the proponents of accommodation theory he held that it is impossible to regard all scriptural references to "natural" things as an adequate description. Accordingly, the biblical utterances concerning natural events were to be regarded as "correct" though "inauthentic."[99]

Writing of Baumgarten's "modest" attempt to mediate the impulses of the new scientific worldview with those of Christian faith, Emanuel Hirsch nonetheless describes Baumgarten's ideas as on a path toward the total dissolution of the entire orthodox system.[100] On the more positive side, Hans-Georg Gadamer writes of German scholarship in the eighteenth century as at the point of breaking free of systematic restraints, a liberation occurring principally through English influence and mediated by Baumgarten, "father of the historical school."[101] In addition, like his teacher Wolff, Baumgarten gave considerable emphasis to the requirement of "fairness" *(Billigkeit)* in interpretation. In his *Unterricht von Auslegung der heiligen Schrift*,[102] he names first "a desire for truth," second "unweariedness," and third "great modesty and fairness" as the attitudes or states of mind required of the interpreter. In the third edition of his work on "theological morality," *Unterricht vom rechtmässigen Verhalten eines Christen oder Theologische Moral*,[103] he includes two paragraphs describing justice or fairness as the attitude to which everyone, and especially the Christian, is obliged, grounding the obligation in the Golden Rule.[104] Incidentally, by allowing for a gap between attributions of intelligibility and rationality and attributions of truth, the hermeneutics of charity recalls Baumgarten's insistence that in respect of human utterance the conclusion can never be drawn that

---

99. Baumgarten, *Untersuchung theologischer Streitigkeiten*, p. 182. See Gottfried Hornig, *Die Anfänge der historisch-kritischen Theologie* (Göttingen: Vandenhoeck & Ruprecht, 1961), pp. 215-19.

100. Hirsch, *Geschichte der neueren evangelischen Theologie*, vol. 2, p. 382.

101. Gadamer, "Einführung," pp. 26-27.

102. Baumgarten, *Unterricht von Auslegung der heiligen Schrift*, 3rd ed. (Auflage, Halle: Johann Andreas Bauer, 1751), p. 218.

103. Baumgarten, *Unterricht vom rechtmässigen Verhalten eines Christen oder Theologische Moral*, 4th ed. (Halle: Johann Andreas Bauer, 1744), p. 283.

104. For discussion of the topic in Baumgarten, see Hornig, "Über Semlers theologische Hermeneutik," in *Unzeitgemässe Hermeneutik*, ed. Bühler, p. 215.

a certain meaning is in error.[105] To what extent Wolff's, Baumgarten's, or their antecedents' "fairness" had Augustine as parent, can only be surmised.[106] The contemporary hermeneutics of charity clearly admits to his influence. Baumgarten died in 1757. From then on, "fairness" would be regarded as a recognized principle of the theological and philosophical concepts of hermeneutics represented at Halle.

105. See Donald Davidson, *Inquiries into Truth and Interpretation* (Oxford: Clarendon, 1984), p. 137; A. K. M. Adam, review of James K. A. Smith, *Fall of Interpretation: Philosophical Foundations for a Creational Hermeneutic, Anglican Theological Review* 85, no. 4 (Fall 2003): 778-79.

106. See Augustine, *On Christian Doctrine,* trans. D. W. Robertson Jr. (New York: Macmillan, 1988), bk. 1, ch. 36, p. 30: "Whoever, therefore, thinks that he understands the divine Scriptures or any part of them so that it does not build the double love of God and of our neighbor does not understand it at all. Whoever finds a lesson there useful to the building of charity, even though he has not said what the author may be shown to have intended in that place, has not been deceived, nor is he lying in any way."

CHAPTER FIVE

Contemporary in Dissent: Johann Georg Hamann

Johann Georg Hamann was born in 1730 and died in 1788 in Königsberg, Prussia, the native city of the friend of his youth, Immanuel Kant. Sent to London in 1756 on a mission for the Berens brothers, merchants in East Prussia and the Baltic, Hamann underwent a crisis that transformed him and in effect rendered him an opponent of the Enlightenment. He began a reading of the Bible on March 13, 1758. Isaiah Berlin, the English historian of ideas, writes that the crisis spelled Hamann's return to the religion of his childhood following a love affair with the Enlightenment — in other words, a return to Lutheran Protestantism — and that his application of this new light "burned for him until the end of his days."[1] Earlier, in 1988, Oswald Bayer of Tübingen wrote that the "knot" was untied on March 31, while Hamann was reading the story of Cain and Abel in Genesis 4, and added that this does not mean Hamann had the experience in an isolated moment or by way of pure intuition.[2] Perhaps, as still another wrote, Hamann's "conversion" can only be referred to in figures, none of which yields more than a single facet of the event, an inaccessibility due to the event as veiled, as God's and Hamann's secret, not even accessible to Hamann himself.[3] At any rate, it was there in London that Hamann experienced while reading the Bible that in reading he was read, that in understanding — through "the descent into the hell of

1. See Isaiah Berlin, *The Magus of the North* (London: Fontana, 1993), pp. 10, 13-14.

2. Oswald Bayer, *Zeitgenosse im Widerspruch: Johann Georg Hamann als radikaler Aufklärer* (München: Piper Verlag, 1988), p. 26.

3. See Harry Sievers, *Johann Georg Hamanns Bekehrung: Ein Versuch, Sie zu Verstehen,* Studien zur Dogmengeschichte und Systematischen Theologie, vol. 24 (Zürich: Zwingli Verlag, 1969), pp. 104, 152, etc.

self-understanding"[4] — he was understood, and understood better, more critically and mercifully, than he could understand himself. In a bundle of pages entitled "Diary of a Christian,"[5] the twenty-eight-year-old alluded to the crisis and the task of his life.

In 1781 appeared Kant's epoch-making work under the title *Critique of Pure Reason.*[6] According to one report,[7] through the offices of the Riga publisher Hartknoch, Hamann assisted in the *Critique* and asked permission to read the proofs. He may thus have been the first reader of the printed copy of Kant's work, and in July 1781 received from the author a bound exemplar. Among Hamann's effects there is a review of the *Critique* that he sketched in July but did not publish. In a letter to his pupil Johann Gottfried Herder (1744-1803), he gave the reason: "I filed it because I did not want to offend the author who was an old friend, and, I must almost say, beneficiary, since I have him almost entirely to thank for my first post."[8] The translation of a work by the Scottish empiricist David Hume (1711-76) that was to accompany the review also did not appear.

Berlin writes of Hamann as

> the first out-and-out opponent of the French Enlightenment of his time . . . the forgotten source of a movement that in the end engulfed the whole of European culture . . . the first writer in modern days to denounce the Enlightenment and all its works . . . the first great shot in the battle of the romantic individualists against rationalism and totalitarianism.[9]

Hamann stated his opposition to the Enlightenment in a four-page letter addressed to Christian Jacob Krauss (1753-1807), professor of prac-

---

4. "Chimärische Einfälle," "Kreuzzüge des Philologen," in Johann Georg Hamann, *Sämtliche Werke,* vol. 2: *Schriften über Philosophie/Philologie/Kritik, 1758-1763,* ed. Josef Nadler (Wien: Im Verlag Herder, 1950), p. 164, line 18.

5. Johann Georg Hamann, "Biblische Betrachtungen eines Christen," in *Londoner Schriften,* ed. Oswald Bayer and Bernd Weissenborn (München: C. H. Beck, 1993).

6. Immanuel Kant, *Kritik der Reinen Vernunft* (Riga: Johann Friedrich Hartknoch, 1781).

7. See Johann Georg Hamann, *Entkleidung und Verklärung: Eine Auswahl aus Schriften und Briefen des "Magus im Norden,"* ed. Martin Seils (Berlin: Eckart-Verlag, 1963), p. 293, n. 1.

8. Quoted in Oswald Bayer, *Vernunft ist Sprache: Hamanns Metakritik Kants, Spekulation und Erfahrung,* Texte und Untersuchungen zum Deutschen Idealismus, vol. 50 (Stuttgart: Frommann-Holzboog, 2002), p. 64.

9. Berlin, *The Magus of the North,* pp. xv, 4, 22, 71, 107.

tical philosophy and statecraft at Königsberg, dated December 18, 1784. The letter is a virtual exegesis of Kant's famous "Was ist Aufklärung?" Hamann saw the source of Kant's error in his use of "the cursed adjective *self-incurred*," a term in the original connoting guilt[10] and on his view falsely applied to the immature or underage. For Hamann the guilt was that of the "wearisome tutor who is the correlative of the immature," a guilt consisting in his blindness while pretending to see. The "tutor" had taken the balcony view, distancing himself from actual life, moving in cold abstraction, a theoretician skulking "in nightcap and behind the stove." He was blind to his separation of thought from actual existence. With his distinction between a public or philosophical and private or ordinary citizen's use of reason, Kant, this self-appointed guardian of the underage, was blind to the political effect of his philosophizing. Hamann insisted that it was the metaphorical discourse of ordinary people that was most adequate to portray what was significant for life. In an ironic twist on Paul's word in 1 Corinthians 14 enjoining women to keep silence in the church, Hamann wrote that at home the women may of course chatter to their heart's content, the private use of reason being their daily bread, then concluded with describing the entire matter of a self-incurred immaturity as something his three daughters would never put up with.

The upshot is that the harshness with which Kant presumed to judge the underage was now directed toward Kant himself, the tutor, or, as Hamann called him, "the Man of death." Hamann was insistent: thought and practical-sensuous existence belong together. The issue is thus to unite "the two natures" of the immature and the guide, the tutor. In the guardianship of the one who lives in the "fear of the Lord," they are in fact united. Irritated by the philosophers' divorcing language from experience, separating what God had joined together, he argued for their reunification. Earlier, in an extended review of Kant's *Critique* entitled *Metakritik über den Purismum der Vernunft,* and included in a letter to Herder in September 1784, Hamann had accused Kant of effecting a division between thought and speech, a divorce reflecting a "purism" that in effect puts reason to death.[11] "Reason is language, *logos*," wrote Hamann, "on this marrow-bone I gnaw, and shall gnaw myself to death on it."[12]

---

10. *Selbstverschuldet.*

11. For an extended analysis of the letter and the *Metakritik,* see Bayer, *Vernunft ist Sprache.*

12. Johann Georg Hamann, *Sämtliche Werke,* vol. 5: *Briefwechsel,* ed. Arthur Henkel

This division between thought and speech in Kant only reflected what had been the principal method of the Enlightenment, that is, a separating of the eternal from the temporal, of the universal truths of reason from the accidental events of history, of thinking from hearing or seeing, of subject from object, of the metaphysical from the historical. The separation had been given classic formulation in the philosophy of Descartes, and repeated in Spinoza, Hegel, Moses Mendelssohn (1729-86), and, to an extent, in Hamann's own pupil, Herder. Hamann called them all *Scheidekünstler,* "artists of separation," and dedicated his life's work in contradiction of the prevailing tendency. In his insistence on the unity of public and private reason in the letter to Kraus, or on the unity of thought and language as the true element of reason made visible in his *Metakritik,* Hamann was working against the background of the Protestant, Lutheran view of the "communication" between the "properties" of the two natures of Christ *(communicatio idiomatum),* or its view of the relation between the visible elements and the invisible grace in the sacrament. Again and again Hamann wrote that this communication of the divine and human idiomata, or properties, is "a basic law and the main key to all our knowledge."[13] The philosophers, on the other hand, wanted to be independent of the sensuous and accidental, but their claim to the timelessness of truth was a chimera; it was mysticism. In the Cartesian separation of subject from object, the subject was without a world, and the world made a pure object, reified. As the medium through which God speaks to humankind, the world, nature, was reduced to total silence. All that interest of the Enlightenment in historical research was not for the purpose of communicating with what was researched, but only for the purpose of gaining a distance from it.

A recent exchange between Isaiah Berlin and James C. O'Flaherty, professor emeritus of German at Wake Forest University in Winston-Salem, suggests the need for caution when describing Hamann as an out and out anti-rationalist. In response to an essay on Hamann by Berlin,[14] O'Flaherty writes of the radical revision Hamann's relation to the Enlightenment has undergone in recent years. Despite Hamann's vehement attacks on reason, states O'Flaherty, he allowed for the legitimate use of

---

(Frankfurt am Main: Insel-Verlag, 1965), p. 177, 18 (in a letter to Johann Gottfried Herder, August 6, 1784).

13. Johann Georg Hamann, *Sämtliche Werke,* vol. 3: *Schriften über Sprache/Mysterien/Vernunft, 1772-1788,* ed. Josef Nadler (Wien: Im Verlag Herder, 1951), p. 27, 12-14.

14. Isaiah Berlin, "The Magus of the North," *The New York Review of Books* 40, no. 17 (October 21, 1993).

reason, and could actually say that "faith has need of reason as much as reason has need of faith." Thus, O'Flaherty concludes, "contemporary scholarship demurs on the charge of irrationalism against 'the Magus of the North.' "[15] Whether or not O'Flaherty's response led him to give greater precision to his characterization of Hamann's stance, Berlin writes that "to call Hamann an anti-rationalist is to say that he attacked the methods by which the great rationalists . . . stated, analyzed, and sought to justify their views," concluding with the statement that "it is this that makes the fact that Hamann is the first and most vehement opponent of the French Enlightenment and its descendants a phenomenon of historical importance."[16] In his characterization of Hamann's perspective, Albert Anderson writes:

> If [Hamann] is now convinced that the ultimate truths of Christianity are revealed in a way essentially different from the suppositions of prevailing epistemologies, then he will refuse to carry on the kind of philosophical discussion of those truths that may mislead a reader by reference to that reader's normal presuppositions. . . . Couple this refusal to mislead with the conviction that every other available means for acceptable or satisfactory enlightenment about reality and truth leads . . . to an unmanageable or undesirable skepticism, and we have the principal directions which Hamann's religious philosophy takes.[17]

What is often missed in an appraisal of Hamann's work is attention to the occasion for the crisis of his youth as extending throughout his life, "until the end of his days." For, once the Bible with its merciful nearness of God had given him conquest of the deadly dissociation, of the philosophers' separations, had given him "marriage" with God, the world, with others, and himself, it became his a priori. So he could write, "another *Dos moi pou sto* I do not recognize or know than his word."[18] For this reason the joining together of what the philosophers had separated began with an apprehension derived from the Bible. He wrote:

15. James C. O'Flaherty, "The Magus of the North," *The New York Review of Books* 40, no. 19 (November 18, 1993).

16. O'Flaherty, "The Magus of the North."

17. Albert Anderson, "Philosophical Obscurantism: Prolegomena to Hamann's Views on Language," *Harvard Theological Review* 62, no. 3 (July 1969): 258.

18. Archimedes' "give me a place where I can stand." Johann Georg Hamann, *Sämtliche Werke*, vol. 5: *Briefwechsel*, p. 333, 16-27 (to Jacobi, 1785); italics added.

> All the phenomena of nature are dreams, visions, riddles, which have
> their meaning, their secret sense. The book of nature and of history are
> no more than ciphers, hidden signs, which need the key made clear by
> Holy Scripture and is the object of their inspiration.[19]

Hamann's belief that the "pictorial" language of ordinary people was most
adequate to portray what is significant for life was not merely reinforced by
but drawn from his understanding of the Bible with its "poetic indirection."
Similarly, his conviction that meaning depended on visualization was not
merely supported by but also derived from the Bible. For this reason he
decided to render his writings similar in form to the language of scripture,
and eschewed the treatise-like shape adopted by his contemporaries, a
form that still irritates and puzzles his readers. Berlin adverts to Hamann's
"hermetic style," his mysterious formulas intended to puzzle, intrigue, and
waken the reader. But, if the poetically indirect or pictorial, if the image
or the metaphor, was the chief ingredient of communication, obscurity
could attach to it and misunderstanding result. Dealing with the problem
of conflicting interpretations, Augustine assesses five views of Genesis 1:1,
concluding that the author's intention is obscure, especially regarding texts
of which God is the author.[20] As for Hamann's "hermetic style" it was de-
liberate, an attempt at imitation of the biblical word.[21]

It was particularly the Old Testament as yielding the union of oppo-
sites that had Hamann's allegiance, an offense to his contemporaries, not
least to Kant. Of the Old Testament Hamann wrote that one could hear
from it "historical truths not only of past but also of future times," that it
is the primer "by which one learns to spell history . . . a living spirit- and
heart-awakening primer of all the historical literature in heaven, on and

19. Hamann, "Biblische Betrachtungen eines Christen," p. 417, 5-9.
20. See *The Confessions of Saint Augustine,* trans. Edward B. Pusey (New York: The
Modern Library, 1949), book XII, para. 23, pp. 290-91: "These things then being heard and
perceived . . . two sorts of disagreements I see may arise, when a thing is in words related by
true reporters; one, concerning the truth of the things, the other, concerning the meaning of
the relater. For we enquire one way about the making of the creature, what is true; another
way, what Moses, that excellent minister of Thy Faith, would have his reader and hearer
understand by those words. . . . But let me be united in Thee, O Lord, and let us approach
together unto the words of Thy book, and seek in them for Thy meaning, through the meaning of Thy servant, by whose pen Thou hast dispensed them."
21. The title of Anderson's essay, "Philosophical Obscurantism," reflects his observation of the poetic and prophetic function of biblical language as furnishing the basis for
Hamann's philosophical reflections.

under the earth." The same applied to nature. The Bible did not exclude nature; it rather included it. But like history nature was a "sealed book, a hidden witness, a riddle that could not be solved without plowing with another heifer than our reason."[22]

In his "Diary of a Christian" Hamann repeats his argument against reason detached from existence, this time in the context of his observations of key biblical passages. On the Pharisees' questioning Jesus' authority in Luke 20:1-8, Hamann writes that they use their reason, draw clever conclusions, presume an ignorance they do not have, all of it the consequence of pacifying "our stupid *(blöde)* reason."[23] Of the voice from heaven recorded in John 12:29, he writes that the crowd's notion of it as thunder or an angel speaking reflects reason's two excesses: explaining the voice of God in terms of natural effects or as a subordinate miracle.[24] On Paul's encounter with the altar to an unknown god recorded in Acts 17:23, Hamann writes that reason is inclined to serve but is infinitely distanced from an unknown God, adding that it refuses to know him, and what is even more amazing, when it does know him, ceases to serve him.[25] On Romans 1:16 he writes that reason might be expected to know and accept this doctrine which of all others is best suited to the imperfection of our nature, and in the easiest and most probable way is raised to a level suited to our inclinations, yet nothing is more difficult and impossible for the natural man than this faith.[26]

If the purism of the rationalist drew Hamann's fire, so did church institution and theology. In "Golgatha und Scheblimini,"[27] which G. F W. Hegel, damning with faint praise, called "the most significant thing that Hamann wrote," he states,

> Dogmatics and church law belong merely to the public institutions of education and administration, as such are subject to governmen-

---

22. Hamann, *Sämtliche Werke,* vol. 3: *Schriften über Sprache/Mysterien/Vernunft,* pp. 305, 2f.; 311, 6-8; Hamann, *Sämtliche Werke,* vol. 2: *Schriften über Philosophie/Philologie/Kritik,* p. 65, 11-13.

23. Hamann, "Biblische Betrachtungen eines Christen," p. 276.

24. Hamann, "Biblische Betrachtungen eines Christen," p. 279, 7-10.

25. Hamann, "Biblische Betrachtungen eines Christen," p. 286, 6-9.

26. Hamann, "Biblische Betrachtungen eines Christen," p. 288, 32-39.

27. The term "Scheblimini" is a transliteration of the Hebrew verb in Psalm 110:1: "The Lord says to my lord, 'Sit at my right hand until I make your enemies your footstool.'" The work appears in Hamann, *Entkleidung und Verklärung.*

tal caprice, and are at times a coarse, and at times a refined external discipline, according to the elements and degrees of the prevailing aesthetic. These visible public, common institutions are neither religion nor wisdom which comes down from above; but earthly, human and devilish.[28]

Hamann was not an exegete in the classical sense of the term. As his "Diary" indicates, his interest lay more in the registering of observations respecting biblical texts. On the other hand, questions dealing with the biblical canon, with scripture inspiration, and with the manner in which the Bible was to be read and understood, as well as its effect, occupied him throughout his life. Respecting the canon, Hamann wrote that it appears to have come about by way of an "enormous detour," despite whatever may have been gained by it. He wrote that the history of canon formation could not be decisive for the Bible's authority. No more than he could trust the Septuagint's becoming canonical through the passages cited by the evangelists and apostles could he trust the power of church fathers and councils to canonize a book. It was precisely the danger of orthodoxy that it was convinced it possessed eternal life in the Scripture, omitting to test it as Christ required (John 5:3). To this principle of tradition Hamann opposed what he called "freedom in Christ." In its witness to Christ lay the importance of scripture.[29]

As to the Bible itself, Hamann defined it as a "few old fragments," as *rudera* (ruins) or rusty shields, reflective of its ancestry in the language and conceptuality of "superstitious paganism and papacy." With its struggle to unite thought and its object in a language intelligible to finite persons, the Bible shows God's great condescension to human beings. Hamann could rhapsodize on the inanition of God's choosing to become an "author":

What proof of divine omnipotence — and humility — that he could and that he willed to breathe the depths of his mysteries, the treasures of his wisdom into such gibberish-like, confused, and menial tongues of human conceptions. . . . Truly, he created us after his image — because we lost it he took on our own image — flesh and blood, just as children have, learned to cry — to babble — to speak — to read — to

---

28. See Hamann, *Entkleidung und Verklärung,* pp. 239, and 241, n. 1.
29. Hamann, "Hierophantische Briefe," pp. 83-85.

compose like a true son of man; imitated us in order to urge us to imitate him.[30]

Since it was not the Bible's early authors who left to posterity their ideas and circumstances, but God, the Spirit of God who revealed himself through them, the conflict of interpretations on the part of the Bible's readers spelled the "death of the author." Measured by time and by its relation to the concepts of the age in which the biblical narrative was written, it could give little pleasure to "heads" that demand explanation or prefer an idea to the truth.[31] It was not a revelation "which a Voltaire (1694-1778), a Bolingbroke (1678-1751), a Shaftesbury (1671-1713) would find worth accepting, which would most please their prejudices, wit, moral, political and magical whims, but a discovery of such truths whose certainty, credibility, and correctness would be laid before the entire human race."[32]

Much of the attention Hamann gave to the Bible had to do with the way in which he believed it should be read. First of all, it had to be read as all other books. No exception was to be made to the rule or precept that applied to other writings, that is, that they be read with and in the spirit of their authors. In the "Diary," Hamann wrote,

> The need to get ourselves as readers into the experience *(Empfind-ung)* of the author before us, to approximate as much as possible his state of mind as we are able to arrive at by the happy use of imagination, and to which a poet or writer of history tries as much as possible to help us, is a rule which by definition is just as necessary as for other books.[33]

Further, the Bible demanded a reading

> with and in the spirit of that theist who as its king, in spite of the soundest and most beneficial morality that united the bloom, salt, and ether of the most exalted Stoicism and Epicureanism, died a shameful, vol-

30. *Johann Georg Hamann, Briefwechsel,* ed. Walther Ziesemer and Arthur Henkel (Frankfurt am Main: Insel-Verlag, 1955), vol. 1, p. 393.

31. *Johann Georg Hamann, Briefwechsel,* pp. 81-83; cf. Hamann, "Über die Auslegung der heiligen Schrift," in *Londoner Schriften,* p. 59, 15-18.

32. Hamann, "Biblische Betrachtungen eines Christen," p. 68, 16-22.

33. Hamann, "Biblische Betrachtungen eines Christen," p. 66, 27-32.

untary, and meritorious death and has allowed to be proclaimed and to resound the good news of his resurrection and redemption and return to world-judgment from the going up to the going down of the sun, from the south pole to the north.[34]

The basic hermeneutical rule was thus to read the Bible in the Spirit of the God to whose revelation it witnesses. As Hamann put it: "The understanding of this book and the faith in its content is to be attained by nothing else than through the same Spirit who moved its authors."[35] If anyone should ask where this witness or testimony is to be found, Hamann referred first of all to the Bible itself. Once read in the Spirit of the God who showed himself to be Creator of heaven and earth, it would be clear how "appropriate" the biblical content is to this God.[36] Or, in simpler terms, "humility of heart" was the indispensable preparation for and the only attitude of mind that belonged to the reading of the Bible. He wrote:

> The inspiration of this book is as great a humiliation and condescension of God as the creation of the Father and the incarnation of the Son. For this reason, humility of heart is the only state of mind that belongs to reading the Bible, and the most indispensable preparation for it.[37]

Hamann read Hebrew, Arabic, Latin, and Greek. His shelves were stacked with works in classical philology and the Near East. But he was convinced that none of it yielded understanding of the Bible. When Johann David Michaelis (1717-91) of Göttingen attempted to give the Bible status in the university through the recovery of ancient Israel as a classical civilization on a par with that of Greece and Rome, thus of Israel's cultural superiority, Hamann thundered:

> Not a lyre! — nor a paintbrush! — a broom for my muse, to clear the threshing floor of sacred literature! — Hail to the archangel over the remains of Canaan's language! — on groomed she-asses he conquers in

---

34. Hamann, "Hierophantische Briefe," pp. 87-88.

35. Hamann, *Sämtliche Werke*, vol. 2: *Schriften über Philosophie/Philologie/Kritik*, p. 43, 21-24.

36. See the editor's notes to Hamann, "Hierophantische Briefe," pp. 87-88.

37. Hamann, "Über der Auslegung der heiligen Schrift," in *Londoner Schriften*, p. 59, 6-10.

the race; — but the wise idiot of Greece borrows Euthyphron's proud steeds for a philological dispute.[38]

Hamann would play the Baptist to Michaelis the Pharisee or Sadducee (Matt. 3:6).

In fact, wrote Hamann, without faith one could not even understand nature, and for this reason would distance oneself from God's Word and will, explain existence through hypotheses and probabilities, and cast doubt on the biblical narrative.[39] This could only mean that to hear the Word of God, more than the text of the Bible was needed. Without the gift of the Holy Spirit one put blind trust in the letter and by way of a doctrine of verbal inspiration did not take seriously the servant-shape of the revelation, or, one attempted by way of method and investigation to free the Word's glorious shape from the lowliness of its revelation.[40] The obscurity, the inanition, required divine alleviation.

In his 1993 essay, Berlin expanded on his description of Hamann's conversion, writing that it was not just to the simple faith of his childhood, but to a doctrine embraced by Protestant mystics according to whom the history of Israel is not merely an account of that nation's history, but a "timeless allegory of the inner history of the soul of each individual man."[41] As to its function, then, the Bible constituted a great universal allegory, as Berlin earlier stated, reflective of "an original, transcendent pattern."[42] So, for example, Hamann wrote that the life of the patriarchs is "full of allegories of the Jewish history . . . in regulating the circumstances of their life God gave a model of the plan by which he intended to lead the Jews."[43] He rendered the story of Ruth contemporaneous in an address to his reader:

> You, poor soul, are the Moabitess who must leave her fatherland, her friends, her sinful habitation and the brood of vipers of the liar and murderer; must wander in a strange land; like Naomi think of the abundance you have lost; [must] feel and mourn your poverty and

38. Johann Georg Hamann, "Aesthetica in Nuce," in Hamann, *Sämtliche Werke,* vol. 2: *Schriften über Philosophie/Philologie/Kritik,* p. 195.

39. Hamann, "Biblische Betrachtungen eines Christen," p. 307, 10-14.

40. See Walter Leibrecht, *Gott und Mensch bei Johann Georg Hamann* (Gütersloh: Carl Bertelsmann, 1958), p. 37.

41. Berlin, *The Magus of the North,* p. 6.

42. Berlin, *The Magus of the North,* p. 118.

43. Hamann, "Biblische Betrachtungen eines Christen," p. 96, 21-24.

the enmity of the one who made you so poor. Go and glean in the fields of the one who will graciously regard you.[44]

On the habit and diet of the Baptist in Matthew 3:4, Hamann stated that grasshoppers frequently appear under the figure of the divine punishment or introduce the hosts of the Almighty, so that the Baptist's diet prefigures the nourishing of the Christian, just as his habit or clothing harks back to Elijah. The reference to John's appearance in the desert, like the wilderness needing to be wandered through before the taking of the promised land, represented the Law, and his call to repentance prefigured the gospel, the way of the kingdom of heaven.[45] References to the Pharisees in the Gospels Hamann interpreted as the supporters of the great dogmatic establishments, the Church of Rome and the French monarchy and its servants in German lands, and references to the Sadducees he interpreted as the freethinkers in Paris or Berlin or Edinburgh. The stories of Paul's navigation and his arrival at an unknown island as recorded in Acts 27–28 Hamann interpreted as prophecies of the spreading of the Christian religion through navigation and its ultimate destiny in America.[46] Summing up, Hamann wrote:

> Every biblical story is a prophecy — which through all the centuries — and in every soul of man is fulfilled. . . . Every story bears man's likeness, a body of earth and ash and is nothing, bears the tangible letters; but also a soul that bears the breath of God and the breath of his mouth, the light and the life that shines in the darkness and cannot be overcome by the darkness.[47]

"Hermetic" or not, Hamann's interpretation of the visit of the Magi in Matthew 2:1-12 is as arresting an observation on a biblical text as he ever wrote. Stating first that he would omit investigating the doctrinal structure of an "obscure sect, and the debris of their theogony and astrology," and rather than imagining a magical star which with either Fontenelle[48]

---

44. Hamann, "Biblische Betrachtungen eines Christen," pp. 146-47, 36-40, 1-2.

45. Hamann, "Biblische Betrachtungen eines Christen," p. 255, 32-39.

46. Hamann, "Biblische Betrachtungen eines Christen," p. 286, 23-26.

47. Hamann, "Betrachtungen über Newtons Abhandlung von den Weissagungen," in *Entkleidung und Verklärung*, p. 247.

48. Bernard de Bovier de Fontenelle (1657-1757), perpetual secretary of the French Academy of Science.

or algebra would not turn out well, he would limit himself to a general observation on the morality of the Magi's journey.

> The mere externals of an action can never reveal its value to us; but the notion of their motives and results as the most natural mediate concepts from which our conclusions along with our applause or displeasure are produced can do so. This law of experience and reason does not seem to favor our pilgrims' journey, if the decision lay with them. The motive for their arrival, from out of their own mouth, forces us to the verdict of a long obsolete delusion, the intimation of a saga to which they had clung as if to a firm prophetic word — to say nothing of the inconvenience and injustice they as citizens dealt their native land through such vast respect for a foreign ruler. As to the result of their undertaking, it can be easily supposed that the mothers who had to mourn the blood bath of their children will have sighed over these foreigners' indiscretion and curiosity. The newborn king of the Jews himself had to take flight because he was betrayed by his worshiper Herod, the reigning antichrist, a liar and murderer from the beginning.[49]

The question of the biblical canon, of the New Testament language as of a piece with the vernacular of its pagan neighbors, of the Gospels as composed of fragments, and the requirement that the interpreter assume a stance on behalf of the text, would be forever asked and answered from Hamann's time on, but with little or no recognition of his having first raised it. And this apart from what has now become axiomatic in contemporary thought, the idea of thought as the use of symbols, of images, of language. As Berlin put it, according to Hamann, "God thinks in trees or battles, or rocks and seas, as well as in the Hebrew and Greek letters of his inspired prophets."[50]

Postscript: Johann Christian Edelmann

German pietism was the answer to the demystification of life brought on by the rationalism of the seventeenth century. It was also the reaction of

---

49. "Die Magi aus Morgenlande," in Hamann, *Sämtliche Werke,* vol. 2: *Schriften über Philosophie/Philologie/Kritik, 1758-1763,* pp. 139-40.
50. Berlin, *The Magus of the North,* p. 80.

feeling to the rationalizing of faith in Lutheran orthodoxy. In other words, it was the counterculture over against the prevailing universal rationalistic tendency of the time. Though at its social and psychological core it spelled retreat from society into religious feeling, it still had its effect on the outside world. It drove Lutheranism into a deep crisis of conscience, and forced a wide wing of moderate Lutheran orthodoxy to adjust to rationalism. At yet another point pietism gave assistance to the Enlightenment. It helped to give broad acceptance to the idea that religion is a private affair.[51] More than thirty years before the fragments of the *Apology* of Hermann Samuel Reimarus (1694-1768) appeared, pamphlets, critiques, "conversations," and confessions came from the pen of a man who peeked into the Enlightenment like Moses on Nebo into the promised land. Unlike Reimarus, despite threats and the burning of his books, in face of injunctions, remonstrances, and perpetual hounding, he could not hide what he had written. The man's name was Johann Christian Edelmann, born in Thuringia in 1689. A subject of considerable recent study, Edelmann began his career hunting for Christians whose lives evidenced authentic rebirth. Orthodox at the outset, he entered on theological studies at Jena preparatory to candidacy in the Lutheran Church. Embittered by orthodoxy's lovelessness, he broke with the church. Drawing a verse from Genesis 12 in the little box of "lots" *(Losungen)* designed to give directions for the day and favored among pietists of the period,[52] Edelmann left for the position of family tutor in Austria. Subsequently attracted to the religious community of Nikolaus von Zinzendorf (1700-1760), he spent only eight days at Herrnhut, repelled by the count's class consciousness. Invited to cooperate in the translation of the Berleburg Bible, the most monumental work of radical German pietism, he left for Westphalia. Out of sorts with the community there, and by this time under indictment for blasphemy, Edelmann left for Neuwied on the Rhine, where he was required to satisfy the local authorities with a confession of faith.

Finally, by way of one detour after another, and earning his bread along the way with potters, bakers, and woodworkers, Edelmann settled in Berlin with the permission of Frederick the Great. The king did not, as

---

51. For a succinct analysis of the period, an enumeration of the various influences that helped to shape Edelmann's life, and quotations and comments, I am dependent on Annagret Schaper, *Ein langer Abschied vom Christentum: Johann Christian Edelmann (1698-1767) und die deutsche Frühaufklärung* (Marburg: Tectum Verlag, 1996).

52. Gen. 12:1: "Go from your country and your kindred and your father's house to the land that I will show you."

often stated, label Edelmann just one more idiot to whom to grant asylum. He said rather that "since he must allow sojourn to so many fools . . . why not furnish space for a reasonable man?" Edelmann spent the last years of his life in Berlin, where he died in 1767.

The influences on this disenchanted, angry man were many and varied. On the journey to Austria he was introduced to the poetry of Barthold Heinrich Brockes (1680-1742), advocate of a theology that expressed a reverential attitude toward nature as well as a religious interpretation of natural phenomena, an attitude new to German poetry.

In Saxony, Gottfried Arnold's (1666-1714) attack on the institutionalizing of Christianity added fuel to the fire of Edelmann's revulsion for orthodoxy. Arnold's *Kirchen- und Ketzer-Historie* was not only sweet music in Edelmann's ears; in the eighteenth century no other book had awakened greater reaction in Protestant Germany.[53] For Edelmann, who had read the *Kirchen- und Ketzer-Historie* in the winter of 1731-32 during a crisis of conscience, this work became incendiary and life altering. That Edelmann had despaired of the Lutheran dogmatic, of the wearisome "reading for and against" on the part of pietistic and orthodox authors, he took to be a sign that he belonged among those whom Arnold had described as the righteous throughout church history. The book tore Edelmann out of his psychic numbness. The number of those awakened by the *Kirchen- und Ketzer-Historie* reaches from unnumbered unknown believers through such a noted pietist as August Hermann Francke (1663-1727) to prominent thinkers including the philosopher Christian Thomasius (1655-1728) and Johann Wolfgang von Goethe (1749-1832), who described the *Kirchen- und Ketzer-Historie* as a "great influence" in his life. Arnold's spiritualistic interpretation of Christianity included a rigorous asceticism that viewed the Lutheran doctrine of faith as morally defective since it implied a summons to sin.

Following his visit to Herrnhut, Edelmann lived in Dresden with a Gichtelian, the member of a group intent on reforming Lutheranism through inner worship of God and celibacy. The Gichtelian introduced him to the writings of Johann Konrad Dippel (1673-1734), a Berleburg hermit who outperformed his pietist comrades by insisting that the substance of the believer was altered in the rebirth. With Dippel, for his generation the most up-to-date radical pietistic author, Edelmann enjoyed more than a

---

53. Gottfried Arnold, *Unpartheyische Kirchen- und Ketzer-Historie, vom Anfang des Neuen Testaments bis auf das Jahr Christi* (Frankfurt am Main: T. Fritschens sel. Erben, 1729), vol. 1, p. 1688 (parts I and II); vol. 2, p. 1699 (parts III and IV), p. 1700.

Lutheran orthodox origin and the study of theology from which both had fallen away. Just as Edelmann in the eighteenth, so Dippel in the seventeenth century had been led on the right path by Professor Arnold.

Next, fascinated by the prophet Johann Friedrich Rock (1678-1749), Edelmann attached himself to the "Inspired" *(die Inspirierten),* a splinter group that fostered revelations amid glossolalia, contortions, shrieking, and whirling. Then in a dream he saw the opening lines of John's Gospel in Greek which he read to mean "In the beginning was reason *(Vernunft),"* and "God was reason." He later separated himself from the "Inspired," and after visits to any number of cities punctuated with false imprisonment, he returned for a time to Berleburg. The first book Edelmann hunted for in the crates of his belongings was Baruch Spinoza's chief biblical-critical work, the *Tractatus Theologico-Politicus,* about which he had read in Arnold's *Kirchen- und Ketzer-Historie.* The *Tractatus,* together with Spinoza's ethics, took Edelmann captive. Spinoza enabled him to strip off the last and heaviest chains binding his thought to the old Lutheran worldview. He surrendered his faith in the divinity of the Bible, thrust that "Bible-idol" *(Bibelgötze)* from the throne to which human superstition had elevated it, and now regarded the writings of the Old and New Testaments as the foundation of one great, thousand-year-old "priests' deception" *(Pfaffen-Betrug)."*

In 1735 appeared the first of fourteen fascicles of Edelmann's *Unschuldige Wahrheiten* ("Innocent Truths"), which indicated the path of his alienation, first from churchly, then also from Christian presuppositions. From this point on, Edelmann bore all the earmarks of a fanatical deist, hostile to church and sect, equating primitive Christianity and rational religion, having his own church in himself, and in imitation of Jesus seeking to live according to the Sermon on the Mount. By virtue of the light dawning on his reason from God, Edelmann felt himself called to prophetic mission. Conscious that God had made it his chief task to tear down, just as it had been Jeremiah's, he wrote:

> Now, like Jeremiah, I have no other calling than to pull out, destroy, and ruin everything that is or is called orthodoxy and false worship of God, Pharisaic prattle-theology, false mysticism and willful sect-patchwork. And to whomever the Lord vouchsafes the same calling besides me, let him confidently do the same.[54]

54. Johann Christian Edelmann, *Sämtliche Schriften in Einzelausgaben,* vol. 5: *Un-*

In 1740, Edelmann began to compose his major work, *Moses mit aufgedeckten Angesicht* ("Moses with Unveiled Face"), divided into twelve *Anblicke,* or "sights."[55] In it he proposed to "peek" a bit more closely than had hitherto occurred under the mask of this infamous leader of the Jews. Following the scheme of the *Unschuldige Wahrheiten,* Edelmann, "lover of light," proceeded to lead the "blind" Bible-believing Lutheran step by step to the knowledge of the Old Testament as a *Pfaffen-Fund* ("priests' invention"). The first three *Anblicke* printed in 1740 barely scraped by a view of the Bible. They leaned on Spinoza's *Tractatus theologico-politicus* and shed doubt on the church's doctrine of the Bible's inspiration. The fifth *Anblick,* which should have appeared first, was actually written last because Edelmann was on the hunt for an ancient source by which he could support his argument that Moses never existed, that Christianity thus rested on a "pure, wicked *Pfaffen-Betrug*" ("priests' deception"). Exodus 34:29-35 functioned as guide since it revealed the essence of the deception.[56] Its narrative of Moses' private conversation with God in the tabernacle was in reality only a relatively simple, politically motivated deception by which better to dupe the people, then still entirely pagan, and to achieve its subjection under a "priestly dictatorship."[57] According to Edelmann, the real Moses was a renegade Egyptian priest who used his position of power to incite a rebellion against the ruling Pharaoh whose religion was unbearably superstitious. The intention was thus to carry out religious reforms by pretending direct contact with God — the most classical of priestly deceptions. Christianity, argued Edelmann, rested on this deception, and the Bible was its basis.

In a marginal remark in his *Tractatus,* Spinoza had suggested that Ezra might have authored the books of Moses. What was marginal for Spinoza became the chief thing for Edelmann. According to his construction,

---

schuldige Wahrheiten: Dreyzehende Unterredung, ed. Walter Grossmann (Stuttgart: Friedrich Frommann, 1970 [1738]), pp. 13-14.

55. Johann Christian Edelmann, *Sämtliche Schriften in Einzelausgaben,* vol. 7: *Moses mit aufgedeckten Angesichte* (vol. 7.1, 1972; vol. 7.2, 1987).

56. "When Moses had finished speaking with them, he put a veil on his face; but whenever Moses went in before the Lord to speak with him, he would take the veil off, until he came out; and when he came out, and told the Israelites what he had been commanded, the Israelites would see the face of Moses, that the skin of his face was shining and Moses would put the veil on his face again, until he went in to speak with him" (Exod. 34:33-35).

57. Edelmann, *Sämtliche Schriften in Einzelausgaben,* vol. 7.2: *Moses mit aufgedeckten Angesichte: Fünfter, sechster, siebenter, achter und achtundzwangzigster Anblick,* p. 27.

after Jerusalem's destruction and the turmoils of the Babylonian captivity, Ezra set himself the task of disciplining "his neglected people" and subjecting it to a new "priestly rule." For this purpose he established a "second dictatorship of the Holy Spirit" among the Jews, after the first Egyptian Moses had disappeared with all his documents. Edelmann wrote,

> [Ezra] knows how to fit his Moses out with this paraphernalia in such style, that we should almost swear the soul of the old Hermes had entered into the Moses of Ezra.[58]

The criterion or interpretive principle by which Edelmann analyzed the story of Moses was plausibility. Whatever did not correspond to the usual experience or the normal course of nature he laid bare, attacked, and rejected as implausible, as a "deception." His comments on the Jews' plundering of the Egyptians preparatory to the exodus offers a vivid illustration of his rationalistic approach:

> At this point Ezra quite shockingly forgets himself by introducing us to the Jews who according to his own report are supposed to have lived in the land of Goshen apart and separated from the Egyptians, and in no other way than as if they . . . had been . . . scattered throughout all Egypt. . . . How then was it possible that these slaves . . . could borrow from [the Egyptians], as their neighbors, the objects of value indicated? . . . Who in his right mind can imagine the Egyptians would have been such fools not only to hand over their silver plate to a heap of beggars ready to leave, but even more, after the last massacre they are alleged to have suffered because of these roughnecks, to have begged them to ask for them, and no differently than as if they had owed them the greatest obligation?[59]

That argument for plausibility was Wolffian. Schaper writes that the synonymy of proving facts and criticizing fictions and fantasies is Wolffian. It corresponds to the spirit of the rationalism operative in the eighteenth century, that is, of coming to no other results than those already known.

---

58. Edelmann, *Sämtliche Schriften in Einzelausgaben,* vol. 7.2: *Moses mit aufgedeckten Angesichte: Fünfter, sechster, siebenter, achter und achtundzwangzigster Anblick,* pp. 90, 91.

59. Edelmann, *Sämtliche Schriften in Einzelausgaben,* vol. 7.2: *Moses mit aufgedeckten Angesichte: Fünfter, sechster, siebenter, achter und achtundzwangzigster Anblick,* pp. 101-5.

The reason why the Wolffian philosophy became popular so rapidly, she continues, lies in the fact that it renders everything manageable.

> Cosmoses become deep plains and the lyrical becomes prose. It is the transition from the bird's-eye view of the mathematician and theologian of the 17th century, no longer accepted by thinkers of the 18th such as Edelmann, to the perspective of the frog.[60]

According to Christian Wolff, the most eminent German thinker between Leibniz and Kant, human reason was equipped with the capacity to reduce any subject to pure demonstration.

According to this demonstrative-deductive method, God would reveal nothing that could be known through reason, and conversely, what God is to have revealed could not be contrary to reason. Thus Wolff could write:

> Because God knew everything that can result from the nature of things and just for this reason brought them forth, so the necessary consequences of the nature of things are God's intentions.[61]

But if Wolff was an ally, Spinoza was the source of Edelmann's hermeneutic, his etiquette of interpretation. If *Moses mit aufgedeckten Angesicht* was the first book in the German language to deny all faith in the Bible, to roundly reject all Christian dogma, it all resulted from Spinoza's teaching about God and the world. As might be imagined, the publication of *Moses* in 1740 set the presses in motion. More than 160 refutations appeared; the purchase of Edelmann's books was forbidden, and in several places his books were burned.

It may have been a deeply inculcated piety and an equally deep rooting in the theological worldview of Lutheran orthodoxy that held Edelmann back from attacking the New Testament. In the fragmentary twenty-eighth *Anblick,* Edelmann tiptoes cautiously around the Gospels by seeking to show that the Christian religion had a poor foundation since the apostles for the sake of its extension had to resort to a deception.

> Phooey! For shame! I can easily imagine what must have moved the leaders of the Christian religion to take flight to such inventions.

---

60. Schaper, *Ein langer Abschied vom Christentum,* p. 208.
61. Quoted in Bayer, *Zeitgenosse im Widerspruch,* p. 92.

Among the heathen they tried to convert they will no doubt have met those who had not yet leased their reason, who, of course, will not have had it in mind to believe in a recently risen God who died a dishonorable death. . . . So they necessarily had to make an attempt as to whether or not they could lead them to believe a delusion from their own prophets or prophetesses, at whose encouragement they would be forced to admit that what happened to Jesus of Nazareth had long since been decreed in the counsel of the gods. And for this the sibyls had to serve them, of whom they no doubt will have known that among the heathen their utterances were still valued.[62]

In his confession of faith, printed in 1746, and roughly translated "A Confession of Faith wrung from me but not forced on others,"[63] delivered at the insistence of the consistory at Neuwied, Edelmann wrote that the Bible should not be approached differently from any other book; its content should rather be examined in the light of reason according to its probability.[64] Accordingly, one tenet after another of orthodox Christianity came under scrutiny. The doctrines of the fall, original sin, Jesus' fulfillment of messianic prophecy, and his death as instrument of redemption fell before the judgment of rationality.[65] Edelmann wrote:

First of all, if one should even want to say that the Lord Jesus preached the forgiveness or removal of men's sins because he himself soon wished to be an atoning sacrifice for them, one clearly makes the dear man into a liar. It is clear to all the world that through the death of the Lord Jesus men's sins were neither removed, nor were they reconciled to God.[66]

62. Edelmann, *Sämtliche Schriften in Einzelausgaben*, vol. 7.2: *Moses mit aufgedeckten Angesichte: Fünfter, sechster, siebenter, achter und achtundzwangzigster Anblick*, pp. 336-37.

63. The complete title reads *Johann Christian Edelmanns Abgenöthigtes Glaubens-Bekenntniss: Aus Verlanlassung Unrichtiger und verhuntzter Abschriften Desselben, dem Druck übergeben, und Vernünfftigen Gemüthern zur Prüfung vorgeleget vom dem Auctore, Anno 1746*.

64. Edelmann, *Abgenöthigtes Glaubens-Bekentniss*, p. 69.

65. Edelmann, *Abgenöthigtes Glaubens-Bekentniss*, p. 243.

66. Edelmann, *Abgenöthigtes Glaubens-Bekentniss*, p. 250. In his *Johann Christian Edelmann from Orthodoxy to Enlightenment* (Paris: Mouton, 1976), Walter Grossmann omits Edelmann's reference to the "Lord Jesus" and thus the semblance of a piety Edelmann seems never to have abandoned. Moenckeberg quotes Edelmann as referring to his many enemies, then adding: "I have an even mightier friend. . . . Now, of course, whether my Lord and Friend wants to use his unworthy servant for something yet to come is hidden from me, but

By contrast, Edelmann wrote that Jesus was a man such as any one of us, endowed with extraordinary gifts, a true Magus or wise man able to know and use nature and its powers. His disciples called him Son of God in recognition of his superiority over others, though he himself called God his Father in no other sense than we. Edelmann continued: Jesus' chief intent was to reunite those separated until now by so many idiotic notions of God. Jesus did not establish a new religion, but uprooted the basis of the old, the notion that sinners must placate an angry God. Thus, Jesus deserved the title "Redeemer" since he removed the barrier between God and men by freeing them from leaders who fattened themselves on their sins, and had to die because the clergy feared he would turn the populace against them. Jesus, wrote Edelmann, rose "spiritually" from the grave and even now appears in thousands of witnesses to judge the living and dead. Finally, he asserted that the Last Judgment consists of one's rising from sleep to recognize God and self and to lead a reasonable life.[67]

In the *Glauben-Bekenntnis* Edelmann developed the idea of an ethics he believed to be morally superior to the Christian. It was this-sided, and reckoned on an earthly requital by way of rebirth. Depending on its moral worth and behavior in a previous existence the soul was fated for a higher or lower form of existence in an eternal alternation between spirit or soul and material or body. Edelmann insisted that the secret intent behind the life story of Jesus was to lead his disciples toward the doctrine of reincarnation, or, as he wrote, to show them

> that God always allows his judgments to be exercised through men against man and, of course, on the very earth on which we at present all dwell; that he is able to alter their state in such way that he can make of a beggar a king, and of a king a beggar. By this means he has intended to found mutual love and mercy among men, to eliminate all horror and inhumanity, in a word, to bless us all both as regards the present as well as the future. . . . This position makes a far deeper impression on souls than all the clerics say of heaven and hell, of future universal world judgment, and imminent eternal damnation.[68]

I know that he always remains my true Lord and God." See Carl Moenckeberg, *Hermann Samuel Reimarus und Johann Christian Edelmann* (Hamburg: G. E. Nolte, 1867), pp. 171-72.

67. Edelmann, *Abgenöthigtes Glaubens-Bekenntniss*, pp. 90, 93, 101, 117, 121, 206; see Moenckeberg, *Hermann Samuel Reimarus und Johann Christian Edelmann*, pp. 171-72.

68. Edelmann, *Abgenöthigtes Glaubens-Bekenntniss*, p. 256.

Hermann Samuel Reimarus (1694-1768), often described as the most forceful Bible critic of the eighteenth century and as the first to attempt the separation of a biblical character from the portrait drawn by later hands, is reputed to have loathed Edelmann.[69] Recent scholarship has turned up compelling evidence of Reimarus's dependence on him, loathed or not. First of all, despite a host of similarities that may simply be put down to the spirit of the age, the manner and force of the two men's use of the critical method are too strikingly similar to plead for coincidence. Second, the similarities between the two in the type of argument and in the vehemence of their criticism are too striking to be dismissed as pure accident. Reimarus's treatment of the exodus narrative, which Edelmann had made the highpoint of his analysis, reads like a page torn from *Moses mit aufgedeckten Angesicht*.[70] As to where or on what occasion Edelmann's copyist(s) might have furnished Reimarus with his work, the circle of deists in Hamburg, to which Reimarus belonged and with whom Edelmann corresponded from the beginning of his Berlin asylum, strongly suggests itself. That circle had clustered around the poet Barthold Heinrich Brocke (1680-1742), with whom Reimarus had discussed his Bible criticism, and to whose natural theology Edelmann had been introduced in his early years.[71]

For one reason or another, Edelmann has eluded classification as the first to undertake radical biblical criticism or to have been "martyred" in its cause. G. E. Lessing, David Friedrich Strauss (1808-74), and the Hegelian Bruno Bauer (1809-82) gave him some attention, though Lessing kept him under wraps, perhaps due to an identification with Spinoza which he himself enjoyed but hesitated to publicize. Strauss guardedly described him as an "alleged precursor," and Bauer waited until 1847 to publish his work anonymously. On meeting Edelmann, Moses Mendelssohn is said to have reached for his hat and scampered off, resolved never again to appear in the company of such a miserable creature. Later, in a letter to Lessing, he conceded that "persecution, misfortune, and difficulties" may have plunged the poor fellow into depression. At the conclusion of his discussion of Edelmann and his work, Emanuel Hirsch writes that while the "frivolous, unprincipled French, free thinker Voltaire could even involve Germany in

69. See Moenckeberg, *Hermann Samuel Reimarus und Johann Christian Edelman,* p. 129.

70. See, for example, Reimarus's *Apologie oder Schutzschrift für die Vernünftigen Verehrer Gottes,* ed. Gerhard Alexander (Frankfurt am Main: Insel Verlag, 1972), vol. 1, pp. 294-95, 300-305.

71. See Schaper, *Ein langer Abschied vom Christentum,* pp. 203-18.

his war against religion and Church, the life of that free, German thinker, ensouled by an upright seriousness toward truth, ebbed away in unnoticed stillness."[72] Reimarus, on the other hand, knew well enough that by revealing his critical views he would have ruined his bourgeoisie existence.

> The writing may remain hidden, for the use of understanding friends. I intend that it should not be made public in print until the times improve. Better that the common herd go astray for a while than that I should annoy it with truths (though I would not be guilty if that happened), and plunge it into a raging religious zeal.[73]

72. Emanuel Hirsch, *Geschichte der neueren evangelischen Theologie*, vol. 2 (Gütersloh: C. Bertelsmann Verlag, 1951), p. 414.
73. Reimarus, *Apologie oder Schutzschrift für die Vernünftigen Verehrer Gottes*, vol. 1, p. 41.

CHAPTER SIX

The Modern Period

Johann Salomo Semler

Johann Salomo Semler, "pioneer of modern biblical science," was born on December 15, 1725, in the Thuringian Saalfeld, son of the archdeacon and later superintendent Matthias Nicolaus Semler. In 1743, at the age of sixteen, he matriculated at the Prussian University of Halle, in this period preoccupied with the intimate connection between theological and general philosophical hermeneutics. While at Halle Semler studied classical languages and history, but soon advanced to evangelical theology, where he came under the influence of Sigmund Jacob Baumgarten, celebrated pupil of Christian Wolff. Under Baumgarten Semler heard exegesis, dogmatics, symbolics, and theological ethics. In 1750 he received his master's degree at Halle, in order to take up an editorial position at Coburg. In the following year, he became professor of history and ancient philology at the University of Altdorf near Nürnberg. After this intermezzo, in 1753 he received the invitation to a professorship in evangelical theology at his alma mater, a chair that he occupied for almost forty years.

Among Semler's works, the two that elicited the most attention and response are his *Vorbereitung zur theologischen Hermeneutik,* appearing between 1760 and 1769, totaling more than 1,200 pages, and his *Abhandlung von freier Untersuchung des Canons,* published in 1771-75.

Viewing himself as a spiritual heir of Reformation principles, Semler noted a surprising neglect of "historical exposition" in post-Reformation, orthodox interpretation of the Bible. Such interpretation, he believed, was unable to convince his critical contemporaries, and threatened to degenerate into intra-confessional polemics or a flattening out by way of naturalism. It was thus necessary, through historical-critical exegesis, to help dogmatics attain to an appropriate scripture interpretation able to convince his contemporaries. To achieve this, he drew a distinction between the Bible and the Word of God that it mediated. Acknowledging that God was sole author of the biblical message or of the Word it contained, and rejecting the idea that the Holy Spirit could be received independently of that Word or prior to its proclamation, Semler nevertheless emphatically rejected the orthodox view, which assigned the divinity of the Bible not only to its content, but to its words, syllables, and letters, extending it even to the Hebrew vowel points. Nor did he agree to the idea of the biblical writers' enjoying a special, discrete inspiration. For their moral changes, for their desire to perpetuate the divine purpose through writing and teaching, the evangelists required inspiration, but for their histories, their language, or their words, they needed none. Obviously, they wrote "in a special frame of mind" but such inspiration was past and did not remain in the words as they are read now.[1] The reason lay in the condition of the biblical texts, that is, in the copies come down to us with their myriad alterations. It was thus not possible that "only this and not that" comprised the number, order, and construction of the actual words. Often whole lines, sentences, and individual words had to be eliminated from the printed text, and some exchanged for others.[2] This rendered the orthodox doctrine with its assertions of the perfection, the uninjured and verbally inspired character of the transmitted text, totally without support.

This judgment denoted a new direction of research, a direction taken by Semler at the encouragement of his teacher, Baumgarten, that of New Testament text criticism. Only now did the term "criticism" come to occupy a place in scientific terminology, and to be used exclusively of text investigation. Semler was conscious of the massive resistance his emphasis on text criticism as an indispensable part of biblical interpretation had to overcome. It meant that the Bible could be assigned no special position over against other ancient literature. It required liberation from the reigning dogmatic assumption that a particular divine providence was to be predicated of the text's transmission. But this meant that there was no hindrance from the side of theology toward the use of reason in Bible

1. Johann Salomo Semler, *Von freier Untersuchung des Canons,* ed. Heinz Scheible (Gütersloh: Mohn, 1967), pp. 83-85.
2. Semler, *Von freier Untersuchung des Canons,* p. 85.

interpretation. In fact, as a suitable, competent, and indispensable organ of knowledge in the search for truth the application of human reason was required for an appropriate exposition of scripture. Semler wrote:

> All readers of Holy Scripture and all who hearken to Christian instruction not only freely retain the entire use of their ability to reason. It is also their great and reverent duty not to relegate to others the use of reason and declare themselves quit of it. Otherwise, reason becomes a human work, the affair of others who imagine they have the right to decide that this or that is and must be the content of the divine teaching.[3]

This also meant that no particular spiritual gift or illumination was required of the Bible interpreter. It was "an old, unreasonable tenet," Semler wrote, "that an unconverted man or one without the Spirit or lacking improvement respecting the direction of his powers of soul can neither understand Holy Scripture nor communicate it usefully to others."[4]

What needed to be understood first of all was that in face of such notions of Holy Scripture according to which its authors functioned as mere tools, scripture and Word of God needed to be radically distinguished. Statements about Holy Scripture as norm could not relate to all the biblical utterances. The "elements," the universal concepts and truths, needed to be separated from the individual, particular concepts, descriptions, and narratives. In concert with the view that reason sufficed for interpretation, those "elements" could not contradict natural, universally moral or related knowledge, albeit having arisen supernaturally.

Semler's insistence on a radical distinction was most evident in his evaluation of the Old Testament. It was inconceivable to him that thoughtful Christians could see the Old Testament as the Word of God.

> It is incomprehensible to me, how it can happen that reflective Christians and even teachers called to aid in the increase of salutary knowledge, can still go wrong on this point and everlastingly confuse the

3. From the larger, three-volume edition of the *Abhandlung von freier Untersuchung des Canons,* quoted by Gottfried Hornig, "Über Semlers Theologische Hermeneutik," in *Unzeitgemässe Hermeneutik,* ed. Axel Bühler (Frankfurt am Main: Vittorio Klostermann, 1994), p. 204.

4. From the preface of Semler's work on Baumgarten, *Unterricht von Auslegung der heiligen Schrift,* cited in Hornig, "Über Semlers Theologische Hermeneutik," p. 205.

holy books or writings of the Jews with the Word of God contained,
communicated, and clothed in them *here and there, not through and
through.*[5]

Semler located the most proximate cause for confusion in the opinion regarding the divine origin of the Septuagint as having spread to Christianity.
The fact that in the teaching style of the time Christ extracted proofs or
inducement from merely a portion of the Old Testament was forgotten,
and thus the Christian community took into its teaching office the entire
canon, "which should belong for Jews *as Jews* alone, and not for all men of
all times once for all."[6] For capable and reflective Christians, Semler added,
the huge amount of writings concerning the *allegationes* of the Old Testament in the New (the so-called scriptural proof) were of no value. In fact,
the old teachers' and rabbis' allegorizing of what according to the literal
sense was never there proves that these books do not contain such divine,
universal truths as require no further enrichment. The new covenant that
God concluded in Jesus Christ enjoys precedence over the old; the New
Testament is to be preferred to at least some Old Testament books that lack
all connection with the teaching of Christ and the apostles' proclamation.
After all, Jesus' own exposition of central passages of the Old Testament
legitimized the distinction between what was or was not of value in it. For
precedent in drawing the distinction Semler turned to Origen as a model
authority. He thought he saw that in regard to the Old Testament historical
sections Origen used only the historical-literal sense in the application,
and for the historical, narrative portions excluded the mystical and moral
senses, by which even the historical sections furnish the basis of knowledge
for Christian faith. A mystical-moral or allegorical interpretation of the
historical sections was thus at bottom an edifying application of the exposition oriented to the literal sense for insightful Christians and a matter
purely for Christian teachers.[7]

Nor did Semler limit distinguishing between what was lesser and
greater to the Old Testament. Agreeing that the New Testament contained
the "genuine documents of the new Christian society," he asserted that
all did not reflect the content of the Christian religion itself. Many pieces

5. Semler, *Von freier Untersuchung des Canons*, para. 10, p. 42f.

6. Semler, *Von freier Untersuchung des Canons*, p. 77.

7. Taken from F. Andreas Lüder, *Historie und Dogmatik: Ein Beitrag zur Genese und
Entfaltung von Johann Salomo Semlers Verständnis des Alten Testaments* (Berlin: Walter de
Gruyter, 1995), p. 84.

have to do with the personality and individual circumstances of the first Christians, which can never lay claim to universality. "The *local* circumstances remain *local* and fall away."[8] Referring to the "discourses of Christ" and the "writings of Paul" as assisting toward a genuine, living faith, he proposed making an "extract" for Christians' practical use. In it those portions should be contained that could be observed as essential parts of the Christian religion.

Naturally, this removed support from the concept of "canon" as a collection of divinely inspired writings transmitted by direct divine intervention. Defining canonical writings as those determined for public reading, Semler proceeded to trace the genesis of their canonicity. At first a certain uniformity in reading and hymnody was observed and distance taken from so-called heretical parties. To this point no overall agreement existed. A more intimate link between churches in several provinces needed forging. This occurred only from the fourth century on. At that time the bishops of the several churches, in part orally, in part by writing, agreed on what books from the so-called Old and New Testaments should make up the *canonicam lectionem* (canonical lection). From now on the uniformity and unalterability of the canon rested on the *iure ecclesiastico publico* (public ecclesiastical right). All of this, Semler insisted, took place primarily for *external* purposes, for which reason the idea that these books had divine origin could only, as every historical witness, be affirmed or denied.[9] After his discovery at a 1770 meeting in Magdeburg of congeniality in thought with Johann Friedrich Wilhelm (Abbe) Jerusalem (1709-89), tutor to the reigning family of Brunswick-Lüneberg-Wolfenbüttel and friend of James Boswell, Semler dedicated his work on the canon to him.[10]

Beneath all this — beneath distinguishing Bible from Word of God and criticism of the text, beneath the summons to the use of reason in interpretation, the resulting evaluation of the biblical witness, and criticism of the canon — there lay total allegiance to the historical task. Consequently, attention to the *sensus litteralis,* a "truly grounded insight into the meaning of the word of Holy Scripture," was the interpreter's first requirement. Second, the interpreter should be able to communicate "the

8. Semler, *Von freier Untersuchung des Canons,* p. 90.

9. Semler, *Von freier Untersuchung des Canons,* pp. 19-20, 23, 25, 31.

10. In *Historie und Dogmatik,* p. 121, Andreas Lüder refers to Karl Aner's description of Jerusalem as the "first German critic of the Pentateuch before Eichhorn"; see Karl Aner (1879-1933), *Die Theologie der Lessingzeit* (Reprographischer Nachdruck der Ausgabe Halle, 1929), p. 313.

historical circumstances of a biblical speech." Only when one sought to understand the biblical texts as reports of particular historical events from their own time could one become conscious of one's distance from them and be able to interpret them appropriately. Only when this historical task had been fulfilled could the actual proclamation of the biblical texts and the Word of God contained in them be taken up. The succession was irreversible: first, historical exposition, then edifying application. In contrast to pietist exposition, these two events could not be mixed.[11]

In the history of theology Semler is referred to as chief representative of the accommodation theory. In order to hold to the thesis of the Bible's verbal inspiration, high and late orthodoxy opted for an accommodation theory according to which the Holy Spirit in dictating to the biblical authors accommodated himself to their style and language. The "critical" theologians did not embrace this idea, but maintained the accommodation of the biblical authors to the ideas of their contemporaries. It is this idea that is present in Semler's accommodation theory, not, however, with reference to the biblical ideas of nature, but to the Bible's various types of speech and ideas. As he wrote in his work on the canon:

> As is clear from the narratives of the evangelists that in his (chosen) delivery and quantity of instruction Jesus always accommodated himself to the varied ability of his hearers, so it is quite certain that in arranging his narrative or instruction an author first sought to be useful to his (then) readers according to their circumstances.[12]

According to Semler, accommodation was pedagogical, for the purpose of easing the acceptance and expansion of Christianity. Proclamation of the Word of God was thus not to be oriented to whatever required accommodation, but to such clear principles as appeared chiefly in John and Paul. The fulfillment of this requirement led to what a later generation would call "demythologizing," the surrender of mythological ideas stemming from pre-Christian religious tradition. According to Semler these included the belief in devils, demons, and evil spirits. More importantly, it included abandonment of the futurist understanding of eschatology since the imminent expectation witnessed to in the New Testament texts represented an accommodation on the part of Jesus and the apostles to the

---

11. Hornig, "Über Semlers theologische Hermeneutik," pp. 195-96.
12. Semler, *Von freier Untersuchung des Canons*, p. 28.

eschatological hopes of contemporary Judaism.[13] The idea of accommodation was not Semler's invention. As Peter Gay reports, the great Isaac Newton did not read the Pentateuch as a literal report but as an account of creation and man's earliest history adapted by the narrator to the limited understanding of his audience. Yet, he did not doubt that despite his use of metaphor and image Moses told the essential truth.[14]

To his successors Semler left a legacy that was considerable if not vast. In face of the suppression of the biblical utterance by an interpretation determined by dogmatics, he defended the independence of exegesis.[15] In contrast to the prevailing notion that the Gospels were written shortly after Jesus' death and resurrection, he insisted that originally there was only oral proclamation, that at least thirty years needed to pass before the oral tradition was fixed in writing.[16] His surrender of the biblical concept of imminent expectation for the sake of a present eschatology could have birthed the modern practice of demythologizing. He refused to direct his historical-critical research toward the attempt to reconstruct the events described in the New Testament or to write a history of the life of Jesus. He wrote, "as soon as we concentrate on the history of Christ without us, outside us, *in abstracto,* as it were, we lose the true connection with the facts."[17] He anticipated research into the contest between Jewish, Palestinian, and Pauline Christianity as reflected in the New Testament documents. He wrote:

> Another party called the Jewish-thinking Christians who were (openly) enemies of all the writings of Paul and thus had books which, for particular praise of Peter, contained narratives of his teaching, travels, and arrangements, in part also contained an apocalypse or prophecies (these books were not accepted or used by the party calling itself Paul's pupils).[18]

13. See the discussion in Gottfried Hornig, *Die Anfänge der historisch-kritischen Theologie: Johann Salomo Semlers Schriftverständnis und seine Stellung zu Luther* (Göttingen: Vandenhoeck & Ruprecht, 1961), pp. 222, 225-28.

14. Peter Gay, *The Enlightenment, an Interpretation,* vol. 2: *The Science of Freedom* (New York: W. W. Norton, 1969), pp. 141-42.

15. See Hornig, "Über Semlers theologische Hermeneutik," p. 202.

16. Semler, *Von freier Untersuchung des Canons,* p. 39; cf. Hornig, *Die Anfänge der historisch-kritischen Theologie,* p. 178.

17. Hornig, *Die Anfänge der historisch-kritischen Theologie,* p. 201.

18. Semler, *Von freier Untersuchung des Canons,* pp. 22-23.

Characteristically, the evaluation of Semler more often has to do with the theological perspective of his criticism than with any accurate appraisal of his work. The assertion that he regarded natural religion as the historical essence of Christianity or was forced into the position of an historical relativist, that his understanding of scripture was modeled after the criteria of rationalism, collapses in face of his relativizing the consequences of his research and their results by emphasizing the abiding value of the New Testament message of salvation. It falls as well by his refusal to distinguish between religion and theology in order to negate or disparage theology but in order to give it shape as a scientific discipline. The criticism that Semler devalued the entire Old Testament or was concerned to prove its inferiority is countered by the fact that he did not judge all Old Testament writings alike. On the other hand, Semler's commitment to the thesis of the clarity of scripture, and his rejection of allegory, his view of the canon as the work of the church, his insistence on the witness of the Holy Spirit as mediated solely through the biblical word, his appeal to Luther's debate with the fanatics in support of his refusal to allow the edifying nature of a text to serve as criterion for proper exposition, all make clear to what extent Semler reflected a Reformation inheritance. At the same time, his distance from the Reformation cannot be ignored. He saw no possibility of bridging the gap between the Old and New Testaments by way of Christological exposition. With respect to Bible interpretation the *sensus litteralis* was for Semler the historical meaning, and not, as for Luther, the meaning oriented to Christ. More, as would Ferdinand Christian Baur (1792-1860) after him, Hegel-like he identified the Christian consciousness with the Spirit of God. He wrote:

> The only proof that totally satisfies an honest reader is the inner conviction through truths encountered in this Holy Scripture (but not in all its parts and individual books), which usually, to put it briefly, has been called in a rather turgid biblical phrase the witness of the Holy Spirit in the reader's heart.[19]

In fine, because of his attempt to avoid the extreme of a fundamentalist authority that regards all biblical data as binding, and that of a modernist relativism that accentuates the time-conditioned and scarcely allows speaking of a valid "Word of God" in the Bible, Semler was reproached by

---

19. Quoted in W. G. Kümmel, *Das Neue Testament: Geschichte der Erforschung seiner Probleme,* 2nd ed. (Freiburg: Karl Alber, 1970), p. 76.

the one extreme for his skepticism and by the other for his relapse into orthodoxy. That was a fate more than one of his successors at the historical-critical task would suffer.

Friedrich Schleiermacher

Friedrich Daniel Ernst Schleiermacher (1768-1834) is often celebrated as the father of the modern theory of interpretation. Upon completion of his studies at the University of Halle, he served two years as a private tutor and two years as a Protestant pastor. He then returned to his alma mater as university preacher and professor of theology, where he remained until his invitation to a chair at the newly founded University of Berlin. It was at Halle that the young professor first gave attention to the problems of biblical interpretation in conjunction with the study and translation of Plato's works. In a letter to a friend, dated November 1806, he wrote:

> Along with Plato I am working on a theologically critical piece on the First Epistle to Timothy. It is to open my actual theological career. Unfortunately, since I do not see when it can now appear, I spend most of the time by far with Plato.[20]

With the publication of the study on 1 Timothy, a fourth volume of the Plato translation appeared together with a review of the neo-Kantian Johann Gottlieb Fichte's (1762-1814) "Characteristics of the Present Age."[21] No doubt, the translation of Plato and the study of 1 Timothy were of mutual influence.

The work on 1 Timothy was not an exegesis or interpretation of the epistle, but an argument against its Pauline authorship. In what amounts to a dedication to a certain J. C. Gass, Schleiermacher reminds his friend of their earlier conversations regarding the authorship of the epistle and of his suspicion:

> You will remember, my most worthy friend, that when we last saw each other, I spoke to you of my suspicion regarding our New Testament

---

20. See Friedrich Schleiermacher, *Kritische Gesamtausgabe*, I/5: *Schriften aus der Hallenser Zeit, 1804-1807,* ed. Hermann Patch (Berlin: Walter de Gruyter, 1995), p. xci, n. 339.
21. "Grundzüge des gegenwärtigen Zeitalters."

First Letter to Timothy, and that as far as I am concerned the matter is fairly settled that it cannot have Paul as its author.[22]

With this suspicion, the phenomenon of "Deutero-Paulinism" in the New Testament made its way into the history of interpretation. Since the argument came by way of the application of an inner, or, as it was then called, "higher criticism," the application itself was new.

In the Halle period, Schleiermacher's ideas respecting interpretation were more or less limited to the classroom. Following his arrival in Berlin, he spun the threads of his study further in a lecture to the public, given in 1809-10 under the title "The General Characteristics of the Art of Exposition."[23] In this period and in the years following, his preoccupation with interpretation began in earnest.

At the outset, Schleiermacher described the interpreter's task as distinguishing the process of understanding from the object of understanding itself. In 1805, in what was perhaps his earliest written comment on the subject, he stated that the act of explanation, which until then had made up a large part of so-called hermeneutical theory, lay outside the task of interpretation. It was one thing to formulate an idea and give expression to it, and quite another to understand what was spoken. Hermeneutics, Schleiermacher insisted, dealt with the latter. In Heinz Kimmerle's rescue of Schleiermacher's lectures and notes on interpretation theory from 1805 to 1829, he states that between the years 1810 and 1819 Schleiermacher began to speak of the process of understanding as an art *(Kunstlehre)*.[24] In his *Brief Outline on the Study of Theology,* published in 1811, Schleiermacher had this to say:

> The perfect understanding of a speech or writing is a work of art, and requires a theory of art or a technique that we describe by the term hermeneutic. We call art, even in a narrower sense, that composite production by which we are conscious of general rules, the application of which in the given instance cannot be reduced again to rules.[25]

22. Friedrich Schleiermacher, *Über den sogenannten ersten Brief des Paulos an den Timotheos: Ein kritisches Sendschreiben* (Berlin: In der Realschulbuchhandlung, 1807), cited in *Schriften aus der Hallenser Zeit,* p. 157.

23. "Die allgemeinen Grundsätze der Auslegungskunst."

24. Friedrich Schleiermacher, *Hermeneutik* (Heidelberg: Carl Winter Universitätsverlag, 1959), pp. 56, 82.

25. Friedrich Schleiermacher, *Kritische Gesamtausgabe,* I/6: *Universitätsschriften. Hera-*

This "art" was not to be restricted to written productions, but was applicable to all life-expressions in language. It was the "translation" of linguistic signs.[26] In his earliest reflection on the subject, Schleiermacher held to the conviction that an individual's thought and entire being was in essence determined through language. "Everything," he wrote, "that [can] be the task of hermeneutics is the member of a sentence."[27] Everything to be assumed and everything to be found in hermeneutics was sheer language, and whatever else was involved had to be discovered from the language. According to Schleiermacher, the approach to that discovery was twofold: on the one hand, it required attention to a speaker's or a writer's articulations in language. To this requirement Schleiermacher most often gave the name "grammatical interpretation." Here, everything dependent on language such as historical conditions, time, circumstances, and whatever falls under the heading of "historical criticism" had the accent. On the other hand, the path to discovery required attention to the form taken on by a speech or text, or "technical interpretation." Schleiermacher was insistent: insight into the relation of an author or speaker to the forms given in articulation in speech or writing was such an essential element of exposition that without it neither the speech nor the writing, to say nothing of the author or speaker, could be properly understood. Thus, with the technical interpretation the speaker's or author's style, type of text, peculiarity of composition, and the setting forth of a theme had the accent. The grammatical approach concentrated on the objective element of speech, and the technical on the so-called subjective element of the author's perspective. The two approaches were indivisible. Just as the grammatical assumed the technical interpretation, so the technical assumed the grammatical interpretation. Both approaches were equal in stature. It would be false, wrote Schleiermacher, to call the grammatical the lower and the technical the higher.

If the path toward understanding life-expressions and their forms in articulated speech or writing required a grammatical and a technical approach, then, according to Schleiermacher, each approach required a method, the method of comparative analysis together with what he called "divination." The comparative method represented "the feminine force"

---

kleitos. *Kurze Darstellung des theologischen Studiums,* ed. Hermann Fischer et al. (Berlin: Walter de Gruyter, 1998), p. 375.

26. Kurt Nowak, *Schleiermacher* (Göttingen: Vandenhoeck & Ruprecht, 2001), p. 199.

27. Schleiermacher, *Hermeneutik,* pp. 17, 64.

in the interpretive art. It sought to comprehend the universal by giving attention to words in their context and comparing all their known uses. The divinatory represented "the masculine force." It sought to comprehend the particular by entering the speaker's or the author's frame of mind. Schleiermacher insisted that the two methods could not be separated. Since logic could not fully account for the workings of understanding, the universal as well as the particular, the comparative as well as the divinatory, were essential. Alone, the comparative would not guarantee unity; alone, the divinatory would degenerate into the fantastic.

What had been missing, according to Schleiermacher, was what one of his interpreters has called "the disposition to examine the foundational act of all hermeneutics: the act of understanding the act of a living, feeling, intuiting human being."[28] Clarity was needed. Did the art of exposition embrace both explication and application, or, in the jargon of the experts, the *subtilitas explicandi* and *subtilitas applicandi* in addition to the *subtilitas intelligendi?* Schleiermacher's answer was a decided "No." Explication and application did not belong to the art of exposition. On the contrary, they actually inhibited it. In the "Academy Speeches" of 1829, he conceded that there had been no lack of instruction in interpretation. For example, the "Principles of Biblical Interpretation" by the Leipzig philosopher-theologian and enemy of Bach, Johann August Ernesti (1707-81),[29] enjoyed great respect since many of the rules set up in it had proved useful. Still, those rules had no basis since they lacked universal principles. "Thus," he wrote, "I had to go my own way."[30] As for the application of this art to a particular discipline such as the study of Christianity, Christian theology itself, wrote Schleiermacher, had to embody the rules of art *(Kunstregeln)* he had outlined, without which harmonious governance of the Christian church was impossible.[31]

The question arose as to whether or not the sacred texts of Christianity require a special art or hermeneutic. Should not the authors of the Old and New Testaments be treated differently because the Holy Spirit spoke

28. Richard E. Palmer, *Hermeneutics: Interpretation Theory in Schleiermacher, Dilthey, Heidegger, and Gadamer* (Evanston, Ill.: Northwestern University Press, 1969), p. 85.

29. Johann August Ernesti, *Institutio interpretis Nov. Test.* (3rd ed., 1778). The fourth edition, *Elementary Principles of Interpretation,* was translated by Moses Stuart of Andover and published in New York by Allen, Morrill and Wardwell in 1842.

30. Schleiermacher, *Hermeneutik,* p. 123.

31. Schleiermacher, *Kritische Gesamtausgabe,* I/6, *Kurze Darstellung des theologischen Studiums,* p. 328.

through them? How could the Spirit be subjected to rules of interpretation? Both orthodox and pietist held that the Old and New Testaments deserved a treatment unlike that given other texts due to their having been "inbreathed" (see 2 Tim. 3:16). In his earliest description of 1811, Schleiermacher replied that the Bible could lay claim to no special hermeneutical principles; it had to be understood according to the same principles as applied to any other moral or written human expression.[32] It was "dogmatic interest" that insisted on viewing the Bible differently from other texts.[33] Further, the distinction drawn between the authors as inspired to write scripture and as otherwise functioning, and thus as guaranteeing scriptural authority, was an error. In *The Christian Faith* Schleiermacher wrote that the impulse to write was nothing by itself alone, that scripture would not have been inspired had not the entire apostolic life been a life from out of inspiration. In fact, even if the authors had been dead instruments, the Holy Spirit could have spoken through them just as they themselves would have spoken.[34] Thus, neither the impulse to write nor the apostolic vocation as such could be separated. As he stated it,

> only when we proceed from an entirely dead view of the connection between idea and word, or between the inner and the outer, can these questions be raised in the sense as usually occurs.[35]

The natural standard here, wrote Schleiermacher, was the analogy of the doctrine of Christ's person. The effect of the Holy Spirit on the biblical authors came as close as possible to the personal union of the divine with the human nature in Christ without eliminating the specific difference between the two ways of uniting. Nothing but an utterly dead scholasticism could attempt to draw a line between the author's impulse to write and the actually written word, or to represent the written word in

---

32. Schleiermacher, *Hermeneutik,* p. 15; see also idem, *Hermeneutik und Kritik,* ed. Manfred Frank (Frankfurt am Main: Suhrkamp, 1977), p. 299.

33. Schleiermacher, *Hermeneutik,* p. 85; cf. idem, *Hermeneutics and Criticism and Other Writings,* trans. Andrew Bowie (Cambridge: Cambridge University Press, 1998), p. 80. (The Bowie translation supplies what Frank's edition lacks respecting application of Schleiermacher's theory to the New Testament.)

34. Schleiermacher, *Hermeneutik,* p. 85.

35. Friedrich Schleiermacher, *Kritische Gesamtausgabe, Schriften und Entwürfe,* I/7: *Der christliche Glaube, 1821-1822,* ed. Hermann Peiter (Berlin: Walter de Gruyter, 1980), p. 234.

its bare externality as a special product of inspiration. There was something Hamann-like in the argument. That "contemporary in dissent" had argued that the question as to whether language was of divine or human origin rent asunder what inseparably belonged together, and, as noted above,[36] accused his old friend Kant of a "purism" that put reason to death with its division of thought from speech.[37] With his conviction that "the *communicatio* of the divine and human *idiomatum*" was "a basic law and the main key to all our knowledge, and of all visible housekeeping,"[38] Hamann may well have prepared for a conception of the Bible's inspiration that would be held for generations to come.

Further, the assumption that since scripture proceeded from the Holy Spirit the biblical text could contain no imperfections was false. In the preface to his study of Luke, published in 1817, Schleiermacher wrote that over against those who had begun to bring the critical study of the biblical books into disrepute, as though it harmed their divine authority, one simple truth should apply, that is, that "the purest, simplest faith and the severest testing are one and the same" since no one anxious to believe what is godly should want to believe deceptions, old or new, alien or home-grown. If, he continued, one regards the activity of the Holy Spirit in the composition of the scriptures as unique, different from the Spirit's working in the church in general or from his universal activity in the disciples of Christ, then one is always in a quandary over deciding wherein such activity should consist respecting the historical writings, and to what kind of subjects one should limit it. In the dedication of this study to his friend and colleague, Wilhelm Martin Leberecht de Wette (1780-1849), later dismissed from his chair for political reasons in 1819, Schleiermacher referred to tensions with other colleagues such as Philipp Marheineke (1780-1846) and August Neander (1789-1850) as well as with the Prussian royal court over the freedom of historical-critical study.[39]

---

36. See p. 84 above.

37. For an extended analysis of the letter and the *Metakritik,* see Oswald Bayer, *A Contemporary in Dissent: Johann Georg Hamann as a Radical Enlightener* (Grand Rapids: Eerdmans, 2012).

38. Johann Georg Hamann, "Des Ritters von Rosenkreuz letzte Willensmeynung," in Johann Georg Hamann, *Sämtliche Werke,* vol. 3: *Schriften über Sprache/Mysterien/Vernunft, 1772-1788,* ed. Josef Nadler (Wien: Im Verlag Herder, 1951), p. 27.

39. Friedrich Schleiermacher, *Kritische Gesamtausgabe, Schriften und Entwürfe,* I/8: *Exegetische Schriften,* ed. Hermann Patsch and Dirk Schmid (Berlin: Walter de Gruyter, 1980), preface, p. 8, and the editor's note on p. xiii.

Regarding scriptural authority as derived from the peculiar inspiration of the biblical authors, in *The Christian Faith* Schleiermacher wrote that respect for Holy Scripture in no way first establishes faith, but quite the opposite: it is faith that gives scripture its unique position. Actually, a faith established by respect for scripture would be quite different from faith as properly understood. It would be reserved for the expert and far removed from the laity.[40] Certainty of faith would exist only where there was ability to prove the divinity of scripture, while all who lacked this degree of "scientific culture" would believe simply on authority. "Thus," wrote Schleiermacher, "piety would spring from, and depend on, science."[41] The general rules governing the art of interpretation applied equally to the biblical canon. Identical rules of exposition underlay all texts, whether of religion, jurisprudence, poetry, or philosophy. Bible interpretation could only involve a special application of those rules. That is, it had only to make those rules more precise in relation to the peculiar language of the canon (Greek and Hebrew), as well as to the particular genre to which the writings belonged.

Schleiermacher's conviction that faith preexisted affirmation of the divinity of scripture extended to the art of its interpretation. If, as he wrote in his "Brief Outline," Christian theology had to embody the rules of the art of interpretation, without a "religious interest" occupation with the New Testament could at worst be only directed against it and at best pursue an alien, vague sentiment. As such the purely philological and historical yield of scripture was not rich enough to attract the investigator. Albeit undertaken by persons of a scientific turn, scripture interpretation was nevertheless undertaken by those desiring to be instruments of the Spirit acting in and through scripture.[42] Thus, religious interest and scientific intelligence united toward theory and practice to the highest degree and in the most possible balance marked the church leader.

This did not mean that the interpretation of biblical texts was easily managed. First of all, there was the matter of the canon, the interpretation of which Schleiermacher described as the most difficult task, in part because it contained materials of a "speculative-religious" sort in a language

---

40. Schleiermacher, *Kritische Gesamtausgabe,* I/8, *Exegetische Schriften,* pp. 221-23, 234.

41. Schleiermacher, *The Christian Faith,* English translation of the second German edition (1830/31), ed. H. R. Mackintosh and J. S. Stewart (Edinburgh: T. & T. Clark, 1948), pp. 593-94.

42. Schleiermacher, *Kritische Gesamtausgabe,* I/6, *Kurze Darstellung des theologischen Studiums,* pp. 250, 276, 279, 328, 379; idem, *The Christian Faith,* pp. 591, 593, 607.

alien to their authors who were by and large from an uneducated class, and was thus liable to infinite misinterpretation, in part because the circumstances that moved the writers to write are unknown and must be guessed at only through the writings themselves.[43] In addition, since neither the time limit of earliest Christianity nor its personnel could be precisely determined, the boundary of the canon could not be fixed. The mere fact that the canon had existed for centuries in the church as a collection did not guarantee that its limits had been irrevocably fixed. For this reason, since each theologian should arrive at his own understanding of the canon, each had to practice the art of canonical criticism, and refuse exposition on authority. For the Roman Catholic, Schleiermacher wrote, such critical questions were of no interest since the canon was a work of the church, and as transmitted in the church had the same value and authority of infallibility as the tradition of the doctrine.[44]

At this point, Schleiermacher drew a line between the Testaments. The Old Testament, because it contained much that was erroneous and had already become alien to the New Testament age, was exempted from the interpretive task. Actually, to include "the Jewish codex" in the canon meant to regard Christianity as a continuation of Judaism, thus mitigating any idea of canon. Only after deluding oneself by unconscious additions and subtractions could a Christian doctrine of God be gleaned from the Psalms and the prophets. The Old Testament law, he contended, lacked the power of the Spirit from out of which Christian life was to emerge. It was not inspired *(eingegeben)*. Of course, historical fidelity and completeness of view demanded that Christ's and his first preachers' references to the Old Testament should be preserved, but such scarcely involved more than the prophetic books and the Psalms. For the sake of these references the entire Old Testament might be taken up in the canon, but the preferred practice was to add only the Psalms and the messianic prophecies to the New Testament as an appendix. Knowledge of the "Jewish codex" constituted an auxiliary study.[45] "The custom now prevailing in the Evangelical Church," said Schleiermacher,

43. Schleiermacher, *Kritische Gesamtausgabe*, I/6, *Kurze Darstellung des theologischen Studiums*, p. 275.

44. Schleiermacher, *Kritische Gesamtausgabe*, I/6, *Kurze Darstellung des theologischen Studiums*, p. 275; idem, *Kritische Gesamtausgabe, Schriften und Entwürfe*, vol. 6: *Kurze Darstellung des theologischen Studiums* (1811), p. 106; idem, *The Christian Faith*, p. 603; idem, *Hermeneutics and Criticism and Other Writings*, p. 210.

45. Schleiermacher, *Hermeneutik und Kritik*, p. 129; idem, *Kritische Gesamtausgabe*,

is by far to be preferred, which only seldom uses Old Testament passages as a basis for public instruction, at most in such cases where what is uniquely Christian is less in retreat; by which it is actively recognized that on both points the Old Testament is inferior to the New.[46]

Clearly, those sections of Schleiermacher's *Glaubenslehre* dealing with the Bible are little more than a digest of Johann Salomo Semler's work on the canon, albeit expanded and in more sophisticated form. The argument that the Old Testament writings owe their place in the Bible in part to the New Testament appeals to it, in part to the historical connection between Christian worship and the Jewish synagogue, merely states in formula the differences between the Testaments already elaborated by Semler. Schleiermacher's explanation for abandoning the old Protestant concept of the canon was precisely that of Semler, that is, that an equally divine inspiration could no longer be claimed for both Testaments. For this reason, Schleiermacher, just as Semler, viewed the Old Testament as the document of a particularistic, national religion. Schleiermacher wrote:

> Even in the prophetic writings most relates to the legal condition and relationships of the people as such; and the spirit from which they proceed is none other than the community spirit of the people, thus not the Christian [Spirit], which as the One [Spirit] was to remove the wall of separation between this people and the others.[47]

Thus, as Semler had argued, it was only in its messianic prophecies that the Old Testament "could share in inspiration in our sense."[48] As to the result of attempting to find Christian faith in the Old Testament, Schleiermacher wrote precisely as did Semler before him:

I/6, *Kurze Darstellung des theologischen Studiums*, p. 272; idem, *Hermeneutics and Criticism and Other Writings*, pp. 609, 611; idem, *Kritische Gesamtausgabe*, I/7: *Der christliche Glaube, 1821-1822*, vol. 2, p. 238.

46. Schleiermacher, *Kritische Gesamtausgabe*, I/7, *Der christliche Glaube, 1821-1822*, vol. 2, p. 239.

47. Schleiermacher, *Kritische Gesamtausgabe*, I/13.1-2: *Der christliche Glaube, 1830-1831*, ed. Rolf Schäfer (New York: de Gruyter, 2003), vol. 2, p. 339.

48. Schleiermacher, *Kritische Gesamtausgabe*, I/13.1-2, *Der christliche Glaube, 1830-1831*, vol. 2, p. 339.

The history of theology shows clearly enough how much this striving to find our Christian faith in the Old Testament has been of disadvantage, in part to our application of the art of interpretation, and in part floods the further formation of doctrine and the contest over its more exact definitions with useless complications.[49]

Schleiermacher did not suggest as did Semler that an extract should be prepared from the Old Testament. Writing that though it could not possibly be for Christians what it was for Jews, nothing militated against the Old Testament's being added in its entirety to the New. Nevertheless, he stated that the matter would be better dealt with if the Old Testament followed the New as an "appendix," lest it be supposed "one must first work through the entire Old Testament in order properly to arrive at the New."[50] Those years in Halle from 1787 to 1789 under Semler had done their work. According to Schleiermacher, not merely their content but also their relation to each other made the biblical texts difficult for exposition. If, due to its inspiration, everything in the Bible were relative to the whole church, the Holy Spirit should have acted more properly and not produced occasional writings. In fact, Schleiermacher contended, the New Testament and the Gospels in particular do not represent a continuous whole, but are constructed of fragments from various periods, a stringing together of various narratives. He wrote that this was especially true of Matthew and Luke, less of Mark, and not at all of John. He stated that individual oral or written accounts from the life of Christ had circulated before the Gospels were written, and that from these the Gospels derived. The New Testament therefore does not contain the original teaching, but has the oral as its basis. More, Schleiermacher wrote that as a rule the New Testament was only designed for those who engaged in oral exchange. Not only the Pauline letters, but even the catholic epistles assume oral proclamation of the gospel.[51]

With respect to the Synoptic Problem, or the problem of the relationship of similarity and dissimilarity between the first three Gospels, Schleiermacher opposed the so-called Use or borrowing hypothesis of Johann Leonhard Hug (1765-1846), Roman Catholic professor of biblical

49. Schleiermacher, *Kritische Gesamtausgabe*, I/13.1-2, *Der christliche Glaube, 1830-1831*, vol. 2, p. 340.

50. Schleiermacher, *Kritische Gesamtausgabe*, I/13.1-2, *Der christliche Glaube, 1830-1831*, vol. 2, p. 341.

51. Schleiermacher, *Hermeneutik und Kritik*, p. 163; idem, *Hermeneutics and Criticism and Other Writings*, pp. 74, 117, 220, 234.

studies at Freiburg im Breisgau. According to Hug, Matthew was the oldest Gospel, Mark was dependent on him, and Luke was dependent on both. He also opposed the so-called Ur-evangelium hypothesis of the "father of modern Old Testament criticism," Johann Gottfried Eichhorn (1753-1827) of Jena and Göttingen, according to which a Gospel anterior to the first three canonical Gospels furnished their writers with their exemplar. Both attempts were wrong, Schleiermacher wrote. The history of the first Christian writing of history had to be thought of as follows. With the distancing of the Christian community from Palestine, and the impending death of the first generation of eyewitnesses, individual collections emerged, greater and smaller, simple and complex, together with miracle stories, speeches, and the passion and Easter narratives, all of which, "by the nature of the case," had to trace back to eyewitnesses.[52] On occasion, in his study of Luke, Schleiermacher seemed to assume the so-called Griesbach hypothesis, named after the Jena New Testament critic Johann Jakob Griesbach (1745-1812), which gave priority to Matthew's Gospel and described Luke as dependent on it and Mark as reliant on both. Nevertheless, in contrast to the various attempts at solving the Synoptic Problem, Schleiermacher's concentration on the individual evangelists was unusual. It freed him from the problems posed by the Use hypothesis, hampered, in Hug's hands at least, by doctrinal commitments, as well as by those posed by the Ur-evangelium hypothesis, with its assumption of an Aramaic or Hebrew original. The editor of the Lucan study states that although Schleiermacher was unable to correct the weaknesses of his predecessors, he helped prepare the way to the ultimately victorious two-source theory, and as a result to the so-called quest of the historical Jesus.[53] In his brief summary of Schleiermacher's scripture interpretation, Emanuel Hirsch writes that Schleiermacher was not so much interested in reforming the church's canon for practical use, but in establishing historical support for understanding the activity of Jesus and the apostles, and from that point determining the true and original nature of Christianity.[54]

Finally, Schleiermacher began to abandon his idea of the identity of language and thought. Though he still held high the grammatical and technical approach, his interest now lay in the "intellectuality" *(Geistigkeit)*

---

52. Schleiermacher, *Kritische Gesamtausgabe*, I/8, *Exegetische Schriften*, p. xx.

53. Schleiermacher, *Kritische Gesamtausgabe*, I/8, *Exegetische Schriften*, pp. xxii-xxiii.

54. Emanuel Hirsch, *Geschichte der neueren evangelischen Theologie*, vol. 5 (Gütersloh: C. Bertelsmann Verlag, 1954), p. 352.

of the author, that is, in a separation of the person from the person's activity, the individual regarded now as a mere organ of speech. It was this axiom, with its reduction of the grammatical-philological and technical to the psychological, in other words, to the separation of understanding from the appreciation of historical particularity, that the later interpreters and critics of Schleiermacher referenced, among them the celebrated historian-philosopher Wilhelm Dilthey (1833-1911) of Berlin. Dilthey's basic idea was that unabridged experience lay at the basis of philosophy. With Kant, self-consciousness formed the conclusion rather than the starting-point of analysis. In fact, in all of Kant's *Critiques* the psychic functions were developed in isolation, resulting in the reemergence of intellectualism. Empiricism was no less abstract. It indulged in an atomistic understanding of psychic life. Interpretation, wrote Dilthey, consisted of "the art of understanding life-expressions." Since it was only in language that the life of the mind was expressed in a way to facilitate its understanding, interpretation consisted in the interpretation of the residue of human existence in fixed, written forms. Philology was based on this art, Dilthey wrote, and hermeneutics was its science. Dilthey eagerly appropriated Schleiermacher's view that real understanding could not be gained simply by pursuing rules. Rather, in addition to the "grammatical" there had to be a "psychological" approach, that is, a text had to be interpreted as a piece from the life of a particular person. For this reason "divination" was required. Just as with Schleiermacher, the divinatory presupposed a kind of "geniality" based on a common, shared humanity that reduced differences between individuals to mere differences of degree. So, to pursue Schleiermacher's goal, that is, "to understand an author better than he understood himself," meant that by projecting oneself back into an historical milieu the interpreter accented and strengthened the writer's inner process of soul while one's own fell into the background, and thus achieved the imitation of an alien life. Dilthey wrote that "understanding the life of an alien soul, in other words hermeneutical understanding," was the object of research.[55] Just as with Schleiermacher interpretation was a work of personal artistry dependent on the geniality of the interpreter, a geniality intensified by living the author's life. Again, what made this art possible was the identity of interpreter and speaker or author, or, as he put

---

55. See *19. Jahrhundert Positivismus, Historismus, Hermeneutik*, ed. Manfred Riedel, *Geschichte der Philosophie in Text und Darstellung*, vol. 7 (Stuttgart: Philipp Reclam jun., 1981), p. 390.

it, the "life-relation" between the two. At two major points Dilthey differed from Schleiermacher. First, he restricted the art of interpretation to the understanding of life-expressions "in fixed written form," thus limiting his inquiry to the author of an actual text. Second, the subject matter about which he inquired into a text was "life." "What is at issue," Dilthey stated,

> is the process from self-reflection to hermeneutics, and from this to the knowledge of nature. But all these relationships have as their most universal basis the relation of life to knowledge, and that of inner experience to thought.[56]

If life was the "given," if every interpretation involved the understanding of a particular historical "life," then thought, thinking, had to be understood as a manifestation of life, and as a result history and historical study assumed first place. Far more significant, it was over the detachment of language from thought that Dilthey followed Schleiermacher's lead. But even here, he took a more radical turn by excluding the grammatical-philological approach altogether from the actual art of understanding. As he wrote,

> First of all, the process of understanding is to be separated from the preliminary grammatical and historical work which with reference to the past, to what is distanced in space or alien in tongue, merely serves to set what is directed toward the understanding of something already occurred into the reader's situation from the author's time and milieu.[57]

The Strauss-Baur School

A welter of approaches to Bible interpretation followed Schleiermacher, but they had less to do with the actual task of interpreting than with the assumptions or presuppositions behind it. The confusing mass takes on a recognizable pattern when it is seen that all, or at least most, interpreters after Schleiermacher viewed history in one way or another as the medium of revelation. Many of these shared the Hegelian assumption that the historical process revealed the movement of the Idea or Absolute Spirit to-

---

56. *19. Jahrhundert Positivismus, Historismus, Hermeneutik,* p. 390.
57. Dilthey, *Die Hermeneutik vor Schleiermacher,* p. 219.

ward self-realization through contradiction and resolution. Many did not share this opinion, but those who did divided roughly into two camps, the "left-wing" and "right-wing" Hegelians, according to how they perceived the Spirit's arrival at self-realization.

In the area of biblical studies, David Friedrich Strauss (1792-1860) was the most strident representative of the "left wing," maintaining that the Idea could only achieve self-realization in a totality, never in a single individual. In his *Leben Jesu* (1835-36) he proceeded to explain the greatest part of the Gospel tradition as "mythical," that is, as composed of "pure myths" or ideas in historicized form, as "sagas" or myths with particular events at their base, or as "poetic" myths or pure fiction. Beneath this "mythical interpretation" lay Hegel's distinction between the "represen-tation" *(Vorstellung)*, and the "conception" *(Begriff)*, the one a mixture of the sensuous with thought, the other free of the sensuous, but needing it to arrive at thought. The result was a life of Jesus totally shorn of the mi-raculous, a study one critic described as the "Iscariotism of our days," and another as "the most pestilential book ever vomited out of the jaws of hell."

On Strauss's epoch-making *Leben Jesu* the spirits divided. Johann Christian Friedrich Steudel (1779-1837), professor of biblical theology at Tübingen, representative of so-called rational supernaturalism, and chief representative of the "older Tübingen School," was the first to go on the attack. As *Superattendant* (principal steward) at the Tübinger *Stift,* or foundation, where Strauss was employed as *Repetent* ("repeater," i.e., tutor employed year by year), he believed it was his particular responsibility to extinguish the torch Strauss had thrown "from his cabinet." The argument of his essay with its enormous title[58] was that the fact of Christianity could not be explained without assuming a historical Christ. Steudel's piece in-troduced a flood of refutations and responses of various sorts, among them that of Ernst Wilhelm Hengstenberg (1802-69), professor of theology at the Berlin University. In a review of Strauss's book, published in the *Tübinger Zeitschrift für Theologie* that Steudel had founded, Hengstenberg described the criticism by Strauss and his successors as a sign of increasing unbelief, a

---

58. "Vorläufig zu Beherzigendes bei Würdigung der Frage über die historische oder mythische Grundlage des Lebens Jesu, wie die kanonischen Evangelien dieses darstellen, vorgehalten aus dem Bewusstsein eines Gläubigen, der den Supranaturalisten beigezählt wird, zur Beruhigung der Gemüther." (In the meantime to be considered in evaluating the question of the historical or mythical basis of the life of Jesus as the canonical Gospels describe it, rendered from the consciousness of a believer numbered among the supernat-uralists for the calming of souls.)

demonically inspired dissolution of Christian foundations. He declared that Christian theology should of course supply the well-intentioned with weapons against doubt, but without forcing its conclusions on those who hate the light because their works are evil. Of such were all who exercised biblical criticism, and who in their appeal to reason against the Word of God were to be left alone. Unredeemable, spiritual abortions existed, Hengstenberg added, men without hearts, and such was Strauss, who had the heart of a Leviathan, hard as flint, and as fixed as the bottommost millstone.[59]

In 1837 appeared the *Leben Jesu* of Johann August Wilhelm Neander (1789-1850), professor of theology at Berlin, among those whom Strauss labeled "the Hegelian right." In the foreword he described himself as occupying a position between the extreme of the supernaturalists and that of Strauss and his adherents, whom he labeled "hypercritics." Neander admitted that inaccuracies, even errors, in the Gospel narratives were possible, and in the individual instance actual. He conceded that Jesus accommodated himself to the popular notions of his day respecting the demon-possessed, maintaining with Schleiermacher that such was an error Christ did not trouble to correct since it did not belong to his calling and was irrelevant to the religious interest. Christian Hermann Weisse (1801-66), professor of philosophy at Leipzig, likewise occupied a middle position, lending it a more sophisticated cast. Believing that Strauss's insights could be improved on without danger to faith, Weisse represented what he called a "differentiated theism," according to which the infinite was not merely one moment in the self-realization of the Absolute but independent, self-sustained. In his two-volume work of 1838, *Die Evangelische Geschichte Kritisch und Philosophisch Bearbeitet,* he conceded that the Gospel narratives often contain unhistorical and mythical elements, but believed he could rescue the greater portion by assuming Jesus' miraculous power which, due to the Spirit's universal power over nature, inhered in him in a special way. The work, perhaps the most lasting contribution of the "Hegelian right" to New Testament research, was celebrated for the comprehensive way in which it set Mark and the Second Synoptic Source Q as the basis for Matthew and Luke.[60]

---

59. Ferdinand Christian Baur, *Historisch-kritische Untersuchungen zum Neuen Testament,* intro. Ernst Käsemann, vol. 1 of *Ausgewählte Werke in Einzelausgaben,* ed. Klaus Scholder (Stuttgart: Friedrich Frommann Verlag, 1963), p. xv; and idem, *Kirchengeschichte des neunzehnten Jahrhunderts,* vol. 4 of *Ausgewählte Werke in Einzelausgaben,* ed. Klaus Scholder (Stuttgart: Friedrich Frommann Verlag, 1970), pp. 364-65.

60. Baur, *Kirchengeschichte des neunzehnten Jahrhunderts,* pp. 369-71, 374-75.

The giant towering above all these, whether supernaturalists or Hegelians to the left and the right, was Ferdinand Christian Baur, leader of the so-called Tübingen School. In a resume of his work in a church history of the nineteenth century he referred to the stimulus he had received from Strauss, but whose "negativity" moved him to ask whether or not the interior of earliest history of Christianity could be penetrated from another point of view, that is, from that of the contradiction between Jewish Christianity and Pauline authority. First Corinthians 1:12 and its reference to the contrasting parties furnished Baur the Archimedean point from which to infer the earliest Christian history. Interpreting the adherents of Paul, Apollos, Cephas, and the Christ people named in 1 Corinthians as comprising two main, antithetical groups, he concluded that contrary to the legends long painted of them these parties had not been united in the beginning, but moved from a contradiction toward a unification still hidden. Here, Baur believed, lay the hermeneutical key that allowed him to orient the New Testament writings to two contrasting poles. Moving on to an investigation of the Pseudo-Clementine *Homilies*, he believed he saw more deeply into the meaning of the contradiction, extending to the post-apostolic period. Following research into gnosticism, which led him to study the pastoral epistles and to deny their authenticity, more work with the Paulines further convinced Baur that the contradiction between Jewish Christianity, or "Ebionitism," as he called it, and Paulinism did in fact penetrate to the heart of apostolic Christianity. As a result, the old "baseless" idea of the closed canon had been forever destroyed. In a series of subsequent essays he opposed Strauss's tactic of attacking the Synoptic Gospels and the Fourth Gospel in one lump, insisting that the contradiction between them was disadvantageous only to John. This, however, did not allow one to conclude that the Synoptics offered pure historical description. On the contrary, each Gospel reflected a tendency of a quite specific type, hence the catchphrase "tendency criticism" *(Tendenz Kritik)* applied to Baur's methodology. Then followed an investigation of Luke's Gospel and a summary of the criticism of the New Testament. In summing up, Baur stated that his criticism had been more methodological than that of his pupil, Strauss, that he had dealt with what Strauss had omitted, that is, with a specifically critical view of those writings that serve as sources for our knowledge of the life of Jesus. Baur wrote,

> in each and every case I believe I can be certain that no view will succeed in creating a more universal recognition than mine, until mine

will be refuted in its totality and with vastly different arguments and proofs that until now have been levied against it.[61]

For this challenge to the restorative orthodoxy of his time Baur would experience resistance soon enough. In the first foreword to his major work, *Das Christentum und die christliche Kirche der drei ersten Jahrhunderte,* Baur described his standpoint as the "purely historical," as conceiving the historically given in its pure objectivity, to the degree possible. Remaining true to this standpoint would protect him "against all those false and hateful judgments inherent in the prevailing tone of an era imprisoned in its limited, particular interests." In the second foreword to the same work he wrote that everything depends on whether one remains true to the recognized principle in the area of historical research, even where it is a matter of its practical application. "Precisely this," he wrote, "is the reef on which one so often shatters."[62] In the foreword to his work on Paul, Baur demurred at the suggestion that he had founded a new critical school, and proceeded to deal with the attack on his method as negating and destroying. He asked, "what would criticism be if it could not negate and destroy?" The question at issue was rather what one negated or destroyed and by what right, further, whether such criticism denounced as negative and destructive was not actually conservative for the simple reason that it rested on the principle of giving each its due, that and only that. Further, no individual element was to be absolutized or negated, but understood as a member of the transition in the context of the immanent historical progress, of the revelation of the Spirit or the Idea moving toward self-realization. This was the meaning of "historical-critical."

> Leave the Protestant Church its inalienable right to be hampered by no deceitful interest, least of all by fear of the truth, of the right to free research in and over the scripture. Whoever does not recognize this right and in practice truly and uprightly recognize it (not merely in an abstract, theoretical generality none dare deny), and in this manner disengages from the foolish prejudice that the striving for truth . . . and the search for it can cause damage to the church, that in the interest

---

61. Baur, *Kirchengeschichte des neunzehnten Jahrhunderts,* p. 399; see also Käsemann's preface to Baur, *Historisch-kritische Untersuchungen zum Neuen Testament,* p. ix.

62. Ferdinand Christian Baur, *Das Christentum und die christliche Kirche der drei ersten Jahrhunderte* (Tübingen: Verlag und Druck von L. Fr. Fues, 1860), pp. iv-v, ix.

of the church one must at least hold back the progress of the Spirit (as if this were possible!) is not a friend and patron of the Protestant Church, but an enemy and destroyer of it.[63]

Strauss "on the left" may have begun the modern phase of theology with his *Leben Jesu,* but as Baur made clear, he had no eye for the differences in kind between the biblical writings. These obviously required more than an interpretation in terms of the split between "representation" and "conception."

Finally, Baur's work seemed to be without effect. For all the ingenuity of his scheme, it assumed, with Hegel, the historian's capacity for a view of history as a totality when at best what is available is only a small nexus or continuum. At any rate, after his death no one thought of himself as his successor; *Tendenzkritik* appeared to have been conquered. Two of Baur's most gifted students, Eduard Zeller (1814-1908) and Albert Schwegler (1819-57), fell victim to the opprobrium heaped on the Tübingen School. Zeller was denied patronage at Tübingen, and after a brief period as theological professor at Marburg, was forced to join its philosophical faculty. Schwegler was from the outset denied an academic career in theology, but subsequently engaged in research into Roman antiquities. As early as in the 1840s, twenty years before Baur's death, there would have been no room for any of his pupils in the theological faculties of the German universities. When he died a mediating theologian was called to his chair.

Georg Heinrich August Ewald

Of all Baur's critics, Georg Heinrich August Ewald waged the longest and bitterest war against him, not even sparing his critics to the left, right, and middle. Heinrich, as he most often signed his name, was born in Göttingen in 1803. At the age of eleven he entered the Göttingen gymnasium, and at sixteen the university, where he studied under Thomas Christian Tychsen (1758-1834) and Johann Gottfried Eichhorn (1753-1827). After three years he earned the doctor of philosophy degree, and entered upon his teaching career, first at the Wolfenbüttel gymnasium, then as *Repetent* (year-by-year

---

63. Ferdinand Christian Baur, *Paulus der Apostel Jesu Christi: Sein Leben und Wirken, seine Briefe und seine Lehre, Ein Beitrag Zu einer kritischen Geschichte des Urchristenthums,* ed. Eduard Zeller and Erster Theil (Leipzig: Fues Verlag, 1866), p. xi.

tutor), associate *(ausserordentlicher)*professor, and full *(ordentlicher)* professor at Göttingen. Ewald spent the major portion of his academic life at Göttingen, interrupted by a ten-year sojourn at Tübingen. He was twice removed from his university chair. In 1838, with the celebrated *Göttinger Sieben,* led by the historian Christoph Dahlmann (1785-1860) and including the brothers Grimm, he protested the annulment of the constitution of 1833 by the new Hanoverian king. The king saw in the behavior of the seven a "revolutionary, high treasonable tendency" and dismissed them from the university. In 1841, following prodigious activity, Ewald was promoted to the nobility, and received an invitation from Tübingen University, Ferdinand Baur heartily consenting, to occupy its vacant chair in orientology. Tübingen and Baur had long heard of Ewald; in fact, the university faculty had officially taken the side of the Göttingen seven during the 1838 protest. After the breach with Baur in the 1840s, Ewald remained in Tübingen until 1848, when he was reinvited to his Göttingen post. In 1867 he refused to swear the prescribed oath of allegiance to the new king of the united Germany, a union he described as a mere tool of Bismarckian politics, and received the order to surrender his office. Forced from his chair in the evangelical faculty, he continued to teach students at his home, where he died in 1875.

The two fronts against which Ewald fought throughout his career were the Tübingen "tendency criticism" of Baur and the orthodox of Berlin, Erlangen, Leipzig, and elsewhere whose perspective, to his mind, reflected the imperialism of godless Prussia. In their first period together at Tübingen, Baur and Ewald were in harness against pietism and church orthodoxy, but after Baur's publications on the Fourth Gospel and Paul in 1844-46, Ewald was horrified by the direction Baur had taken. He went on the attack with the *Jahrbücher der biblischen Wissenschaft,* the journal of which he remained almost sole contributor throughout its twelve volumes. Linking Baur to his notorious pupil, David Friedrich Strauss, that "stupid, harassed bird"[64] who had ruined south Germany, he wrote that their philosophical patron Hegel deserved his place alongside Kant and others, but to import him into matters of religion was a huge error. "What was the effect of the Strauss affair," Ewald asked:

> A young scholar . . . writes a book about a Life of whose unique height and truth he has no idea. He points out others' deficiencies, thinks he

---

64. Heinrich Ewald, *Worte für Freunde und Verständige* (Basel: In der Schweighauser'schen Buchhandlung, 1838), p. 45.

alone is right, creates nothing because he understands nothing of the truth of his subject, and ends with a view that must convince even the blindest of his terrible error.[65]

Tübingen had become the world's disgrace. That such a movement as Strauss-Baur could appear indicated what kind of scientific spirit reigned there. After the Franco-Prussian War (1870-71) Ewald wrote that "with its evil science and dark purposes goes the misery breaking forth over Germany, over people and congregation, state and church, and which one tries vainly to obscure by a victory over the French."[66] In the second volume of his *Die Lehre der Bibel von Gott,* he wrote of the Strauss-Baur school as confusing what strict history teaches, whether according to its immanent or its transcendent, divine side, and as good as seeks to destroy all historical certainty of the biblical narratives,[67] and added to the list of those who denied the invisible the name of Ludwig Feuerbach, a "logical consequence of the Strauss-Baur school."[68] This "purely heathenish" school was ruled by a type of "German science" entrenched not so much because of its scholarship as of the general and deep penetration of "principles" harking back to the time of Napoleon, in other words, the principles of the Hegelian School.[69]

Ewald's ire toward the orthodox was no less protracted and caustic than that against Baur. It was even more protracted since he and Baur had originally joined forces. The list of enemies was long. It included Ernst Wilhelm Hengstenberg (1802-69) of Berlin; Gottlieb Christoph Adolf von Harless (1806-79) of Erlangen and Leipzig; Carl Friedrich Keil (1807-88), student of Hengstenberg, and celebrated author of commentaries on the Old Testament together with Franz Delitzsch (1813-90), also of Erlangen and Leipzig; Theodor Kliefoth (1810-95), president of the superior ecclesiastical court of Mecklenburg-Schwerin, their supporters, and their successors. These were the "demagogues" who searched for an epithet

---

65. Heinrich Ewald, *Über einige wissenschaftliche Erscheinungen neuesten Zeit auf der Universität Tübingen* (Stuttgart: Krabbe, 1846), p. 12.

66. Heinrich Ewald, *Die Bücher des Neuen Bundes übersetzt und erklärt,* vol. 1: *Die drei ersten Evangelien und die Apostelgeschichte,* part 2 (Göttingen: In der Dieterichschen Buch-handlung, 1872), p. ix.

67. Heinrich Ewald, *Die Lehre der Bibel von Gott, oder Theologie des alten und neuen Bundes,* vol. 2: *Die Glaubenslehre,* part 1 (Leipzig: Verlag von F. C. W. Vogel, 1873), p. 31.

68. Ewald, *Die Lehre der Bibel von Gott,* vol. 2, part 1, p. 39.

69. Heinrich Ewald, *Die Lehre der Bibel von Gott,* vol. 4: *Über das Leben des Menschen und das Reich Gottes* (Leipzig: Vogel, 1876), p. 172.

whenever something new or different appeared, creators of a division originating with "the later Luther," adherents of a "merely traditional, sterile conception of Christianity which, despite its love for refutation, could not refute the enemy in a learned way. If the Hegelians wanted to dissolve the church in the state, these "Hengstenbergers," casting suspicion on a science they scarcely comprehended, wanted to dissolve the state in the church.[70] Internal collapse, ruin, would result if one had to choose between the Christianity of Hengstenberg and the atheism of the Strauss-Baur School.[71] Of the Erlangen New Testament scholar Hermann Olshausen (1796-1839) Ewald wrote that if he had lived in the time of the apostles, he would have been one of their "coldest and most noxious persecutors and crucifiers."[72] On occasion, Ewald would align the orthodox with those otherwise their enemies. In the preface to his second volume on the Johannine literature, he wrote of Baur's assigning the Apocalypse to an apostle, and of the gratitude of "our pietists" for this "reverencing of the Ludwigsburg atheist."[73] Such unholy alliance involved more than theological faculties. The Hengstenbergs and their ilk belonged with Edwin Freiherr von Manteuffel (1809-85) and Otto von Bismarck (1815-98) and all the rest who had brought Germany to its current horrific state.[74] In the essay on his second dismissal from office Ewald wrote:

> The basic idea of Prussia has been . . . a single German people with the right to expand its rule in Germany at others' expense. The right

---

70. Ewald, *Worte für Freunde und Verständige,* p. 6; idem, "Über die Ungeschichtlichkeit evangelischen Geistlichen in Deutschland, mit einem Worte über Die Evangelische Kirchenzeitung," in *Theologische Studien und Kritiken* (Tübingen, 1845), p. 29; idem, *Über einige wissenschaftliche Erscheinungen neuesten Zeit auf der Universität Tübingen,* pp. 14, 20; idem, *Über die Sittlichkeit und Religion der deutschen Wissenschaft* (Stuttgart: Krabbe, 1847), p. 6.

71. Heinrich Ewald, *Über seinen Weggang von der Universität Tübingen mit anderen Zeitbetrachtungen* (Stuttgart: Krabbe, 1848), p. 41.

72. Heinrich Ewald, *Die Dichter des Alten Bundes,* vol. 3: *Das Buch Job,* 2nd ed. (Göttingen: Vandenhoeck & Ruprecht, 1854), p. xxii.

73. Heinrich Ewald, *Die Johanneischen Schriften übersetzt und erklärt,* vol. 2: *Johannes Apocalypse* (Göttingen, 1862), p. viii.

74. Heinrich Ewald, *Die Dichter des Alten Bundes,* vol. 1, part 1: *Allgemeines über die Hebräische Dichtkunst und über das Psalmenbuch,* 2nd ed. (Göttingen: Vandenhoeck & Ruprecht, 1866), p. 294. Edwin Freiherr von Manteuffel (1809-85), Prussian, monarchist, Roman Catholic, commander of a division during the Hanover campaign, and occupier of Wurzburg during the Franco-Prussian war, was an eminent target.

is purely imaginary. This basic idea is illegal, ungodly, unGerman, derived from the French . . . the Bismarcks . . . will be the life of our public benefactors, the Hengstenbergs . . . but also the Strausses . . . will be the spirit of our divines. Will the German people permit this?[75]

Orthodox applause for the circumstances created since Prussia's invasion of Saxony, Hanover, and Hesse was proof they did not differ from Strauss and the atheists of his stripe, extolling what the Bible and Christianity forever eschewed.[76]

As for their scholarship, despite their ungodly trust in the Bible, their veneration of its letter and assigning it a sanctity by which to replace God, they all succeeded in giving "the most upright, the most Christian attempt at a certain understanding of the whole Bible a bad name."[77] They treated the books of the New Testament more superficially than those of the Old, happily since anyone of unbiased mind knew they did not possess the most rudimentary knowledge and ability necessary for Old Testament study. In fine, it was the guilt of these evangelicals that hindered a perfecting of the German Reformation, and gave no guarantee of resisting the Strauss-Baur School.[78]

In an extended essay on the Bible, Ewald traced the route leading to its sanctity. Initially, the oldest and most important books were not in the least authored and published with the intent of being held sacred. It was inherent in the original nature of all sacred scriptures that they were sacred without intentionally wanting to be so. Ewald noted that the more pure and perfect a religion the greater in power and permanence this sacredness of its writings. Over time, however, older pieces or larger writings came more and more to be regarded as such. For this reason, in Isaiah 34:16 a writing prophet could call the piece on which he was working "the book of

75. Heinrich Ewald, *Dr. H. Ewald über seine zweite Amtsentsetzung an der Universität Göttingen* (Stuttgart, 1868), p. 54.

76. Heinrich Ewald, *Die Propheten des Alten Testaments*, vol. 2: *Jeremja und Hezeqiel mit Ihren Zeitgenossen* (Göttingen: Vandenhoeck & Ruprecht, 1868), pp. xv-xvi.

77. Heinrich Ewald, *Die Propheten des Alten Testaments*, vol. 3: *Die Jüngsten Propheten des Alten Bundes mit den Büchern Barukh und Daniel* (Göttingen: Vandenhoeck & Ruprecht, 1868), pp. 491-92.

78. Heinrich Ewald, *Sieben Sendschreiben des Neuen Bundes übersetzt und erklärt von H. Ewald* (Göttingen: Verlag der Dieterichschen Buchhandlung, 1870-), p. vii; idem, *Die Lehre der Bibel von Gott*, vol. 4: *Über das Leben des Menschen und das Reich Gottes* (Leipzig: Vogel, 1876), p. ix.

the Lord" by appending it to the older book of Isaiah (chapters 28–33). Or, as in the case of the book of Daniel, the writer spoke in the name of an older man of God. In the second century the need for a more precise historical investigation had not yet dawned among the people of the "true religion," leading to an overevaluation of the biblical writings and the emergence of allegory by which every conceivable passage was related to Christ. If such a method had prevailed, Ewald wrote, the historical sense of the Old Testament would have been destroyed. By contrast, Christ could say that "the scripture cannot be annulled" (John 10:35), yet with the greatest freedom sharply distinguished what is temporary and what is eternal in it. Ewald added that the term *theopneustos* ("God breathed") in 2 Timothy 3:16[79] was unintelligible as applied to scripture since only the word or Spirit could be described in such fashion, and nowhere in the Bible was scripture identical to word or Spirit. This error of Sacred Scripture most probably arose in times of transition from antiquity to the Middle Ages, when Christians borrowed the concept from the Jewish community, for which the holy letter constituted the last genuine remnant of all its sanctuaries. For this reason, Ewald argued, the Reformation would have been entirely different if one had understood the Bible more perfectly and accordingly had known to limit its sanctity. The essay ended with asking, who will deny that today we understand the Bible and thus also its sacredness incomparably better than our best reformers themselves?[80]

Elsewhere, Ewald could describe the Bible as "the bright mirror in which we recognize all the conditions and levels of the perfect, true religion," as neither ambiguous nor uncertain in meaning, yet capable of infinite application.[81] At the same time, he could insist that not all biblical passages were of the same clarity, and thus distinguished three levels, the first consisting of passages that encounter us as truths but have taken on a hardening from an earlier time when they were livelier and fresher; the second consisting of passages "in the middle" where the great truths of God himself lie; and the third level consisting of passages containing darker secrets or mysteries, not on a level with what is sunny-clear.[82] Ewald could

---

79. "All scripture is inspired by God, and is useful for teaching, for reproof, for correction, and for training in righteousness."

80. Heinrich Ewald, "Über die Heiligkeit der Bibel," *Jahrbücher der biblischen Wissenschaft,* vol. 7 (Göttingen, 1854-55), pp. 68-100.

81. Ewald, *Die Propheten des Alten Testaments,* vol. 3, p. xiv.

82. Ewald, *Die Lehre der Bibel von Gott,* vol. 1, pp. 468-70; idem, *Die Lehre der Bibel von Gott,* vol. 2, pp. 1-5.

refer to the many differences in authors and concepts, to the contradictions that were nevertheless less significant than appeared to those who "deliberately err," and to the "lacunae," to what was lacking of basic truths and views of the Bible. Regarding the application of the term "myth" to anything in the Bible he raised objection, writing that what is correctly called myth is of a heathen spirit, whereas the Bible despite its mass of sayings of the most diverse sort contains no myths.[83]

The interpreter's first task, wrote Ewald, was to recognize as accurately as possible every biblical passage, every biblical word according to its original sense and value, and according to its age. For since every prophetic word sprang from its time and was destined for it, we can comprehend it when we envision the time of its birth and from that point understand what it meant for its time and what it means for eternity. Such knowledge of meaning and context, Ewald continued, prepared the way for all other questions respecting age and author. Ownership of this "purely historical arrangement" would always belong to his teacher J. G. Eichhorn, a thing "vilely disdained in his time."[84] It was possible now to understand the Bible in the same light and sense in which its authors wrote — an impossibility for the church fathers or the sixteenth-century Reformers.[85] Such investigation, of course, required that "for a moment in thought" the interpreter had to be removed from the object in order to see it reflected from the outside.[86]

Since the Bible contained what Ewald called "two halves," that is, a historical half and a "remainder," the interpreter had to guard against confusing the one with the other, against mixing explanation in the strict, historical sense with application. Explanation had to do with investigating and establishing the author's original meaning. Application, on the other hand, could be infinite, and only when the author's original meaning was investigated could application be made.[87] Ewald likewise distinguished two types of "lacunae," "historical lacunae" and lacunae attaching to the "remainder." With regard to the former Ewald never tired of stating that the lack of external sources could be supplied. For example, though there were no external sources available for study of the Psalms, the collection itself offered a mass of means and evidences, provided one knew where

83. Ewald, *Die Lehre der Bibel von Gott*, vol. 2, p. 215.

84. Ewald, *Die Propheten des Alten Testaments*, vol. 1, pp. 84-85.

85. Ewald, *Die Propheten des Alten Testaments*, vol. 3, p. xiv.

86. Ewald, "Über die Ungeschichtlichkeit evangelischen Geistlichen in Deutschland," pp. 49-50.

87. Ewald, *Die Lehre der Bibel von Gott*, vol. 1, pp. 460-61.

and how to find them.[88] As for lacunae attaching to the "remainder," such could be removed by the application of general truths when the particular case was observed in its peculiarity. The hermeneutical rule was thus to interpret what was lacking or obscure from those pieces that yielded the basic truths, preeminent among which were the "voices of the prophets and of Christ himself."[89] Or again, as Ewald stated,

> where we are confronted with a piece that is difficult to understand and moreover is larger, there our most important task is from out of all the details grasped as correctly as possible to arrive at a certain view of the whole, since in the last analysis we are intent only on the whole, and the perception of a mass of detail remains uncertain as long as the view of the whole is in the main not yet firmly defined.[90]

This perception of the whole as illumining the individual detail and the detail illumining the whole comprises "the joyous circle in which our work moves once it is based on firm ground."[91]

According to Ewald, the interpreter's task did not end with observing whatever ideas or truths each biblical passage contained. Inasmuch as biblical content consisted of a braid of the historical and doctrinal, it was necessary to proceed toward recognizing the doctrinal content and purpose served up by each piece. Obviously, not every piece contained doctrinal material, but whether or not it did could only result from serious historical investigation. On the other hand, every passage, or at least every piece of historical writing, was to be evaluated as doctrinal when it contributed to an understanding of what corresponds to all perfect true religion, that is, to the "voices of the prophets and of Christ himself."[92]

Beneath it all, beneath the summons to what he believed to be exact historical research, and thus his impatience with the Strauss-Baur or Hengstenberg School's lack of historicity, lay Ewald's conviction of a divine history behind everything visible. All the customary narratives, he argued, do not suffice to describe the working of the divine power

---

88. Ewald, *Die Dichter des Alten Bundes,* vol. 1, p. 242.

89. Ewald, *Die Dichter des Alten Bundes,* vol. 1, pp. 465, 471; idem, *Die Lehre der Bibel von Gott,* vol. 2, pp. 7, 9, 33.

90. Ewald, *Die Dichter des Alten Bundes,* vol. 1, p. vii.

91. Heinrich Ewald, *Die Sendschreiben an die Hebräer und Jakobus' Rundschreiben übersetzt und erklärt* (Göttingen: Verlag der Dieterichschen Buchhandlung, 1870), p. viii.

92. Ewald, *Die Lehre der Bibel von Gott,* vol. 2, pp. 15, 17, 26.

active in history. The Bible does not embrace everything one wishes to know and experience of God. On the contrary, it speaks of mysteries. But these mysteries of the divine activity do not remain forever so. "Every real progress in revelation" throws new light on them. After the fulfillment of all the revelation of antiquity by Christ, the apostles, said Ewald, made the most unexpected progress in this direction. Yet not even they saw everything. Even "the single great hero of our history" who with certain hand undid the fetters "by drawing from the magical vessel of genuine written tradition one of the highest truths" left the Reformation half finished. Not even we, engaged in the "most precise continuation and fulfillment" of sixteenth-century study, who see individual things clearer than were seen in the last pages of the Bible, have penetrated the darkness. But it is possible to understand more closely "the light of that primal history of eternal religion." For this reason history needs retrieving as nearly as possible, and for it no single book of the New Testament suffices. In fact, the New Testament itself directs us toward what stands above it. Only when we are reminded of that fact and allow ourselves to be seized, enlightened, and led by the beams of that great light that once appeared on earth and alone can lead us into the future through the darkness of the times toward an ever higher salvation does the Bible retain its profit and its treasure.[93]

The Americans

Jonathan Edwards

During this period, Bible interpretation in North America was anything but insular. With Jonathan Edwards, first to deserve mention regarding seventeenth- and eighteenth-century Bible interpretation in America, English influence was obvious. He was indebted to such British commentators as Matthew Poole (1624-79) and Matthew Henry (1662-1714), and for his "Blank Bible," to Philip Doddridge (1702-51) and John Locke, the most prominent author cited in that work. Locke's *Essay Concerning Hu-*

---

93. Ewald, *Die Lehre der Bibel von Gott*, vol. 2, p. 213; idem, *Die Lehre der Bibel von Gott*, vol. 4, p. vii; idem, *Das Sendschreiben an die Hebräer und Jakobus' Rundschreiben übersetzt und erklärt*, p. vi; idem, "Über die Ungeschichtlichkeit evangelischer Geistlichen in Deutschland," pp. 7, 12-13.

man Understanding is alleged to have had pivotal intellectual influence on Edwards. The allegation is a typical one since the exegetical dimension of Edwards's thought has been largely ignored by American historians and thinkers. In this respect, he has suffered the same fate as Johann Georg Hamann. The allegation is also in error, for while it is true that Edwards came upon Locke's famous essay early in his academic career, it was the British philosopher's commentaries on the Pauline epistles that aroused his attention and are cited extensively in his biblical notebooks.[94]

Jonathan Edwards (1703-58) was born in East Windsor, Connecticut, the son of a Harvard-educated minister. At the age of thirteen he entered Yale College, and in 1720 received the baccalaureate degree. After two years of graduate study he spent nine months ministering to a small Presbyterian congregation in New York City. In September 1723 he delivered his thesis at the Yale commencement and received the M.A. degree. A month later he concluded negotiations with the nearby town of Bolton and in November signed the town book agreeing to settle there as pastor. From 1724 to 1725 he worked at Yale as tutor, then as assistant from 1726 to 1729. In November 1726 Northampton, Massachusetts, invited him to "settle" as colleague to his grandfather Solomon Stoddard, and he was ordained the following February. Stoddard died in February 1729, and Edwards assumed the entire round of pastoral duties. In 1750 he was dismissed from the Northampton congregation for demanding that only those who displayed demonstrable signs of Christian faith could receive communion. From Northampton he retreated to an obscure parish in Stockbridge where he ministered to the native Americans. In 1757 he was elected president of the College of New Jersey. On March 22, 1758, at the age of fifty-four, two months after assuming the presidency at Princeton, he died from a smallpox inoculation.

Edwards saw the church as imperiled from three sides. First, claims on behalf of reason and natural religion were gaining ground in New England. The claim that religion must contain nothing contrary to reason led to radical conclusions, reinforced by the ideas of the Irish free-thinker John Toland (1670-1722) and the deists Anthony Collins (1676-1729) and Matthew Tindal (1657-1733). Toland had challenged the view that miracles testified to the truth of revelation; Collins argued that none of the Old Testament prophecies had been fulfilled, thus undermining the ev-

94. Jonathan Edwards, *The "Blank Bible,"* ed. Stephen J. Stein, The Works of Jonathan Edwards, vol. 24 (New Haven, Conn.: Yale University Press, 2006), part 1, p. 67.

idential value of prophecy; and Tindal asserted that a purely rational religion had no place for supernatural revelation. Second, enthusiasts were offering visions and private revelations as authentication of their religious experience. Edwards himself had figured prominently in the "First Great Awakening" of 1725-50, but he believed the idea of the Spirit as imparting immediate revelations confused what was occasioned by the Bible and what was properly derived from it. Third, Roman Catholic practice and dogma constituted a threat to biblical revelation. Edwards was no less certain than Luther that the pope was the antichrist. Regarding Jesus' prediction of the tribulation in Matthew 24, he wrote, "'tis probable that Christ has not only respect to those false Christs and false prophets that arose at or near the time of the destruction of Jerusalem, but that he has especial respect to the great Antichrist, to the Pope and his clergy."[95]

Edwards's response to the peril is contained in those extensive notebooks that he called "Miscellanies," "Notes on Scripture," and the "Blank Bible," a book-like, leather-bound manuscript with a small, interleaved edition of the King James Version, with observations made during Edwards's last years in Northampton and his years in Stockbridge. To the rationalist's challenge Edwards replied that though nature reveals much of God, God is not really known from nature, further, that nature does not reveal whether God will damn or save, and even if it did such would not alter hostility toward God. A special revelation was needed, a revelation witnessed to in the Bible, the Word of God. Between that Bible and right reason existed the most perfect harmony. No other religious book offered a rational way of peace with God. As Edwards wrote, "men are reasonable. . . . The Bible does not ask [them] to believe things against reason."[96] More important, the doctrines of the Bible are "the foundation of all useful and excellent knowledge," revelation thus "that light . . . from whence has beamed forth not only the knowledge of religion, but all valuable truth . . . the fountain of that light which has lightened the understandings of men with all sorts of knowledge."[97] Clearly, the new scholarship derived from

95. Jonathan Edwards, *Notes on Scripture,* ed. Stephen J. Stein, The Works of Jonathan Edwards, vol. 15 (New Haven, Conn.: Yale University Press, 1998), p. 255.

96. Jonathan Edwards, Sermon on Isaiah 3:10, cited in John H. Gerstner, "An Outline of the Apologetics of Jonathan Edwards, Part IV: The Proof of God's Special Revelation, the Bible — Continued," *Bibliotheca Sacra* 133 (July–December 1976): 293.

97. Jonathan Edwards, *The "Miscellanies," a-500,* ed. Thomas A. Schafer, The Works of Jonathan Edwards, vol. 13 (New Haven, Conn.: Yale University Press, 1994), p. 425.

the Enlightenment was not without its effect, but it was nuanced, warped to the Protestant principle of the centrality of the biblical revelation. God would have us wholly dependent on the scriptures, wrote Edwards, since the greater our dependence on them the more direct and immediate our dependence on God himself. Moreover, those scriptures were infallible, inspired by the Spirit of God. For example, of Moses, author of the Pentateuch, Edwards could write:

> [He] was so intimately conversant with God and so continually under the divine conduct, it can't be thought that when he wrote the history of the creation and fall of man, and the history of the church from the creation, that he should not be under the divine direction in such an affair.[98]

In addition, Edwards regarded the boundaries of the biblical canon as beyond debate, and accepted the traditional authorship of the various books. Of the New Testament he wrote that God had ordered that such and such books be included in it, and of the Old that none were received by the "Jewish church" and handed down in its canon but what was his word and "owned by Christ."[99]

In his interpretation of the text, Edwards affirmed its plain, rational sense. But in contrast to the Reformation accent on the sufficiency of the Bible's single, literal sense, he could assign it a multiplicity of senses, or could speak of its sense as including "various distinct things." Thus,

> it is becoming of him who is infinite in understanding and has everything in full and perfect view at once . . . so to speak infinitely more comprehensively than others, and to speak so as naturally to point forth many things.[100]

In this connection, Edwards's "Notes on Scripture" documents his fascination with typology, a method linking the two Testaments by way of correspondences between "types" in the Old Testament and "antitypes" in the New. To illustrate, in his interpretation of Isaiah 33:17 ("Your eyes will see

98. Edwards, *The "Miscellanies," a-500*, p. 427.
99. Edwards, *The "Miscellanies," a-500*, p. 431.
100. Jonathan Edwards, *The "Miscellanies," 833-1152*, ed. Amy Plantinga Pauw, The Works of Jonathan Edwards, vol. 20 (New Haven, Conn.: Yale University Press, 2002), p. 80.

the king in his beauty; they will behold a land that stretches far away"), he wrote that the things chiefly intended here were "spiritual," for when the Jews were carried away into Babylon no king reigned in Zion in peace and prosperity. Thus, the word of being carried off into a "land that stretches far away" appears to apply to the "eternal rejection and banishment of hypocrites." At the moment these persons dwell in Zion, in God's church among his people, but the time will come when they will be removed at the utmost distance from it and be eternally banished. Finally, the king here spoken of, whom the eyes of the true citizens of Zion will see in all his beauty, is Jesus Christ, "even David their king, as he is called."[101] More than once, Edwards furnished justification for his typological interpretation. For example, in the first volume of his "Miscellanies" he wrote:

> God had a design and meaning which the penmen never thought of, which he makes appear these ways: by his own interpretation, and by his directing the penmen to such a phrase and manner of speaking, that has a much more exact agreement and consonance with the thing remotely pointed to, than with the thing meant by the penmen.[102]

Above all, it was prophecy that served Edwards as a hermeneutical clue in support of the unity of the Testaments and the Bible's integrity. In the word of the prophet or in Jesus' word Edwards saw more than one future or fulfillment. "'Tis a common thing in Scripture," he wrote, "that things are said to be fulfilled that have been spoken of in the same context when they are only fulfilled in their type, and not in that which is ultimately intended."

For example, in the text of Matthew 16:28 ("There are some standing here who will not taste death before they see the Son of Man coming in his kingdom") Edwards saw multiple comings of the Son of Man. Thus, the descent of the Spirit at Pentecost, the destruction of Jerusalem, the time of Constantine, the destruction of antichrist, and the end of the world were all steps in the fulfillment of the same great event. Jesus' promise that some should witness it before they died was fulfilled, "in the beginning of it," that is, "in a glorious degree, though not in its most glorious degree." In fact, Jesus' manner of speaking led the disciples to expect that the event should be fulfilled in another manner since he was wont to speak to them in

101. Edwards, *Notes on Scripture*, p. 146.
102. Edwards, *The "Miscellanies," a-500*, pp. 347-48.

"mystical language."[103] Or again, in his interpretation of Matthew 24:21-22[104] Edwards wrote that the days to be "cut short" were those of the siege of Jerusalem, cut short "for the sake of the elect," that is, for those Christians in Jerusalem unable to flee the siege, or for the unborn who "were to come out of the loins of Jews then in Jerusalem," or for the unbelieving Jews then living, but afterward to be brought in. "But," he added, "perhaps that time . . . is not meant only [of] the days of Jerusalem's siege, but also the days of tribulation that precede or accompany other comings of Christ, viz., at the overthrow of the heathen empire, at the destruction of Antichrist, and the end of the world."[105]

Since Edwards could write of the prediction of the coming of the Son of Man that "as much was fulfilled or accomplished as answered [the disciples'] expectation,"[106] he appeared to affirm the idea of accommodation, here on the part of Jesus toward his disciples. In the last volume of his "Miscellanies," he clearly embraced the idea, stating that

> although in many of the promises in Moses and the Prophets, wherein God speaks to Israel as a nation, there is truly respect to something further than God's dealings with them as a nation and in things temporal, yet those things which related to 'em as a nation were so much regarded, that *it naturally occasioned the language and manner of speaking to appear more legal and more accommodated to the nature of that national covenant.*[107]

Edwards penned no text on interpretation, but throughout his writings devoted considerable space dealing with the exegetical task. In concert with many of his age, he accented pursuit of the historical meaning of the biblical text, making use of the philological method in attending to the original language, its words and phrases, and employing rational analysis in the process. According to commentarial tradition,

103. Edwards, *Notes on Scripture*, pp. 117-19.

104. "For at that time there will be great suffering, such as has not been from the beginning of the world until now, no, and never will be. And if those days had not been cut short, no one would be saved; but for the sake of the elect those days will be cut short."

105. Edwards, *The "Blank Bible,"* part 2, p. 867.

106. Edwards, *Notes on Scripture*, p. 119.

107. Jonathan Edwards, *The "Miscellanies," 1153-1360,* ed. Douglas A. Sweeny, The Works of Jonathan Edwards, vol. 23 (New Haven, Conn.: Yale University Press, 2004), p. 530; italics mine.

such analysis would involve identifying and reconciling conflicting elements within the canon, clarifying obscurities, finding coherence in
what appeared incoherent, harmonizing elements that appeared discor-
dant, and proposing moral possibilities where the text appeared to approve immoral action. This constituted what Edwards called "the mental
matter." Further, he encouraged acquaintance with whatever customs
prevailed with non-biblical authors since the "penmen of Scripture"
spoke in the same manner. Over all, whatever afforded a "just argument
to reason" could be made full use of since the manifest design of God in
scripture was to "speak so plainly as that the interpretation should be
more independent than that of any other book." The only question was
that of the proportion of "weight of argument" between the Bible and
other factors, the danger being that of not laying sufficient weight on
what was to be found in scripture. For this reason scripture should be
interpreted by scripture.[108]

According to Edwards, this pursuit and analysis constituted "the
mental matter." It was scripture rationally understood, a speculative knowledge accessible to all, and though a matter on which the Spirit could work
an awakening faith, it was without redemptive value. The efficacious use of
this knowledge required a second step beyond mastery of the literal sense.
It required a "spiritual sense," a new heart and mind worked by the interaction of the Word and the Spirit of God. In the "Miscellanies" Edwards
wrote of scripture as "falling in with the natural stream of one's thoughts,"
provided one was "affected" with the things of which it speaks. "There is
that disposition of the mind," he continued, "that when it comes to be put
forth into action, raises such a series and succession of thoughts, as sweetly
corresponds and harmonizes with the expressions of God's Word."[109] It
has been noted that Edwards used this concept of "spiritual sense" in a
second way, to denote a profounder understanding of the Bible resulting
from that sense of the heart implanted by God, and for which he could use
the term "mystical" or "allegorical." The practical effect of this accent on
the spiritual sense was Edwards's restiveness over concentrating on the
literal meaning of a passage, and to his giving range to typology beyond

108. Jonathan Edwards, The "Miscellanies," 501-832, ed. Ava Chamberlain, The Works
of Jonathan Edwards, vol. 18 (New Haven, Conn.: Yale University Press, 2000), pp. 538-39;
cf. Stephen J. Stein's introduction to Edwards's Notes on Scripture, p. 6; and Conrad Cherry,
The Theology of Jonathan Edwards (Bloomington: Indiana University Press, 1990), p. 49.
109. Edwards, The "Miscellanies," a-500, p. 290.

its conventional bounds.[110] Nevertheless, for both the analytical element, the "mental matter," and for the "spiritual sense," or in modern jargon, the existential element, the reception of faith, of grace, was the indispensable principle. On the one hand, the "holy rape of the soul" could not take place without a rational apprehension of the revelation:

> No speech can be any means of grace, but by conveying knowledge. Otherwise the speech is as much lost as if there had been no man there, and he that spoke, had spoken only into the air. . . . He that doth not understand, can receive no faith, nor any other grace; for God deals with man as with a rational creature.

On the other hand, interpretation involved more than the discovery of objective truth. It required the molding of the interpreting self by the truth discovered.[111] The paragraph above thus had to end with the words, "and when faith is in exercise it is not about something he knows not what."[112]

With respect to the presuppositions underlying Edwards's interpretation, the assumption that the testimony of our senses can be depended on was primary. John Locke had written:

> I cannot . . . conceive how bodies without us can any ways affect our senses, but by the immediate contact of the sensible bodies themselves,[113]

and at least in this respect gave impetus to the development of the "common sense" tradition in English thought. Edwards, as has been made clear, was no Ramist, no follower of the Parisian Pierre de La Ramée (1515-72), opponent of Aristotelianism, as were many of his Calvinist contemporaries. He did not believe that God had planted certain principles in the mind which exactly duplicated elements within the material world and the mind of God, and which, united to empirical experience, could yield access to

110. See Stephen J. Stein's "The Quest for the Spiritual Sense: The Biblical Hermeneutics of Jonathan Edwards," *Harvard Theological Review* 70 (January–April 1977): 109-11.

111. See Samuel T. Logan Jr., "The Hermeneutics of Jonathan Edwards," *Westminster Theological Journal* 43 (Fall 1980): 92-93.

112. From Edwards's essay "The Importance and Advantage of a Thorough Knowledge of Divine Truth," cited by Cherry, *The Theology of Jonathan Edwards*, p. 51.

113. John Locke, *An Essay Concerning Human Understanding*, ed. Alexander Campbell Fraser, vol. 2 (New York, 1959), p. 184.

the nature of God himself. The interpretive task involved more than mental flights into the mind of God.[114] But he held rigorously to the belief that sense impressions are the basic reality.

Next, Edwards interpreted the Old Testament Christologically. In his interpretation of the Genesis flood narrative, for example, he writes that just as the ark contained the church of God, and was made for the church's salvation, "so Christ, God-man, Mediator, was made for the salvation of his church, to save it from that destruction and woe that is denounced against this wicked world, and that deluge of wrath that will overwhelm all others." Pursuing the refuge motif, he adds a chain of verses from Psalm 46, Psalm 124, and Isaiah 43, which he also interprets in terms of the church's safety, but then of Christ himself in his suffering:

> This also represents to us how Christ was kept from sinking under his sufferings. It was impossible that Christ should fail in the great work that he undertook; and though his sufferings were so great, though the deluge that came upon [him] was so very great, the billows of wrath so mighty, enough to overwhelm a whole world, and to overwhelm the highest mountains, to overtop the stoutest and mightiest, yet Christ did not sink and fail, but was kept above water.[115]

In his interpretation of the Old Testament, particularly of the Psalms and prophets, Edwards would give this Christological principle such latitude as is reflected, say, in his interpretation of Isaiah 25:11 ("though they spread out their hands in the midst of it, as swimmers spread out their hands to swim") "which," Edwards wrote, "was the posture that Christ was crucified in."[116] That principle would open Edwards to the charge of challenging the uniqueness and integrity of the historic Jewish community by imposing a Christian category on it, of diminishing the historical intention and integrity of the Hebrew Bible by transforming it into an Old Testament whose ultimate purpose and meaning depended on the New.[117] But however "immense" the latitude, as such that Christological principle was hardly Edwards's invention. It was part and parcel of his Reformation heritage.

114. See Logan, "The Hermeneutics of Jonathan Edwards," pp. 84, 85, 92.

115. Edwards, *Notes on Scripture,* pp. 268-70.

116. Edwards, *Notes on Scripture,* p. 76.

117. See the introduction of Stephen J. Stein to Edwards, *The "Blank Bible,"* part 1, p. 30.

Third, Edwards's doctrinal commitment was capable of influencing his exegesis. For example, in the "Notes on Scripture" his treatment of Romans 8:28 ("We know that all things work together for good for those who love God") suggests an interpretation in the service of theodicy. His first point is that everything may issue in some good to every saint, but not to the utmost degree of good possible. There is no reason to suppose that every circumstance of every saint is the best God could have arranged. His second point is that the phrase "all things work together for good" cannot refer to everything, negative as well as positive. Nothing in the context suggests that all dispensations of providence that are merely negative also work for good. All that God does is for the good of the saint, but it does not follow that all his forbearing to do is also for his good. From these two positions it follows that not all that is called the sin of the saints works for their good, to the extent that it was better for them to have sinned. A thing may be for the good of the saints, "and yet that thing may not be for the best, or better for them than anything else could have been." Thus, with respect to "negative disposals," Edwards writes, "some benefit, in some respect or other, will ever accrue to the saints . . . though sometimes the benefit will not be equal to the benefit withheld." Finally, being overcome by temptation may be an occasion for the saints' gaining greater strength, but it is nowhere promised that "in the general it should prove better for them that they are foiled so much." Thus, Edwards concludes, "nothing can be inferred from that promise in Rom. 8:28, tending to set aside or abate the influence of motives to earnest endeavors to avoid all sin."[118]

Finally, Edwards's interpretation could be seen as in service to the moral or ethical. In *The "Blank Bible"* the request of Queen Esther that "the ten sons of Haman be hanged on the gallows" (Esth. 9:13) suggested a "revengeful spirit" totally out of character. Edwards recognized the ethical tension and defended Esther's request:

> The reason why Esther desired that Haman's ten sons might be hanged probably was not from a revengeful spirit, desiring to revenge Haman's injury on his sons, but that she might fulfill the will of God concerning the Amalekitish nation declared in Ex. 17:14.16. And probably she did it by Mordecai's direction, that he gave by the direction of the Spirit of God.[119]

118. Edwards, *Notes on Scripture,* pp. 539-47.
119. Edwards, *The "Blank Bible,"* part 1, p. 425. In his *Notes on Scripture* Edwards

In summary, in the defense of Christian, Protestant, Calvinist faith over against the threefold threat of rationalism, enthusiasm, and Roman Catholic dogma and practice, Edwards combined the analytic and intuitive. As one contemporary has put it, to the question whether or not we must choose between the analytic, currently represented by the logical positivists, formalists, and structuralists, and the intuitive, currently represented by the existentialists and phenomenologists, Edwards once said "No."[120] The question is whether or not anyone since has succeeded at unifying the two.

Moses Stuart

Moses Stuart was born a farmer's son on March 26, 1780, in Wilton, Connecticut. Following the usual primary education he entered the sophomore class at Yale College in 1797, and two years later graduated at the head of his class. After two teaching positions at Easton and Danbury, in 1801 he left to prepare for a career in law, and moved to Newton, where he studied in private. Admitted to the bar in 1802, he was invited back to Yale as tutor. In that same year a revival swept the campus under the leadership of Yale's president, Timothy Dwight (1752-1817), grandson of Jonathan Edwards. Stuart was converted in the revival, formally joined the Church of Christ at Yale College in 1803, and abandoned his law studies and prepared for the ministry. For two years he remained at Yale as tutor and divinity student. In 1804 he resigned as tutor and after a brief period of travel he returned to New Haven, was invited to assist James Dana (1735-1812), the pastor of Center Congregational Church, and was installed in 1806. Some two hundred individuals were added to the church under his brief ministry, among them the celebrated Noah Webster (1758-1843). In 1809 Stuart was called to Andover, the first incorporated, endowed institution for theological education, and charged with the responsibility for teaching the entire Bible and related disciplines.

At an auction in 1812 Stuart bid for a copy of J. G. Eichhorn's *Einleitung in das Alte Testament,* and entered on the pursuit of a language and type

---

identified Haman with the antichrist or the pope, writing that "Europe, which has been the house of Antichrist, shall be in the possession of Protestants, and all his power and dominion shall be given to the saints," p. 63.

120. Logan, "The Hermeneutics of Jonathan Edwards," p. 94.

scholarship that would forever mark his vocation as scholar. From Eich-horn Stuart learned the method of "critical defense," the application of the higher criticism as employed by Baumgarten, Semler, and others in defense rather than in attack. His interest in interpretation likewise developed early in his career. After acquiring the *Hermeneutik* of the orthodox theologian Georg F. Seiler (1733-1807) of Erlangen, he became acquainted with the moderates as well as the extremists of German opinion. Among the former, the most acceptable was Johann August Ernesti (1707-81), philologist and theologian at Leipzig, whose *Institutio interpretis Novi Testamenti,* first pub-lished in 1761, became required reading in the Latin for all his students. In 1842 Stuart published his translation of Ernesti's hermeneutics.[121] Among Stuart's many publications those deserving special mention are his Hebrew grammar (1821), a commentary on Hebrews (1827-28), a grammar of the New Testament (1834), the translation and publication of Johann August Ernesti's volume on interpretation (1842), and a volume on prophecy that he titled "Hints" (1842). *A Hebrew Grammar with a Copious Syntax and Praxis* was the first full-length manual of the Hebrew language for Amer-icans. Wilhelm Gesenius (1786-1842) of Halle served as its main source, though Georg Heinrich Ewald was given mention in the fourth edition. Initially published at his own expense, this edition was republished in En-gland by Edward Pusey (1800-1882), Regius Professor of Hebrew at Oxford. The *Commentary on the Epistle to the Hebrews,* for a good century and a half without precursor, was lauded by *The London Evangelical Magazine* of 1828 as "the most valuable philological help ever published in the English lan-guage." Characteristically, *The Grammar of the New Testament Dialect* drew on German scholarship, as did, of course, the translation of Ernesti and Stuart's *Hints on the Interpretation of Prophecy* and in particular Georg B. Winer's (1789-1858) *Grammatik des neutestamenlichen Sprachidioms.*

Stuart, like Edwards, saw the Christian community imperiled by the claims on behalf of reason and rational religion. The form these claims assumed was that of Unitarian liberalism which itself turned to the Bible to support its challenge to Calvinist orthodoxy, and in doing so drew from the higher criticism of Europe. On the other hand, Stuart's entire study of German scholarship was calculated to strengthen the orthodox position, first, by extracting the best of German scholarship, and second, by refusing the more radical German criticism. Principal among the Unitarians was

---

121. Johann A. Ernesti, *Elementary Principles of Interpretation* (Andover: Allen, Mor-rill and Wardwell, 1842).

William Ellery Channing (1780-1843), pastor of the Federal Street Church of Boston and foremost Unitarian preacher of the century. In response to the status Channing had assigned to reason in the interpretation of the scriptures, Stuart insisted that "the sole office of reason in respect to them is to act as the interpreter of Revelation, and not in any case as a legislator."[122]

Additionally, like Edwards, Stuart had his differences with orthodox colleagues and their classification of German scholarship as skepticism. In Lecture Fourteen of his unpublished Andover "Lectures on Hermeneutics," delivered from 1822 on, Stuart acknowledged his indebtedness to German scholarship, particularly to Eichhorn, and issued a manifesto:

> If the investigation in which we have been engaged served to convince you that the Bible does not shrink from the examination of critical inquirers; that the result of such examination fairly conducted will always be favorable to the word of God; and that the genuineness and canonical credit of the Old Testament rest on better grounds than you had even imagined; in a word, if your rational faith in the sacred scriptures is strengthened, and you feel with more weight your obligations to obey a book, which bears the incontestable stamp of heaven upon it, then will the time and labour which we have expended upon this subject, not be lost.[123]

If Stuart was not the first among the orthodox who functioned as colporteurs for volumes by foreign critics, he was earliest. He is said to have ordered cases of books from abroad and nervously to have awaited their arrival, each day scanning the Yale Seminary weathervane to see if the wind was favorable for a ship's arrival.[124] In a volume devoted to criticism and defense of the Old Testament, Stuart wrote that the battle raging over the documentary hypothesis in Europe had at last reached America, for which reason none could decline the "contest." Stuart challenged those who stood aloof from acquaintance with "German productions" and fretted over such suspicious import to "show their faith by their works." "What I mean is," wrote Stuart, "have we not a right to expect that they will enter into the battle which is going on, clad with the panoply of days of yore,

---

122. Quoted in John H. Giltner, *Moses Stuart: The Father of Biblical Science in America* (Atlanta: Scholars, 1988), p. 60.

123. Quoted in Giltner, *Moses Stuart*, p. 33.

124. Roland Bainton, *Yale and the Ministry* (New York: Harper and Brothers, 1957), p. 92.

which they regard as the only trusty armor? . . . It does not look well for them to shrink from the contest."[125]

Perhaps the greatest difference between Stuart and his orthodox contemporaries had to do with the interpretation of prophecy, a subject that consumed most if not all his reflection on interpretation. In his *Hints on the Interpretation of Prophecy* Stuart wrote that while it was not his purpose to reproach those urging the churches to engage in speculation, "there is nothing in sacred hermeneutics that casts such a stain on English and American expositors, as the character of their interpretation of some parts of the prophets." Then he added,

> if the Bible is not to be interpreted by the common principles of language, it cannot be interpreted at all, except by inspired men. Is there any promise to the church of such a class of interpreters? If not, then our only safety lies in adopting and following out the common, well-known, and well-established principles of interpretation.[126]

Of the numbers-symbolism applied to prophecy by Tübingen's Johann Albrecht Bengel[127] Stuart stated that though the great scholar was a "pillar of the higher order in the temple of God," nonetheless, à la Prospero's speech in Shakespeare's *Tempest,* "the baseless fabric of his vision has not left a wreck behind."[128]

Stuart delivered his first lectures on hermeneutics in 1822.[129] In Lecture One he stated that the "Andover Creed" would be the fundamental consideration to be kept in mind in relation to what followed. The creed read that "the word of God, contained in the scriptures of the Old and New Testaments, is the perfect rule of faith and practice." He went on to state that the differences and disputes over scripture, its alleged contradictions,

---

125. Moses Stuart, *Critical History and Defence of the Old Testament Canon* (London: William Tegg and Co., 1849), pp. 364-65.

126. Moses Stuart, *Hints on the Interpretation of Prophecy* (Andover: Allen, Morrill and Wardwell, 1842), pp. 149-50.

127. See pp. 41-42 above.

128. Stuart, *Hints on the Interpretation of Prophecy,* p. 149.

129. For the substance of Stuart's lectures, not available on loan, I am indebted to Giltner's volume *Moses Stuart,* cited above, to his unpublished doctoral dissertation ("Moses Stuart: 1780-1852"), submitted to Yale University January 1956, and to Mark Granquist's essay, "The Role of 'Common Sense' in the Hermeneutics of Moses Stuart," *Harvard Theological Review* 83, no. 3 (1999), as well as to his notes gleaned from the lectures.

were not occasioned by the Bible but by its interpretation. He inquired, "has then the Bible, different and opposite meanings in the same passages, as party exegesis would represent them? Does the same fountain send forth water that is brackish and sweet?" The lecture ended with an answer to the question as to how hermeneutics was to be regulated: "To the question which is the test by which different principles of hermeneutics are to be tried, I answer without hesitation, Reason."

In Lecture Two Stuart stated that the Bible is subject to the same principles of interpretation as those applied to other books. He rejected the orthodox doctrine of literal, verbal inspiration as an antiquated view, and held to "plenary inspiration." According to this view, the words of the Bible were not dictated, which would rob the writers of their integrity, but allowed that "the inspired man ascends an intellectual and moral eminence so high, that his prospect widens almost without bounds, and what is altogether hidden from ordinary men is more or less distinctly within his view."[130] So, on the one hand, everything about the "manner" of the Bible is human, capable of error, though such is of small import. On the other hand, the "matter" of the Bible is of divine authority. For this reason not all the hermeneutical principles respecting the Bible can be shared with other writings since "a specialties of hermeneutics" attaches to it. But in the last analysis, the Bible contains such revelation from God "as may be understood in everything not strictly experimental, by all men, who use in a proper manner their reason and understanding." That reference to "everything not strictly experimental" implies that something in tandem with reason is needed for genuine interpretation. At any rate, Stuart's embrace of "plenary inspiration" was calculated to balance the assignment of "divine influence" to the biblical canon, and the application of historical method to its interpretation. This balance was key to whatever he thought or wrote concerning interpretation.[131]

In Lecture Three Stuart enunciated the rule that the interpreter's "simple question" is always "which idea did the writer mean to convey?" Then followed Lecture Four in which he reaffirmed his earlier argument in Lecture Two, that revelation had to be intelligible in its single, literal sense. This meant challenging the mystical-allegorical and "double sense" interpretation of his orthodox contemporaries. For example, Ernst Hengstenberg's argu-

---

130. Moses Stuart, *A Commentary on the Apocalypse* (Andover: Allen, Morrill and Wardwell, 1845), vol. 1, p. 168.

131. See Giltner, *Moses Stuart,* p. 249.

ment for a double sense in prophecy on the basis of a presumed visitation of the Spirit on the prophets was a faulty reading. Revelation was by definition intelligible in its single, literal sense, to both writer and interpreter.

In Lecture Six Stuart summed up his theory of interpretation, combining both reason and "feeling" or "sympathy":

> The one true method of finding the sense of the Bible . . . consists of the grammatico-historical principle of interpretation . . . [combined] with such a state of feeling and sympathy with the writer, on the part of the interpreter, as may enable him to transfer himself into a condition similar, in all respects, to that of the author, when he wrote that which is the subject of his exegesis.

As to the presuppositions underlying Stuart's hermeneutic, those references to reason or "common sense" suggest something other than an ordinary understanding of the terms. When, for example, he wrote that "the origin and basis of all true hermeneutical science is the reason and common sense of men, at all times and in all ages, applied to the interpretation of language either spoken or written,"[132] or when he insisted that the principles of interpretation based on reason or common sense were superior to those based on the "analogy of faith," he was drawing on a tradition on which Jonathan Edwards also drew, according to which sense perceptions were the basic reality. Back of Stuart's hermeneutic lay the same discrete, identifiable epistemology that characterized Edwards's confidence in sense perception. If neither was directly dependent on or aware of a particular philosopher, both embraced the view given classical expression in the Scottish thinker Thomas Reid's (1710-96) *Inquiry into the Human Mind on the Principles of Common Sense.* In his attack on the "new" theory of ideas held by René Descartes (1596-1650), Locke, and Hume, Reid had written:

> When I perceive a tree before me, my faculty of seeing gives me not only a notion or simple apprehension of the tree, but a belief of its existence, and of its figure, distance, and magnitude; and this judgment or belief is not got by comparing ideas, it is included in the very nature of the perception. . . . Such original and natural judgments are . . . a part of that furniture which Nature hath given to the human understanding. They are the inspiration of the Almighty. . . . They serve to direct us in

132. Stuart, *Hints on the Interpretation of Prophecy,* p. 310.

the common affairs of life, where our reasoning faculty would leave us in the dark. . . . They make up what is called the *common sense of mankind.*[133]

When Stuart writes,

> the principles of interpreting what we hear or read are instinctive, they belong to our rational nature, or why do the proper principles of Hermeneutics address themselves to all intelligent men with an imperative force? The answer is, that they are imperative, because they are the laws of our communicative nature and faculties — because we find the basis of them within ourselves, and are conscious therefore of their binding force,[134]

what is that but an echo of Reid's reference to "such original and natural judgments" as part of the furniture given by nature? In his biography of Stuart, his student, William Adams, wrote, "if I should undertake to condense [Stuart's] principles and practice concerning Biblical exegesis . . . I should characterize it by common sense."[135]

Whether or not Stuart considered reason and common sense as separable functions,[136] there is no question that the one or other demanded an interpretation amenable to scientific organization by way of specific rules. That is, it demanded the grammatico-historical method, precisely for the sake of which he had translated Ernesti's *Institutio.* Though the linkage of his career to German scholarship drew fire from his contemporaries, to his mind that scholarship, absent its speculative passion, or "neology," as he called it, best reflected what reason or common sense demanded. Interpretation involved pursuit of the meanings of words and of the meanings of things. That is, it required use of philological and grammatical analysis, giving attention to the *usus loquendi,* or customary usage, of terms and their meaning in other contexts, and a reading of the author and his audience in their historical, geographical, and religious setting.

In the preface to his 1828 commentary on Hebrews, Stuart stated,

133. *Thomas Reid's Inquiry and Essays,* ed. Ronald E. Beanblossom and Keith Lehrer (Indianapolis: Hackett, 1983), p. 118.

134. Stuart, *Hints on the Interpretation of Prophecy,* pp. 10-11.

135. William Adams, *A Discourse on the Life and Services of Professor Moses Stuart* (New York: John F. Trow, 1852), p. 310.

136. See Granquist, "The Role of 'Common Sense' in the Hermeneutics of Moses Stuart," pp. 313-15.

to translate, so as to make an author, who has composed in another language, altogether intelligible, and yet preserve all the shades, and colouring, and nice transitions, and (so far as may be) even the idioms themselves of the Original, is the very highest and most difficult work which an interpreter is ever called to perform.[137]

Yet again, in 1833, Stuart elaborated on the method required for writing a commentary. Its aim was to explain the words, phrases, and idioms of the text according to the rules of grammatico-historical interpretation. This required clear and simple translation; philological analysis of doubtful or ambiguous passages; comparison of words used in the passage with use of the same words in other passages; and an exegetical and descriptive paraphrase, in which all "the difficulties of grammar, idiom, phraseology, peculiar style, geography, antiquities, history, etc." are made clear. The commentator was then to present the results in logical fashion, and finally suit the work to its intended audience.[138]

Though he gave much less emphasis to "feeling and sympathy" than to the grammatico-historical method, Stuart nonetheless reserved a place for it in interpretation. In Lecture Two of the hermeneutics he allotted a greater understanding to the one who studied "with poetic feeling and imagination," and, as noted above, in Lecture Six stated that when combined with the historical method, feeling and sympathy would result in true understanding. In an article published in 1832, Stuart wrote that "religious feeling" is as necessary to an understanding of "the meaning of the sacred writers" as is "poetic feeling" to an understanding of Milton, or a "mathematical feeling" to a comprehension of Laplace.[139] In his study of the coming of the Son of Man in Matthew 24, he asserted that "the Bible is put into our hands in languages that are intelligible, and in a style that needs nothing more to be understood, than a sympathizing heart and a well-informed and common-sense power of exegesis."[140] Whether Stuart considered the role of reason as the equivalent of historical method, and

137. Moses Stuart, *A Commentary on the Epistle to the Hebrews* (London: John Miller, 1828), vol. 1, p. xii.

138. Giltner, *Moses Stuart,* p. 103.

139. Moses Stuart, "Are the Same Principles of Interpretation to Be Applied to the Scriptures as to Other Books?" *American Biblical Repository* 2 (January 1832): 135-36.

140. Moses Stuart, "Observations on Matthew 24:29-31, and the Parallel Passages in Mark and Luke, with Remarks on the Double Sense of Scripture," *Bibliotheca Sacra* 9, no. 34 (July 1852): 467.

the role of common sense as the equivalent of sympathetic understanding,[141] clearly, sensitivity to the author's point of view had to be harnessed to rational investigation. How that sensitivity was to be defined Stuart had already made clear in his reference to the Andover Creed as the underlayment for whatever came within range of interpretation.

Stuart's principles were clearly reflected in his exegesis. In his interpretation of the Genesis creation narrative he stoutly opposed the position of his geologist friend Benjamin Silliman (1779-1864). Silliman had attempted to reconcile current geological theory with the Mosaic creation account, interpreting "day" in each stage of the creation as denoting an indefinite period of time. Stuart conceded the *anthropopathic* form of the narrative, that is, as accommodated to views current in the Mosaic period, but with no intent to mislead. "The Bible," he wrote, "was not designed to teach the Hebrews astronomy or geology." The text had therefore to be taken according to its literal sense. In the face of what he conceived to be philological license, Stuart added that Moses wrote "day," and "if [he] . . . contradicts geology, then be it so; but to violate the laws of exegesis in order to accommodate a geological theory . . . is not acting in accordance with the precepts of Scriptural Hermeneutics." Stuart may have nursed the hope that ultimately geologists would come around to accepting the biblical view of the days of creation, but as things currently stood, the contradiction between contemporary theory and biblical narrative had to remain. Again, in what for Stuart spelled a philological contortion, Silliman's pupil, the congregational clergyman Edward Hitchcock (1793-1864), argued that between God's creating heaven and earth and the first "day" there lay unknown periods of geological time. In support of his theory he rendered the Hebrew particle in verse 1 "afterward" so as to make the verse read, "In the beginning God created the heavens and the earth. *Afterward* the earth was waste and void," all for the purpose of implying a long passage of time. Again, Stuart insisted on the simple and direct meaning of the particle, writing that no reputable scholar, German or not, would allow for the construction. Years after his death Stuart would win recognition for his insistence that the philologist, not the scientist, was to be the final arbiter respecting the meanings of ancient texts.[142]

141. From Granquist's notes gleaned from the hermeneutics lectures, p. 1.

142. See Giltner, *Moses Stuart*, pp. 66-74. Note the omission of the particle and substitution of the temporal adverb in the Revised Standard Version translation of Genesis 1:1 ("In the beginning *when* God created the heavens and the earth, the earth was a formless void"), presumably arguing for simultaneity versus chronological sequence.

In his "observations" on Matthew 24:29-31,[143] Stuart opens with a criticism of contemporary orthodox interpreters who either concede or are silent regarding David Friedrich Strauss's imputation of error to the evangelists. Arguing that philology neither demands nor allows one to enter on such a path, that the authority of the New Testament is at an end if it can be shown that Christ or the evangelists embraced or taught error, he proceeds to describe the collapsing of the Last Judgment into the destruction of Jerusalem as strange and forced. "Thousands of sober readers," he writes, "have been misled by want of a familiar acquaintance with the tropical diction of the Scripture. . . . It strikes them, that such imagery as Matt. 24:29-31 employs, cannot be meant for any mere temporal or worldly occurrences." Insisting that so many objections render improbable if not impossible an exegesis that finds the Last Judgment in these verses, he asks "what other book on earth . . . ever requires or admits a *double-sense* theory of interpretation?" The "neologists," obviously, appeal to this double-sense approach, reflecting the apostles' *Unkündigkeit,* or "unknowingness," as proof of their lack of inspiration. Totally disallowing any such double-sense interpretation Stuart concludes,

> I am unable to perceive how we can avoid being driven to and fro, while we are in a state of mere conjecture as to an *under sense,* or what can prevent our being tossed on every wave of doctrine, when we are cut loose from the sheet-anchor of simple historic-grammatical and common-sense exegesis.[144]

Thirty years later, in his remarks on Galatians 3:6-21,[145] Stuart again attacked the assignment of a dual sense to a biblical passage. He insisted that once it was understood that persons, actions, and words in the Old Testament serve to establish a principle, a precedent, or to declare a doctrine that is applicable to more than one thing or person, much of the obscurity vanishes. Similarly, when a New Testament author cites or applies passages of such a type, stating that they are fulfilled by one event or another in the new dispensation, the same principle of action is involved as is set forth in the Old Testament. "This," he writes, "would save all the

---

143. Stuart, "Observations on Matthew 24:29-31," p. 454.

144. Stuart, "Observations on Matthew 24:29-31," p. 465.

145. Moses Stuart, "Remarks Exegetical and Doctrinal on Gal. III, 6-21," *The Quarterly Review of the Methodist Episcopal Church, South* 6, no. 2 (April 1852).

anti-hermeneutical and indefensible appeals to a double sense," concluding that "the sense is not double; but the application of a principle, or of
a significant action or truth, is double, i.e. it is more than once repeated."[146]

In his commentary on Romans, Stuart entered into controversy with
Charles Hodge of Princeton over the interpretation of chapter 5, verses 12
to 21.[147] He found repugnant the idea represented by Hodge, according to
which the sin of Adam is imputed to the entire human race. He stated first
that since none is righteous without active involvement in penitence and
faith, so none is constituted sinner without active participation. In other
words, self-conscious involvement was necessary to moral responsibility.
Second, he emphasized the existence of a universal sense of justice and
fairness. Both points were an obvious reflection of his commitment to
common sense realism, to what Thomas Reid had called those "original
and natural judgments" given by nature to human understanding. "I have
only to add," Stuart wrote,

> that the supposition of men's own personal sins not being reckoned to
> them, while they perish by the imputation of another's sin, is a position
> so revolting with respect to the justice, and goodness, and impartiality
> of the sovereign Judge, "who will render to every man according to his
> works," that it should not be made out.[148]

Acknowledging that some connection existed between Adam's sin and that
of every man, a connection not made explicit in the epistle, Stuart left the
problem unresolved.[149]

For the biblical scholar of Stuart's time, the slavery question was
inextricably tied to the hermeneutical question. Nowhere, perhaps, was
Stuart's fidelity to the grammatico-historical method so restrictedly applied as in his defense of gradual emancipation of the slave. In 1835 an
anti-slavery rebellion broke out among the students at Andover Seminary,
after which rules were passed forbidding the formation of anti-slavery so-

146. Stuart, "Remarks Exegetical and Doctrinal," p. 182.
147. The passage begins: "Therefore, just as sin came into the world through one
man, and death came through sin, and so death spread to all because all have sinned. . . ."
148. Moses Stuart, *A Commentary on the Epistle to the Romans, with a Translation and
Various Excurses* (New York: J. Leavitt, 1832), p. 19.
149. See Stephen J. Stein, "Stuart and Hodge on Romans 5:12-21: An Exegetical Controversy about Original Sin," *Journal of Presbyterian History* 47, no. 4 (December 1967):
345-46.

cieties. The situation grew more tense when an anti-slavery orator whom William Lloyd Garrison (1805-79) brought to the United States visited Andover during a Massachusetts tour. On the occasion of this event Stuart assayed a defense of the moderate position in a lecture to the students, of which only an abstract remains.[150] Attempting to avoid the error of the abolitionist who judged the claims of scripture by an independent conscience or higher law, and that of the slave-holder who violated the ethical principles of the gospel, Stuart agreed that slavery carried with it the possibility of great moral evil, but insisted that the abolitionists' definition of it as an evil in itself *(malum in se)* could not be justified. The Bible never declares it to be such. To the question whether or not the Bible allows of slavery in any form he answered that the Old Testament replied in the affirmative. He cited Leviticus 25:44-46,[151] according to which Israelites were allowed to purchase slaves, as refuting the *malum in se* argument. Noting also that Exodus 21:2[152] and Deuteronomy 15:12[153] allowed the purchase of Hebrew slaves, Stuart asked whether or not the gospel had changed these rules, and answered that since the New Testament contains nothing directly bearing on the subject, slavery may only be described as a *malum prohibitam,* not a *malum in se.* Stuart concluded that affirmation of the truthfulness of the biblical text and the certainty of the revelation led to affirmation of gradual emancipation. It was this that remained true to those gospel principles, yet avoided calling slavery a sin — an affirmation that made more political sense and did less violence to the text.[154]

Later, when the Compromise of 1850 rekindled conflict between

---

150. See John H. Giltner, "Moses Stuart and the Slavery Controversy: A Study in the Failure of Moderation," *The Journal of Religious Thought* 18, no. 1 (Winter–Spring 1961): 30.

151. Lev. 25:44-46: "As for the male and female slaves whom you may have, it is from the nations around you that you may acquire male and female slaves. You may also acquire them from among the aliens residing with you, and from their families that are with you, who have been born in your land; and they may be your property. You may keep them as a possession for your children after you, for them to inherit as property. These you may treat as slaves, but as for your fellow Israelites, no one shall rule over the other with harshness."

152. Exod. 21:2: "When you buy a male Hebrew slave, he shall serve six years, but in the seventh he shall go out a free person, without debt."

153. Deut. 15:12: "If a member of your community, whether a Hebrew man or a Hebrew woman, is sold to you and works for you six years, in the seventh year you shall set that person free."

154. See Robert Bruce Mullin, "Biblical Critics and the Battle over Slavery," *Journal of Presbyterian History* 61, no. 2 (Summer 1983): 210-17.

abolitionists, slave-holders, and moderates, Stuart again took a stand on the subject. In March 1850, Daniel Webster (1782-1852), a personal friend of Stuart, rose in Congress to make his celebrated speech in favor of the compromise proposed by Henry Clay. The speech angered abolitionists and slave-holders, but was cheered on by a thousand supporters, Stuart among them. With both Webster and his supporters now under attack, Stuart replied in a pamphlet entitled *Conscience and the Constitution with Remarks on the Recent Speech of the Hon. Daniel Webster on the Subject of Slavery*. Referring to the controversy over Deuteronomy 23:15-16,[155] allowing freedom to slaves escaped from heathen masters, Stuart wrote,

> when a fugitive bond-man, then, comes to us of the North, from a master at the South, in what relation do we of the North stand to that southern master? Are our fellow citizens and brethren of the South, to be accounted as heathen in our sight? . . . The Mosaic law does not authorize us to reject the claims of our fellow countrymen and citizens, for strayed or stolen property.[156]

Further, to the contention that "the higher law" of Christian conscience demanded the abolition of slavery, even disobedience to the Constitution should it protect it, Stuart cited Paul's letter to Philemon in which the apostle did not injure Philemon's "vested rights," but returned the fugitive to his master. The "higher law" thus lay only in the "passions and prejudices" of those who urged it, and as for that "Christian conscience" it was "wholly subjective."[157]

Stuart's strict application of the grammatico-historical method to the issue of slavery led to what his principal biographer has described as a failure to give true moral guidance to the moderate cause,[158] a failure rehearsed in John Greenleaf Whittier's "A Sabbath Scene." In it Whittier describes his dream in which a fugitive slave girl, fleeing to a church for protection, is handed over to her pursuer by the parson himself. In a stanza later removed, Whittier wakes and exclaims:

155. Deut. 23:15-16: "Slaves who have escaped to you from their owners shall not be given back to them. They shall reside with you, in your midst, in any place they choose in any one of your towns, wherever they please; you shall not oppress them."

156. Stuart, *Conscience and the Constitution,* pp. 31-33, cited by Giltner, "Moses Stuart and the Slavery Controversy," p. 34.

157. Quoted in Giltner, "Moses Stuart and the Slavery Controversy," p. 36.

158. Giltner, "Moses Stuart and the Slavery Controversy," p. 38.

My brain took fire: "Is this," I cried, "the end of prayer and preaching?"
Then down with pulpit, down with priest, and give us Nature's teaching! I woke, and lo! The fitting cause of all my dream's vagaries — Two
bulky pamphlets, Webster's text, with Stuart's commentaries!

Retiring from Andover in 1843 due to ill health, Stuart died in January
1852. His epitaph in the old burial ground at Andover in part reads that "he
is justly entitled to be called among the scholars of his native country, The
Father of Biblical Science."

Charles Hodge

Charles Hodge was born in Philadelphia on December 28, 1797, of a family
rooted in the Great Awakening of 1733 and the Great Revival of 1742-43. In
1812 he entered the College of New Jersey at Princeton. There, as a first-
year student, he witnessed the installation of Archibald Alexander (1772-
1851) as the first professor of the newly founded seminary. In 1815 he was
converted in a campus revival, and decided for the ministry. He entered
Princeton Seminary and graduated in 1819. In 1820 he was appointed assistant instructor in biblical languages and two years later named professor
of oriental and biblical literature. In October 1826, Hodge sailed for Paris
to study oriental languages under the linguist Antoine de Sacy (1758-1838).
He soon moved on to Germany, studying under Wilhelm Gesenius and
Friedrich August Tholuck (1799-1877) at Halle, and under Ernst Hengstenberg, Johann August Neander, and Alexander von Humboldt (1769-1859)
in Berlin. After two years in Europe Hodge returned to Princeton, and in
1840 moved to the chair of systematic theology while continuing to teach
the New Testament.

In the conflict within Presbyterianism between the so-called New
and Old Schools, the Princetonians laid claim to Presbyterianism of the
Old School, with Hodge and the two sons of Archibald Alexander, Joseph
Addison (1809-60), and James Waddell (1804-59) in the phalanx.

Hodge's most important contributions include his establishment of
the *Biblical Repertory* in 1825, which became the *Princeton Review* in 1877;
the republication of his principal essays in *Essays and Reviews* (1857) and
in the *Princeton Theological Essays* (1878); and the projection of a popular
commentary on the Bible together with the two Alexanders, of which his
volume on Romans published in 1835 is best known, commentaries on Ephe-

sians and the two Corinthian epistles, and his famous "three volumes" of systematic theology, published between 1871 and 1873. In April 1872 the fifti-eth anniversary of his election to professorship was observed with between four and five hundred in attendance. Hodge died at Princeton in June 1878.

Hodge's career was marked first of all by what he perceived to be the perils facing the Christian community in the United States. One, in the words of his son, Alexander Archibald, was the church's convulsion "with the controversies growing out of the intrusion into a community deriving its Presbyterianism from Scotland and the Westminster Assembly, of the new anthropology of the New England School."[159] To engage the champi-ons of this "New Theology," among them Moses Stuart of Andover, he es-tablished the *Biblical Repertory* and to it contributed the bulk of its articles. Another peril facing the church was the moral extremism resulting from a radical change in the understanding of the nature of the conversion experi-ence. According to Hodge, too many elements in American evangelicalism led toward the absolutizing of goals, principal among them insistence on the abolition of slavery.

Like Stuart, Hodge also turned his attention to European, particularly German, scholarship. In a lecture addressed to the students of Princeton Seminary, he described the orthodox, the rationalists, and the pantheists as the leading parties in Germany. He noted that once historical criticism had been applied to the ancient classics, Semler and his school were led to pursue the same course with respect to the Bible, resulting in a loss of faith in the scriptural word. Now, however, orthodoxy was enjoying a new spring. In Germany, severe national and private afflictions had begun to turn the minds of all classes of men toward God, thus to the doctrines of the Bi-ble. Among the orthodox Hodge listed his friend Friedrich August Gottreu Tholuck, the pietist apologist of Halle with whom he often corresponded. Among the "rationalists" Hodge listed Baumgarten and Ernesti, whom he accused of explaining away the doctrines of scripture. These, he continued, were followed by such as Semler and Eichhorn. In his *Systematic Theology* Hodge described the "rationalists'" system as taking its first serious blow from Immanuel Kant, who "undertook to show that reason is incompetent to prove any religious truth."[160] In his article on inspiration occasioned by a

159. Alexander A. Hodge, *The Life of Charles Hodge* (New York: Reprint edition by the Arno Press, 1969), p. 272.

160. Charles Hodge, *Systematic Theology*, 3 vols. (New York: Charles Scribner and Company, 1872), vol. 1, p. 43.

series of discourses on the subject by a Dublin scholar, Hodge gave considerable space to an attack on "pantheism." He wrote,

> this new philosophy makes the world and history a process, a development of God, in which process there is no room for any special intervention of God. . . . The fundamental idea that God and the world are one, however distinguished; that God is the life of the world, and that all history is the self-evolution of God, determines the nature of all the doctrines of religion.[161]

Hodge explained that the new philosophy taught that religion is not a form of knowledge, not a mode of action, but a life, a peculiar state of feeling. Hence, if the "spinal cord" of Neander's historical study was that Christianity is a new life, in Schleiermacher that new life was a form of pantheism.[162] Hodge continued the attack in his *Systematics,* stating that according to Schleiermacher inspiration was the intuition of divine truths due to the excitement of the religious nature, thus denying it as a form of knowledge. According to this theory, Hodge concluded, the Bible had no normal authority as a rule of faith.[163]

The Bible, Hodge wrote, was one book, the "evolution through successive centuries, and in the use of a multitude of writers, of one great system of truth."[164] It was, accordingly, "the product of one mind."[165] For this reason, he contended, no one book of the Bible could be understood by itself. This very organic relation of the Bible's different parts argued in favor of its divine origin.[166] As Hodge wrote in *The Way of Life,* a work produced in 1841, republished in England, and circulated in 35,000 copies in America, such an admission required a faith that rested on the internal demonstration of the Spirit. No amount of external evidence could produce it, and to make the testimony of others to the truth of Christianity the basis for faith was inadmissible. There was, therefore, "no way of justifying the universal, immediate, and authoritative demand that the Bible makes

---

161. Charles Hodge, "The Inspiration of Holy Scripture, Its Nature and Proof," *The Princeton Review,* no. 4 (January 1857): 688. The eight discourses were delivered before the University of Dublin by William Lee, M.A., Fellow and Tutor of Trinity College.

162. C. Hodge, "The Inspiration of Holy Scripture," p. 689.

163. C. Hodge, *Systematic Theology,* vol. 1, p. 177.

164. C. Hodge, "The Inspiration of Holy Scripture," p. 663.

165. C. Hodge, *Systematic Theology,* vol. 1, p. 166.

166. C. Hodge, *Systematic Theology,* vol. 1, p. 38.

on our faith, except by admitting that it contains within itself the proofs of its divine origin."[167]

This faith, according to Hodge, assumed the Bible's inspiration, that is, its emergence under supernatural influence, an influence distinguishable from God's universal providential agency, from the operation of the Spirit on the heart of the believer, or from spiritual illumination. What constituted the Bible's uniqueness was its subject matter and design.[168] Further, inspiration extended to the entire Bible, to historical and geographical details as well as to religious or moral teaching. Hodge wrote that "church doctrine" opposes the notion that some parts of the Bible are inspired and others are not; that a higher degree of inspiration belongs to some portions rather than to others; or that inspiration is confined to the moral and religious truths in the Bible.[169] More, the influence of the Spirit extended to the words no less than to the thoughts of the writers. As he stated, "how any one can hold that the sacred writers were inspired as to their thoughts, but not as to their language, is to us perfectly incomprehensible. . . . By a law of our present constitution, we think in words."[170] Hodge conceded that there was little for inspiration to accomplish respecting the historical portions of the Bible beyond the selection of materials and accuracy of statement, but that the end to be accomplished would have failed had the Spirit left the mode of selection and accuracy to the "uninfluenced" mind of the author.[171]

Hodge was intent on distinguishing his view of "plenary inspiration" from a mechanical dictation theory. He wrote that it was a perversion of the doctrine to represent it as reducing the inspired authors into mere machines. All wrote and spoke in full possession of their faculties. Their self-consciousness was not suspended, nor their intellectual powers superseded. Nor did their inspiration interfere with the free exercise of their distinctive mental characteristics. "It is, therefore," Hodge wrote, "a perversion of the common doctrine, to represent it as reducing the inspired penmen into mere machines,"[172] and a few pages later queried,

167. Charles Hodge, *The Way of Life*, ed. Mark A. Noll (New York: Paulist, 1987), pp. 54, 55.

168. C. Hodge, *Systematic Theology*, vol. 1, p. 154.

169. C. Hodge, "The Inspiration of Holy Scripture," p. 664.

170. C. Hodge, "The Inspiration of Holy Scripture," p. 677.

171. C. Hodge, "The Inspiration of Holy Scripture," p. 675; idem, *Systematic Theology*, vol. 1, pp. 154, 163.

172. C. Hodge, "The Inspiration of Holy Scripture," p. 673.

if then the providential and the spiritual agency of God may control human action, and leave the agent free, why may not the Spirit of God, as the spirit of inspiration, guide the mental operations of the sacred writers, so that while they are unconscious of his power, they yet speak as they are moved by the Holy Ghost?[173]

Hodge was likewise intent on distinguishing inspiration from revelation. As he stated in the Lee review, they differed as to their goal. The goal of inspiration was to render men infallible in the communication of truth; the goal of revelation was to impart knowledge. Accordingly, many received revelations who were not inspired to communicate them, and many who were inspired were not recipients of revelation.[174] Further, the two phenomena differed respecting their effects: "The effect of revelation was to render the recipient wiser. The effect of inspiration was to preserve him from error in teaching."[175] These two gifts might be enjoyed by the same person, but were often separated.[176] The authors of the historical books of the Old Testament may have received no revelations, in fact, were in need of none for the facts they recorded.[177] Discrepancies and inconsistencies in the Bible were dismissed as for the most part trivial. It was unreasonable, Hodge stated, to deny the Bible's inspiration because one writer speaks of 24,000 and another of 23,000 men slain in battle. A Christian should be allowed to tread such objections under foot. Other inconsistencies were merely apparent or attributable to copyists. In light of all the errors in the transcription of the biblical text, and in light of present ignorance respecting the history contemporary with the events recorded, it was rational to admit ignorance in the face of what could not be satisfactorily explained. And in the ultimate, such discrepancies were remarkably, miraculously, few in number.[178] By way of summing up, in his *Systematic Theology* Hodge stated that neither in the Bible nor in other writings was there a simpler or clearer statement of the doctrines of revelation and inspiration than in 1 Corinthians 2:7-13.[179]

173. C. Hodge, "The Inspiration of Holy Scripture," p. 677.
174. C. Hodge, "The Inspiration of Holy Scripture," pp. 665, 680-81.
175. C. Hodge, *Systematic Theology*, vol. 1, p. 155.
176. C. Hodge, "The Inspiration of Holy Scripture," p. 680.
177. C. Hodge, "The Inspiration of Holy Scripture," p. 675.
178. C. Hodge, "The Inspiration of Holy Scripture," pp. 682-87; idem, *Systematic Theology*, vol. 1, pp. 169-70.
179. C. Hodge, *Systematic Theology*, vol. 1, p. 162.

Consequent upon this "doctrine" of inspiration was that of the in-fallibility of the biblical authors. That is, inspiration as an *ab extra* divine influence rendered the biblical authors infallible as organs of the Spirit.[180] Hodge insisted that they were protected from error in what they wrote, but, as he made clear, only in what they wrote. Infallibility thus extended only to the nature of the object to be accomplished.[181] It did not imply infallibility in the authors' understanding of what they communicated, nor did it imply that they did not differ in the degree in which they under-stood what they communicated.[182] "It is preposterous," Hodge wrote, "to attempt to reduce the sacred writers to a dead level — to place Isaiah and Amos upon the same footing as to their subjective state."[183] In an article written together with Benjamin B. Warfield (1851-1921) of Western Theo-logical Seminary at Allegany, Hodge made clear that inerrancy applied only to the original autographs of the Bible. Throughout the article, Hodge and Warfield repeatedly distinguished the "common text" from the "orig-inal autographic text," of which no error could be asserted. They wrote,

> in all the affirmations of Scripture of every kind, there is no more error in the words of the original autographs than in the thoughts they were chosen to express.[184]

The two conservative theologians admitted to inconsistencies in the Bible, either with scientific fact, with facts of history, or with other statements. Such instances, however, were to be expected in "imperfect copies of an-cient writings." Yet, candid inspection of "all the ascertained phenomena of the original text of Scripture" would indicate that the books were without error.

In face of what he believed to be merely the alleged conflict between science and the Bible, Hodge expressed his optimism that reconciliation between the two surely lay ahead. Of the latest challenge to the biblical record from geology, Hodge wrote that it would "soon be found side by side with astronomy in obsequiously bearing up the queenly train of God's

---

180. C. Hodge, "The Inspiration of Holy Scripture," p. 680.

181. C. Hodge, "The Inspiration of Holy Scripture," p. 668; cf. idem, *Systematic The-ology*, vol. 1, p. 165.

182. C. Hodge, "The Inspiration of Holy Scripture," pp. 669, 670, 671.

183. C. Hodge, "The Inspiration of Holy Scripture," p. 672; cf. p. 684.

184. Charles Hodge and Benjamin Warfield, "Inspiration," *The Presbyterian Review* 6 (April 1881): 233.

majestic word."[185] Writing that it was unwise for theologians to insist on an interpretation of scripture that brings it into collision with the facts of science, he recalled that for ages the Bible was read in terms of the Ptolemaic system, whereas now it is read in terms of the Copernican system without doing it the least violence. "Christians," he wrote, "have commonly believed that the earth has existed only a few thousands of years. If geologists finally prove that it has existed for myriads of ages, it will be found that the first chapter of Genesis is in full accord with the facts."[186] The moral of the story was thus to allow science to take its course, assured of the Bible's accommodation to all well-authenticated scientific facts.

Respecting the task of interpretation, Hodge stated that the duty of the biblical theologian was to ascertain and state the facts recorded in the Bible. Accordingly, the exegete worked inductively, collecting data from the Bible just as the scientist collected data from nature. As natural science was a chaos until the principle of induction was admitted, so theology "not worth a straw" when the same principle was not applied to the study of the Word of God. In neither case, then, were the principles derived from the mind and imposed on the facts. These, then, were the rules of interpretation. First, the words of scripture were to be taken in their plain historical sense, that is, in the sense attached to them in the age and by those to whom they were addressed. Second, scripture was to be explained by scripture, a rule sometimes called "the analogy of scripture" or "the analogy of faith." Finally, scripture was to be interpreted under the guidance of the Holy Spirit, a need Hodge would describe as "of an inward supernatural teaching," or as a "congeniality of mind." But if the Bible is perspicuous, that is, able to be understood by the individual Christian, then for Hodge it inevitably followed that all must agree in their interpretation where "essential matters" were concerned. For the individual Christian to dissent from such agreement, or as Hodge titled it, from "the faith of the universal Church," was tantamount to dissent from the scriptures themselves.[187] Of course, in their interpretation of the Bible theologians were not infallible. It could happen that an interpretation long received had to be modified or abandoned. But the scriptures themselves remained infallible.[188]

Hodge's actual exegesis is graphically illustrated, first of all, in his

185. C. Hodge and Warfield, "Inspiration," p. 283.
186. C. Hodge, *Systematic Theology*, vol. 1, pp. 56, 171.
187. C. Hodge, *Systematic Theology*, vol. 1, p. 184.
188. C. Hodge, *Systematic Theology*, vol. 1, p. 59.

conflict with Moses Stuart over the interpretation of Romans 5:12-21. The steps leading to the battle between the interpreters began with an article released in 1830 by Archibald Alexander defending the Princeton viewpoint regarding the imputation of Adam's sin to all humankind. To this defense Stuart anonymously replied with a sharp attack in articles published in 1830 and 1831. These articles in turn evoked Hodge's response, to which Stuart replied six months later. These hostile exchanges formed the context within which Stuart's commentary on the epistle appeared in 1832, followed by Hodge's denunciatory review and the publication of his own commentary in 1835.

Preliminary to his discussion of the Romans passage in the 1835 commentary Hodge refers to such German interpreters as are free of the guilt of perverting the Word of God, who allow the Bible to mean what it says despite refusing to submit to its teaching. By implication Stuart and those who agree with him fall only under the latter category. Turning to the passage in question Hodge asks "where it is said, or where proved, that the many die for the offence of one, if not in ver. 12, and vs. 13, 14?" He insists that if any consistency is to be maintained among the several parts of the apostle's argument, it must be contained in verse 12. The analogy is destroyed, he writes, if anything in us is assumed to be the reason for the infliction of the evils described. Thus to assume that these verses refer to men as actual sinners, or as subject to an inherent, hereditary depravity, gives no satisfactory sense. Rather, Paul's argument is that

> by one man sin entered into the world, or men were brought to stand in the relation of sinners to God; death consequently passed on all, because for the offence of that one man they were all regarded and treated as sinners.[189]

Under the section headed "Doctrine" Hodge refers to the objection that this interpretation "contradicts the essential principles of moral consciousness," obviously a reference to Stuart's position, whom he then quotes as stating that "a transfer of moral turpitude is just as impossible as a transfer of souls." Noting the frequent appearance of this idea in Stuart's Romans commentary, Hodge states that like others of its kind it is based on a misapprehension of the doctrine in question. Imputation,

---

189. Charles Hodge, *Commentary on the Epistle to the Romans,* new ed. (Edinburgh: Andrew Elliot, James Thin, 1864), p. 175.

Hodge writes, is never represented as affecting the moral character, but merely the relation of men to God and his law. Thus, to impute sin is to regard and treat as sinner, just as to impute righteousness is to regard and treat as righteous.[190]

At this point Hodge refers to the position of the sixteenth-century Reformers, who describe "original sin" as an accident, not as an essential attribute of human being. They in fact speak of original sin as a corruption of nature, but not as the infusion of anything in itself sinful, but rather as a tendency or disposition. Hodge then quotes Jonathan Edwards to the effect that original sin as the "absence of positive good principles" is sufficient to explain all the corruption within human existence. Hodge concludes,

> how large a portion of the objections to the doctrine of original sin is founded on the idea of its being an evil positively infused into our nature, "as poison is mixed with wine," may be inferred from the exclamation of Professor Stuart, in reference to the passage just quoted from President Edwards. He says it is a "signal instance, indeed, of the triumph of the spontaneous feelings of our nature over the power of *system!*"[191]

If, in this contest, the highest tribunal for Stuart was the bar of philology, and for Hodge the witness of an accepted authority, the distance between Hodge's understanding of "original sin" as accident versus the orthodox Calvinist understanding of it as total depravity was evidence of "an evangelical *Tendenz*" permeating his commentary.[192]

Respecting the slavery question, Hodge's position was similar to that of Stuart, though it was given more space and emphasis. In a review of the book *Slavery* by William Ellery Channing (1780-1842), the country's foremost Unitarian preacher, Hodge produced a piece originally intent on only the scriptural view but eventually expanded due to the abolitionists' appeal to "general principles of morals."[193] Following lengthy remarks designed to aid the reader in forming "a just moral judgment," Hodge at last gives attention to the biblical text. Stating that it is too clear to admit of denial or doubt that the scriptures sanction slaveholding, he notes that under the

190. C. Hodge, *Commentary on the Epistle to the Romans,* pp. 180-81.

191. C. Hodge, *Commentary on the Epistle to the Romans,* p. 185.

192. See Stein, "Stuart and Hodge on Romans 5:12-21," pp. 347, 350.

193. Charles Hodge, "Art. VI. — Slavery. By William E. Channing. Boston: James Munroe and Company, 1835," *Biblical Repertory* 8, no. 2 (April 1836): 297.

old dispensation it was permitted by divine command, and under the new it is nowhere forbidden or denounced but acknowledged to be consistent with the Christian character and profession. For this reason, he concludes, to declare slaveholding a heinous crime is to impeach the Word of God, a stance that can only result in national and ecclesiastical disunion. "We shall become two nations in feeling, which must soon render us two nations in fact." Hodge continues that the extinction of slavery and the amelioration of the laws protecting it are as sincerely desired by him and his supporters as by any abolitionist. "If," writes Hodge,

> any set of men have servants bond or free, to whom they refuse a proper compensation, for their labour, they violate a moral duty. . . . Again, if any man has servants or others whom he forbids to marry, or whom he separates after marriage, he breaks as clearly a revealed law as any written on the pages of inspiration, or on the human heart. . . . [I]f he deliberately opposes their intellectual, moral or religious improvement, he makes himself a transgressor.[194]

Hodge concludes his review by conceding that should the slaves attain to such improvement as to become freemen, the next step in their progress is that they should become citizens, but in a last footnote states, "we have said nothing of African colonization, though we regard it as one of the noblest enterprises of modern benevolence."[195]

Later, in his 1851 review of Stuart's *Conscience and the Constitution*,[196] Hodge avers that the discussion has taken a new turn, that the abolitionists assume the legislation regarding the return of fugitive slaves to their masters is unconstitutional, or, if not contrary to the Constitution, contrary to the law of God. Hodge stipulates that since government is a divine institution obedience to its laws is a religious duty, that such obedience is due in all cases in which it can be rendered in good conscience, that the great body of the people regard the fugitive slave law as consistent with the Constitution and the law of God, that therefore all resistance to its operation must be without excuse.[197] The similarity of Hodge's position to

194. C. Hodge, "Art. VI. — Slavery. By William E. Channing," p. 303.

195. C. Hodge, "Art. VI. — Slavery. By William E. Channing," p. 305.

196. Charles Hodge, "Art. V. — Conscience and the Constitution. By Moses Stuart," *The Princeton Review,* no. 1 (January 1851).

197. C. Hodge, "Art. V. — Conscience and the Constitution. By Moses Stuart," pp. 154-55.

that of Stuart led to a similar result, to the absence of any reexamination of the biblical record and its interpretation.

On the other hand, if intended to single him out among his orthodox, northern contemporaries as in essence sympathetic to the "peculiar institution," reference to Hodge's article as "notorious" is unfortunate.[198] His refusal to declare slavery a *malum in se,* his insistence that the institution be distinguished from its possible misuse, that its encroachments of rights is analogous to those of other social institutions, that the abolitionists court national and ecclesiastical disunion, that slave labor deserves compensation, that the slave's improvement could eventuate in citizenship, even the suggestion of colonization, scarcely differs from that of Stuart and his Andover colleagues, and not one whit from the position held by Abraham Lincoln and other Whigs or Republicans prior to the Civil War. But the truth remains, neither Hodge nor Stuart, neither Princeton nor Andover, resolved the biblical question. Both had reached an impasse.

In Hodge's interpretation of the Bible, the commitment to Scottish common sense philosophy is evident throughout, but so also is his emphasis on the necessity of faith for a genuine interpretation. In *The Way of Life,* published in 1841, and written to combat "sophistical objections against the doctrine of the Bible," and in the introductory section of the *Systematic Theology* these two factors or accents appear in a kind of *pas de deux,* the one continually supplementing or complementing the other. In *The Way of Life* Hodge writes that if the Bible contained anything contrary to reason or right moral feeling, belief in its divine origin would be impossible. On the other hand, "positive internal evidence" of its divine origin gives power and authority to the Bible's claims.[199] Or again, two things are needed to produce conviction regarding the biblical evidence. The first is that the evidence be attended to, and the second that it be understood or "really apprehended."[200] Violence must be done all modes of argument; people must believe moral impossibilities and irreconcilable contradictions before they can intelligently become infidels, but at the same time they must harden their hearts to "the excellence of the Saviour."[201] Ten years later, in the *Systematic Theology,* Hodge summons us to "rely on our

---

198. Leonard J. Trinterud, "Charles Hodge (1797-1878)," in *Sons of the Prophets: Leaders in Protestantism from Princeton Seminary,* ed. Hugh T. Kerr (Princeton, N.J.: Princeton University Press, 1963), p. 35.

199. C. Hodge, *The Way of Life,* p. 56.

200. C. Hodge, *The Way of Life,* p. 58.

201. C. Hodge, *The Way of Life,* p. 75.

senses, within the sphere of our sense perceptions; on our reason within the sphere of rational truths."[202] Since the "intuitive judgments of the mind" or "laws of belief" have been implanted in our nature, or, more to the point, since "the truths revealed in the Bible have the same adaptation to our souls that the atmosphere has to our bodies,"[203] we cannot refuse to assent to evidence when clearly perceived; we are forbidden to believe the impossible.[204] But again, "let us rely . . . on God, and God alone, in all that relates to the things of God," for "in believing we affirm the truth of the proposition believed."[205] And lest the impression be given that these two factors or accents are somehow in competition, Hodge states that we can affirm nothing of that of which we know nothing, that faith cannot be required without evidence.[206]

However Hodge might protest, the idea that there is "the most perfect agreement between all the precepts of the Bible and the highest dictates of reason," that there is "no command in the word of God of permanent and universal obligation, which may not be shown to be in accordance with the laws of our own higher nature," as he put it in his review of Stuart's *Conscience and the Constitution*,[207] reflects an "overly confident view of the power of induction," a "naïve scientism," a "Baconian turn," which could result in the intellectualizing of belief, in assuming that the truths of the Bible are there for all to see when approached with the proper methodological rigor.[208] At best, assigning to this member of the duet such a signal role would leave Hodge's interpretation mired in ambiguity.

202. C. Hodge, *Systematic Theology*, vol. 1, p. 48.

203. C. Hodge, *Systematic Theology*, vol. 1, pp. 52, 167.

204. C. Hodge, *The Way of Life*, p. 56; idem, *Systematic Theology*, vol. 1, p. 52.

205. C. Hodge, *Systematic Theology*, vol. 1, pp. 48-49.

206. C. Hodge, *Systematic Theology*, vol. 1, pp. 49, 53.

207. C. Hodge, "Art. V. — Conscience and the Constitution. By Moses Stuart," p. 136.

208. See Mark A. Noll's introduction to C. Hodge, *The Way of Life*, pp. 27, 28, 36.

CHAPTER SEVEN

The Twentieth Century

Karl Barth

In its encounter with the Enlightenment, nineteenth-century Protestant theology had adopted a defensive position. It held that the truth of Christian faith could be proved by demonstrating the presence of a religious a priori or God-consciousness, that all previous historical religions comprised a ladder with Christianity at the topmost rung. Christianity was thus the irreplaceable means for humanizing humanity, the expression of humanity's noblest need, the highest certainty to be discovered in oneself. It was a position that could only lead to the assertion of a Ludwig Feuerbach (1804-72), student of Hegel become materialist and onetime docent at Erlangen, to the effect that theology was nothing but anthropology. If the revelation that established and legitimized all others lay in the human breast, then human need was the criterion by which what was time-bound in the Bible had to be distinguished from what was still valid. But how to distinguish hull from kernel?

In 1914, Europe was at war. The entry of ninety-three German intellectuals into the propaganda front marked a turning point. Either one had to continue to establish God from the perspective of the human and distance oneself more and more from what was specifically Christian, or one had to take seriously the revelation witnessed to in the Bible. In the beginning weeks of the war, a group of young clergymen met in one of the villages of the Aargau for their usual conference. Most decided to postpone theological issues until calmer times. Karl Barth was convinced that theological work needed doing more now than ever.

Barth was born May 10, 1886, in Basel, Switzerland. In that year his father, Johann Friedrich ("Fritz") (1856-1912) had been called to the school of homiletics *(Predigerschule)* in that city. Like his father, his mother, Anna Katharina Sartorius (1863-1938), was the child of a Basel pastor. Three years after Karl's birth, the Barths left Basel for Berne, where the father took up duties as instructor *(Privatdozent)* at the university. In 1904, after successfully completing his studies at the gymnasium in Berne, Karl entered the university. Two years later he completed the *Propädeuticum,* or first stage of university study qualifying Swiss students for study abroad. Eager to continue his studies at Marburg, but opposed by his father who preferred the more "positive" Halle or Greifswald, the two compromised on Berlin. There Barth attended the New Testament seminars of Adolf von Harnack (1851-1930), who drew the young scholar like a moth to the flame. Sent to Tübingen in 1907 by a father now grown anxious concerning his son's drift toward liberalism, the young Barth had nothing but scorn for the faculty to the right or the left. By 1908, the father gave up his attempts at control, and the son made his way to Marburg, or, as he called it, "my Zion." There he came under the influence of Wilhelm Herrmann (1846-1922), a Kantian and pupil of the younger Schleiermacher, and whom he latter called *"the"* theological teacher of his student years. In 1909, after successfully completing the required university examinations in theology, Barth left Marburg to begin a two-year internship *(Vikariat)* in Geneva, followed by a call to serve as pastor in the village of Safenwil in the Aargau. In that same year, Barth was betrothed to Nelly Hoffmann (1893), a member of his first class in religious instruction. She bore him five children.

What launched Barth on his career was a commentary on the Epistle to the Romans, completed in 1918 at Christmastide in Safenwil, written on twenty nine-by-seven tablets, each with forty-eight pages of twenty-four lines. After three Swiss publishers rejected the manuscript, Barth's wealthy businessman friend Ruedi Pestalozzi secured its publication with a company in Berne, in an edition of one thousand copies. When the capacity of the Swiss market appeared exhausted with the sale of three hundred copies, the book was discovered by a Munich pastor, Georg Merz (1892-1959), and the remainder bought up by Christian Kaiser Verlag. The author then decided upon a revision, which was completed in eleven months. In his own words, "of its original state, scarcely one stone remained on the other."[1] The

---

1. Karl Barth, "Vorwort zum Nachdruck dieses Buches," in *Der Römerbrief, Erste Fassung* (1919), ed. Hermann Schmidt, in Karl Barth, *Gesamtausgabe* (Zürich: Theologischer Verlag, 1985), II, p. 6. Hereafter referred to as *Römerbrief, Erste Fassung.*

first edition soon became a bibliographical rarity, but it was to this edition that Barth owed his call in 1921 to a newly founded chair in Reformed theology at Göttingen, Germany. In the foreword of the reprint of the first edition in 1963 he wrote,

> if I am to be seriously researched as an "object of scientific theology," then, for good or ill, the second "Romans" must be investigated — but then, and hardly to be avoided beside it, the first as well.[2]

After the disaster of World War I, betrayed by the prevailing theological method, it was not a foregone conclusion that a young pastor in a tiny Swiss village would turn to the Bible or to Romans for a remedy. Barth had no revelation, no "tower experience," no experience of a heart "strangely warmed." In the last year of his life, in an epilogue to a Schleiermacher anthology, he gave a survey of the early history, the reasons for and the emergence of his two interpretations of Romans. Years before, he said, his old friend Eduard Thurneysen (1888-1977) had whispered into his ear that what was needed for preaching, teaching, and the care of souls was an "entirely different" basis. The decision to begin with the Bible was a purely practical one. It contained the theological ABC's. On the morning after the day Thurneysen had whispered into his ear, Barth turned to Romans under an apple tree. The choice of tree was accidental, too soon for allusions to Newton. The choice of Romans was not. In 1901, in confirmation class Barth had heard that it involved something crucial. "I began to read it as though I had never read it," he said, "and not without slowly writing down point by point what I had discovered. . . . I read and read and wrote and wrote."[3] He read the Bible in the original. More to the point, the very thing from which he was struggling to get free, the "Schleiermacher-Ritschl-Herrmann line," which spelled the "plain destruction of Protestant theology and the Protestant Church,"[4] had taught him where to go. Schleiermacher wrote that the Holy Scriptures were the first member in the series and the norm for all successive presentations of the Christian faith.[5] Albrecht Ritschl (1822-89) wrote that

---

2. Barth, *Römerbrief, Erste Fassung,* p. 7.

3. The editor's foreword ("I. On the Origin of the Book"), in Barth, *Römerbrief, Erste Fassung,* pp. ix-x.

4. Karl Barth, *Church Dogmatics,* I/1 (Edinburgh: T. &. T. Clark, 1936), p. x.

5. Friedrich Schleiermacher, *The Christian Faith,* English translation of the second German edition (1830/31), ed. H. R. Mackintosh and J. S. Stewart (Edinburgh: T. & T. Clark, 1948), p. 594.

instituting a community on behalf of a universal religion required a content stamped by the person and work of its founder. To construct a theology from this "material," a norm that bound theology to Holy Scripture offered a "special criterion."[6] Herrmann wrote that the Christian's communion with God rested on "the witness to a life set free within the community of God, a witness that meets one nowhere else in such fashion as in Holy Scripture."[7]

The first edition reflects Barth's chrysalis stage, his struggling to get free of the idealistic perspective and whatever drew life from it — the church, experience, morality. He wrote of the church as "the grave of the biblical truth,"[8] insisted that grace was not an "experience," that the certainty given our spirit is not to be dragged down into the murk of subjective moods and feelings,[9] and that morality had always been an especially powerful support of the dark powers.[10] Since the throne shared an identical hunger with the altar, representing the kingdom of God on earth, it too was a target for attack,[11] as was also German socialism, for which reason more than one observer has seen in Barth's first exposition of Romans 13 a passionate dialogue with Lenin.[12] Nothing escaped attack, whether pietism —

faith cuts off the detour pietism takes by way of the psychic. It begins with what pietism at best shakily ends, with the confidence and defiance that rests on God's Word[13]

the theology of the last generation —

Oh, this theology of the nineties with its arid contrasts! The Spirit of God is a Being, a transcendent presupposition. . . . We do not have the

6. Albrecht Ritschl, *Die Christliche Lehre von der Rechtfertigung und Versöhnung*, vol. 2: *Der biblische Stoff der Lehre* (Bonn: A. Marcus und C. Weber's Verlag, 1900), pp. 13, 19.

7. Wilhelm Herrmann, *Der Verkehr des Christen mit Gott* (Tübingen: J. C. B. Mohr, 1921), p. 34.

8. Karl Barth, *Der Römerbrief* (Zürich: EVZ-Verlag, 1963), pp. 268, 288, 341.

9. Barth, *Der Römerbrief*, pp. 79, 149, 237, 215.

10. Barth, *Der Römerbrief*, p. 215.

11. See the quotation from Gottfried Menken (1769-1831), evangelical pastor and representative of the *Erweckungstheologie* movement, in Barth, *Der Römerbrief*, p. 239: "God preserve us from the meanness of the view for which things are so good on earth that it will not have them otherwise or better, as if in the face of eternal damnation itself!"

12. See F. W. Marquardt cited in Nico T. Bakker, *In der Krisis der Offenbarung: Karl Barths Hermeneutik* (Neukirchen: Neukirchener Verlag, 1974), p. 68.

13. Barth, *Der Römerbrief*, p. 115.

Spirit of God, but the Spirit has us, whoever we are, for you in Rome as well as for us in Corinth![14]

religion —

> at issue is neither "religion" nor "morality," nor "our" decisions or the two combined, neither "autonomy" nor "heteronomy," but the lordship and freedom of God in the real sense[15]

and whatever it was that birthed them all:

> so the standpoints of religion, church, school, Judaism, Christianity, morality, and all the idealisms, insofar as they contrast the divine with the human purely in terms of demand, are at bottom dispatched, disposed of.[16]

In the preface to his second edition, Barth quotes the Greek of Galatians 1: "Nor did I go up to Jerusalem . . . but I went away at once into Arabia." These words mark the end of the chrysalis stage. Twelve times in the second edition Barth made clear that he had thrown off whatever had clung to him in the first. There he had written of a "secret tendency for good" inherent in all that occurs and is to be, so that it must "cooperate . . . toward restoring the life of the world and men in the peace of God," of an "organic growth-like way of change," of the divine in our existence appearing as "nature, gift, and growth,"[17] of salvation as "process."[18] Hegellike he wrote that whoever has moved with God from an earlier to a new stage of his activity knows best that "the entire movement must one day again be of benefit to the elements now left behind."[19] In the second edition that synthesis of revelation and history, identified with nature, with its innumerable references to growth and process, was abandoned for their antithesis, with its reference to origin, decision, and crisis. But if the divine, if the kingdom of God, was not nature, growth, and process, then the notion of reality derived from nature, then the idea of the real as sprung

14. Barth, *Der Römerbrief,* p. 227.
15. Barth, *Der Römerbrief,* p. 235.
16. Barth, *Der Römerbrief,* p. 181.
17. Barth, *Der Römerbrief,* p. 218.
18. Barth, *Der Römerbrief,* p. 255.
19. Barth, *Der Römerbrief,* p. 318.

from the perceptible, had to give way to an idea of reality as linked to the unseen and imperceptible. Then whatever occurs in the world can never be a "divine beginning or seed or kernel," but only a signpost, a parable of the divine. The first edition would never contain this statement:

> [There is] no concrete thing which does not point beyond itself, no observable reality which is not itself a parable. . . . All human doing or not-doing is simply an occasion or opportunity of pointing to that which alone is worthy of being called "action," namely, the action of God.[20]

If what occurs here exists only as parable, then there is no direct point of contact between here and there, now and then, time and eternity, history-nature and revelation, humanity and deity. In the first edition Barth had written,

> God can be searched out and known to those who seek him. There is, of course, that impenetrability, immeasurability, and inexhaustibility with which he reveals in ever new freshness and freedom a new wealth of his power, a new wisdom of his intentions, a new knowledge of his ways and means to those who seek him day by day and hour by hour.[21]

But in the second,

> "The depth of the riches and the wisdom and the knowledge of God" is — correcting here what was written in the first edition of this book — unfathomable. The Epistle moves round the theme . . . that in Christ Jesus the Deus absconditus is as such the Deus revelatus.[22]

Finally, election and rejection, Isaac and Ishmael, Jacob and Esau, could no longer be "the momentary expression of a movement, like a bird in flight,"[23] no longer part of an organic process in which the one or other was merely a stage and never the process itself. But then, whatever else Isaac and Ishmael, Jacob and Esau, election and reprobation, might be, they express the unfathomable mystery of the sovereign freedom of God:

---

20. Karl Barth, *The Epistle to the Romans,* trans. Edwyn C. Hoskyns (Oxford: Oxford University Press, 1933), pp. 275, 432.

21. Barth, *Der Römerbrief,* pp. 344f.

22. Barth, *The Epistle to the Romans,* p. 422.

23. Barth, *Der Römerbrief,* p. 286.

The God of Esau is known to be the God of Jacob. There is no road to the knowledge of God which does not run along the precipitous edge of this contradiction.[24]

In his preface to the second edition, Barth described its connection with the first as the extension of the first edition's position to points further ahead.[25] This reference to continuity between the two editions needs correcting. The second edition is an entirely new book, and whatever connection exists between the two is purely formal. Both are concerned with the same object — the Epistle to the Romans, and both with the same subject matter — the kerygma of Paul.[26]

What created the difference between the two editions was not another influence that needed shrugging off, something in addition to the idealism with which the nineteenth century attempted to defend itself against the Enlightenment. It was Barth's clearer sight of that influence and the degree to which it had left its mark on him that created the difference. He was helped toward that sight, especially, perhaps, by Franz Overbeck (1837-1905), friend of Friedrich Nietzsche (1844-1900), agnostic, and one-time professor of theology at Basel, according to whom contemporary theology had no right to speak for genuine, original Christianity:

As a rule, theologians are Christians, though not at all plain Christians, persons whose relation to Christianity is simple and unequivocal. . . . Viewed in the most propitious light they are negotiators of Christianity with the world, and for this very reason no one really trusts them. . . . Christianity itself despises negotiators, and since it is absolute in its claims, does not recognize a world alongside itself. . . . Theologians as negotiators may enjoy standing with the world, may even appear almost indispensable, but without on that account having to overcome the stigma of their profession. Now and again, the service they suppose they can render is accepted with most courteous thanks, without ignoring the basic detriment of their service, that is, that they come from the same sector as assigns a merely relative value to Christianity.[27]

24. Barth, *The Epistle to the Romans,* p. 350.
25. "Die damals gewonnene Stellung wurde auf weiter vorwärts liegende Punkte verlegt." Barth, *Römerbrief, Erste Fassung,* p. vi.
26. See Bakker, *In der Krisis der Offenbarung,* p. 72.
27. Franz Overbeck, *Christentum und Kultur* (Darmstadt: Wissenschaftliche Buchgesellschaft, 1963), p. 273.

Once the *Römerbrief* became available, the question of identity was raised. Was this commentary an exegesis? Adolf Jülicher (1857-1938), Barth's former professor at Tübingen, smirkingly greeted the first edition as a model of acceptable, devotional material.[28] Jülicher took issue with Barth's construing the noun *pistis* in Romans 1:17 as a divine attribute, thus translating it as "the *faithfulness* of God," all the while calling into question Barth's expertise in the Greek, the manuscript tradition, and New Testament *Wissenschaft* in general.[29] Paul Wernle (1872-1939), who more than any other typified what it was to which Barth had been in thrall, labeled him a "Biblicist" who glided smoothly over all the hurdles to modern consciousness posed in Romans, adding that nothing in Paul appeared to give Barth trouble.[30] Von Harnack indicted "Herr Kollege Barth" for mixing scientific theology and edifying discourse:

> The scientific theologian who *begins* with setting aflame and edifying brings strange fire to his altar. Just as there is only *one* scientific method, so there is also only *one* scientific task — the pure knowledge of its object.[31]

Not even the two who most shared his position — Adolf Schlatter (1852-1938) and Rudolf Bultmann — spared him. Earlier, Schlatter had insisted on distinguishing the historical and dogmatic tasks, not because the self could be split into two separate centers of thought, but because those tasks represented two functions, both of which required a certain independence. When, Schlatter added, in biblical exposition we turn our gaze immediately to what concerns us in the present, we risk breaking off observation at the point where our interest does not reach. Then he asked, "can we perform a genuine act of surrender to what has been given, so that our eyes are open to something not ourselves?"[32] Of Barth's second edition Schlatter wrote,

> In the first two chapters of this epistle Paul stated what plunges Greek and Jew into guilt and death. . . . Of [this] . . . we hear nothing in

28. *Anfänge der dialektischen Theologie*, ed. Jürgen Moltmann, Theologische Bücherei, vol. 17, part 1 (München: Chr. Kaiser Verlag, 1974), p. 89.
29. Moltmann, ed., *Anfänge der dialektischen Theologie*, pp. 91-94.
30. Barth, *Römerbrief, Erste Fassung*, p. 643.
31. Barth, *Römerbrief, Erste Fassung*, Note 1.
32. Adolf Schlatter, *Zur Theologie des Neuen Testaments und zur Dogmatik,* Theologische Bücherei, vol. 41 (München: Chr. Kaiser Verlag, 1969), p. 213.

[Barth's] exposition. . . . You, reader, are the Greek and you are the Jew. . . . But is it Paul we hear when Greek or Jew have disappeared from Romans? . . . For a Pauline community the question of its relation to Israel's destiny was crucial. But in Barth's opinion these events tell us nothing. . . . Israel disappears and the "church" is spoken of in chapters 9–11 without a qualm. Is Paul's word still left inviolate?[33]

Rudolf Bultmann, with whom Barth corresponded over forty years and admitted the great impression "Romans II" had made on him, nevertheless agreed that the commentary had done violence to the individuality of Romans and Paul. Further, the commentary reflected the "impossible assumption" that every word and sentence in Romans had done justice to its theme, resulting in the total absence of any critical measuring of the text by its subject matter.[34]

Barth's reply to Paul Wernle sufficed for the majority of his critics:

I went to the text firmly assuming that everything I read there must make sense. . . . Paul knows what he wants and what he is saying, and can be understood. Of course, whether or not I succeed is a question, but I must still make every effort to understand. This is the difference between my exegesis and what was taught us at the university, and which we correctly though ignorantly found to be totally boring and worthless. . . . Many of us did not find so much as one modest, *intelligible* residue in what the current theological faculty said about the Bible. We do not reproach you for your criticism, but for a lack of criticism over against the shapeless rubble-heap of disconnected, relative truths which you offered us as the result of your scholarly work on the New Testament.[35]

Was it exegesis? In his second preface, Barth had formulated what he believed was indispensable to biblical interpretation:

The Word ought to be exposed in the words. Intelligent comment means that I am driven on till I stand with nothing before me but the enigma of the matter; till the document seems hardly to exist as a doc-

---

33. Moltmann, ed., *Anfänge der dialektischen Theologie*, p. 144.
34. Moltmann, ed., *Anfänge der dialektischen Theologie*, pp. 140-41.
35. Barth, *Römerbrief, Erste Fassung*, pp. 643-44.

ument; till I have almost forgotten that I am not its author; till I know the author so well that I allow him to speak in my name and am even able to speak in his name myself.[36]

Was it exegesis? Schlatter replied in the affirmative: "His own life-situation and that of his contemporaries gives content to the otherwise empty words of Paul. It was thus among the old interpreters and it is thus with Barth."[37]

It is often argued that Barth's *Römerbrief* inaugurated a new era of biblical interpretation. The statement should be altered to read that it inaugurated a new era of interpretation for some. It is not majority opinion that interpretation consists of a conversation between author and reader about God, Christ, and the human condition to the point where the distance between them is erased. Nor was Barth the first to insist on the exegesis of the New Testament as the foundation for an openness to its claim. An entire host had earlier expressed the same conviction — Wilhelm Dilthey (1833-1911), Schleiermacher, Bengel, Luther, Calvin. But it was Barth who gave dignity and force to a position that the nineteenth century had abandoned in its attempt to define religion by conceding the agenda to its critics.

Following the publication of "Romans I and II," Barth's rise in the theological world was meteoric. Subsequent to the invitation to Göttingen in 1921, the evangelical faculty at Münster in Westphalia awarded him the doctor of theology degree. In 1925, at the close of the summer semester in Göttingen, Münster called him to the chair of dogmatics and New Testament exegesis. Five years later, the University of Bonn invited him to the chair of systematic theology. In 1935, three days after being removed from his chair at Bonn for refusing to swear the oath of allegiance to Hitler required of university faculties as officials of state, Barth received the invitation to occupy a specially designed chair at the University of Basel, which he occupied until 1962. After six productive years as emeritus professor, Barth was buried in the Basel Hörnli cemetery in December 1968.

Rudolf Bultmann

Rudolf Karl Bultmann was born on August 20, 1884, at Wiefelstede, in the archdukedom of Oldenburg, Germany, the first child and son of Arthur Ken-

---

36. Barth, *The Epistle to the Romans*, p. 8.
37. Moltmann, ed., *Anfänge der dialektischen Theologie*, p. 140.

nedy and Helene (Stern) Bultmann. In 1890 his family moved to Rastede, and from there to Oldenburg, where Rudolf was enrolled in the gymnasium. He was confirmed in Oldenburg in 1899, in 1903 made his *Abitur,* passed his final examinations qualifying him for university study, and matriculated at Tübingen. There, he heard the Ritschlians Johannes Gottschick (1847-1907), professor of New Testament, ethics, and practical theology, and Karl Müller (1852-1940), church historian in the tradition of Ferdinand Christian Baur and Carl Heinrich Weizsäcker (1822-99), in addition to the New Testament scholar Adolf Schlatter. Of these Müller impressed Bultmann most and Schlatter least. In 1904, he left Tübingen for Berlin, where he heard Julius Kaftan (1848-1926), occupant of Schleiermacher's chair in theology, the historian Adolf von Harnack (1851-1930), and the Old Testament scholar Hermann Gunkel (1862-1932). In the fall of 1905 he left Berlin for Marburg, where he heard the systematician Wilhelm Herrmann (1846-1922), and the three New Testament scholars Wilhelm Heitmüller (1869-1926), Adolf Jülicher (1857-1938), and Johannes Weiss (1863-1914). After successfully passing his university examinations, he served as instructor in the upper grades *(Oberlehrer)* at the Oldenburg gymnasium from October 1906 to September 1907. In 1907 he was invited to serve as *Repetent,* or tutor, in New Testament at Marburg. At the end of that service, in 1910, he submitted his doctoral dissertation on the preaching of Paul and the Cynic-Stoic diatribe *(Der Stil der paulinischen Predigt und die kynisch-stoische Diatribe),* which led to his promotion as licentiate (licensed to teach) rather than as doctor of theology, according to the prevailing custom at Marburg. His *Habilitationsschrift,* or second dissertation, on Theodore of Mopsuestia qualified him for university professorship. In 1913, he entered upon a four-year teaching responsibility at Marburg as *Privatdozent,* a non-salaried lectureship supported from student fees. In 1916, the year of his engagement to Helene Feldmann, he received an invitation to the University of Breslau to serve as associate professor of New Testament *(Extraordinarius),* and four years later was invited to Giessen as full professor *(Ordinarius).* Since only the holder of a doctorate could share in the promotions process there, the dean of the Giessen faculty requested that the Marburg faculty grant Bultmann the requisite doctorate, which it did *honorus causa.* One year later, Bultmann was called as full professor to his alma mater, where he taught until his retirement in 1951. He died twenty-five years later, on July 30, 1976.

Bultmann's most signal contribution to twentieth-century biblical research was his existential interpretation. First of all, it was a type exposition that did not allow for a special hermeneutics. As he wrote, "the interpretation of the biblical writings is not subject to other conditions of understanding than any other literature."[38] Nor, as he stated in his 1925 address to the students and faculty of Göttingen, did it allow for a "pneumatic exegesis" or appeal to an inner light.[39] It was not a new method intended to replace the old.[40] In fact, it spelled the surrender of any method that presumed to arrive at objective results.[41] More than once Bultmann would list the types falling into this category. The "older rationalism" regarded the doctrines of scripture as universal truths whose validity was decided before the bar of reason. Its offspring, "historical explanation," replaced the contrast between the contingent and the universally valid with a view of the individual as instance of the universal. Naturalistic, "biological" interpretation limited itself to a history of the nature of human being, and the psychological reduced all utterances to an expression of a particular psychic life, proceeding according to law. The idealist inquired after the text's reflection of a given stage of the Spirit's self-unfolding, saw nothing that encountered him as authority. In all these types, Bultmann contended, the original posture was surrendered by which the text makes its claim on the reader; in all the text was viewed from a distance without inquiring whether history contains essential realities that can be seen when observation from a distance is abandoned.[42] The task of understanding appeared to be achieved by following certain hermeneutical rules.[43] By contrast, existential interpretation sought to understand "in what respect the text is the exposition of its author regarding his understanding of his existence, as the authentic possibility of existing."[44] Bultmann wrote, "we

38. Rudolf Bultmann, "Das Problem der Hermeneutik" (1950), in *Glauben und Verstehen, Gesammelte Aufsätze von Rudolf Bultmann,* vol. 2 (Tübingen: J. C. B. Mohr, 1952), p. 231.

39. Rudolf Bultmann, "Das Problem einer theologischen Exegese des Neuen Testaments" (1925), in *Neues Testament und christliche Existenz,* ed. Andreas Lindemann (Tübingen: Mohr Siebeck, 2002), p. 37.

40. Rudolf Bultmann, "Die Bedeutung der 'dialektischen Theologie' für die neutestamentliche Wissenschaft" (1928), in *Glauben und Verstehen,* vol. 1, 2nd ed. (Tübingen: J. C. B. Mohr, 1954), p. 132.

41. Bultmann, "Das Problem einer theologischen Exegese des Neuen Testaments," p. 23.

42. Bultmann, "Das Problem einer theologischen Exegese des Neuen Testaments," pp. 13-18, 21.

43. Bultmann, "Das Problem der Hermeneutik," p. 214.

44. Bultmann, "Das Problem einer theologischen Exegese des Neuen Testaments," p. 28.

will therefore only finally understand a text when we are finally clear about the possibilities of human existence."[45]

This approach did not mean dispensing with the means by which those old methods assayed to achieve objectivity. To the interpretation of the biblical writings there unquestionably applied the old hermeneutical rules of grammatical interpretation, formal analysis, and interpretation by way of historical conditions. For example, understanding of late Jewish literature and religion was essential if the New Testament was not to be isolated from the rest of earliest Christian literature. The literature of Hellenistic syncretism required attention as well. Precise knowledge of the form of ancient letters was necessary to distinguish fixed, traditional form from the individual author's own shaping, to seeing that in moral instruction and edification, prayer and polemics, fixed forms soon took shape reflecting community tradition. In this connection, Bultmann hailed the appearance in 1919 of Martin Dibelius's (1883-1947) *Formgeschichte des Evangeliums*.[46] The difference between himself and such contemporaries as Hans Lietzmann was that they wanted to separate the historical viewed from the perspective of faith and the historical as scientifically researched, whereas he believed the historical and the "theological" study of history belonged together.[47] This alternation between literary-critical analysis, religious-historical reconstruction, theological interpretation, and his own premises of interpretation in working out the sense of the text would help to secure his exposition from criticism from either side.[48]

Existential interpretation began in earnest with what Bultmann called *Sachkritik,* with content criticism. Such criticism was essential to a revelation veiled in the human word, which required raising the utterance of the text to the conceptuality of the present.[49] Content criticism thus inquired into the matter of which the text speaks, of the issue to which

45. Bultmann, "Die Bedeutung der 'dialektischen Theologie' für die neutestamentliche Wissenschaft," p. 119.

46. Rudolf Bultmann, "Die neutestamentliche Forschung im 20. Jahrhundert" (1919), in *Theologie als Kritik*, ed. Matthias Dreher and Klaus W. Müller (Tübingen: Mohr Siebeck, 2002), pp. 96-97, 100; Bultmann, "Das Problem der Hermeneutik," p. 231.

47. Kurt Aland, "Rudolf Bultmann," in *Glanz und Niedergang der deutschen Universität: 50 Jahre deutscher Wissenschaftsgeschichte in Briefen an und von Hans Lietzmann (1892-1942)* (Berlin: Walter de Gruyter, 1979), p. 967.

48. See Konrad Hammann, *Rudolf Bultmann: Eine Biographie,* 2nd ed. (Tübingen: Mohr Siebeck, 2009), p. 306.

49. Bultmann, "Das Problem einer theologischen Exegese des Neuen Testaments," p. 36.

it refers, as well as into its meaning for the interpreter. Both questions, wrote Bultmann, belonged to the actual work of the exegete. Bultmann allowed that the differentiation between what a text says and what it means was "primitive, provisional," since inquiring into what a text says implies a neutral exegesis, a virtual impossibility. In fact, the distinction between what the text says and what it means was insufficient, insofar as no exegesis intended or was able merely to reproduce the wording of a text without in some sense intending to say what is meant.[50] In view of the differences within the New Testament concentration on the matter or issue of the text was unavoidable. The kerygma and its disclosure of the self-understanding in which faith is explicated could not be achieved by the mere reproduction of the theological sentences of the New Testament. Such sentences could not be the object of faith; they are situational and incomplete. As more or less appropriate explications of believing self-understanding they are subject to continual *Sachkritik*. The criterion by which the *Sache* was to be measured or evaluated Bultmann described as "the decisively basic idea of the New Testament, or, better perhaps, the intention of the message resonating in the New Testament," and in parentheses added Luther's criterion (*was Christum treibet* [what bears or carries Christ]). To the possible objection that this *Sachkritik* might in fact be Lutheran and thus at risk, he queried whether or not any exegesis could be without it.[51]

Respecting the text itself and its status within the interpretive process, Bultmann was insistent. Since exegesis takes its criterion from the matter created by the text, it has no prior control. Put theologically,

> the work of the exegete does not come about through his presuppositions and his method, but through its object, the New Testament. His character as theologian consists in the fact that the church has directed him toward the New Testament he is to explain. Not what he can do by dint of his presuppositions, his methodology, his possible spirituality renders his work theological. Research of the New Testament is just as profane as the research of any kind of historical source as such. Responsibility for the theological character of his work is

50. Bultmann, "Das Problem einer theologischen Exegese des Neuen Testaments," pp. 20-22.

51. Rudolf Bultmann, "In eigener Sache" (1957), in *Glauben und Verstehen*, vol. 3 (Tübingen: J. C. B. Mohr, 1965), p. 186.

borne by the New Testament itself which he merely serves. What he hears as researcher is profane; only the word that stands written is Holy.[52]

Once the matter of the text lay beyond mere report, once the text was not used as a source for reconstructing a piece of the past but interpreted as witness to an understanding of existence disclosing the possibility of a new self-understanding, the question emerged as to the presuppositions underlying the interpreter's encounter with the text. Bultmann gave his answer in a few theses.

First, genuine understanding presupposes a life-relation *(Leben-zusammenhang)* of the interpreter to the matter directly or indirectly coming to expression in the text. As he wrote,

> a particular understanding of the matter on the basis of a life-relation is always presupposed in exegesis, and insofar no exegesis is presupposition-less.[53]

That is, understanding assumes an interest within the life of the interpreter which is somehow alive in the text to be interpreted, and which thus connects text and interpreter. For this reason, the individuality of the interpreter and the author of the text are not in opposition. Both enjoy the same relation to the matter or the issue since both are in the same life-relation.[54] In his review of Karl Barth's *Römerbrief,* Bultmann registered basic agreement with Barth's recommendation that the interpreter must move in a relationship of trust toward the author. As he wrote:

> From this book it became decisively clear to me (1) that the essence of Christian faith does not consist in an attitude of the soul, but in its relation to its object, God's revelation; and (2) that the interpretation of a text presupposes a personal relation to the matter of which the text speaks.[55]

---

52. Bultmann, "Die Bedeutung der 'dialektischen Theologie' für die neutestamentliche Wissenschaft," p. 133.

53. Rudolf Bultmann, "Ist voraussetzungslose Exegese möglich?" (1957), in *Glauben und Verstehen,* vol. 3 (Tübingen: J. C. B. Mohr, 1965), p. 146.

54. Bultmann, "Das Problem der Hermeneutik," p. 217.

55. *Theologie als Kritik,* appendix 1, no. 5, p. 513.

Second, this means that every interpretation is borne along by a certain preliminary understanding *(Vorverständnis)* of the matter of the text. "Clearly," he wrote, "I can only understand such a text [as involves me, my existence] when I already bring to it a preliminary understanding of the matter of which it is speaking."[56] Or again, "only on the basis of such a preliminary understanding is . . . interpretation as such possible."[57] This preliminary understanding, Bultmann continued, is grounded in the question about God which is alive in human life.[58] In other words, one's question about good fortune, salvation, the meaning of the world, or the genuineness of one's existence always reflects a knowledge of God.[59] This is not an understanding the interpreter creates. It is rather assumed, and, moreover, outside of faith. In this connection he frequently quoted the familiar line from book I of Augustine's *Confessions:* "Thou hast formed us for thyself, and our hearts are restless until they find their rest in thee."

Third, interest in the matter or content of the text results in the formulation of the question, or, as Bultmann often termed it, in its "Whither" *(Woraufhin).*[60] The formulation of the question may be identical with the intention of the text and thus communicate the matter or issue of the text directly. When not identical with the text's intention it communicates the matter indirectly. The formulation of the question may be fed by a psychological or an aesthetic interest. It may be fed by interest in history as the context for human existence, in which it achieves and shapes its possibilities, and in reflection on which it achieves understanding of self and its own possibilities. Genuine understanding thus involves listening to the question put to the text and to the claim encountering the interpreter. It involves a "supplementing" of one's own individuality by way of a richer and deeper disclosure of possibilities, a being summoned forth from oneself. Obviously, texts most suitable for such a formulation of the question are those of poetry, philosophy, and religion.[61] Bultmann readily acknowledged that this concept of understanding as "existential," as belonging to the broad structures of human being, and of interpretation as the "cultivation of understanding," as an encounter between interpreter and text that discloses

---

56. Bultmann, "Die Bedeutung der 'dialektischen Theologie' für die neutestamentliche Wissenschaft," p. 125.

57. Bultmann, "Das Problem der Hermeneutik," p. 216.

58. Bultmann, "Ist voraussetzungslose Exegese möglich?" pp. 146-47, 149.

59. Bultmann, "Das Problem der Hermeneutik," p. 233.

60. Bultmann, "Das Problem der Hermeneutik," pp. 229-21.

61. Bultmann, "Das Problem der Hermeneutik," pp. 226-28.

a possibility of existence demanding a "Yes" or a "No," affirmation or denial, was given "decisive clarity" by Martin Heidegger (1889-1976) in his
so-called phenomenological analysis of Dasein.[62]

Bultmann was quick to make clear that this concept of understanding
and interpretation had its forerunners, principally in Schleiermacher and
Dilthey. Schleiermacher, wrote Bultmann, saw that genuine understanding
could not be gained by following the traditional rules. The composition
and unity of a work could not be grasped solely by the categories of formal
logical and stylistic analysis. The work had to be understood as the moment
of life of a particular person. Thus, to grasp the "outer form" an "inner
form" needed adding, involving not an objective but a subjective, "divinatory" interpretation. Exposition was thus an "imitation" made possible by
virtue of the author's and interpreter's sharing a common human nature
and thus a commonality of understanding. Dilthey appropriated Schleiermacher's idea, arguing that individual distinctions were not conditioned
by qualitative differences but merely through differences of degree, that
interpretation as "the art of understanding written, fixed life-expressions"
was conditioned by the congeniality of author and interpreter, resting on a
relationship heightened by a life entering in with the author. In his 1910 *Habilitationsschrift* on Theodore of Mopsuestia (ca. A.D. 350-428) Bultmann
wrote that the "profoundest artistry" of the exegete consists in

> allowing oneself to be addressed by the writing at the point where
> it furnishes nourishment *(Lebensmittelpunkt),* from out of which it
> appears as a living unity; to discover the point of crystallization in
> the understanding of which the lines of the inner structure are shown
> clearly to the eye.[63]

Further, to disclose the "inner life" of a writing, two tasks were involved.
The one required grasping the ideas underlying it, and the other observing
what was individual or peculiar in their expression, entailing the writing's
historical situation, and particularly the "personality of the author."[64]

The problem with Schleiermacher's concept of understanding, as
Bultmann saw it, was that it was applicable only to philosophical and po-

---

62. Bultmann, "Das Problem der Hermeneutik," pp. 226-27.

63. Rudolf Bultmann, *Die Exegese des Theodor von Mopsuestia,* ed. H. Feld and K. H.
Schelkle (Stuttgart: W. Kohlhammer, 1984), p. 83.

64. Bultmann, *Die Exegese des Theodor von Mopsuestia.*

etic texts. Historically related to Johann Joachim Winckelmann's (1717-68) interpretation of works of art, and to Johann Gottfried Herder's (1744-1803) "feeling oneself into the souls of periods and peoples," the interpretation of a mathematical or medical text could not possibly emerge from Schleiermacher's tracing psychic episodes in the author. As for Dilthey, his concept of interpretation was limited to literary documents. More, his restriction of the matter or issue of the text to "life" ignored other matters or issues depending on how one formulated the question.[65] With respect to the presupposing of a life-relation, Bultmann reserved a good word for Johann Christian Konrad von Hofmann (1810-77). The Erlangen theologian had seen what was decisive, insofar as he insisted that biblical hermeneutics was not an independent science, but presupposed a general hermeneutics. Moreover, it was a science that did not simply consist in the application of its method to the Bible but presupposed a relation to the biblical content since both expositor and author existed within the same life-relation.[66]

In his essay on hermeneutics, Bultmann dealt with Karl Barth's vigorous resistance to his idea of the bond between text and interpreter in terms of a preliminary understanding. The matter of which Holy Scripture speaks, Barth stated, is an activity of God of which there can be absolutely no preliminary understanding. Only through the revelation of God, through his activity, can one know of him. In response Bultmann stated that to understand events as historical, and not merely as occurrences of whatever kind, there must be a prior understanding of the historical possibilities from which these occurrences take their meaning and thus their character as historical events. Agreed, he continued, this knowledge need not be explicit, but to understand reports of events as activities of God assumes a prior understanding of what an activity of God might be. To Barth's objection that prior to the revelation one cannot know who God is or what an activity of God may be, Bultmann replied that one "can very well know who God is, that is, in the question about him." If existence were not moved by the question of God in terms of the Augustinian *"tu nos fecisti ad te"* ("thou hast formed us for thyself"), one would not recognize God as God in any revelation of God. He went on to write that in human existence an *existentielle* knowledge of God is alive, that is, a knowledge impinging on my own existence. It is as alive as the question about "luck" or "salva-

65. Bultmann, "Das Problem der Hermeneutik," pp. 214-16.
66. Bultmann, "Das Problem der Hermeneutik," p. 217.

tion," about the meaning of the world, of history, about the authenticity of my own existence. Though the right to describe such questioning as the question about God may be gained only from faith in the revelation of God, the phenomenon as such is the relation of the matter or issue to the revelation. To Barth's argument that a theological statement can only be valid when proved to be a genuine component of the Christian understanding of human existence, that it cannot be reduced to a statement about the inner life of man, Bultmann replied that existential interpretation and its understanding of existence has nothing at all to do with the "inner life of man." It rather intends to see and understand the human being's true, historical existence, an existence in a life-relation to what is different from self, an existence in encounters, and thus with an analysis concerned with the appropriate conceptuality in which such can occur.[67]

With Bultmann, "historical-temporal interpretation" takes on new definition. In contrast to an interpretation that views everything from a distance, sees nothing in history that raises a claim and is thus encountered as authority, existential interpretation is determined by the *tua res agitur* ("the matter has to do with you"). Bultmann writes,

> Precisely this is the decisive question: whether we encounter history in such fashion that we recognize *its claim on us,* that it has *something new* to say to us.[68]

Or again, "that word which we speak about history is necessarily also a word about ourselves."[69] For such an interpretation, Bultmann continued, encounter with history is itself a temporal event in which the word of the text retains its temporality.[70] At issue, he concluded, is simply "historical understanding, historical science." Just as every new situation in life subjects me to inquiry and yields the possibility of understanding myself anew, so every text. The modern understanding of historical reality therefore consists in seeing it as "the reality of the historically existing person."[71]

---

67. Bultmann, "Das Problem der Hermeneutik," pp. 231-34.

68. Bultmann, "Das Problem einer theologischen Exegese des Neuen Testaments," p. 17.

69. Bultmann, "Das Problem einer theologischen Exegese des Neuen Testaments," p. 21.

70. Bultmann, "Das Problem einer theologischen Exegese des Neuen Testaments," p. 29.

71. Bultmann, "Die Bedeutung der 'dialektischen Theologie' für die neutestament-

"Objectivity" as well takes on new definition with Bultmann. Objectivity, in terms of neutral observation, of determining historical reality by means of method, had to be abandoned.[72] On the other hand, knowledge appropriate to the object when set within a particular formulation of the question was "objective." In this instance, Bultmann stated, to call the formulation of the question "subjective" would be senseless. As he wrote,

> the requirement that the interpreter must silence his subjectivity, must extinguish his individuality in order to arrive at objective knowledge, is thus the most senseless thinkable. It has meaning and right only insofar as it means that the interpreter must silence his personal desires respecting the result of the interpretation. . . . The "most subjective" interpretation is in this case the "most objective," that is, only the one moved by the question of his own existence can listen to the claim of the text.[73]

With Bultmann, the slogan "dialectical theology" likewise took on new definition. "Dialectical theology" did not denote a method of research, but rather "insight into the historicity of human existence," or into "the historicity of speaking about God."[74] But again, because God was not an objectively ascertainable world-phenomenon, that speaking about God had to be speaking of human existence.

Bultmann was clear: the results of interpretation could not be guaranteed or controlled as a methodological exegesis assumed. The possibilities of understanding the text were as inexhaustible as the possibilities growing out of the I-Thou encounter.[75] For this reason, preliminary understanding could never be closed off, nor could the understanding of a text ever be ultimate, since the text "speaks into existence" and requires an ever new response.[76] In a letter to Karl Barth sent in December 1935,

---

liche Wissenschaft," pp. 128, 132; idem, "Zum Problem der Entmythologisierung" (1963), in *Glauben und Verstehen,* vol. 4 (Tübingen: J. C. B. Mohr, 1965), p. 129.

72. Bultmann, "Das Problem einer theologischen Exegese des Neuen Testaments," p. 24.

73. Bultmann, "Das Problem der Hermeneutik," p. 230.

74. Bultmann, "Die Bedeutung der 'dialektischen Theologie' für die neutestamentliche Wissenschaft," p. 118.

75. Bultmann, "Das Problem einer theologischen Exegese des Neuen Testaments," p. 30.

76. Bultmann, "Ist voraussetzungslose Exegese möglich?" p. 149.

Bultmann described Barth's sermons as difficult to endure. "With you," he wrote,

> the text is interrogated according to a dogmatic formula and does not speak with its own voice. After a few sentences we already know everything you are going to say, and only on occasion ask, now, how is he going to extract all that from the following words of the text? . . . I am not engaged by this exegesis; the text does not speak to me. Instead, the cover of dogmatics is thrown over it.[77]

Exegesis thus functions as guide, but it is also a question the answer to which must always be new. If, Bultmann wrote, understanding a text means grasping the text's own understanding of existence from out of the exegetes' openness toward their own existence and its possibilities, then, in the given instance, a conclusive *(abschliessendes)* understanding of a text is basically possible. But then he added,

> of course, such an understanding is never a "result of science," such as is possessed and handed on. It always has "dialectical" character. . . . Scientific work is, of course, infinite because our conceptuality is constantly developing and thus in each generation the task of interpretation is taken up afresh.[78]

Again, since the interpreters' understanding could only correspond to the degree of their openness to their existence, their understanding could never have the character of a result of research. Rather, it was "dialectical," not because it would be limited or supplemented by an opposing sentence, but because it had to be won ever anew.

Thus far, what Bultmann wrote of historical understanding applied to interpretation as such. In his 1925 essay on the problem of a theological exegesis, he wrote that what is peculiar to New Testament interpretation is that it may remain within the circle of so-called profane exegesis, but that it is met by the assertion of the New Testament that on one's own no one controls existence even to the point of being able to put the question of existence. This, Bultmann insisted, would be possible only for faith.

---

77. Quoted in Hammann, *Rudolf Bultmann: Eine Biographie,* p. 320.

78. Bultmann, "Die Bedeutung der 'dialektischen Theologie' für die neutestamentliche Wissenschaft," p. 123.

The decisive question for understanding the New Testament would then be whether or not the requirement of faith is met. But this would render the exegete's situation a total impossibility since the New Testament not only denies that the interpreter is capable of making this decision, but actually asserts that by oneself one cannot know what faith is since such knowledge results only from an exegesis that proceeds from faith. Even the question put to the text, if it is to be proper, must proceed from faith. So then, Bultmann asked, would readiness for a question derived from faith have to be assumed with the exegete? This would require leaping over one's own shadow. Everything, the entire enterprise, is for nothing when viewed in the way just described, when viewed "in principle," since the exegete is still being observed in the abstract preferred by the "profane exegete." The situation is this: exegesis of the New Testament is a task for the one who stands in the tradition of the church of the Word. Only when this means I am not observed from the outside as an individual historical datum, but that together with my existence I stand in the tradition of the Word, is there such preparedness for an exegesis from out of faith. The possibility of a theological exegesis of the New Testament "in principle" does not exist. Proper inquiry into the text can only be one of faith, that is, grounded in obedience to the authority of scripture. Theological exegesis would thus be an exegesis for which faith is a presupposition, but then it can only be ventured and never rooted or grounded since the interpreter has no control over the presupposition. In his Göttingen lecture Bultmann stated that in method the exegesis of the New Testament must follow the universal standards of scientific text interpretation, but it becomes a meaningful undertaking only insofar as, as a theological exegesis, it presupposes faith. In so doing it corresponds to "theology as such," which likewise presupposes faith without bringing this presupposition under control.

Exegesis is thus in the same situation as theology, meaningful only under the assumption, under the presupposition, of faith.[79] Later, Bultmann would write that faith may see in a given event an action of God, and, in a quite specific sense, in the appearance of Jesus Christ. This, wrote Bultmann, spells paradox, that is, the assertion that an event that touches me in my existence is able to touch me or become present to me in quite another sense, and thus becomes "eschatological event." Naturally, since God is not objectively ascertainable, and thus his activity can only be spo-

79. Bultmann, "Das Problem einer theologischen Exegese des neuen Testaments," pp. 32-33.

ken of in such fashion that human existence is also spoken of, that is, "analogically," the understanding that one is called to life and borne by God's almighty power can only be expressed as confession.[80]

Bultmann gave the clearest illustration of his interpretive method in what is often labeled his "demythologization program," a procedure originally intended merely to arouse discussion without offering a final solution. Bultmann first used the term "demythologizing" in a 1934 review of a volume by Heinz-Dietrich Wendland (1900-1992) of Heidelberg on Jesus' understanding of the kingdom of God.[81] Five years later, at a conference in Denmark in 1939, and at another at Frankfurt am Main in 1941, and at still another in Alpirsbach of the same year, he gave meaning to the term in his celebrated lecture on "The New Testament and Mythology." In it he stated that the worldview of the New Testament and its description of the saving event are mythological, its central motifs those of Jewish apocalyptic and the gnostic redeemer myth. Since this worldview has become obsolete in the twentieth century, mythological language exceeds credibility. The worldview of natural science and modern self-understanding rule out adherence to the mythological ideas of the New Testament. But unlike natural science, which eliminates the mythological, historical science must interpret it, must put the question concerning the meaning of mythological language, itself an historical phenomenon. Though the mythological may run contrary to its real intent through naively objectifying what is beyond *(jenseits)* as on this side *(diesseits),* thus through conceiving transcendence as spatially distant, "demythologizing" intends to give validity to the actual, genuine intention of the myth, that is, to speak of a reality that lies beyond the objectifiable and observable but is nevertheless of decisive significance for human life. It intends to speak of the world and human existence as having their basis and limit in a power beyond their control.[82] Behind the term "demythologizing," demonstrably liable to considerable misinterpretation, thus better represented by the phrase "existential interpretation," lay the intention to render the New Testament proclamation intelligible to twentieth-century readers and hearers. This analysis, Bultmann added, did not presume to establish a relation between the interpreter relative to the interpreter's own existence and the reality to be understood. That

---

80. Bultmann, "Zum Problem der Entmythologisierung," pp. 135-36.

81. See Bultmann, *Theologie als Kritik,* p. 309: "In the first chapter (the idea of God and the kingdom of God) the concept of the kingdom of God is in essence removed from the sphere of the mythological. . . . This demythologizing is not executed consistently."

82. Bultmann, "Zum Problem der Entmythologisierung," pp. 133-34.

relation was rather assumed. Again, interpretation of the Bible assumed the question about God alive in human life. What this analysis did do was to clarify the character of genuine historical decision and thus the decision of faith in encounter with the biblical proclamation.[83] Among the New Testament motifs Bultmann declared to be out of date *(erledigt)* and in need of reinterpretation he listed the story of Christ's ascension, faith in spirits and demons, miracles as actual events, the mythological eschatology, the idea of the supernatural activity of the Spirit and the sacraments, the notion of death as punishment for sin, Christ's death as satisfaction, and the understanding of the resurrection as a physical event. In a sermon on the text of Luke 5:11, preached in July 1941, Bultmann stated that Christian faith did not require of anyone a *sacrificium intellectus,* specifically, a holding to the New Testament miracles as historical events, contrary to all experience. Christian faith consisted rather in faith in Jesus Christ as liberator from law and death.[84] Respecting earliest Christianity's expectation of Christ's imminent return, as early as 1917 he stated that such eschatological consciousness was a historically necessary yet time-conditioned cover for early Christianity's psychic state but not essential to New Testament religion.[85]

All in all, as he himself stated, Bultmann's hermeneutic or approach to interpretation represented an attempt to unite the "decisive knowledge of so-called dialectical theology with the inheritance of so-called liberal theology," at the same time retaining a critical relation to both.[86] In his statements on exegesis and interpretation he acknowledged indebtedness to the standards of liberal theology touching historical research, and to the basic hermeneutical reflections laid down for Bible exposition by his teachers Gunkel and Weiss, as well as by William Wrede (1859-1906), a chief representative of the History of Religions School. From Weiss he learned that the "ultimate goal of exegesis" is not "to be acquainted with the basic ideas but rather to grasp the individual phenomena, the individual writing, the individual sentence."[87] Among the six books that he described as of decisive significance for his own work as theologian and New Testament interpreter he listed the work of another representative of

83. Bultmann, "In eigener Sache," pp. 179-82.
84. Quoted in Hammann, *Rudolf Bultmann: Eine Biographie,* p. 329.
85. Rudolf Bultmann, "Die Bedeutung der Eschatologie fur die Religion des Neuen Testaments," *Zeitschrift für Theologie und Kirche* 27 (1917): 81.
86. Bultmann, "In eigener Sache," p. 178.
87. Quoted in Hammann, *Rudolf Bultmann: Eine Biographie,* p. 50.

the History of Religions School, namely, Carl Heinrich Weizsäcker's *Das apostolische Zeitalter der christlichen Kirche*.[88] In the outline of his *Theology of the New Testament* he was indebted in not a few instances to the work of Wrede and Wilhelm Bousset (1865-1920), the other chief representative of the History of Religions School. Finally, respecting his own philosophical premises of interpretation he was guided by Søren Kierkegaard (1813-55), but especially by the phenomenological analysis of Dasein of onetime colleague Martin Heidegger.

Finally, a great gulf separated Bultmann and Barth, the two giants of twentieth-century theology, over the matter of presuppositions in the interpretation of the Bible. But their struggle to interpret its message for what Bultmann called "the aggravatedly modern man" urges a certain similarity, called up, for example, from an homage paid to Barth by Paul Louis Lehmann (1906-94), student of Barth and intimate of the martyred Dietrich Bonhoeffer (1906-45), professor of ethics and systematic theology at Princeton Theological Seminary, Harvard Divinity School, and Union Theological Seminary in New York. Lehmann may not have been the first, but he was certainly among the few to describe Barth's deliverance of theological language and conceptuality from bondage to propositional logic by joining them again to poetry. In the first section of his homage to Barth entitled "Dogmatics and Language," Lehmann wrote that Barth's early critics were confused by this move, owing to their conviction that rational coherence buttressed by scientific empirical verifiability was the surest liberation of theology from verbal and textual inerrancy. "What Barth was exploring," Lehmann continued, "was the metaphorical content and meaning of the language of dogmatics," an exploration reflected in his injunction to the higher critical interpreters of scripture as contained in the preface to his second edition of the *Commentary on Romans:* "Lassen die Kritiker noch kritischer werden!" The secret behind this hostility, Lehmann contended, lay in ignorance of Barth's pioneering a metaphorical interpretation of the knowledge and obedience of faith. In support of his argument, Lehmann referred to the opening sections of the *Church Dogmatics,* to extended sections on "Legend and Story," "God's Time and Ours," "The Miracle of Christmas," "The Divine Perfections," "The Angels," "Election and Ethics." "These dogmatic labors," Lehmann continued, "brought [Barth] to the transforming edge of the world of today and of the church of today and tomorrow in their need and search for 'an essential

---

88. See Hammann, *Rudolf Bultmann: Eine Biographie,* p. 443.

metaphor.'" In a final paragraph of this section, Lehmann summarized the results of those labors:

> Among fellow-seekers on the left have been those who, having left the faith behind, strangely find themselves in the vestibule of faith and in search of a center of meaning, purpose and hope for their lives.[89]

To the authors in the presentation volume prepared for his eightieth birthday, as well as to those listed in the *Tabula Gratulatoria,* Bultmann replied:

> but I am also ashamed and can only conclude my thanks by recalling words from the Bible with which I once ended my lecture at leaving office: Gen. 32:10; I Cor. 4:7.[90]

Chicago, Harvard, Yale, Union, Princeton

The Chicago School

In the "first generation" of the Chicago School (1892-1920), advocates of historical criticism as well as its opponents regarded the attack on biblical authority as an assault from the outside.[91] William Rainey Harper (1856-1906), who may be said to have inaugurated the Chicago School, passionately concerned for scripture, for its rightful place as the basis of faith, and hence for its correct interpretation, concentrated on the Old Testament as the locus of imminent threat. In an editorial of 1889 he wrote:

89. Paul Lehmann, "The Ant and the Emperor," in *How Karl Barth Changed My Mind,* ed. Donald K. McKim (Grand Rapids: Eerdmans, 1986), pp. 41-42.

90. Gen. 32:10: "I am not worthy of the least of all the steadfast love and all the faithfulness that you have shown to your servant"; 1 Cor. 4:7: "For who sees anything different in you? What do you have that you did not receive? And if you received it, why do you boast as if it were not a gift?"

91. For the material in this section, I am heavily indebted to two essays delivered at the annual meeting of the Society of Biblical Literature in Chicago, 1975, the first by Robert W. Funk (1926-2005), entitled "The Watershed of the American Biblical Tradition: The Chicago School, First Phase, 1892-1920," and the other by Ernest Cadman Colwell (1901-74), entitled "The Chicago School of Biblical Interpretation."

The cry of our times is for the application of scientific methods in the study of the Bible . . . if the methods of the last century continue to hold exclusive sway, the time will come when intelligent men of all classes will say, "If this is our Bible we will have none of it."[92]

Though aware of the threat posed by the new science, Harper did not view it in the same terms as did, for example, the conservative William Henry Green (1825-1900) of Princeton. He was actually prepared to capitalize on it, and in 1887 gave an optimistic assessment of it:

We speak of a revival of interest in the study of the Bible. Are we in the midst of it? We are rather on the eve of it. For the present is as night in the brilliance of that day, not far distant, when the Bible shall be more widely known and its authority more widely recognized.[93]

After moving his work to Yale in 1886, where he held chairs in the Graduate Department and Divinity School and later a third in Yale College, he returned to Chicago in 1892. Interest in biblical study dictated the shape of the new Chicago divinity faculty, but since the Americans were largely defenseless in face of the German criticism, Harper set to work to meet the challenge. He held out the high standards of German scholarship and encouraged Americans to emulate them, while warning against "destructive criticism." Enthusiastic in his estimate of the constructive possibilities of higher criticism, Harper never lost his conviction that "evangelical truth" would triumph and the divine word be vindicated. In *The Hebrew Student,* inaugurated in 1882 when agitation over critical study of the Old Testament was at its peak, he wrote that the prejudices against higher criticism were unreasonable, and to be deprecated. "The church," he stated, "is challenged to meet the issue. It is a call of Providence to conflict and to triumph of evangelical truth. The divine word will vindicate itself in all its parts."[94] Again and again he reiterated his conviction that after higher criticism had its erosive effect on the human element in scripture, a residuum of the divine would remain. "We confidently affirm," he wrote, "that there is such a residuum which stamps the Scripture as an authoritative rule of faith and practice."[95] He argued that

92. William Rainey Harper, *The Old and New Testament Student* 9 (1889): 1f.
93. William Rainey Harper, *The Old Testament Student* 6 (1887): 193.
94. William Rainey Harper, *The Hebrew Student* 2 (1882-83): 218.
95. William Rainey Harper, *The Old Testament Student* 8 (1888-89): 162.

respecting those portions of scripture whose authenticity is not confirmed by criticism and whose truth cannot be verified by experience one could appeal to the experience of others for whom that teaching was confirmed and then infer that other matters in the same document were also true.[96] In this way, Harper could affirm the normative, authoritative character of scripture and yet indulge the full rights of the higher critic. It was clear, however, that by "higher criticism" Harper meant philological expertise. Philological expertise, the immediate issue of which was translation into the current idiom, furnished the solution to the hermeneutical problem. It was in this domain that Chicago scholarship represented little more than a rehearsal of German theories. Yet this was the point of the most hostile contact with orthodoxy on the one side, and the realm that offered the greatest hope for the reconciliation of science and biblical religion on the other. The consequence of this accent on method, on philological expertise, was that the problem of scriptural authority was never addressed on internal grounds. Moreover, the posture was anti-theological, intent on divesting itself of pre-modern dogmatic theology, though anxious to win academic respectability. The Chicago School of biblical interpretation was so sure it was empirical (i.e., scientific) that it felt no need of philosophy or theology. This confidence rested on the obvious soundness of its methodology and the expertise of its champions in pioneering research. In his preface to the Chicago Faculty's 1916 publication *A Guide to the Study of the Christian Religion,* Gerald Birney Smith (1868-1929) wrote:

> The only common presuppositions of the various portions are the acceptance of the historical method and the belief that the interpretation of Christianity must be in accord with the rightful tests of scientific truthfulness and actual vitality in the modern world.[97]

Interest in theology was taboo.

When Harper returned to Chicago in 1892, he needed a New Testament counterpart, and chose Ernest DeWitt Burton (1856-1925). It was Burton who gave the first explicit statement respecting the direction the Chicago School of biblical interpretation would take. The statement was titled "The Function of Interpretation in Relation to Theology."[98] Inter-

96. William Rainey Harper, *The Biblical World* 11 (1898): 228.
97. (Chicago: University of Chicago Press, 1916), p. vii.
98. Ernest DeWitt Burton, "The Function of Interpretation in Relation to Theology," *The American Journal of Theology* 2 (1898).

pretation, Burton wrote, has its object in the uncovering of meanings. The truth of interpretation, however, has nothing directly to do with theological truth. The interpreter does not ask whether the testimony of a witness is true in the theological sense, but only whether it is true to the intention of the witness. If, in fact, the interpreter raises the question of ultimate truth, "he is in danger of vitiating his own work."[99] By thus forcing the truth question upon it, the interpreter would be treating the Bible with "gross irreverence," making it echo his own convictions. It is a legitimate function of the biblical interpreter to determine the thoughts of the biblical authors, but in this form the interpretation has nothing whatever to do with the truth of these thoughts.[100] On the other hand, literary interpretation could not accomplish the whole task; it needed to be supplemented by the interpretation of facts.[101] To the question of how the interpreter was to determine the facts, say, in distinction from the thoughts of the biblical authors, Burton responded that biblical criticism was the process by which to determine the facts.

> With the facts before him, dealing no longer with records, but with events, searching no longer for thoughts, but for truths, his task will be to find in this unparalleled history the great truths of divine revelation. Then will he be able, on solid and substantial ground, to construct the doctrine of scripture, the doctrine, that is, of the nature of revelation made in the Bible, and of the character of the books that the Bible contains. On the basis of such a doctrine he will be able to rear the complete and solid structure of the truth of God revealed in the Bible. And not only so, but he will also be able to verify the results thus reached by an independent process of investigation. For the same material and the same process by which he will reach this doctrine will enable him, in large measure at least, to reach independently the other truths which he seeks concerning God and man in their mutual relations.[102]

Thus, if one first uses the biblical documents together with such extrabiblical sources as are available in order to establish the correlative history, he may then employ the correlative history to establish the biblical

---

99. Burton, "The Function of Interpretation," p. 53.
100. Burton, "The Function of Interpretation," p. 58.
101. Burton, "The Function of Interpretation," pp. 61ff.
102. Burton, "The Function of Interpretation," p. 69.

documents. The argument was circular, and reflected Burton's resistance to orthodoxy's excluding the narrative portions in favor of the didactic portions of the Bible as the direct, unmediated thoughts of God,[103] and his desire to give priority to the narrative history as well as to emphasize the human element in biblical interpretation. In making these moves Burton was reversing the position of Harper and his orthodox predecessors, and preparing for what has been termed "the second Chicago generation."

In fine, the first generation of the Chicago School was grounded in philological expertise. Its members had mastered lower and higher criticism. Edgar Johnson Goodspeed (1871-1962) may be taken as a representative product of the Chicago School in its earlier days. Of the 251 books and articles listed in his 1948 bibliography, 169 were published before 1927. Of these 103 were technical philology, for the most part the study of manuscripts and linguistic data. In the list of books, 10 of the first 11 are technical philology.

To that "second Chicago generation" Shailer Mathews (1863-1941) belonged. Appointed by Burton, Mathews became chief representative of the modernist movement emanating from Chicago. He joined with Burton in shifting the authority of the Bible as text from the text itself to the men who wrote the texts. Modernists, Mathews wrote, "believe "in the inspiration of men, not of words. Men were inspired because they inspire."[104] In other respects Mathews echoed Burton. For example, he wrote that the modernist strives to determine the facts, to arrange the texts in chronological order, and to place each document in its wider historical context.[105] When this is done, the meaning of the Bible clearly emerges. Wanting to have the best of both worlds, Mathews insisted that "revelation must conform to the realities of the universe,"[106] and that the Bible is "a trustworthy record of the human experience of God."[107] In view of his understanding of the social process he was completely at one with Harper and thus qualified assumed the deanship of the Divinity School in 1907. The systematician-philosopher George Burman Foster (1858-1919), of whom his colleagues stood in awe, disdained to deliver Christian faith into the hands of the biblical critics, not merely because they were likely to settle for a fixed quantum like Jesus, Paul, or the primitive church, but because religion then would

---

103. Burton, "The Function of Interpretation," pp. 63f.
104. Shailer Mathews, *The Faith of Modernism* (New York: Macmillan, 1925), p. 52.
105. Mathews, *The Faith of Modernism*, pp. 37ff.
106. Mathews, *The Faith of Modernism*, p. 47.
107. Mathews, *The Faith of Modernism*, p. 47.

be understood as knowledge, technical skill, something to be taught and learned.[108] Biblical criticism served to drive us from false objects, wrote Foster,[109] but it could never provide faith with its true object. Certainty in historical science could not effect or affect religious certainty.[110]

The most radical of the second-generation scholars was Shirley Jackson Case (1916-65). Trained at Yale by Benjamin Wisner Bacon (1860-1932) and Frank Chamberlain Porter (1859-1946), he directed his fire at German and American liberals and orthodox alike. He pointed out that the higher critics' interest in the authorship and date of documents, the two-document solution to the Synoptic Problem, even form criticism, was highly deceptive, unless it was all to be understood as preliminary to the real task.[111] However important the documents, it was the social context that deserved attention.[112] In other words, the interpreter's task was to focus on the social process attaching to the evolutionary or developmental understanding of Christianity. The work of higher criticism, therefore, was only preparatory to the work of the modern historian. The student of the New Testament should abandon the techniques of traditional scholarship. Clearly, Case had moved steadily away from the New Testament toward defining his discipline as the social history of early Christianity. From Mathews's continued concern with social action Case turned to scholarship. This shift explains the minimal role played by Mathews in the continued development of the Chicago School after 1925. Together with G. B. Smith, Case set the stage for the emergence of the second major phase at Chicago, and put an end to the dominance of the biblical question. Whereas Harper and Burton had specialized in the biblical languages, written grammars, and produced commentaries, now such studies were conspicuous by their absence. Philological expertise died, and the older forms of scholarship were rejected, including the literary-critical work of contemporary German scholarship. For once the Bible was abandoned as the anchor of the tradition, there was no reason to continue with disci-

108. George Burman Foster, *The Finality of the Christian Religion* (Chicago: University of Chicago Press, 1906), p. 282.

109. Foster, *The Finality of the Christian Religion*, p. 403.

110. Foster, *The Finality of the Christian Religion*, pp. 329f.

111. Shirley Jackson Case, *The Social Origins of Christianity* (Chicago: University of Chicago Press, 1923), pp. 21-32; idem, *Jesus: A New Biography* (Chicago: University of Chicago Press, 1927), pp. 73ff., 94f., 103f.

112. Shirley Jackson Case, "The Historical Study of Religion," *The Journal of Religion* 1 (1921): 4.

plines oriented primarily to its interpretation. From now on, the Chicago School was basically sociological-historical. Since the New Testament was created by that social movement called Christianity, social-historical study provided the only sound approach to the New Testament. In 1925 the original concern with philological studies had passed its peak. Burton was no longer teaching, and the loss of philological interest created by his absence was not compensated for. Case shared his older colleagues' desire to communicate the authentic meaning of scripture to the public in a usable way. But his particular dedication was to the establishment of the "authentic meaning" by way of socio-historical methods. Thus, in the Chicago School, the concept of man or woman was social, epistemology was social, Christian ethics was social, theology was social psychology. This limitation brought an end to the Chicago School. With the waning of exegetical theology and the study of the biblical languages the authoritative or normative function of scripture in theology was abandoned.

Harvard

The trajectory charted by Mathews and Case did not affect the course of biblical scholarship in America. The "second generation" was unable to perpetuate itself. Harper survived and came to prevail nearly everywhere but at Chicago. In general, biblical scholars were largely preoccupied with textual and literary criticism, often relegating the hermeneutical question to random comments in the margins. There were exceptions, among them Kirsopp Lake and Henry Joel Cadbury of Harvard.

Kirsopp Lake was born in Southampton, England, in 1872. He attended St. Paul's School in London and Lincoln College at Oxford. After ordination into the Church of England he was curate of St. Mary the Virgin, Oxford, from 1897 to 1904. At Oxford Lake began his academic career, publishing *The Text of the New Testament*.[113] In 1904 he became professor of early Christian literature at the University of Leiden, and remained there until 1913. In 1914 he was invited to join the faculty of Harvard University, and five years later was appointed to a chair as Winn Professor of Ecclesiastical History, a position he retained until his retirement in 1938. Lake's interest in archaeology resulted in several excavations in the Near East, projects that were interrupted by World War II. His contributions to bib-

---

113. Kirsopp Lake, *The Text of the New Testament* (London: Rivingtons, 1900, 1943).

lical study include the five-volume study entitled *The Beginnings of Christianity,* co-authored with F. J. Foakes-Jackson (1855-1941), from 1916 to 1934 Briggs Professor of Christian Institutions at Union Theological Seminary in New York, and his separating out from the so-called Western family of New Testament texts a group now known as Family I or the Lake group. Lake died in South Pasadena, California, in 1946.

In what was greeted at the time as a magisterial volume on Paul's earlier epistles, Lake paid tribute to Ferdinand Christian Baur and the Tübingen critics, writing that "there is no school to whom we are so much indebted. . . . Largely owing to their efforts we are able in many respects to improve on their results."[114] In *The Beginnings of Christianity* Lake included a preface advocating application of "the imaginative faculties" in the analysis of the biblical materials.[115] Such comments were largely relegated to the margin, with preeminence given textual and literary matters.[116] Lake, however, did not dismiss the questions of interpretation out of hand. In a volume dealing with the evidence for Christ's resurrection[117] he gave considerable space to the problem of interpretation. First of all, in arguing the authenticity of Jesus' appearances to his disciples, he suggested that "spiritual experience" can throw light on the meaning of events historically vouched for by other means. But, he added, since such experience cannot replace those means, the problem of Christ's resurrection deserves analysis by way of historical research. After recounting the reports of the resurrection in Paul, the Synoptists, John, the apocryphal literature, and earliest Christian tradition, Lake arrived at his discussion of the facts behind that tradition in the chapter entitled "The Facts which are behind the Earliest Tradition." There he concluded that the narrative of the empty tomb, as well as the reference to "the third day" were "improper" inferences drawn from the "fact" of the resurrection. That fact is defined objectively, not as

114. See Kirsopp Lake, *The Earlier Epistles of St. Paul* (London: Rivingtons, 1914), p. 116, n. 3.

115. See F. J. Foakes-Jackson and Kirsopp Lake, *The Beginnings of Christianity* (London: Macmillan, 1922), I, vol. 2, pp. vi-xi.

116. The reference to the contribution of Baur and the Tübingen School appears in a footnote. In an introduction to the New Testament co-authored with his wife, Lake states that the book "gives the general basis of the modern study of the New Testament, but makes no attempt to build on it, or to deal with the theological, philosophical or ecclesiastical problems which are either its cause or effect"; see Kirsopp Lake and Silva Lake, *An Introduction to the New Testament* (New York: Harper & Brothers Publishers, 1937), p. ix.

117. Kirsopp Lake, *The Historical Evidence for the Resurrection of Jesus Christ* (London: Williams & Norgate, 1922).

the resuscitation of a material body ("many of us . . . would not welcome the prospect of the resuscitation of that body of flesh and blood which is so often a hindrance"), but as the survival of human personality after death, and its power under certain circumstances to communicate with the living. In support of his definition, Lake appealed to recent psychic research, in particular to Frederic William Henry Myers (1843-1901), pioneer in the subliminal regions of consciousness. He then proceeded to define the fact subjectively, in terms of an unconscious thought that suddenly reaches the plane of consciousness, and manifests itself there in the form of "appearances." Thus, although criticism and philosophy may give reason for describing as unhistorical or subjective the appearances of Christ as related in the tradition, they cannot impugn the fact of those appearances, at least the fact as defined above. By means of this objective-subjective view of the resurrection, Lake demythologized earliest Christian tradition in face of a generation "hesitating whether it will hear or whether it will forbear, on any purely theological argument or on the accuracy of the narratives of any event in the past."[118]

Questions of biblical interpretation were given even greater attention by Lake's Quaker colleague, Henry Joel Cadbury (1883-1974). The celebrated founder and leader of the American Friends Service Committee was born in Philadelphia in 1883. He graduated from Haverford College in 1903, then attended Harvard University from which he received his Ph.D. degree. In 1910 he returned to Haverford to teach biblical literature. In 1918, for speaking out against the American "orgy of hate" against Germans, a large group of the Haverford alumni demanded his resignation, newspapers attacked him as a German dupe, and the United States Attorney's office threatened to arrest him on sedition charges. Under fire at Haverford, he resigned his teaching position, but was subsequently hired by the administrators at Harvard, where he taught from 1919 to 1954, interrupted by a six-year term at Bryn Mawr (1925-34). Cadbury spent his last twenty years at Harvard as Hollis Professor of Divinity.

For the most part, Cadbury's comments on interpretation did not appear in his major or best known works, such as *The Making of Luke-Acts* or *The Peril of Modernizing Jesus,* but rather in his essays and reviews. These make clear that the questions of interpretation did not enjoy pride of place with him. In an essay near the beginning of his career he wrote that "the interpretation of the New Testament is not in itself a branch of criticism

118. Lake, *The Historical Evidence,* pp. 4, 244-46, 258-59, 272, 274-76, 278.

but merely a tool," then added that the researches of an earlier century had been delayed and were still being delayed "by artificial theories and presuppositions about interpretation."[119] Toward the middle of his career he wrote that textual criticism was the "most obvious area for both specialization and collaboration,"[120] and toward its end wrote that since a total understanding of the New Testament ultimately depended on what it says or means, "one cannot but claim some credit for him whose interest is the pedestrian one of the grammarian, or for the translator, whose occupation is most frustrating."[121]

Having made clear where his priority lay, Cadbury proceeded to give space to the questions and problems attaching to Bible interpretation. One aspect that interested him was what he termed the "social translation of the gospel." Whether or not it reflected influence from the side of the "second generation" of the Chicago School, Cadbury did not state. In any case, he described the social task of the church as "the leading religious question of the day," a question that required the process of translation. In an essay entitled "The Social Translation of the Gospel," Cadbury first noted that the teaching of Jesus as recorded in the oldest and most reliable strata of the tradition was not primarily social; what social motive there was, with its apparent individualism, was more or less alien to contemporary readers. Next, Cadbury registered a lack of a definition of "collective duty," and finally noted the absence of "social motive" in the Gospels. As he put it, "nearly every form of social ideal is conspicuous by its absence." He then proceeded to list what was needed for a social translation. At the outset, it demanded study of "the underlying basis." No educated minister, he wrote, dare evade it. This meant that one could not accept the "second-hand" work of others, but had to study the life and teaching of Jesus, keep constantly qualified to consult the original, and as far as possible live in its atmosphere and spirit. These three, then, were the first objects of study: the problems of Jesus' time, Jesus' attitude toward them, and the problems of contemporary life. This basis established, the task of interpretation followed. Cadbury wrote:

119. Henry Joel Cadbury, "Divine Inspiration and the New Testament," in *Outline of Christianity,* The Story of Our Civilization in Five Volumes, vol. 4 (New York: Bethlehem Publishers; Dodd, Mead, 1926), p. 373.

120. Henry Joel Cadbury, "New Testament Study in the Next Generation," *The Journal of Religion* 21 (1941): 419.

121. Henry Joel Cadbury, "Current Issues in New Testament Studies," *Harvard Divinity School Bulletin* 51 (1954): 53.

Translating the gospel socially is one that is worthy of exceptional mental powers, exceptional moral earnestness, exceptional fidelity and honesty. Translation in the case of books in foreign languages too often means expurgation, paraphrase, — the watering down of the original to the effete or prudish tastes of our day. The social translation of the gospel must be accurate and unadulterated, true to the spirit of Jesus, and never shrinking to declare the whole counsel of God.[122]

Cadbury did not make clear how such "translation" should occur. Elsewhere, he would make repeated reference to the interpreter's task as understanding the "mind" of the biblical writer, allowing the inference that any "social translation" or "translation" of any other type would come by way of that understanding. "It is surely gain," he wrote in "The Social Translation of the Gospel," that "we can often think our way into the pulsing heart of the early Church and its leaders."[123] In "Divine Inspiration and the New Testament," he wrote that the modern critic "wishes to understand the writer's mind," for which reason "the underlying basis" needed tending to.[124] In "New Testament Study in the Next Generation," he described the task as "thorough acclimatization into the temper and mentality of the ancient world," adding that since, for example, in the Pauline letters, the apostle's "distinctive personality shines out in many traits that are psychological rather than religious or literary," an attractive task awaited scholars.[125] In the same article he spoke of the opportunity "to live more profoundly into the human experience behind the early records."[126] The interpretive task, then, took on a psychological cast. "I find myself," Cadbury wrote, "much more intrigued with curiosity about how the writers got that way than with knowing who they were. These problems are psychological rather than literary." Here, he added, lay a relatively neglected area, though the Germans had given it attention a generation earlier in the *religionsgeschichtliche* (History of Religions) study of the New Testament.[127] To this interpretive approach Cadbury gave the name "motive criticism."

122. Henry Joel Cadbury, "The Social Translation of the Gospel," *Harvard Theological Review* 15 (January 1922): 13.
123. Cadbury, "The Social Translation of the Gospel," p. 393.
124. Cadbury, "Divine Inspiration and the New Testament," p. 374.
125. Cadbury, "New Testament Study in the Next Generation," p. 415.
126. Cadbury, "New Testament Study in the Next Generation," p. 418.
127. Cadbury, "Current Issues in New Testament Studies," p. 54.

Just as Form-Criticism is a stage prior to Source-Criticism, so what I may call Motive-Criticism should precede them both. In looking at an item in the gospels one should ask systematically — what motive led to the preservation and shaping of this item? . . . How helpful it would be — but how difficult — if we could see ourselves and our prejudices, as we try to see the interests of earlier scholars and even those of the evangelists![128]

Despite these hints at a psychological approach, Cadbury did not flesh them out. In fact, they might even be subsumed under the literary-critical task. For example, in *The Making of Luke-Acts,* he wrote that "the revelation of the author's own personality and point of view must be reckoned as an historic contribution of the first importance," adding that though the writer does not bring his own personality into his writings, it can in part be recovered from them, but then referred to the recovery as occurring by way of "careful literary analysis."[129]

As Cadbury viewed it, the interpretive task was twofold. The historian had to give attention to the "mind of the writer," predicated on attending to that "underlying basis." In other words, the interpreter as historian had to pursue "purely scientific aims." On the other hand, that pursuit needed supplementing in a "strong religious, not to say apologetic, prepossession." As he put it, "the motive of scholarship in this field is still as it has been a combination of search for pure truth and, at least frequently, an expectation of religious serviceableness."[130] Clearly, two interpretive motives were emerging, hence the question, "which shall we choose?" Cadbury replied, "that we are dealing here with a fundamental philosophical enigma of the relation of fact and value must be evident to all of us," but begged leave "not to deal exhaustively with such a problem."[131] "Not to deal exhaustively," however, did not mean to ignore the problem altogether. "There is a sense," he stated, "in which fidelity to the strictest stands of scholarship about the Bible demands all the more from us a responsibility for constructive forces that would counterweigh any destructive, unspiritual results of our labors." This meant that while the "translator" had to be faithful to the "cold standards of history and literary criticism," there could

---

128. Cadbury, "Current Issues in New Testament Studies," pp. 57-58.

129. Henry J. Cadbury, *The Making of Luke-Acts* (London: SPCK, 1968), p. 5.

130. Henry Joel Cadbury, "Motives of Biblical Scholarship," *Journal of Biblical Literature* 56 (1937): 8.

131. Cadbury, "Motives of Biblical Scholarship," p. 13.

be no indifference to the moral, spiritual values and needs of contemporary life. "Fidelity to the best in our professional tradition," he wrote, "both of piety and of open-minded, honest quest for the truth, may prove in the end one of the most satisfying motives for us all."[132]

Cadbury was aware of the perils attendant upon the dual task. "The danger of attempting to combine pure scholarship with an edifying motive" was apparent to all.[133] In an earlier generation the attempt had led to submerging the apocalyptic element in an idea of progress defined as a slow-moving development, "a kind of escalator forever leading us upward." World War I had "badly jolted" this theory. Consequently,

> It might have been well if, instead of our modern evolutionary optimism, we had shared a little in the apocalyptic forethought and watchful anxiety of him who asked, "When the Son of Man cometh, shall he find faith on the earth?"[134]

Further, the task of interpretation had "singularly neglected and abused" the ethical material in the Gospels. According to Cadbury, "even modern and liberal scholars have hurried to apply it, like casuist rules, to present-day issues, or to overlay it with our own social viewpoint."[135] More, dependence on ancient attempts at harmonizing the Gospels driven by the dogma of their uniformity proved unnecessary and fruitless in the face of modern conceptions of unity in diversity, progressive revelation, and development in doctrine.[136] Finally, interpretation was prey to the twin perils of modernizing and archaizing the biblical text. Cadbury wrote of the "over-ready" attempt to modernize Bible times, of the necessity for curbing the "morbid tastes of superficial lay book readers who prefer to hear from us some new guess than some old fact," of keeping ourselves fully *en rapport* with our own time, deliberately placing ourselves and the ancient mentality over against each other.[137]

Archaizing by far, however, constituted the greatest peril. However necessary sympathetic imagination to an understanding of the past, the

132. Cadbury, "Motives of Biblical Scholarship," pp. 14-16.
133. Cadbury, "Motives of Biblical Scholarship," p. 10.
134. Cadbury, "The Social Translation of the Gospel," p. 11.
135. Cadbury, "Results of New Testament Research," p. 389.
136. Cadbury, "Results of New Testament Research," p. 393.
137. Cadbury, "Motives of Biblical Scholarship," p. 11; idem, "The Peril of Archaizing Ourselves," *Interpretation* 3 (1949): 336.

insistence of the "archaizers of Christianity" that the unmodern cosmology of the Bible should be adopted, their mistaking of dramatization for experience, their failure to emulate the confusing but human multiplicity of biblical religion, and their verbalism or embrace of the doctrine of mechanical inspiration, of the biblical text as inspired "literatim et punctatim, as well as verbatim," thus their insistence that "the Bible is either all true or all false" — it all threatened genuine interpretation.[138]

This "tendency" to archaize, Cadbury asserted, had its reflection in the biblical theology movement, essentially different from the ancient brand. It was "Neo-orthodoxy" masquerading as neo-biblicism, a "so-called biblical theology" particularly inappropriate in relation to the Gospels.[139] Here, at least, Cadbury did not separate the emerging biblical theology movement from neo-orthodoxy or dialectical theology, and as he himself admitted, the latter's connection with New Testament criticism eluded him.[140] Proceeding with his criticism he wrote that it is one thing when Paul wrote casual letters to churches with "little allusion" to the life and career of the historical Jesus, but quite another when "a twentieth century theology dealing systematically with the nature and destiny of man shows apparently greater indifference to the content of our Gospels." In Cadbury's mind, Reinhold Niebuhr's (1892-1971) *Nature and Destiny of Man* (1941) marked him as a proponent of the biblical theology movement.[141] The attempt at the imitation of Jesus has had a curious history, wrote Cadbury. It set out in quest of the primitive Christian pattern, believing we could project ourselves directly into the New Testament era. It loosed the bands by which we were fettered to the mentality of the present and strove to free us from the alterations and perversions of modern philosophy, psychology, and science. It rejoiced to feel the life and movement following Pentecost come to us by way of this reversion and to see us retreating to meet Jesus. "But," he asserted, "we do not stay; we pass his time by, and return to our

---

138. Cadbury, "The Peril of Archaizing Ourselves," pp. 332, 336; idem, "Motives of Biblical Scholarship," pp. 4-5.

139. Cadbury, "The Peril of Archaizing Ourselves," p. 333.

140. See Cadbury's statement in "The Present State of New Testament Studies," in *The Haverford Symposium on Archaeology and the Bible* (New Haven: The American Schools of Oriental Research, 1938), p. 109, n. 25. "The significance of Barthianism for New Testament criticism is discussed in an essay which I do not profess to understand, 'Die Bedeutung der dialektische Theologie für die neutestamentliche Wissenschaft,' in R. Bultmann, *Glauben und Verstehen* (Tübingen: J. C. B. Mohr, 1933), I, pp. 114ff."

141. Cadbury, "The Peril of Archaizing Ourselves," p. 334.

own."[142] Cadbury went on to state that though "in a sense a legitimate part of history" biblical theology was a system constructed out of the fragments of thoughts, and regarded as requisite for modern Christians. An aloof or objective attitude to scripture is deprecated. "These theologians," he argued, "claim that only in so far as we share the New Testament belief ourselves can we understand the New Testament," a belief that for them is a permanent standard and norm. "In other words," he added, "the historical approach to religion as we have known it here at Harvard and generally in modern Biblical study is actually challenged by the new approach."[143] That the hard-won achievements of a century of scientific approach should be surrendered for the supposed values of biblical theology involved a loss that Cadbury reckoned deserved more consideration than it had received. Agreeing with biblical theology that religion is to be appreciated only as one recognizes the religious experience as one's own, Cadbury nevertheless saw it as a threat to genuine interpretation. At the end of his article on current issues in New Testament studies, he had this to say:

> I have expressed my apprehension of the deleterious effect of Biblical theology on sound Biblical learning. . . . I have some fear of its effect on the promotion of true religion. We seem to be reverting in it to the pre-scientific treatment of the Bible as the one-track norm of religion. Here, as elsewhere, we are reverting to an extreme of Protestantism. Among the causes for the rise of Biblical Theology I could have included the powerful but indirect influence of Barth.[144]

Cadbury's aversion to the biblical theology movement had nothing to do with anti-European sentiment. He made generous use of the form-critical method pioneered by Martin Dibelius, Karl Ludwig Schmidt (1891-1956), and Rudolf Bultmann. If he did not understand the significance of dialectical theology he was nevertheless thoroughly at home in the new field of research that addressed itself to the question of what lay behind the written record. In what was perhaps the first review of form criticism to appear in this country,[145] Cadbury wrote that for the recovery of the various stages of Gospel history it was time to examine the Gospels themselves

142. Cadbury, "The Peril of Archaizing Ourselves," p. 335.
143. Cadbury, "Current Issues in New Testament Studies," p. 61.
144. Cadbury, "Current Issues in New Testament Studies," p. 63.
145. Henry J. Cadbury, "Between Jesus and the Gospels," *Harvard Theological Review* 16 (1923): 81-92.

and "compel them to divulge the secrets of their past." He then proceeded to summarize the work of Dibelius, Schmidt, and Bultmann, noting the differences and similarities between them in the matter of classification, understanding of origins and influences behind the written documents, and their subsequent editorial treatment. He wrote that such fresh study of the early history of the Gospel material had effects on our understanding that are "generally sound and are most significant." "Synoptic study," he said, "has been excavating the upper strata; we need now to dig down into the older archaeological layers underneath." Finally, he concluded,

> the surpassing interest of the field in which this literary excavation is being carried on should tempt many more workmen of all lands and creeds to join in the search and should rouse the sympathetic attention of those who perforce remain only spectators.[146]

More significant, in *The Making of Luke-Acts,* Cadbury not merely referred to but made extensive use of form-critical method.[147] Robert Funk's statement, to the effect that biblical scholarship in America was virtually untouched by theological developments in Germany, must be restricted to the yet undigested dialectical theology of a Karl Barth or a Rudolf Bultmann.[148] In matters of textual, literary, and form criticism, the opposite was true.

Following his retirement in 1954, Cadbury lectured at Haverford College and Temple University, and for twelve years served as chairman of the board of directors at Bryn Mawr. He died in Haverford in 1974.

Yale

If the scholars at Harvard did not share the conviction that the hermeneutical question could be solved solely through philological expertise,

146. Cadbury, "Between Jesus and the Gospels," p. 92.

147. See Cadbury, *The Making of Luke-Acts,* chapter IV: "Motives in the Transmission of the Material"; chapter V: "Forms in the Transmission of the Material"; and chapter XI: "Popular Forms." Here Cadbury associated form-critical method with that of the Yale scholar Benjamin Bacon (1860-1932), who urged what he termed the "aetiological" study of the Gospels; see Roy A. Harrisville, *Benjamin Wisner Bacon: Pioneer in American Biblical Criticism* (Atlanta: Scholars, 1976).

148. See Funk, "The Watershed of the American Biblical Tradition: The Chicago School, First Phase, 1892-1920," p. 27.

for which reason philosophy or theology as vehicle was to be eschewed, it was also not shared at Yale. During the tenure of Chicago's "first-" and "second-generation" scholars, a Yale professor and former teacher of Shirley Jackson Case was at work engaging the hermeneutical task through furnishing a supplement or complement to the higher criticism. If Frank Chamberlain Porter was not the first American scholar to furnish a supplement, the degree of his concentration on the task set him apart from his contemporaries and justifies assigning him the status of pioneer.[149]

Frank Chamberlain Porter, son of William, great-grandson of Jonathan Edwards, was born on January 5, 1859, in Beloit, Wisconsin. In 1874 he enrolled at the Academy or "Prep" and entered Beloit College in 1876. Of the two curricula offered, the philosophical and the classical, Porter chose the latter. Toward the end of his college career, he became acquainted with the work of Julius Wellhausen (1844-1918), the great German biblical scholar and orientalist, through the writings of the Scottish orientalist W. Robertson Smith (1846-94), and owed much to the exposition of the new approach to biblical studies through the articles of Henry Preserved Smith (1847-1927) of Princeton. Porter graduated from Beloit College in 1880, studied at Chicago Theological Seminary in 1881-82, two years later earned an M.A. degree at Beloit College, and spent a year (1884-85) at the theological school in Hartford, Connecticut. At year's end Porter entered the Divinity School of Yale University, and completed his undergraduate course in 1886. He then reentered the Divinity School to pursue doctoral studies. In 1889 he received his Ph.D. following completion of a dissertation on the subject of Jewish belief in life after death and in the fall of that year took up duties as instructor in biblical theology at the Divinity School. In the spring of 1891 Porter was appointed to a new chair in biblical theology, and was joined in marriage to Delia Wood Lyman. In the fall of 1891 he began lecturing on Old and New Testament theology and chaired a seminar on Judaism. During the summer semester of 1892, he visited several European universities, and in 1895 was ordained and appointed the Yale Divinity School (Trowbridge) librarian. In the spring and summer of 1908 he traveled to Europe again. He remained in Berlin for the summer, spent September in England, delivered an address at the Third International Con-

---

149. For a more extensive study of the life and work of Porter, see Roy A. Harrisville, *Frank Chamberlain Porter: Pioneer in American Biblical Interpretation* (Missoula, Mont.: Scholars, 1976). Some of the material cited is from Porter's extensive collection of notes, often in his own type of shorthand, its pagination left to guesswork.

gress of Comparative Religions in Oxford, and resumed work at Yale in the academic year 1908-9. In August 1924 Porter had his first sabbatical leave after thirty-five years of teaching, and with his wife sailed for China, lecturing at Beijing. From Beijing he visited India, Ceylon, Egypt, Palestine, Constantinople, and Athens, and by way of Montreal sailed for home.

At the outset, Porter acknowledged the necessity of historical criticism. He insisted that knowledge of Greek was requisite to an understanding of the life and teachings of Jesus, and that Hebrew was indispensable for special research into the background of Gospel history. Porter clearly admitted that the historical method necessitated a reconsideration and restatement of theological positions. He regarded opposition to attempts to recover the historical Jesus as tantamount to a rejection of the historical-critical method, reserving bitterest judgment for the "Princeton Theology." The sacrifice of faith in the human mind and its capacity to reach the truth for the sake of faith was a "dangerous form of unbelief in God."[150]

Porter frequently referred to the historical method as an emancipation, a twofold liberation from dogma or dogmatic use of the Bible. First, it rendered scripture kin to all other literature,[151] and second, it freed the interpreter from the assumption of the Bible's uniqueness and hence its authority.[152] On the credit side, Porter contended that the historical method yielded a view of the Bible that reflected a great advance.[153] That is, it furnished an understanding of the great personalities of the Bible, above all, that of Jesus.[154] Again and again Porter emphasized that historical criticism was consonant with the religion of Jesus, who "did not intend to give us definiteness, but freedom."[155]

---

150. Frank Chamberlain Porter, "Princeton Theology," *Yale Divinity Quarterly* 9 (March 1913): 131-34.

151. From an untitled fragment on the Spirit, unpublished (n.d.), p. 9.

152. From an untitled piece on the relation of the New Testament to Jesus, unpublished (n.d.), pp. 4, 7, 11, 13, 15f., 20, 22f.

153. From an untitled piece on the relation of the New Testament to Jesus, unpublished (n.d.), p. 23; Porter's shorthand review of Theodore Munger's biography of Horace Bushnell, unpublished (n.d.), p. 1.

154. Frank Chamberlain Porter, "The Mysticism of the Hebrew Prophets," in *At One with the Invisible,* Studies in Mysticism, ed. E. Hershey Sneath (New York: Macmillan, 1921), p. 34; an untitled fragment on the Spirit, unpublished (n.d.)

155. Frank Chamberlain Porter, "The Historical and the Spiritual Understanding of the Bible," in *Education for Christian Service,* by members of the faculty of the Divinity School of Yale University; a volume in commemoration of its one-hundredth anniversary (New Haven, Conn.: Yale University Press, 1922), pp. 37, 46.

Porter was more specific respecting the yield of historical criticism when it came to miracles. He characterized his own time as unable to believe in the intervention of supernatural powers, and as regarding the position of our earth within the universe as insignificant. The term "miracle" itself constituted an offense to the modern mind.[156] Consonant with this view Porter interpreted the visions and auditions of the Old Testament prophets in terms of mental or emotional experiences seen in retrospect as a means for reaching the truth. As for Jesus, his consciousness of messiahship did not derive from ecstatic emotion or objective vision. His religion could not be seen to consist in any external or prodigious quality, but rather in a radical inwardness. Porter entertained a like aversion to the apocalyptic element in the Bible, and his reflections on the question of Jesus' messianic consciousness tended to negative results.[157] In response to the question why, then, apocalyptic should have emerged at all, he stated that Jesus' sayings were soon carried by early tradition into the area of eschatology.

Porter was not unaware of criticism's limitations. Even if historical science could get back to Jesus, such a return would satisfy only the intellectual sense. More, an inevitable uncertainty attached to the results of critical research. Historical studies rendered certain data insecure. Faith, therefore, could not rest on the results of scholarly activity;[158] it required certainty. It had to be liberated from dependence on anything science might shake.[159]

Historical criticism was thus not the "highest and fittest use" to which the Bible could be put. It required a supplement that could be achieved in various ways: getting into the "mental atmosphere" of the author, having "insight" or "sympathy," yielding a "spiritual response," showing "tact," or sharing "communion of soul."[160] Repeating the question of Matthew

156. From an untitled fragment on the Spirit, p. 4; Frank Chamberlain Porter, "Christ the Miracle of Christianity," *The Congregationalist and Christian World,* December 1909, p. 916.

157. Frank Chamberlain Porter, "Some Recent Critical Studies in the Life of Christ," unpublished, 1902, pp. 9f., 12.

158. Frank Chamberlain Porter, "The Place of the Sacred Book in the Christian Religion," *Yale Divinity Quarterly* 5, no. 4 (March 1909): 262, 265.

159. Frank Chamberlain Porter, "Crucial Problems in Biblical Theology," *Journal of Religion* 1, no. 1 (1921): 80; idem, "Some Recent Critical Studies in the Life of Christ," unpublished (1902), p. 1.

160. Frank Chamberlain Porter, "The Jewish Literature of New Testament Times: Why Should It Be Studied?" *The Old and New Testament Student* 9 (1889): 77; idem, "Ought a Minister to Know Hebrew?" *The Congregationalist,* May 4, 1899, p. 633; idem, "Paul's Belief

Arnold, "Shall we enjoy the Bible?" Porter spoke of a "simpler and more direct use of the book as it is," an "emotional appreciation of its qualities," or a "more inward response to the spirit that moves in it."[161] All of this meant turning to the Bible's character as literature. As to the species of literature to which the Bible belonged, "poetry" chiefly described its character.[162] In harmony with this emphasis on the poetic character of the Bible and the appreciative approach toward it, Porter turned to Aristotle, to the Greek rhetorician Longinus (first century A.D.), and to William Wordsworth (1770-1850). In Aristotelian terms, poetry, thus the Bible, expressed the universal element in human life. It disclosed the universal in the particular, represented things as they ought to be. To Longinus, presumed author of *On the Sublime* (*Peri hypsous*), the reading of great works required "transport and wonder." Wordsworth made clear that the poet was concerned to relate things in an ideal order and unity, rather than relating events as they occurred. The poetry of Samuel Taylor Coleridge (1772-1834) reflected one aspect of the Aristotelian theme, namely, that truth is higher than fact, but it was Wordsworth who most completely represented the ancient ideal.

"Truth higher than fact," "transport and wonder," "giving the charm of novelty to things of every day" — such dicta for Porter described the horizon of the interpreter's task. Moreover, they were "moral qualities" that impinged on critical study and were superior to intellectual powers and training.[163]

To the charge of subjectivism and modernizing, Porter replied that when the object of study is the understanding of a person one must have the courage to insist on a subjective path toward an objective goal. It is more important for the historian to be "courageously subjective" than to be in bondage to the word "scientific." The more truly and deeply subjective the interpreter, the better. As for "modernizing," it was a virtue, not a vice, provided it meant that "spiritual means can only be spiritually discerned."[164]

---

in Life after Death," in *Religion and the Future Life,* ed. E. Hershey Sneath (New York: Revell, 1922), p. 238; idem, "The Bearing of Historical Studies on the Religious Use of the Bible," *Harvard Theological Review* 2 (July 1909): 259.

161. Porter, "The Place of the Sacred Book in the Christian Religion," p. 262.

162. Porter, "The Place of the Sacred Book in the Christian Religion," p. 264.

163. Frank Chamberlain Porter, *The Mind of Christ in Paul,* Light from Paul on Present Problems of Christian Thinking (New York: Charles Scribner's Sons, 1930), pp. 9, 11; idem, "The Intellectual Value of Theological Training," unpublished (n.d.), p. 8.

164. Frank Chamberlain Porter, "Toward a Biblical Theology for the Present," in *Contemporary American Theology,* Theological Autobiographies, ed. Virgilius Ferm, Second

To the question, what remained once the supplement had been furnished, Porter replied: "The inner life of the divine and of man." Such inward appropriation of the Old Testament, for example, undermined the notion of a canon. Jesus' parables reflected that inward quality to the highest degree. At this point, Porter was sharply critical of Bultmann's interpretation of the parables as purely supernatural or eschatological.[165] Adolf Jülicher's position was more to his taste. Accordingly, Jesus used the parables in simple, homely, and everyday fashion needing no interpretation.

Nowhere were the results of Porter's appreciative method more transparent than in his exposition of the epistles of Paul. The apostle, wrote Porter, applied two "tests" to all Christian thought. First, Christian thought must be according to the historical Jesus, and second, it must be "natural" or "true" to one who has the "mind" of Jesus.[166] Given these "tests," Paul's method was to trace the Christological categories he had inherited back to the historical Jesus, conforming them to his character.[167] Referring to Colossians 1:15-17 as standing in the strangest isolation, he did not eliminate the verses but argued that though Paul could affirm the words of the hymn, he was more interested in Christ's place in the church than in the universe. He wrote in essentially the same fashion of the hymn in Philippians 2. By applying it to Jesus the apostle changed it from its original purpose and employed it as "neither myth nor theology," but as a hymn to Christ and his self-sacrificing love. Whatever residue in Paul remained after his tests had been applied was to be construed after the rule of the relation between "reality and form," thus as "poetry."[168] Paul's "hard sayings," in which he identified the Christian with Christ's suffering, death, resurrection, and glory, were to be interpreted in terms of love, friendship, and morality. The

Series (New York: Round Table, 1933), pp. 200, 234f.; idem, "The Historical and the Spiritual Understanding of the Bible," p. 23.

165. At the same time, Porter thought he detected a fundamental inconsistency in Bultmann's parable interpretation, namely, an exclusion and an affirmation of the present kingship of Jahve, a spiritualizing of Jesus' teachings, and yet a naturalizing of the Gospels. These comments are contained in Porter's copy of Bultmann's *Jesus and the Word; New Testament Theology: Supplementary Material*, unpublished (1923-24), p. 20; idem, "The Place of the New Testament in the Christian Religion," unpublished (n.d.), p. 57.

166. Porter, *The Mind of Christ in Paul*, pp. 95f.

167. Frank Chamberlain Porter, "History of Biblical Conceptions: Christology," unpublished (1924), p. 27.

168. Porter, "The Place of the New Testament in the Christian Religion," pp. 6, 8, 10; idem, *The Mind of Christ in Paul*, p. 163; idem, "Paul and the Spirit of God," unpublished (n.d.), p. 43.

second of the Pauline tests, that Christian thinking should be natural to one who has the mind of Christ, was thus identical with the ethical or moral.

In summarizing the thought of Paul, Porter spoke of him as the "great prophet of the Spirit." The term "Spirit" solved the problem of the relation between the external and inward, the revelation of Jesus as objective and as inwardly experienced. When Porter came to distinguish Paul from the Synoptists he reached for Longinus's contrast between transport and wonder. The Gospels fell under the rubric of transport, whereas John fell under that of wonder. Since John's idea of the spiritual presence, viewed as the returning Jesus or as his spiritual "substitute," makes up the Gospel's chief thought, it assumes its proper place as successor to the Pauline idea. Porter admitted that he knew of no clearer recognition of that primary element in Paul's conception of Christ and the Christian than in Jonathan Edwards's "Treatise on Grace," and summarized Edwards's conception of the Christian religion as the entrance of the Divine Love into human beings and making them his own.

In support of his choice of the term "Spirit," Porter appealed to a "typical modern theologian," Auguste Sabatier (1839-1901) of the Sorbonne, and a "typical modern philosopher," Rudolf Eucken (1846-1926) of Jena. The former rejected authority in religion as outmoded and seized on the word "spirit" to name the religion that is free. The latter rejected the current "monism" because of its tendency to materialism and found the term "spirit" conducive to a "higher realm."[169]

Porter was discontented with urging an appreciative approach as supplement. He sought a more precise definition of the adjustment between historical study and appreciative method. The Ritschlian, for example, in his insistence on the historical Christ as ultimate revelation, ran the risk of contending "the better the historian, the better the Christian," whereas the liberal was in danger of contending "the better the philosopher, the better the Christian." Both avoided making the living Christ essential to faith. Porter concluded that the two "ways" need not be mutually exclusive. Referring to Rudolf Hermann Lotze (1817-81) and his description of the long dispute between men's spiritual needs and the work of science, Porter quoted the Berlin metaphysician to the effect that each has its own right and that the mediation between them is to be found "in showing how absolutely universal is the extent and at the same time how completely subordinate the significance of the mission which mechanism

169. Porter, untitled fragment on the Spirit, p. 16.

has to fulfill in the structure of the world."[170] When Porter applied Lotze's rule to the Bible he found that it yielded science an absolutely unrestricted freedom and yet allowed the worth of the book to the spiritual nature of man to remain unimpaired and supreme. It was a "true life" or "faith" that solved the problem of the relation between the historical and religious uses of the Bible. So the religious value of a historical record is itself a fact with which the historian must reckon. The value or power which the record possesses and which is due to the power the facts once had over the biblical author may be valid evidence of the actuality of the events. In another connection, Porter could describe the adjustment in terms of the relation between "form and spirit."[171]

Despite these frequent references to Aristotle, Longinus, Words-worth, Lotze, Sabatier, and Eucken, Jonathan Edwards occupied as large a place as any other in Porter's published and unpublished pieces. It was Edwards who had spent his life attempting to forge a link between "the objective good" as the "irresistible sequence of law" and the "inherent good" as the "perception of expediency or pleasure."[172] This struggle with the "two gigantic issues of modern philosophy" lay at the heart of Porter's work as well. Porter's quarrel was the same as Edwards's: the reason scientific research could not furnish the basis for religious uses was that rationality was but one aspect of genuine religion. Porter deplored what he alleged to be the contention of his Princeton adversaries, namely, that a knowledge of Christ's death apart from the perception of its ethical character and effect constituted true faith. Porter, too, pressed home the necessity of keeping faith abreast of present knowledge, above all for the sake of those who could not agree to the claims of a religion expressed in unintelligible language.[173] Porter as well as Edwards saw the synthesis of the two opposing worlds in what can only be termed the aesthetic factor. For Edwards it was beauty that achieved the union between sensation and thought. The same aesthetic-affective aspect underlies Porter's thought:

170. Porter, "The Historical and the Spiritual Understanding of the Bible," p. 22; idem, "Toward a Biblical Theology for the Present," pp. 210, 216; idem, "The Word of God and the Spirit of God," unpublished (n.d.), pp. 20f.

171. Frank Chamberlain Porter, letter to Mr. Chas. Wingate, July 19, 1886.

172. See Perry Miller, *Jonathan Edwards* (New York: Meridian, 1959), pp. 98, 112, 117, 149, 180, and Roland Andre Delattre, *Beauty and Sensibility in the Thought of Jonathan Edwards* (New Haven, Conn.: Yale University Press, 1968).

173. Porter, "The Intellectual Value of Theological Training," p. 13; idem, "Some Recent Critical Studies in the Life of Christ," p. 1.

"wonder and worship, trust and love, naturally express themselves in the language of feeling, the language of poetry, not in that of explanation and definition."[174] For both, "Spirit" constituted the sum and substance of a life's work. For Edwards, everything hinged on identifying beauty with the essence of the divine as Spirit. For Porter, "Spirit" characterized a "right return" to the religion of Jesus.[175] Above all, it signalized the synthesis between the objective and the subjective, the particular and the universal, between the Jesus of history and Jesus in Christian experience. It tokened the union between inwardness, freedom, the interpretation of Jesus by Spirit, and love, the interpretation of Spirit by Jesus. The similarity to Edwards is unmistakable.

Of course, the appearance of scientific, biblical research required a retranslation of the Edwardsean sense-thought question and in an idiom Porter best understood. Now the antinomy was not represented by the views of Locke and Hume, but by the History of Religions School on the one hand and the liberal schools of the continent on the other. The one attempted to demonstrate that the Gospels contain something that can be accepted as certain fact, the other maintained that Christianity does not consist in the acceptance of an historical datum but of an ideal or principle. For Porter, the History of Religions School appeared as principal protector of the right to criticism, and he freely used its comparative method, as, for example, in his psychological interpretation of Jesus' exorcisms, a tactic familiar to the *Religionsgeschichtler* since the days of Wilhelm Bousset. It is just as obvious, however, that Porter was at odds with that school, not merely for its vaunted optimism over the results of its criticism or its tacit assumption that the better historian was the better Christian. Something else lay at the root of his irritation: a commitment, a pledge to ideas or notions, which led Porter to a drastic revision of his Edwardsean heritage.

First of all, Porter was committed to Christianity as an ideal. That ideal took its shape less from Locke, Hume, the English Puritans, and Edwards than from Lessing, Kant, and the Romanticists. The task was not to concentrate on a particular action of God or to exclude Jesus from the "development" the historian had to trace, but rather to distinguish the idea, the "eternal truth beneath the accidents and incidents of human life and

---

174. Porter, *The Mind of Christ in Paul*, p. 160.

175. Frank Chamberlain Porter, "The Place of Christ in the Christian Religion," unpublished (n.d.), p. 72.

thought."[176] Why, then, the "return to Jesus" or to his religion, if not to establish some historical datum on which faith might rest? For Porter the answer was simple: the idea, the eternal verity, was symbolized in persons. If, as Arnold had written, the personality of Jesus was "the revelation of the Eternal, not ourselves, which makes for righteousness,"[177] then the explanation to Christianity was to be found in that personality, a contention reinforced by the Göttingen scholar of ancient Greek religion and gnosticism Richard Reitzenstein (1861-1931), cited by Porter as often as any other continental.[178]

Given the inability of the single symbol as creed to reflect the entire truth, it was a small thing for Porter to draw the conclusion that Jesus as symbol must himself be subordinate to the "ideal," or to state flatly that historical study was clearly subservient to the religious uses of the Bible. Ultimately, then, the "actuality" of Jesus, in contrast to his "picture" or "impression," was expendable. In support of his conclusion Porter cited the British philosopher Francis Bacon (1561-1626), Lord Verulam, to the effect that poesy

was ever thought to have some participation of divineness, because it doth raise and erect the mind by submitting the shows of things to the desires of the mind, whereas reason doth buckle and bow the mind into the nature of things.[179]

At some point, however, Porter was compelled to retain particularity. For example, the prophets had to be spared a certain uniqueness, and a certain uniqueness lay with the wisdom literature. More, it was from prophetism and Wisdom, not from law and apocalyptic, that Jesus and Paul drew their strength.

Still and all, what Edwards had joined together Porter had put asunder. He conceived his task as separating the imaginative truth expressed

176. Frank Chamberlain Porter, "The Spirit of Christianity and the Jesus of History," unpublished (n.d.), p. 30; idem, "The Ideals of Seminaries and the Needs of Churches," *Yale Divinity Quarterly* 3 (March 1900): 30.

177. Matthew Arnold, *Literature and Dogma: An Essay Towards a Better Apprehension of the Bible* (London: Smith, Elder & Co., 1873), p. 230.

178. See Frank Chamberlain Porter, "The Place of Apocalyptical Conceptions in the Thought of Paul," *Journal of Biblical Literature* 41 (1922): 186; idem, *New Testament Theology*, p. 142; idem, *The Mind of Christ in Paul*, p. 166; idem, shorthand notes on the works of Benjamin W. Bacon.

179. Porter, "The Place of the New Testament in the Christian Religion," p. 109.

in the language of feeling from its occasion in historical fact. The stories of Jesus' birth, the nature miracles, and references to the physical aspects of the appearance of the risen Christ — all these required the "unembarrassed application of standards of literature," that is, were to be construed in a "poetic" sense. Paul's "ingenious arguments" concerning the end of the law, above all the Christologies in Romans 8, 1 Corinthians 8, Philippians 2, and Colossians 1, were not literally but poetically true, true as imagic, true as the language of "lofty emotion." They were also reproducible. That moral effort that Porter demanded as the "chief test" of a truly religious life was an imitation achieved through the appreciation of forms. Some forms that appeared to be eschatological or apocalyptic in reality were not. Paul himself had prepared for their "weakening," and such interpretations as that of Albert Schweitzer (1875-1965) were a "mistake," resulting from too great anxiety over modernizing the New Testament.[180] Yet, Porter's greatest objection to the eschatological lay in his belief that its fixing a future and outward goal betrayed the moral and inward quality of Jesus' teaching. This was the entire burden of Porter's interpretation of the temptations and the Lord's Prayer.[181] The eschatological-apocalyptic needed to be reinterpreted, if not relegated to the category of what Matthew Arnold (1822-88) had once called "extra-belief," or *Aberglaube*.[182]

Porter had some acquaintance with the neo-orthodoxy just being introduced to the United States. How well he was acquainted with it is difficult to tell. He had read Bultmann's *Jesus* in English translation, and something of Barth. His references to the two men were infrequent and reflect only an understanding of their similarities, nothing of their differences. But whatever Porter had read of them he did not like because they lacked a truly "natural" theology, that is, they denied that universal, "humanistic character" of Jesus' thought and of all true religion. Barth and his confreres were thus described as trying to force theology off from sympathy with a belief in every way in which man seeks God, and Bultmann fell under the same judgment.

Porter retired in 1927, and two years later made his third trip to Eu-

---

180. Frank Chamberlain Porter, "The Christian Hope in Times of War," in *Religion and the War*, by members of the faculty of the School of Religion, Yale University, ed. E. Hershey Sneath (New Haven, Conn.: Yale University Press, 1918), pp. 50f.; idem, "The Place of Apocalyptic Conceptions in the Thought of Paul," pp. 185f.; idem, "Biblical Theology of the New Testament," unpublished (1923-24), p. 64; idem, "New Testament Theology," unpublished (ca. 1924), pp. 74-77; idem, *The Mind of Christ in Paul*, pp. 166, 312.

181. Porter, "New Testament Theology," pp. 34-36.

182. Arnold, *Literature and Dogma*, pp. 93, 105f., 152, 190.

rope. On July 17, 1931, Yale awarded him a second doctorate *honoris causa,* as did Beloit College earlier, in 1897. Delia Lyman Porter died in 1933, preceding her husband in death by thirteen years. Porter died on January 24, 1946, at the age of eighty-seven.

Union in New York

Following the conflict between "Old School" Presbyterianism, represented by Hodge of Princeton, and "New School" Presbyterianism, represented by Charles Augustus Briggs (1841-1913), from 1876 to 1913 Davenport Professor of Hebrew at Union Theological Seminary in New York, a conflict climaxing in the Briggs trials (1891-1893) and eventuating in Union's cutting its denominational ties, the following generation of Union's biblical department embraced current critical methods and directly or indirectly, sporadically or continuously, addressed the problems of interpretation.

One who dealt obliquely with the problems of interpretation was F. J. Foakes-Jackson. Despite extensive research devoted to *The Beginnings of Christianity* and other works, his attention to questions of interpretation was occasional and minimal, due in great part to his concentration on matters of text and form. Whenever he did touch on questions of interpretation, his stance was clear and more or less precise. For example, while acknowledging the embarrassment of many over adopting the Old Testament for liturgical use, he asserted that "no Christian can have the slightest hesitation in acknowledging that the basis of all religious instruction must be the New." From that point he proceeded to indicate the difference between "the moral difficulty" in both instances:

> Instead of having to excise or explain away many passages in the books of the Old Covenant as not inculcating a sufficiently high standard of morality, we find in those of the New so lofty a view of man's duty to God and to his neighbor, that we are disposed to question whether it is within the powers of human nature to attain to it.[183]

Of the Gospels Foakes-Jackson stated that whereas in former times interpreters were content to detach one from the other and regard each in

---

183. F. J. Foakes-Jackson and B. T. Dean Smith, *A Biblical History for Schools* (Cambridge: W. Heffer and Sons Ltd., 1913), p. ix.

isolation, earnest endeavor was now being made to understand the Gospels together as parts of a "scheme of teaching."[184] Respecting the Gospel miracles he agreed that more was at stake in their regard than regarding those recorded in the Old, but despite whatever questions might be put respecting their cause, they may be regarded as a "manifestation of that which we now recognize to be in accordance with natural laws."[185] In connection with what once was dubbed a *pia fraus* in the writer's adopting the name of another, more noteworthy personage, say, that of a prophet or apostle, Foakes-Jackson wrote that the idea of literary honesty current "in those days" was vastly different from our own; an author might feel justified in assuming another's name for the purpose of defending that person's faith. Then he added, "if this be thought to detract from its claim to be an inspired work, we must be prepared to recognize degrees of inspiration within, as well as the action of the Holy Spirit without, the covers of the New Testament."

Apart from any extended discussion of the interpretive task, Foakes-Jackson could accent its necessity as he did in question form prefaced to a work by P. Gardner-Smith (1888-1985), dean of Jesus College, Cambridge:

> To what extent does criticism compel a revision of the traditional theology of the Church? . . . Can the ideas and ideals of the first century be applied to meet the needs of the twentieth? Is Christianity necessarily an historical religion, and if so, in what sense? . . . if [such questions] are ever to be answered, the first necessity is that the Gospels should be read and studied with utmost care.[186]

Frederick Clifton Grant (1891-1974), Robinson Professor of Biblical Theology at Union from 1938 to 1954 and participant in the 1947 revision of the New Testament, devoted the bulk of his reflection on interpretation to three books published during his retirement. In the third and last[187] he traced the emergence of concentration on the literal meaning of scripture from Nicolas of Lyra (d. 1340) in the early part of the fourteenth century to the sixteenth-century Reformers. It was Lyra, Grant wrote, whose emphasis on the literal meaning contrasted with the traditional fourfold interpretation

---

184. Foakes-Jackson and Smith, *A Biblical History for Schools,* pp. x-xi.

185. Foakes-Jackson and Smith, *A Biblical History for Schools,* p. ix.

186. F. J. Foakes-Jackson, preface to P. Gardner-Smith, *The Christ of the Gospels* (Cambridge: W. Heffer & Sons Ltd., 1938), p. v.

187. Frederick Clifton Grant, *Translating the Bible* (Greenwich: Seabury, 1961).

favored in the West, an interpretation summarized in the rule *littera gesta docet* ("the letters teach what happened"), *quid credas, allegoria* ("allegory, what you believe"), *moralis, quid agas* ("the moral, what you do"), *quid spes, anagogia* ("the anagogic, what you hope"). As a result, interpreters and preachers gave wide scope to their imagination, with often bizarre results. With Lyra began a movement toward simplicity and directness, destined to grow until the Reformation insisted on the plain and simple interpretation of the Bible and the literal, historical meaning of its language. Grant went on to cite the use of allegorical interpretation in the ancient world, first by the interpreters of Homer and the Greek myths, by Christian expositors of Alexandria in contrast to those of Antioch, then by medieval interpreters under Augustinian influence, until with the Reformation the allegorical together with the moral and anagogic senses finally fell into disuse.[188]

According to Grant, "pure rabbinism," "bibliolatry," "biblicism," or "literalism," was the enemy of authentic interpretation. Writing that expert historians wrote as if history had no meaning, he saw this view reflected in modern theology as a result of the biblicism long characteristic of religious thought, and beneath which lay the assumption that the "truth" of the Bible is identical with its historical accuracy. That "truth," Grant asserted, is not a mere accurate record of historical events, capable of interpretation in a dozen different ways or not at all, but rather the meaning for humankind's salvation attaching to those events.[189] The church, he wrote, does not require that the Bible be interpreted literally, or in the fundamentalist sense, nor does it lay down a fixed and predetermined explanation of scripture.[190] In fact, one of the most tragic results of a literal interpretation was the support it gave to anti-Semitism, "one of the blackest and most ineradicable blemishes upon the modern world."[191] He noted that Christian resistance to the tide of anti-Semitism may be of little account, but it had to begin with a frank acknowledgment of the seriousness of the situation within the New Testament itself. He wrote,

> The clergy and other leaders of the church should realize how far-reaching are the inferences people draw from the passages heard or

188. Grant, *Translating the Bible*, pp. 53-54, 144-45.

189. Frederick C. Grant, *An Introduction to New Testament Thought* (New York: Abingdon-Cokesbury, 1950), pp. 49-50.

190. Frederick Clifton Grant, *How to Read the Bible* (New York: Morehouse-Gorham Co., 1956), p. 47.

191. Grant, *An Introduction to New Testament Thought*, p. 94.

read at church, and how serious are the practical consequences of our acquiescence in the inherited prejudices which the New Testament seems to support.[192]

Concomitant with anti-Semitism was the rupture of the relation between the two Testaments, a relation the early church understood but was obscured by later centuries.[193] The "modern proposal" to omit the Old Testament, Grant wrote, was impossible on every ground. The New Testament could not be understood without reference to the Old, for the reason that it was the supplement to the Jewish sacred book. Both Testaments were thus indispensable parts of the record of divine revelation, the New presupposing the Old, with its ideas, history, teaching, and prophecies on almost every page. Fortunately, continuity between the Christian church and the Jewish synagogue had lately come to be more widely recognized than at any time since the Reformation.[194]

Grant was convinced: literalism with its adverse results offered no way out of the hermeneutical impasse. Only enlightened historical scholarship provided the interpretation needed, a task that could not be left to the secular historian.

> We cannot leave it to others to distinguish within them [the scriptures] between what is permanent and what is passing, between the central and the peripheral, the essential and the existential, the eternal and the temporal, between the divine revelation which they enshrine and the external, the adventitious, the phenomenal, the transient elements in the record of that revelation.[195]

Grant conceded that objective scholarship might lack some of the qualities needed to understand a sacred book, but in contrast to literalism or fundamentalism, which made "capital of a few selected texts," it could supply what was indispensable to exposition.[196] For one thing, it enabled one to see that revelation was progressive, that interpretation and reinterpretation characterized the entire course of its long history.[197] For another,

192. Grant, *An Introduction to New Testament Thought,* p. 97.
193. Grant, *How to Read the Bible,* pp. 154-55.
194. Grant, *How to Read the Bible,* pp. 126, 154.
195. Grant, *An Introduction to New Testament Thought,* p. 98.
196. Grant, *An Introduction to New Testament Thought,* p. 93.
197. Grant, *An Introduction to New Testament Thought,* p. 88.

it made clear that the Bible's inspiration was occasional, not constant. As Grant phrased it, it was pure rabbinism and bibliolatry to claim that every word in the Bible is inspired since the Bible itself made no such claim.[198] As he wrote,

> The old-fashioned Protestant view that every detail of scripture (even the punctuation points, some argued!) was inspired and infallible, that its primary message was to the individual in the privacy of his own chamber, where he meditated and was still, and that his salvation depended upon strict obedience to the very letter of scripture — all this, while profoundly moving as an example of piety, not only has passed away in much of the modern world, but must be recognized as something quite different from the historic position of the great churches of Christendom.[199]

The use of the historical method also facilitated an understanding of the "closest religious milieu of early Christianity," that is, the thought-world of Jewish apocalyptic.[200] Anyone, therefore, for whom "I believe in the holy Catholic Church" was a vital article of the Creed or confession of faith, need have no fear of following the reconstructive efforts of modern criticism.[201]

In view of the relevance of the historical method the interpreter's task was clear. Grant could go on in some detail regarding the interpreter's inheritance from the ancient church fathers and councils, from the Schoolmen and the Reformers of a conception of theology that demanded accurate, exhaustive definition, which insisted that truth needed stating in propositional form, in statements of fact and principle subject to the fullest examination, attack, and defense by human logic.[202] Later, he added that the revelation contained in the Bible did not consist solely in factual statements or propositions, but in wide-embracing principles that gather up and interpret those facts.[203] Specifically, the interpreter needed to get accustomed to take seriously what the earliest Christians took seriously,

---

198. Grant, *An Introduction to New Testament Thought*, p. 66.
199. Grant, *An Introduction to New Testament Thought*, pp. 87-88.
200. Grant, *How to Read the Bible*, pp. 102-3.
201. Grant, *How to Read the Bible*, p. 144.
202. Grant, *An Introduction to New Testament Thought*, p. 73.
203. Grant, *How to Read the Bible*, p. 88.

"to see the world through their eyes."[204] For example, like all other books of the Bible the poetical books had to be read in the light of their own times and conditions, as well as of their authors' intention and purpose.[205] Further, the interpreter had to be a student of all Greek literature, especially of ancient Greek, as well as of the formal inscriptions and the popular papyri. "In brief," he added, "he must study all ancient Greek if he is to acquire an accurately balanced judgment in interpreting the text before him," and in this connection could quote Philipp Melanchthon to the effect that "every good theologian and faithful interpreter of heavenly doctrine must of necessity be first a grammarian, then a dialectician (weighing different possible interpretations), finally a witness."[206]

Grant did not end there. The historical method required a supplement. As Millar Burrows (1889-1990), from 1934 to 1958 Winkley Professor of Biblical Theology at Yale, had demonstrated, the authenticity of the revelation witnessed to in the Bible could not be established by external testimony, by its claim as having been inspired, nor by the unique mode of its deliverance. "This," wrote Grant, "is a matter of faith and of insight, the inner testimony of the Holy Spirit in the individual, as Calvin said." "In other words," he added, "the scripture must 'find' me and speak to me, to be true for me — a testimony as old as the *Theologia Germanica,* at least, and one strongly emphasized by Coleridge and other Christian thinkers of more recent date."[207] In a kind of valedictory Grant wrote,

> although none of the writers was aware that he was writing scripture, God nevertheless spoke through their words, not only to their contemporaries but also to Christians of later ages; and He still so speaks, if we attentively listen to His voice.[208]

He was quick to add that this testimony in the individual in turn required a supplement in the context of a community. It was this community that gave to the biblical books their sacrosanct character. This community exercised the right to choose, select, and approve a body of literature appropriate for reading at worship, a collection authoritative in setting forth the true, original Christian faith, unsullied by heretical accretions

204. Grant, *An Introduction to New Testament Thought,* p. 56.
205. Grant, *How to Read the Bible,* p. 89.
206. Grant, *How to Read the Bible,* pp. 18, 42.
207. Grant, *An Introduction to New Testament Thought,* p. 87.
208. Grant, *How to Read the Bible,* p. 132.

or by gnostic or other misinterpretations, and to which appeal would be made in the attempt to settle whatever questions emerged at a later date. Accordingly, if one insisted that it was the power of these books to reach and speak to the individual that lay behind their use, it was not the individual in solitariness but as one caught up within the fellowship of the church that made the choice and selection effective. The claim of historical, scientific exegesis to be heard was thus balanced by the authority of the church to interpret its scriptures.[209] After a productive and distinguished career, Frederick Clifton Grant died in 1974 at his home in Gwynedd, Pennsylvania.

Grant's colleague, John Knox (1901-1990), from 1943 to 1966 Baldwin Professor of Sacred Literature, whose major contribution to biblical scholarship may have been his *Marcion and the New Testament*,[210] published the majority of his reflections on interpretation in two monographs entitled *Criticism and Faith* and *Myth and Truth*.[211] The former concentrated on what Knox termed the "event" or "happening." "The Bible has value," he wrote, "only because it brings us a firsthand account of that happening. The event is the important thing, not the account; and we must interpret the account to recover the event."[212] Recovery of the event spelled "looking through" rather than "looking at" the Gospels, an impossible activity until one was ready and willing to allow for "the defects of the medium."[213] Allowing for the defects meant distinguishing essentials and nonessentials, the less and more important elements of the event.[214] Protestant fundamentalism or dogmatism with its hankering after an a priori harmony might attempt recovery of the event, but blurred the sharp edges of the biblical books, muted their distinctive notes, and obscured or distorted their characteristic structures and shapes.[215] This detachment of the event from history denied its historicity in the moment of affirming it, and perpetrated a worse error than any negative historical conclusion.[216] As for

209. Grant, *How to Read the Bible*, pp. 87-88, 92.
210. John Knox, *Marcion and the New Testament* (Chicago: University of Chicago Press, 1942).
211. John Knox, *Criticism and Faith* (Nashville: Abingdon-Cokesbury, 1952); idem, *Myth and Truth* (Charlottesville: University Press of Virginia, 1964).
212. Knox, *Criticism and Faith*, p. 80.
213. Knox, *Criticism and Faith*, p. 77.
214. Knox, *Criticism and Faith*, p. 86.
215. Knox, *Criticism and Faith*, p. 85.
216. Knox, *Criticism and Faith*, p. 91.

Roman Catholicism, it blurred the distinction between event and church, resulting in constituting the church the norm of its own life, an error the Protestant sought to avoid by setting the church under the authority of the Bible.[217]

The only way of escape from either peril was to apprehend the event in its "original character and impact."[218] This meant discerning the way in which fact and interpretation interacted as the event occurred.[219] But in view of the indissoluble fusion of the two it did not mean that the interpreter was under any religious or theological pressure to separate nicely between fact and meaning, to say precisely where the one left off and the other began.[220] This fusion of fact and meaning was a factor often neglected in biblical as well as in historical scholarship generally with its emphasis on the ascertaining of facts to the exclusion of meanings and values. It was a neglect Knox described as "a phase of the devotion to objectivity" characteristic of modern historiography.[221] By contrast, the historian needed to be not only critical, but also creative, that is, needed not merely to "get down" to the facts, but "reach up" to their meaning.[222]

All throughout, Knox was insistent that the task of interpretation was not the affair of the solitary individual. As he wrote:

> If scripture must in the nature of the case be interpreted, any authority it has must be its authority as interpreted; and if every individual is free to interpret it as seems best to him, it ceases to have authority at all. As against this contingency the Roman Church takes its firm and characteristic stand: the Bible has authority only as it is interpreted by the church.[223]

At the same time, in some sense and degree the integrity of the event had to be distinguishable from and normative for the community:

> If the scriptures are to be interpreted simply and only in the light of the church's continuing experience or by the authority of its self-

217. Knox, *Criticism and Faith*, p. 79.
218. Knox, *Criticism and Faith*, p. 82.
219. Knox, *Criticism and Faith*, p. 84.
220. Knox, *Criticism and Faith*, p. 38.
221. Knox, *Criticism and Faith*, p. 94.
222. Knox, *Criticism and Faith*, p. 95.
223. Knox, *Criticism and Faith*, p. 80.

perpetuating hierarchy, the event is on the way to losing its integrity and its authority.[224]

Thus, the Roman Church was mistaken in identifying the church with its own hierarchy, but not mistaken in setting the church above the individual. Accordingly, the Protestant was mistaken in supposing that when speaking of the Spirit he was not also speaking of the church, but not mistaken in emphasizing the role of the Spirit and in preferring the Spirit's voice to episcopal vote.[225]

In *Myth and Truth,* Knox reflects his acquaintance with European scholarship, particularly with Bultmann's existential interpretation of the mythical, and advances his own perspective relative to it. Myth, writes Knox, denotes a narrative dealing with a cosmically significant act of God of decisive importance for the world, its origin in the common life of a particular community, prized for its accounting for something distinctive in human existence, and finally inseparable and indispensable to the community's life.[226] Myth, accordingly, does not create or alter the fact, but rather interprets it.[227] When used of facts, such as the life of Christ or its consequences in history, the term is misleading, but when used of what is beyond the factual, such as the incarnation or the atonement, "we enter . . . a quite different world of discourse."[228] Knox explains:

> In saying, "Christ died for us," we may be thinking of him as meeting the enemy Death in an agonizing, but finally victorious struggle. . . . Or we may be thinking of him as paying a debt we owe. . . . But in either case we are not stating the historical fact but are trying to express the meaning that fact has proved to have.[229]

Myth, then, denotes that "different world of discourse," an expression of the meaning the fact "has proved to have."

To the suggestion that the term "story" is preferable to "myth," Knox responds that myth has a narrower, more specific meaning, and connotes an "objective truth" that the term "story" does not convey. Knox gives

---

224. Knox, *Criticism and Faith,* p. 82.
225. Knox, *Criticism and Faith,* pp. 80-81.
226. Knox, *Myth and Truth,* p. 35.
227. Knox, *Myth and Truth,* p. 70.
228. Knox, *Myth and Truth,* p. 61.
229. Knox, *Myth and Truth,* p. 64.

considerable space to W. Norman Pittenger (1905-97), process theologian at the General Theological Seminary, and his distinction between "myth" as connoting events before or after "history," and "story" as linked to a specific historical event, thus the difference between the "myth" of creation and the "story" of the incarnation or the atonement. Knox replies that such a distinction was unknown to the biblical authors for whom time extended before or after history. Moreover, such a distinction would break up the unity of the whole picture of God's dealings with men. Thus, creation, incarnation, and atonement all belong to one all-inclusive myth or story.[230]

In a discussion of the relation between myth and legend, Knox denies that it is possible objectively to determine sharply and certainly in which of the two categories any item of the Gospel tradition belongs, but affirms the possibility of a distinction in principle since in the one instance we encounter a fact creating a myth or story, and in the other a story or myth creating a fact.[231] To inquire whether the nativity stories or the resurrection appearances belong to the category of history or legend is to put them outside the category of myth since they can be validated by investigation, whereas myth is not amenable to historical or scientific inquiry. But if legends, amenable to historical or scientific investigation, are for this reason nonmythological and thus nonessential to faith, myth, though not amenable to investigation, is not without contact with actual fact, but the fact with which it is connected is "experienced or existential." Knox writes, "the 'light' God made is the light we see, and the 'Son' God sent is the Jesus whom the Church remembers and still knows."[232]

Finally, in regard to the demythologizing program that was initiated by Bultmann and that furnished the occasion for the reflections contained in this essay, Knox writes that if by "demythologizing" we mean doing our best to interpret the myth, there can be no doubt of its legitimacy. "By this 'interpreting,'" he states, "we shall mean . . . recognizing and identifying the character, or possibility, of our actual existence to which it points and of which it is the symbol." Then he hastens to add that a further thing needing to be said and to which Bultmann should have devoted more clarity is that the "existence" of which the myth is the expression is the existence of the church.[233] It was the same theme as was struck in *Criticism and Faith*,

---

230. Knox, *Myth and Truth,* pp. 52-62.
231. Knox, *Myth and Truth,* pp. 68-69.
232. Knox, *Myth and Truth,* p. 73.
233. Knox, *Myth and Truth,* p. 49.

to the effect that interpretation can never be the affair of the lone expositor. Knox died at his home in Medford, New Jersey, at age eighty-nine.

Samuel Terrien (1911-2002) taught at Union Seminary from 1941 to 1976, first as instructor in Old Testament, then as Auburn Professor, finally as Davenport Professor of Hebrew and Cognate Languages. Best known for his work on the Psalms, Terrien registered his reflections on the problems and tasks of interpretation in a monograph entitled *The Bible and the Church*,[234] and in an extensive biblical-theological study entitled *The Elusive Presence*.[235]

For Terrien, use of the historical approach is axiomatic, its legitimacy residing in its object, the God who intervenes in history, but more particularly, the Christ who appears in the person of Jesus.[236] This approach Terrien stipulates as "literary aesthetics," that is, as alertness to the nuance of verbs, sensitivity to the writer's "verve," awareness of literary articulation and of the embrace between thought and form. These are the first prerequisites of Bible interpretation. But they require supplementation in the interpreter's "enlistment," that is, in a theological activity involving the spirit and will beyond the emotions or the intellect. This enlistment was often ignored by the medieval and Renaissance church despite its careful preservation of the Bible.[237] Such a theological interpretation or "interpretation of history by faith" is not to be confused with biblicism, an aberration that takes the Bible as an end in itself, makes of it an absolute, and confuses it with God. Terrien writes:

> The theological interpreter . . . will be profoundly aware of the mystery of divine Presence that pervades the Bible. He will enter its world with awe and open expectation. But such an attitude shall never be confused with intellectual obscurantism. Reverence and humility will prevent the reader of the Bible from interpreting with the illusion of omniscience, but they must never be divorced from intellectual integrity.[238]

Negatively, such integrity requires the refusal to explain away by use of allegorical, spiritual, or mystical interpretation such "anecdotes" respecting the biblical characters as reflect strange levels of belief or morals. Positively, it requires recognition of the Bible as a "true and live myth." Myth, Terrien

234. Samuel Terrien, *The Bible and the Church* (Philadelphia: Westminster, 1962).
235. Samuel Terrien, *The Elusive Presence* (New York: Harper and Row, 1978).
236. Terrien, *The Bible and the Church*, p. 90.
237. Terrien, *The Bible and the Church*, pp. 68, 70-71, 73-74.
238. Terrien, *The Bible and the Church*, p. 77.

writes, denotes a form of discourse intent on describing a truth that cannot be adequately formulated by rational thought. Thus, any depiction of truth that cannot be measured or empirically observed belongs to the myth-making process. The Bible is a "true and live myth" through which the universe and the history of humankind are brought within the compass of the divine activity. Whereas pagan myths are "space myths," that is, attempts at describing the status quo in spatial terms, the Bible is a "time myth," that is, it is related to a dynamic view of history that moves from creation to re-creation through incarnation. The incarnation thus assumes central place in Terrien's hermeneutic. Recognition of the incarnation, Israel's gift to Christianity, as the central event of history, is key to understanding the Bible, its unity, and its relevance. Or again, to see the story of the birth, ministry, death, and glorification of Jesus as "history introduced into myth," in contrast to, say, the story of Adam and Eve in the garden as "myth introduced into history," is indispensable to theological interpretation.[239] Ten years later, in his *Anatomy of Criticism*, the Canadian literary theorist Northrop Frye (1912-91) would echo Terrien's study, writing of the book of Isaiah that its theme epitomized the theme of the Bible as a whole, "as the parable of Israel lost, captive, and redeemed."[240] In the same volume Frye wrote that a "genuine higher criticism of the Bible would be a synthesizing process which would start with the assumption that the Bible is a definitive myth, a single archetypal structure extending from creation to apocalypse."[241] Frye then noted that from the poetic point of view, the action of the Bible included the themes of the three great epics, the destruction and captivity of the city in the *Iliad,* the return home in the *Odyssey,* and the building of the new city in the *Aeneid.*[242]

Since recognition of the incarnation or a dynamic view moving from creation to re-creation through incarnation spells discernment of a homogeneity attaching to the biblical books, and since this homogeneity points to a continuity between the "Covenants," as Terrien puts it, this recognition must (pace Cadbury) move the interpreter to put the question of "the possibility, the legitimacy, and perhaps even the inevitability of biblical theology."[243] Recent discussion, Terrien writes, has shown the weakness of various attempts at constructing an Old Testament theology on the cov-

239. Terrien, *The Bible and the Church*, pp. 78-79, 82-83, 87.

240. Northrop Frye, *Anatomy of Criticism* (Princeton, N.J.: Princeton University Press, 1971), p. 56.

241. Frye, *Anatomy of Criticism*, p. 188.

242. Frye, *Anatomy of Criticism*, pp. 316, 319.

243. Terrien, *The Elusive Presence*, p. 33.

enant motif or on such "central" but in fact "peripheral" or at least "partial" notions as election, kingdom, redemption, community, or eschatology. It has also revealed the difficulty of presenting Israel's various testimonies respecting the successive waves of historical challenge and response, and this, Terrien adds, despite the "valuable and even brilliant" work of the Heidelberg Old Testament scholar Gerhard von Rad (1901-71), celebrated developer of the "tradition-historical" approach. Biblical theologians, he writes, have become increasingly aware of the relativity of historical research, and the dangers of historicism. They recognize the need for becoming critically explicit regarding their epistemological presuppositions, their limitations in attempting to penetrate scriptural meaning and remain faithful to it while rendering it in the current cultural worldview. They also recognize that responsibility toward the work of the systematic theologian requires a "descriptive task," which goes beyond the mere cataloguing of mythopoetic formulations of the biblical documents.[244]

In the midst of these concessions Terrien submits his own construction, which he calls a "theology of presence." The religion of the Hebrews, he writes, of Israel, of post-exilic Judaism, and of the early Christians is permeated by the experience, the cultic recollection, and the proleptically appropriated expectation of the presence of Yahweh among humankind. It was this "Hebraic theology of presence" that dominated all the interpretations of the person of Jesus, from Mark to Revelation. In his own words:

> It is the Hebraic theology of presence, not the covenant ceremonial, that constitutes the field of forces which links — across the biblical centuries — the fathers of Israel, the reforming prophets, the priests of Jerusalem, the psalmists of Zion, the Jobian poet, and the bearers of the gospel. The history of biblical religion hinges upon the growth and transformation of the Hebraic theology of presence.[245]

And, Terrien argues, it was this reality of divine presence as the constant element of distinctiveness throughout the centuries of biblical history that produced the power of a "canonical" scripture.[246]

This sense of presence, Terrien continues, is persistently compounded with an awareness of absence. In the whole of scripture, he writes, the motif

---

244. Terrien, *The Elusive Presence*, pp. 33, 472-73, 39.
245. Terrien, *The Elusive Presence*, p. 31.
246. Terrien, *The Elusive Presence*, p. 42.

of presence induces a "magnetic field of forces" that maintains a dynamic tension between divine self-disclosure and divine self-concealment. The proximity to God creates a memory and an anticipation of certitude, but it always defies human appropriation. "The presence remains elusive."[247] Terrien illustrates by way of psalm interpretation. Noting the laments that complain of the veiling of the Deity as confessions of sin, he refers to Psalm 22 as an exception. He observes that if the hero of the poem was not a king but a single member of the community, his plight must have been the more intolerable since he had no answer to the question "why," and found neither justification nor meaning in his agony. But after his ordeal he looked back and understood that "absence was presence deferred." The psalmists in general, Terrien continues, exhibited theological maturity because they were forced to recognize their true selves vis-à-vis God, even when God hid from them. By avoiding them, God became more and more manifest to them. It was an avoidance that disclosed to them not only the meaning of their existence but the intrinsic quality of divinity. "The God of the psalmists made them live in this world, and they lived without using him. . . . The *Deus revelatus* is the *Deus absconditus.*" When God no longer overwhelmed the senses of perception and concealed himself behind the adversity of historical existence, those who clung to the promise were still aware of God's nearness in the veil of his seeming absence. For them, Terrien concludes, "the center of life was a *Deus absconditus atque praesens.*"[248]

In an essay on T. S. Eliot (1888-1965) entitled "The Pantomime Cat: T. S. Eliot and Hebrew-Christian Dynamic," Terrien faults the American-born, English poet for his fear of sexuality, his scorn of the democratic form of society, his disparaging of ecumenical rapprochement, and his rejection of the reality of time, hence of history. He writes:

Faith without vision is precisely the memory and the hope of an Elusive Presence, when infinite reality appears to be hidden or absent. Eliot ignores the *Deus Absconditus,* the God concealed within history (Isa. 45:9), whose power human faith apprehends calmly, tenaciously, triumphantly. Instead of saying, "Redeem the time!" Eliot flatly states, "All time is unredeemable."[249]

247. Terrien, *The Elusive Presence*, pp. 29, 43.
248. Terrien, *The Elusive Presence*, pp. 323, 325-26, 470.
249. Samuel Terrien, "The Pantomime Cat: T. S. Eliot and Hebrew-Christian Dynamic," *Theology Today* 44, no. 4 (January 1988): 7.

In a final paragraph Terrien refers to Amos, "kidnapped from behind his flock by the God of the poor," to the singer of Job who cried to the hidden God, to the poet who saw Wisdom as mediatrix between creature and Creator, to Jesus "who filled the Void of the Holy Place" as practicing an introspection as complex as that of Sophocles (497/496 B.C.–406/405 B.C.), Shakespeare (1564-1616), or Eliot, but who did not "proceed from unreality to unreality," did not reject time.[250]

Accordingly, that dedication of self that theological interpretation requires as supplement to the "critical faculties of the mind" is the "celebration of presence," its obverse side the affirmation of time, of history. It is a celebration "in the midst of the community of faith." It is thus not an isolated but a "cultic commemoration of presence" and "expectation of its renewal," a commemoration extending from the "theophanic past" to the "epiphanic end" of history. "Divine presence," whether perceived or deferred, experienced or elusive, the reality that produced the power of a "canonical" scripture, demands pride of place in authentic interpretation. *The Elusive Presence* concludes with the question whether "the Hebraic theology of presence" provides a legitimate approach to a genuine theology of the entire Bible, and ends with the answer that "contemporary trends" suggest "this may well be the case."[251]

Princeton

Up to and following World War II, occupation with questions of interpretation among scholars in the United States was easily equaled if not actually exceeded by that of Otto A. Piper of Princeton Theological Seminary. In a host of essays, books, and reviews, the exile from Hitler's Germany addressed the problems attendant on Bible interpretation.

Otto Alfred Wilhelm Piper was born on November 29, 1891, in Lichte, Thuringia. After attending the Erfurt gymnasium he began university studies at Jena, where he remained from 1910 to 1913, with a short semester break at Marburg. At Jena he studied with Heinrich Weinel (1874-1936), Adolf Jülicher (1857-1938), and Hans Lietzmann (1875-1942). In 1913 Piper spent eight months in Paris, studying simultaneously at the Sorbonne and the Faculté Libre de Théologie Protestante. In France

250. Terrien, "The Pantomime Cat," p. 9.
251. Terrien, *The Elusive Presence*, pp. 41-42, 470.

he was attracted to the religious life of the minority French Reformed Church and to the ministry of the preacher and ecumenical pioneer Wilfred Monod (1867-1943). One year later he spent a brief period at Heidelberg, studying economics and political theory, after which he took his ordination exams. With the outbreak of World War I in 1914, he went into the army and was sent to the front as an officer. On August 15, 1915, he was seriously wounded. He spent the closing months of the war in Munich, taking courses at the university, and attended the circles of such Protestant thinkers as Johannes Müller of Elmau (1864-1949), with whom he remained a lifelong friend. He then moved to Göttingen, focusing on the writings of Luther and the Reformers and on the work of Swabian biblical scholars. In 1920, he took his doctorate with a thesis analyzing the concept of religious experience in the thought of Schleiermacher. He taught first at Göttingen as *Privatdozent,* then at Münster as full professor and successor to Karl Barth. Because of its concern for the needs of the working classes, Piper openly joined the Social Democratic Party, an engagement that would seriously inhibit his career. In 1927 he was a delegate to the Lausanne Conference on Faith and Order, and in 1928, 1930, and 1931 traveled to France to further inter-church contacts. In 1930 the Theological Faculty of Paris awarded him an honorary doctorate. In 1933, after having delivered a course of lectures on state and church ("Kirche und Politik"), which, together with his advocacy of a "common confession of German Protestantism on questions of public life," contributed toward the formation of the Confessing Church (Bekennende Kirche),[252] he was dismissed from his teaching post and no longer allowed to hold a professorship in Germany. In November 1933 he spent a year as refugee in the Quaker College at Woodbrooke, Birmingham, England. In 1934 Swansea University in Wales invited him as "guest of the college." He was later invited to the College of North Wales in Bangor. In 1937-38 he was offered a visiting professorship in systematic theology by John Alexander Mackay, president of Princeton Theological Seminary. In 1941 he was offered a permanent chair as the first Helen P. Manson Professor of New Testament Literature and Exegesis, and one year later became a naturalized U.S. citizen. Both Piper's sons were drafted, the elder killed in the Battle of the Bulge. Serving as founder and president of the American Emergency Committee for German Protestantism, in 1960 he received the Officer's

---

252. See Friedrich Wilhelm Graf, "Lutherischer Neurealismus, Otto Piper — ein früher Pazifist," *Lutherische Monatshefte* 27 (1988): 361.

Cross of Merit from President Heinrich Lübke of the Federal Republic of Germany. Piper retired in 1962, and died on February 13, 1982.

Piper's list of the impediments to genuine Bible interpretation was unusual, if only in length. On the one side, lay orthodoxy and fundamentalism or biblicism, and on the other, an aggregation of methods and perspectives from earliest Christianity to contemporary thought. Of orthodoxy Piper wrote that it represented a shift from Reformation perspective to an idea of the Bible as a collection of infallible doctrines existing outside of time, useful for dogmatic propositions, thus reflecting a suspicious tie to the "human forms of knowledge of a particular period of church history." The result was an interpretation of biblical authority in legal terms, an authority resulting from the omnipotence and sovereignty rather than the saving activity of God. Piper was insistent: the Bible did not possess legal but saving authority, and only such authority constituted the object by which the *vera doctrina* was to be normed. This meant that the content of the Bible, not the historical forms of its ideas, was normative. Thus, with the Bible's nature as communication disregarded, its historical character neglected, and its content assumed to be known ahead of any interpretation — an enterprise in which the exegete always found his special brand of theology — in orthodoxy the Bible as "instrument of uncreated truth" became "a created truth sufficient unto itself," its truthfulness subject to the test of logical consistency. Nor did pietism escape Piper's attack. Its exclusive focus on personal redemption and the practice of devotional life resulted in a similar truncation.[253]

Analogously, fundamentalism or biblicism, in its peculiar American form, gave to the Bible an uncreated sanctity of its own, reducing the biblical revelation to an idolatrous worship of the text of the King James Version. By this means the Bible was allowed to take God's place, was treated as an oracle, and its instrumental character and thus the mediate character of its truth ignored. But such adherence to an infallible text never guaranteed infallibility of interpretation. The view of scripture as sole and infallible rule of faith and life obviously did not suffice to prevent serious disagreements in biblical exposition. Conversely, it produced a paucity of exegetical results. Ironically, the fundamentalist appeared satisfied with the

---

253. Otto A. Piper, *Gottes Wahrheit und die Wahrheit der Kirche* (Tübingen: J. C. B. Mohr, 1933), pp. 41-42, 77-79, 80-81; idem, "Die Mittelbarkeit der christlichen Ethik," *Zeitschrift für Evangelische Ethik* (May 1957): 203; idem, "Biblical Theology and Systematic Theology," *Journal of Bible and Religion* 25, no. 2 (1957): 106; idem, *Protestantism in an Ecumenical Age* (Philadelphia: Fortress, 1965), p. 100.

few ideas that had been the stock-in-trade of an earlier century.[254] Piper noted that for fear of an erroneous appropriation of God's Word Judaism had resorted to a theory of mechanical inspiration of the Old Testament, and attempted to gain knowledge of all truth through literal interpretation. It had committed the error of identifying the Bible with the Word of God. Piper did not go on to state, but allowed the inference, that such views of the Bible as orthodoxy and fundamentalism reflected already existed in the primitive church since the attraction of Jewish patterns of interpretation could not be altogether excluded.[255]

Piper's list of impediments alternative to orthodoxy and fundamentalism was noticeably longer. He wrote of the dominating influence of Greek philosophy and mentality on the thought of the church, as a result of which the biblical message was obscured. As an accompaniment of that influence allegory deserved jettisoning since it was no exegesis at all.[256] "We have no right," he wrote, "to disregard the historical content of Old Testament prophecies as is done, for instance, in allegorical interpretation."[257] He noted the influence of nominalism on the Reformers, an "incomplete" perspective that denied the reality of the spiritual world, handicapped theological discussion of history, and led to the one-sided insistence on justification by faith.[258] He diagnosed modern Gospel interpretation as persistence in reproducing eighteenth-century rationalism. Among the rationalists only Lessing saw that such an interpretation was incompatible with the nature of the documents since it ignored the unique historical position assigned to Jesus in the Gospels. The humanists Goethe, Friedrich Schiller (1759-1805), and Robert Browning (1812-89) likewise held that the historical element in the Gospels was not to be neglected. Yet, where the rationalist regarded the nature and significance of biblical and non-biblical phenomena as identical, the humanist reduced the significance of Jesus to an impersonation of the idea of the truly reli-

---

254. Piper, *Gotteswahrheit und die Wahrheit der Kirche,* p. 77; idem, foreword to J. C. K. von Hofmann, *Interpreting the Bible,* trans. Christian Preus (Minneapolis: Augsburg, 1959), p. vi; idem, *Protestantism in an Ecumenical Age,* pp. 99, 123.

255. Otto A. Piper, *God in History* (New York: Macmillan, 1939), pp. 30-31; idem, "Biblical Theology and Systematic Theology," p. 6; idem, "Protestant Theology's Predicament," *Theology Today* 20 (1963): 483-84.

256. Piper, *Protestantism in an Ecumenical Age,* p. 50; Otto A. Piper, "Principles of New Testament Interpretation," *Theology Today* 3 (1946): 199-200.

257. Piper, *New Testament Theology,* part II, unpublished (n.d.), p. 39.

258. Piper, *God in History,* p. 53.

gious life, a view modified by Ernst Troeltsch (1865-1923) of Berlin who assigned him a merely relative absoluteness.[259] The "scientific biblicism" of many of his contemporaries Piper described as insufficient as a naïve biblicism. He noted the confidence of the "school" leading from Timothy Colani (1824-88) of Strasburg and the French theorist Ernst Renan (1823-92) to Edgar Johnson Goodspeed of Chicago, Morton Scott Enslin (1897-1983) of the University of Pennsylvania, and Ethelbert Stauffer (1902-79) of Erlangen. All were mistaken in supposing they had rediscovered the objective historical reality. Similarly, members of the History of Religions School *(Religionsgeschichtliche Schule)* lacked understanding of the significance of holy history *(Heilsgeschichte)* for the remainder of history, and on the "open sores" of whose historiography Ernst Troeltsch attempted to stick the "plasters of an anemic speculation."[260] Karl Barth, Piper added, reacted strongly to this deplorable development but stopped only halfway. At the other extreme of fundamentalism, that "pragmatic version" of seventeenth-century repristination theology, lay the existentialism of Bultmann, with his method of demythologizing, or of Friedrich Gogarten (1887-1967) of Göttingen, co-founder of the so-called dialectical theology movement. All were anxious at any price to obtain a humanistic rather than a historical gospel.[261] In short, in its reaction to the conceptualism into which the theology of the West had lapsed at an early age, modern Protestant theology took it for granted that God should enter into direct relation with humankind, that it should be directly confronted with God's redemptive will. For Bible interpretation this could only mean that it was left to anyone to decide how much of the Bible, if anything, should be accepted.[262] In fact, some scholars, Piper wrote, pursued modern criticism so intensively that little of the Bible had been left intact. In this fashion the Bible's authority was radically and fatally questioned, and Protestantism cut the very tie that should bind it to the other partners in the ecumenical encounter.[263]

Despite the space given to what he believed to be the impediments

259. Otto A. Piper, "Christology and History," *Theology Today* 19 (1962): 327-28; idem, *New Testament Theology,* part I, unpublished (n.d.), pp. 40, 46.

260. Piper, *God in History,* pp. xvii-xviii.

261. Piper, foreword to *Interpreting the Bible,* p. vi; idem, *Protestantism in an Ecumenical Age,* p. 191; idem, *New Testament Theology,* part II, p. 47.

262. Otto A. Piper, "The Virgin Birth: The Meaning of the Gospel Accounts," *Interpretation,* no. 2 (1964): 143; idem, foreword to *Interpreting the Bible,* p. vi.

263. Piper, "Protestant Theology's Predicament," p. 484.

to authentic interpretation, Piper gave the lion's share to his description of the interpreter's task. First of all, he spent little time justifying the historical-critical method, writing that the origin of biblical criticism not only antedated the rise of neo-Protestantism but the Reformation as well. "Without exception," he stated, "the great interpreters of the Scripture have employed the critical treatment of the biblical text as an indispensable tool of exegesis."[264] Nor was much space given the argument that the biblical books in no wise require a special, unique method of interpretation over against that required respecting other literature. The argument could be stated in a single sentence:

> The Protestant exegete does not employ different methods in the processes of exegesis proper and of comprehension from those used in the interpretation of any non-biblical document.[265]

The greater part of the discussion was left to an outlining of the interpreter's task and the underlying assumptions. To that task belonged awareness of "the basic unity of the New Testament."[266] In his inaugural address at Princeton in 1942, Piper included among his hermeneutical axioms awareness of the Christocentric purpose of the biblical revelation. This purpose gives to the Bible its unity despite its diverse expressions. Piper wrote,

> It is out of his free sovereign grace that God speaks through [the Bible]. and there is only one subject he wants us to understand from the bottom of our heart, namely, the fact that he has come to rescue us from the bondage of sin, death, and the devil, and to make us certain of the fact that in Jesus Christ his purpose is accomplished.[267]

The Bible's purpose was thus Christocentric. Clearly, this raised the question of the significance of the Old Testament and its relation to the New. Piper's response was that the Old Testament required interpreting in light of the ministry of Christ and our experience of its effects. In the concrete, this meant assigning to the Old Testament persons and events the status of

---

264. Piper, *Protestantism in an Ecumenical Age*, p. 119.
265. Piper, "Die Mittelbarkeit der christlichen Ethik," pp. 202-3.
266. Piper, "Principles of New Testament Interpretation," p. 197.
267. Otto A. Piper, "Modern Problems of New Testament Exegesis," *Princeton Seminary Bulletin* 36 (1942): 9.

types. As types they indicated the operation of an invisible reality whose manifestation still lay ahead, but which, as "the forming factor," was "superior to its imprint."[268] Constant use of Old Testament passages in the New might suggest that the New Testament was merely a fulfillment of the prophecy of the Old. At this idea Piper demurred:

> No, everything in the Old Testament — history, law, sacrifice — find their fulfillment in the New Testament. Because none of them is an end in itself, they become, as seen from the New Testament, types of the things to come. This is why from the Christian viewpoint the Old Testament must be understood both historically and typologically.[269]

Piper was quick to add that this did not mean the Old Testament was to be used *only* typologically. It had to be used historically. It was the event itself, in its actuality, and the divine purpose behind it, its structures, not its details, that urged typological interpretation.[270] In an article entitled "Unchanging Promises: Exodus in the New Testament," Piper illustrated his point. The framework within which the material of Mark's Gospel was arranged footed on a typological use of the book of Exodus. That is, the original pattern of the Gospel story saw the Exodus narrative as the preparation and first step of God's saving work. In the selection of motifs from Exodus the Gospel writer clearly followed Jewish tradition according to which Israel's religion was molded more by that book than by any other. From its emphasis on exodus Israel's religion received "teleological character with an historical goal." The sequence was clear: from the exodus event, its historicity signaling an invisible reality yet to be manifest, to the event's recording in a book giving shape to Israel's religion, to its giving teleology and a historical goal to that religion from the emphasis given it, to its giving shape to the original pattern of the Gospel story, to its furnishing the framework of the Gospel of Mark.[271]

The task did not end with attention to the Bible's unity. The interpreter needed to understand. To understanding or "comprehension" belonged the mastery of two tasks: first, it meant locating each idea in its specific place within the author's total view of life and reality, and second,

---

268. Otto A. Piper, "Unchanging Promises: Exodus in the New Testament," *Interpretation* 11 (1957): 10.

269. Piper, *New Testament Theology*, part I, p. 50.

270. Piper, *New Testament Theology*, part I, p. 52.

271. Piper, "Unchanging Promises," pp. 19-21.

determining the relation between the idea of the document and our own ideas.[272] Mastery of the first task involved getting at the document's "life movement," at the move from author to intended reader. Beginning with the author, "reproducing as far as possible the mental process going on in the author's mind at the time of his writing" was primordial.[273] But "life movement" was more complex than authorial intent. It involved the movement of the author's ideas, the discernment of his forms of speech and style. Poetry, for example, "the paramount type of art and thus . . . the mode of purest expression," had been a never-ending source of misunderstanding for modern exegetes. There was even more to getting at "life movement." The interpreter needed to get beyond verbal expressions to visualize the realities with which the words were concerned. It was to this part of the task, Piper wrote, that Wilhelm Dilthey gave a significance that could hardly be overrated.[274] Hence the demand for attention to the author's use of images, the special value of which lay in the fact that they influenced the mind to a greater degree than mere sense experience or conceptual language.[275] The list of requirements kept tumbling out. As to the author's background, to limit research to the Mishnah and similar rabbinical sources, or to turn exclusively to Jewish apocalypticism was a methodological error. There never was a time, wrote Piper, when the two trends were so completely separated. As for the author's use of "secular informations," they needed attending to as a means by which the author expressed his revealed insight into the divine purpose in terms of the natural knowledge available to him.[276] Not in addition, perhaps, but in summary of this aspect of the task Piper wrote that understanding the literal sense of the text involved coming to grips with the author's "general scale of values," a phrase he used in tandem with the author's "worldview."[277]

Coming to grips with the author's scale of values obviously meant dealing with the miraculous. Since modern scientific thinking was built on the axiom of an unchanging, uniform, and universal order of nature,

---

272. Piper, "Principles of New Testament Interpretation," p. 197.

273. Piper, "Principles of New Testament Interpretation," p. 193.

274. Piper, "Principles of New Testament Interpretation," pp. 194, 195; idem, *God in History*, p. 64; idem, "Biblical Theology and Systematic Theology," p. 107.

275. Otto A. Piper, "The Transforming Power of the Gospel," *Theology Today* 12, no. 4 (1956): 448-49.

276. Piper, "Unchanging Promises," p. 21; idem, foreword to *Interpreting the Bible*, p. viii.

277. Piper, "Principles of New Testament Interpretation," pp. 198, 200.

miracle construed as a temporary suspension of the order of nature was bound to give offense. But, Piper added, this implied a "vexing antinomy." When applied to the religious view of life and this world, the axiom demanded either that this was the best of all possible worlds, or that it was totally devoid of meaning due to its ineradicable evils.[278] Piper held to an alternative. Reasons for believing in the historicity of a narrative, thus of a miracle, could be weightier than those supporting its denial. He asked:

> Will not the historian test the reliability of a document by inquiring whether effects of an alleged event can be found when its historicity cannot be apprehended directly?[279]

The issue took on particular relevance with regard to the miracle of the Virgin Birth. "From the historian's point of view," Piper wrote, thus by implication apart from any "leap of faith," the truthfulness of the birth narratives of Jesus deserved to be affirmed.[280]

Piper devoted considerable space to the interpretation of symbol and myth. In his 1942 inaugural lecture, he conceded that in some instances it would be difficult to determine whether an event was to be understood literally or as symbol, but asserted that in others the event was obviously to be taken symbolically. For example, the cursing of the fig tree in Mark 11:12-14 required symbolic interpretation: "The Jewish people had been granted half a millennium since their return from the Exile to get ready for the coming of the promised Messiah. Will he now find fruit?" Reference to the "desolating sacrilege" in Mark 13:14 was hardly intended to remind the reader of Caligula's (A.D. 12-41) unsuccessful attempt to desecrate the Temple. The evangelist rather intended to stress the "symbolical character of the expression." Reference to the cosmic events in Mark 13:24 was not to "astronomical catastrophes" but rather to a "manifest termination of the earthly order of values." The escape of the naked young man in Mark 13:51-52 symbolized "what happens to a person who in the hour of danger withdraws from Jesus." Piper denied the arbitrariness of symbolically interpreting the rending of the Temple curtain in Mark 15:38, and read the crowd's daring Jesus to come down from the cross in 15:51-52 as a summons to descend to its level.[281]

---

278. Piper, "The Virgin Birth," p. 146.
279. Piper, "The Virgin Birth," p. 142.
280. Piper, "The Virgin Birth," pp. 140-41.
281. Piper, "Modern Problems of New Testament Exegesis," pp. 171-74.

In *God in History,* and in his lectures on New Testament theology, printed exclusively for class or seminar, Piper dealt at some length with the problem of myth. First of all, he asserted that it should no longer be denied that in the first chapters of the Bible, human pre-history was narrated in mythical language. He then went on to define myth as follows:

> A myth is a story by which events in the spiritual world are described in terms of earthly occurrences, or earthly events are shown in relation to their spiritual roots.[282]

Humankind had forever struggled to give verbal expression to the supernatural. Mythical language was used to solve the problem. It speaks of the supernatural in concrete terms as if it were similar to the natural world. At the same time, it reflects the peculiar character of the supernatural world by the absence of the limitations the same objects would have if they designated phenomena of the natural world. For this reason, Piper stated, the interpreter had to keep in mind that mythical usage always carried the proviso that the words used pointed to a reality of a nature different from and superior to that of sense experience. He was eager to add that the mythical view was based on facts. Describing realities that transcended the categories of space and time, as well as our imagination, myth was nevertheless real. It was, he asserted, "the genuine form of revelation."[283]

Piper was not so sanguine as to believe this part of the task could be perfectly executed in every conceivable instance. For example, of the Bible's symbolic terms he could write that the "simplicity" of biblical language could facilitate agreement over the essential truths among all who understood the spiritual nature of those terms, yet the "profundity" of those terms left room for diversity, depending on the nature and degree of the interpreters' spiritual insight.[284] He could express the concession more pointedly, baldly stating that "an increasing number of points in the document must be left unexplained because they transcend the mental stature of the exegete."[285]

At one point, at least, Piper stressed that getting at the life movement, at the scale of values or the worldview of an author, transcended

---

282. Piper, *God in History,* p. 61.

283. Piper, *God in History* p. 61; idem, *New Testament Theology,* part I, pp. 44, 78; idem, *New Testament Theology,* part II, pp. 56-57.

284. Piper, "Modern Problems of New Testament Exegesis," p. 9.

285. Piper, "Principles of New Testament Interpretation," p. 199.

whatever may have been in the author's mind. That point was the point of prophecy. With particular reference to the Old Testament authors he wrote that it would be erroneous to suppose that the meaning of a prophecy was exhausted by whatever the writer himself thought at the moment. Whatever the writer wrote was full of potential beyond its reference to a given historical situation.[286]

According to Piper, mastery of the second part of "comprehension" involved "the determining of the relationship between the ideas of the documents and the ideas of our own mind."[287] If the statement appears skeletal, Piper could give it flesh and blood: "The interpretation of a document consists of two different though closely related processes — exegesis and appropriation." Or again, "a true interpretation must be both historical and spiritual."[288] Piper commended Barth's commentary on Romans for insisting that the biblical books presented themselves as revelation and "demanded of the reader to accept them as divine truth." He likewise commended Bultmann, who taught that as divine truth the Bible addresses itself "not merely to my intellect but primarily to my very self." Through the Marburger's insistence on the self-transcendence of the text, he wrote, we will learn to understand how "all biblical texts point beyond our level of understanding of the divine realities."[289] In other words, the "openness" required of the interpreter presupposed recognition of the Bible as God's Word, as the divine Word of truth to be held in supreme authority.[290] Piper gave further specificity to this openness when referring to Old Testament interpretation. By itself, apart from discovery of its spiritual meaning in Jesus Christ, the Old Testament remained a collection of laws of the ancient Jews that no longer placed us under obligation.[291]

"Appropriation," "spiritual interpretation" construed as acceptance of the biblical books as revelation, as divine truth, as God's Word, or the "discovery" of the meaning of the Old Testament was not an attitude or posture simply to be assumed, but occurred only through faith. As Piper

---

286. Piper, *New Testament Theology*, part II, p. 39.

287. Piper, "Principles of New Testament Interpretation," p. 197.

288. Piper, "Principles of New Testament Interpretation," p. 193; idem, *New Testament Theology*, part II, p. 39.

289. Piper, "Biblical Theology and Systematic Theology," p. 109; idem, *Protestantism in an Ecumenical Age*, p. 192.

290. Piper, *Protestantism in an Ecumenical Age*, p. 191; idem, "Principles of New Testament Interpretation," p. 202.

291. Piper, *God in History*, p. 23.

wrote, "the claim of the Biblical books to contain a divine message of supreme importance for all men cannot be appreciated except by faith."[292] This meant that the interpreter was to approach the Bible as a learner:

> Gone is the presumption that one already knows everything of the nature and purpose of the Father of Jesus Christ. One will rather read it in a state of constant expectancy and, when the light of truth dawns upon one's heart, be prepared to give up any view of God and human life previously held.[293]

To Piper's mind this "openness," interpreted as "search for the present Christ who speaks to us through the Bible," had hardly begun in Protestantism.[294]

More, the task was not to be undertaken in isolation. Interpretation needed to occur within the context of the believing community. The interpreter's subjective insights needed checking by "the spiritual insights of the Church as a whole." Piper wrote that those who attempt interpretation can only do acceptable work when they recognize how they have been conditioned by, and are responsible for, the spiritual life of the church. Though denominational standards or confessions can never be absolutely binding, their heuristic value for interpretation is beyond question.[295] On the other hand, the conclusion of the form-critical scholars respecting the creative role of the church in the matter of handing on, supplementing, and enlarging the Jesus-tradition required radical revision. "The time has come," wrote Piper, to demythologize the myth of a creative collectivity called *die Gemeinde.* The documents of the New Testament confirm the findings of sociology and anthropology to the effect that collectivities are receptive, not creative entities. In fact, without the authority of the apostles who counteracted the centrifugal tendencies in the congregations, the church would have disintegrated.[296]

Threading through all his work was Piper's commitment to a school that may initially have attracted him during his first stay in Göttingen, the

---

292. Piper, "Principles of New Testament Interpretation," p. 203.

293. Otto A. Piper, "How I Study My Bible," from the series "What the Bible Means to Me," *The Christian Century* 43, no. 10 (March 1946): 301.

294. Piper, *Protestantism in an Ecumenical Age,* p. 215.

295. Piper, "Modern Problems of New Testament Exegesis," pp. 13-14.

296. Otto A. Piper, "The Origin of the Gospel Pattern," *Journal of Biblical Literature* 78, no. 2 (1959): 123.

school of *Heilsgeschichte,* of holy, sacred, or redemptive history. Principal representatives of the school were the Württemberg scholars Johann Albrecht Bengel, Johann Tobias Beck (1804-78), and Karl August Auberlen (1824-64), as well as the Erlanger Johan Christian Konrad von Hofmann. Roots of this school reached back to the reflections of the Swiss reformers Huldrych Zwingli (1484-1531) and his pupil Johannes Oecolampadius (1482-1531), to the "federal theology" of the Dutch theologians Jan Cocceius (1603-69) and his follower Campegius Vitringa (1664-1772), and, it is argued, concepts foundational to the school can be traced to the writings of Irenaeus and Augustine. In America the school's earliest representative may have been Jonathan Edwards. A century later the school's principal representatives were the Hodges, Charles and Alexander (1828-86), Benjamin B. Warfield (1851-1921), Gerhardus Vos (1862-1949), and J. Gresham Machen (1881-1937) — all of Princeton.

Piper did not devote much space to justifying the attraction that *Heilsgeschichte,* the offspring of what he called "biblical realism," had for him. It was enough, for example, simply to quote Rudolf Bultmann to the effect that interpretation of the Bible begins with a *Vorverständnis,* with a preliminary understanding of its subject matter.[297] That preliminary understanding involved comprehension of the Bible's truth as contained in a "process," rather than in an infallible doctrine.[298] Piper insisted that the biblical writers themselves were not so much interested in developing a system of religious notions as in "bearing witness to facts of experience and to the significance of those facts for our redemption."[299] Now, in his own time, guided by "biblical realism," scholars had come to see that Irenaeus and the school of holy history were on the right track in emphasizing the purposeness of God's activity.[300] Lutheran and Reformed theologians had espoused views of Christ's work in which the Gospel story had lost almost all significance. With their understanding of history as the realm of the contingent, Johann Gottlieb Fichte, David Friedrich Strauss, and the Anglican William Inge (1860-1954), dean of London's St. Paul's Cathedral, construed faith as the attempt to bring the eternal into one's life, thus saw the Gospels as a narrative of the birth of the divine in the human, its growth, conflicts, and fulfillment. The result was the total irrelevance of the historicity of

297. Piper, *Protestantism in an Ecumenical Age,* p. 141.
298. Piper, "Biblical Theology and Systematic Theology," p. 109.
299. Piper, *Protestantism in an Ecumenical Age,* p. 49.
300. Piper, *Protestantism in an Ecumenical Age,* p. 51.

the New Testament events. Harnack of Berlin espoused an "unhistorical mysticism" with his view of the Old Testament as able to be preserved only when spiritualized and reinterpreted. Piper's Union Seminary contemporary, John Knox, likewise spurned the historical with his understanding of the Christian hope as resting on an indefinable "Christ-event."[301]

To be sure, though the *Heilsgeschichtler* were the only group in Protestant theology to maintain the central significance of holy history, they committed a major error. In essence they simply repeated the stories of the biblical records, and confined themselves to investigating the underlying principles and supernatural structure of the biblical history. What was needed now was to see that the authors of the biblical books recorded events for a contemporary public aware of what was going on in the world around them. To make proper use of the biblical records the biblical narratives had to be delivered from their isolation and set within the whole of history.[302] The reason for it was simple: the making of the biblical books in almost every respect resembled that of any other book, and the historical events they record did not occur in a vacuum but in the context of the ancient Near East and the Hellenistic age. Clearly, in the Old Testament the entire process of history is described as rooted in the world process.[303]

If, finally, the truth of the Bible lay in a "process" rather than in a dogma of infallibility, if it consisted of a series of events from creation through redemption to consummation as reflective of a divine purpose, a process with a purpose witnessed to and interpreted by the biblical authors, then the witness and interpretation of that holy historical, redemptive process implied revelation in a word spoken and received. As Piper wrote,

> The religion underlying holy history is preeminently a religion of the Word . . . the Word that God has spoken to His chosen ones and by which He has manifested His purposes.[304]

---

301. Piper, "Christology and History," p. 326; idem, *New Testament Theology,* part II, pp. 44-45; Otto A. Piper, "Praise of God and Thanksgiving: The Biblical Doctrine of Prayer (1)," *Interpretation* 16, no. 1 (1959): 158.

302. Piper, *God in History,* pp. xix-xx.

303. Piper, foreword to *Interpreting the Bible,* p. v; idem, *New Testament Theology,* part I, p. 17.

304. Piper, *God in History,* p. 69.

CHAPTER EIGHT

Summing Up

To whom or what belongs the distinction of having invented or pioneered the historical-critical method? If the ancient Greeks with their penchant for metaphysics and the Jews with their love of Haggadah inhibited the historical interpretation of texts, then perhaps the beginnings of that method, however inchoate, should be assigned to the Christian community, since Christian faith draws its power from the past and from the fact that the content of this past is given in a book. But if Theodore of Mopsuestia, as Bultmann suggested, is one of the earliest interpreters to pay attention to the nature of Christianity as historical religion, then he has a host of imitators. In that case, Augustine, Faber, Lyra, Luther, Calvin, Müntzer, Flacius with his two-volume *Clavis* — an entire host of successors — deserve the title of pioneer.

If the question is limited to the invention of the historical-critical method as currently construed, one figure stands head and shoulders above the rest: Baruch Spinoza. If none besides Edelmann or Semler publicly acknowledged dependence on Spinoza and his idea of the (ultimate) coherence of reason and revelation, it would hardly be a genetic fallacy to state that every interpreter to follow walked in his shoes, however great the absorption of his influence in the general mélange of the Enlightenment. Spinoza's assigning to religion a place entirely apart from reason, whatever the motivation, would spark debate over the question whether or not Bible interpretation demanded its own set of rules. The distinction between the Bible and the Word of God; opposition to the imposition of what was alien or foreign, whether of metaphysics or dogma; insistence on the Bible as due a reading for its own sake (anciently dubbed *scriptura sui ipsius interpres*), on extracting data from it as parallel to mining facts from nature; emphasis on the "purpose and core" of the biblical tradition (anciently dubbed the *scopus*), on distinguishing the greater from the lesser; the place of the Old Testament; the question of words and their referents in the distinction between "sense" or "meaning" and "truth"; the condition of the original text and the transmitted tradition; the "practical" end it was all to serve (for Spinoza, "peace and freedom") — all of this had Spinoza for a father, whatever the nuance or "spin" given his program. Schleiermacher might be celebrated for birthing the distinction between understanding and interpretation, and Moses Stuart for fathering "biblical science" in the United States, but those two and everyone between was "Spinozistic," whether or not he used or demonized the method. In the hands of a Wolff, a Baumgarten, or a Semler the method might raise the hackles, but who would dare call Jonathan Edwards impious even though he believed that between the Bible and human reason existed "the most perfect harmony" — just one more variation on Spinoza's theme that, at its purpose and core, the biblical revelation cohered, agreed with that "natural light" common to all?

From the pre-critical period to the twentieth century, almost all the interpreters cited saw the Bible as imperiled from one direction or another. The greater number saw the peril as within the community of faith. Luther read it in terms of the collective subjectivity of the Roman Catholic tradition and the individual subjectivity of the enthusiast. He believed that both pope and enthusiast introduced a criterion into interpretation alien to its concern; thus both reflected the human penchant toward the subjective. Calvin saw the peril in a belief that spelled blind submission to the church. Müntzer read the peril in terms of advocacy of the status quo in view of Christ's delay. For Flacius the peril lay in the false methods applied to Bible interpretation on the part of Roman Catholics and such Protestants as Philipp Melanchthon. According to Bengel, a non-historical, orthodox, anti-apocalyptic dogmatic crippled exposition. Locke regarded the threat as consisting of theological systems. For Hamann the danger inherent in orthodoxy was the notion that it possessed eternal life in the scripture without testing it as Christ required. According to Edelmann, orthodoxy, "the old Lutheran view," comprised the chains that needed throwing off. For Semler, the neglect of historical exposition in post-Reformation orthodox interpretation spelled ruin. Schleiermacher had no taste for orthodoxy's divorcing the Bible from the remainder of world literature with its special hermeneutic. Baur avowed that he was conscious of no other striving than of a purely historical standpoint, a consciousness that would protect him against "all those false and hateful judgments inherent in the prevailing tone of an era imprisoned in its limited, particular interests."[1] Ewald nursed hatred for Ferdinand Christian Baur's "tendency criticism," but was no less caustic toward the orthodox with their "ungodly trust in the Bible," their veneration of its letter, all of it giving any Christian attempt at understanding scripture a bad name. Moses Stuart saw the peril in Unitarianism as well as in orthodoxy. Hodge saw it in the anthropology of the New England school, in a moral extremism derived from a radical misreading of the conversion experience, and singled out Semler and his school as pursuing a course that led to loss of faith in the scriptural word. For Barth, the Schleiermacher-Ritschl-Hermann line spelled danger. At Chicago, theology was Harper's bugbear. Burton had no time for orthodoxy's choice of the didactic over narrative as the direct, unmediated thought of God; Case directed his fire at liberals and orthodox alike, and Shailer Mathews read the peril in inattention to the social context. For George Burman Foster the peril faced in the opposite direction: in the reduction of faith to technical skill in the hands of the critics. Cadbury saw what he called "archaizing" as the "greatest peril," a tendency reflected in the biblical theology movement. Miracle, the intervention of supernatural powers, visions and auditions of the Old Testament worthies, Jesus' consciousness of messiahship, and apocalyptic — all the phenomena essential to orthodoxy — screened danger as Porter saw it. Grant saw the peril in what he called "pure rabbinism, bibliolatry, biblicism, [and] literalism" with its anti-Semitic strain.

A few saw the threat as from without, or from within and without. For Wolff and his follower Baumgarten, the peril lay in the pitting of reason against faith. Hamann saw the peril in the Enlightenment thought of his friend Immanuel Kant. The peril for Ewald was a combination of the political and theological. The disaster attendant on Bismarck's unification of the German states on the one hand, and the orthodoxy of the Henstenberg stripe with its obverse side the "atheism" of the Baur-Strauss school on the other — in Ewald's mind the two indissolubly connected — spelled disaster. Among the Americans Edwards saw the church imperiled from three sides: from the claims on behalf of reason and natural religion; from enthusiasts offering visions to authenticate their religious experience; and from Roman Catholic practice and dogma. In the first generation of the Chicago School, the critics regarded the attack on biblical authority as from the outside.

Bultmann listed five external and internal perils: the older rational-

---

1. Ferdinand Christian Baur, *Das Christentum und die christliche Kirche der drei ersten Jahrhunderte* (Tübingen: Verlag und Druck von L. Fr. Fues, 1860), pp. iv-v.

ism, with its doctrines of scripture as universal truths whose validity were to be decided before the bar of reason; historical explanation, rationalism's offspring, with its idea of the individual as an instance of the universal; naturalistic, biological interpretation that limited itself to a history of the nature of human being; psychological method that reduced everything to an expression of a particular psychic life; and idealism with its inquiry into the text as reflecting a given stage of the Spirit's unfolding.

All in all, Protestant orthodoxy, whatever the variety, fared worst with these critics. Seldom, almost nowhere, in the writings of the interpreters referenced can a good word be found for the theological systems of the post-Reformation era. In some instances, the animus had its direct cause in personal experience. Müntzer's attachment to apocalyptic, to the point of giving it political expression, finally cost him his head, and Wolff's perspective earned him dismissal from his professorship, though it was later restored. Edelmann despised the orthodoxy he had once embraced, from, as he put it, inability to encounter one genuine Christian amid all the believing and confessing. For Ewald, as noted, orthodoxy was merely Prussian hegemony disguised, and for his attack on it he twice lost his chair. With the exception of Charles Augustus Briggs and the conflict swirling about him, American experience seldom matched that of the Europeans. Whatever caused their resistance to orthodoxy, whether in the home, school, or church, they largely left unsaid. Beneath the biblicism of modern theology and its identification of biblical truth with historical accuracy Grant saw commitment to current historiography whose advocates wrote as if history had no meaning. He may have witnessed firsthand the anti-Semitism he insisted was a direct consequence of holding the orthodox position. His colleague Knox simply wrote that fundamentalism detached the event from history, thus denying its historicity in the moment of affirming it. According to Piper, in fundamentalism the Bible as instrument of uncreated truth became a created truth sufficient unto itself, and as for pietism, its exclusive focus on personal redemption and the practice of devotional life resulted in a similar truncation.

In the end, it may have been Bengel's arrangement of manuscripts into historically and geographically circumscribed text families that did more damage to the orthodox position than did any of his predecessors or followers. The arrangement broke the back of the *Textus Receptus,* the version to which the orthodox had assigned verbal infallibility, forcing them to a drastic revision of their position by affirming infallibility only of the original *autographa* or *ideocheira.*

To fend off the peril, and in whatever guise, allegory had to be done to death. The Antiochenes had done it, with their rejection of the exegesis of the Alexandrians. With Luther, the doing took time, but in the end the Quadriga of Cassian[2] and others was reduced to one single, indivisible *scopus* or goal. Calvin's indictment read that allegory twisted scripture this way and that, and Semler wrote that commitment to the clarity of scripture demanded the rejection of allegory.

Canon in terms of a sacred, discrete collection also needed putting to the blade. Hamann wrote of it as having come about "by way of an enormous detour," thus the history of its formation could not be decisive for biblical authority. Regarding the Old Testament, Semler was not as coarse in his attack as Edelmann, but saw absolutely no bridge from it to the New. As he saw it, the Christian community had appropriated a canon that belonged to the Jews as Jews alone, not to all men of all times once for all.[3] For Schleiermacher the canon posed a difficult task. In light of the fact that the biblical text was in a language alien to its authors, thus liable to infinite misinterpretation, and since the circumstances moving them to write were unknown, the boundary of canon could not be fixed. As for the Old Testament, it was not inspired, though Christ's and the apostles' reference to it should be preserved — which scarcely meant more than the prophets and the Psalms. In Bultmann's volume on *Primitive Christianity in Its Contemporary Setting*,[4] the Old Testament appeared only to reflect a history of shipwreck. For Porter, "inward appropriation of the Old Testament" undermined the idea of a canon.

2. Whether or not Cassian's Quadriga was dependent on thirteenth-century Jewish exegesis, the fourfold types of interpretation in the period of the Zohar (PRDS) were surely a precursor ("P" for *peshat,* the simple, literal; "R" for *remez,* the search for suggestions contained in the text; "D" for *derush,* the homiletical interpretation; and "S" for *sod,* the theosophical interpretation, the uncovering of mysteries hidden beneath the letter). See Frederick C. Grant, *An Introduction to New Testament Thought* (New York: Abingdon-Cokesbury, 1950), pp. 82-84.

3. In the same period, at Göttingen, Johann David Michaelis, captive to the notion of a Golden Age derived from classical studies, assigned the canonical Old Testament to a race in irreversible decline. Authored by Jews who could not be identified with the ancient Israelites, it thus lacked any spiritual authority over Christians and had no place in modern intellectual inquiry. The language itself, "Euro-Hebrew," was more than a millennium removed from the ancient tongue. "What a decline from the old," Michaelis exclaimed, "and what a swarm of new meanings!" (cited in Michael Legaspi, *The Death of Scripture and the Rise of Biblical Studies* [Oxford: Oxford University Press, 2010], p. 87).

4. Rudolf Bultmann, *Primitive Christianity in Its Contemporary Setting* (Thames and Hudson, 1956).

More, reason deserved a place in Bible exposition. By effort of reason Augustine made his way through ambiguity (almost the entire third book of *De doctrina Christiana* is devoted to it) through consulting what was plain together with church authority, and taking as figurative whatever did not relate to good morals or true faith. Calvin's dialectic in construing the Bible as Word of God and human word resulted in unparalleled philological investigation. Müntzer accented the necessity of scholarship, despite or along with his insistence that whoever relied on the mere letter had been abandoned by God. Flacius's use of the "Lydian Stone" was only an application of logical rules to determine the emphasis of a given text. Bengel's assumption that the biblical history and the course of human history corroborated each other hardly came by way of revelation, nor did Locke's dividing the content of the Bible into four discrete categories. For Wolff reason and revelation were not merely connected but consonant; thus the text was a phenomenon of nature, perceptible through human understanding. His pupil Baumgarten averred that God's intention with the Bible was to unite people to himself in a fashion agreeing with their rationally free condition. Hamann's distaste for the Enlightenment did not spell the exile of reason. Calling canon into question, insisting on the New Testament language as of a piece with the vernacular of its pagan neighbors, taking the Gospels as composed of fragments — all aspects of his thought long unrecognized — meant putting reason in its proper place. Edelmann, another eluding classification among the historians, was nothing if not a rationalist, and did what he did by virtue of the light dawning on his reason from God. For Semler, the application of human reason in Bible interpretation was indispensable, and according to the "early Schleiermacher," technical interpretation dealing with authorial perspective occurred by way of comparison and "divination," a "divination" he did not yet define as construing a text from its author's experience or feeling. For Ewald envisioning the origin of a given prophetic word and from that point understanding what it meant for its time and what it meant for eternity prepared the way for all other questions. Edwards avowed that "the holy rape of the soul" could not take place without a rational apprehension of the revelation. Revelation, wrote Stuart, had to be intelligible. There was rationality in the orthodox Hodge's concession that inspiration had little to accomplish respecting the historical portions of the Bible beyond the selection of materials and accuracy of statement, however warranted by the Spirit. There was something Spinozistic in Hodge's assertion that the exegete worked inductively, collecting data from the Bible just as the scientist from nature. The argument between Barth and Bultmann over "preliminary understanding of the subject matter" of the biblical text *(Vorverständnis)* was nothing if not a conflict over the place of reason in existence apart from faith. In that argument, according to Bultmann, Barth was the irrationalist. The Chicago School's confidence in method, thus in higher criticism as the solution to the hermeneutical problem, goes without saying, as does the Harvard Cadbury's trust in the "social translation of the gospel." Porter was not a rationalist, but the decision to turn to the Bible as literature, more, to poetry, and his choice of models for the needed supplement to historical criticism belonged to what his great-grandfather Edwards had called the "mental matter." According to Grant, "objective scholarship" could supply what was indispensable to exposition. For Terrien use of the historical approach was axiomatic, and the "understanding" that Piper demanded had to do with "locating," "determining," and "reproducing."

As to the nature or character of the text with which they were dealing, the interpreters gave various descriptions. For Augustine and the Reformers, the Bible was the Word of God, according to Calvin dictated by the Spirit, but also a human production, at times incorrect respecting matters of fact. Müntzer described the Bible as an external word of God, distinguishable from the Word of God still to be heard here and now, "external" comprising the letter. According to Flacius, God spoke through the scriptures, its authors functioning as instruments without loss of personality. Bengel acknowledged the Bible to be the Word of God, then proceeded to solve the problem of its ambiguities. Locke wrote of the Bible as divinely inspired though written by fallible beings. According to Baumgarten, understanding of the Bible as "God breathed" extended to language and usage as well as to subject matter and content, albeit applicable only to the original languages. For Hamann the Bible was key to the books of nature and history, by themselves merely ciphers, hidden signs. Edelmann saw the Bible piled high with improbability, even deception, requiring repair through reason. Semler radically distinguished Word of God and Bible which required no gift or illumination for its interpretation. Schleiermacher could write of the "divine authority" of scripture, of the Bible as the "divine word," which, however, did not mean that anyone off the street could prove its books contained divine revelation.[5] For Ewald "God-breathed" was unintelligible as applied to scripture since only the

5. Friedrich Schleiermacher, *Der christliche Glaube nach den Grundsätzen der evangelischen Kirche,* part IV (Gotha: Friedrich Andreas Perthes, 1889), pp. 16, 26.

word or Spirit could be described in such fashion. He wrote that "no intelligent person will somehow equate the Holy Scripture . . . with Christ," and that "no true prophet, indeed, not even Christ himself, spoke and lived in such a way that he wanted to be sacred," but in the end "became sacred without wanting to be, [so] how much more must the same be true of the scriptures!"[6] Though Stuart, like Edwards, could write that everything about the manner of the Bible is human, he still could state that "the matter of the Bible" was of "divine authority." According to Hodge, the Bible was the "product of one mind," for which reason it was infallible morally and religiously, as well as historically and geographically. Later interpreters had no objection to a definition of the Bible as Word of or from God, though that definition underwent a hundred and one variations. When, for example, Terrien wrote that the Bible reflected a "divine presence" that demanded pride of place in interpretation, that statement could be construed as inferring divine origin.

From Luther on there was common allegiance to the Bible as its own interpreter, in Reformation parlance *scriptura sui ipsius interpres*. Despite his view's formal similarity with the Reformation axiom, Spinoza stood the principle on its head. Since, he wrote, we have no certain knowledge of the things reported in the Bible, the Bible must be its own interpreter:

> It should be observed that Scripture frequently treats of matters that cannot be deduced from principles known by the natural light; for it is chiefly made up of historical narratives and revelation. . . . Therefore knowledge of all these things — that is, of almost all the contents of Scripture — must be sought from Scripture alone.[7]

Whether or not to counter challenges to the doctrine of the Bible's inerrancy, a goodly number entertained the idea of its accommodation to given times and circumstances. Calvin, for instance, asserted that the biblical text accommodated itself to the perceptions of its recipients in analogy to the divine condescension in the incarnation. Spinoza devoted considerable space to applying the idea of accommodation to the revelation itself, writing that the signs intended to validate the prophet's word

---

6. Heinrich Ewald, "Über die Heiligkeit der Bibel," *Jahrbücher der biblischen Wissenschaft*, vol. 7 (Göttingen, 1854-55), pp. 69, 78.

7. Baruch Spinoza, *Theological-Political Treatise* (Gebhardt edition), trans. Samuel Shirley (Indianapolis: Hackett, 2001), p. 87.

were suited to the prophet's beliefs and capacity.[8] He stated that the same conclusions were to be drawn respecting Christ's "reasonings." In convicting the Pharisees' obstinacy and ignorance and in exhorting his disciples to the true life "he adapted his reasonings to the beliefs and principles of each individual."[9] In the end, however, Spinoza's concept of accommodation was meant to serve his axiom that "almost all the contents of Scripture . . . must be sought from Scripture alone" since its revelations, albeit adapted to the views of its recipients, surpassed human understanding.[10] The idea of accommodation lay beneath Baumgarten's restriction of inerrancy to the Bible's chief content, thus his admission of chronological, geographical, and historical errors in the Bible. With Hamann, accommodation was writ large. The Bible's struggle to unite thought and its object in a language intelligible to finite persons did not simply render it analogous to the condescension of the absolute majesty in the incarnation. It was itself a divine humiliation and condescension.

> He created us after his image — because we lost it he took on our image — flesh and blood, just as children have, learned to cry — to babble — to speak — to read — to compose like a true son of man.[11]

Nor did Hamann's view serve, Spinoza-like, to set the biblical text apart, cut off from nature. Hamann wrote that one could hear from the Old Testament "historical truths not only of past but also of future times," that it is the primer "by which one learns to spell history . . . a living spirit- and heart-awakening primer of all the historical literature in heaven, on and under the earth." The same applied to nature. The Bible did not exclude, it rather included it. But nature like history was a "sealed book, a hidden witness, a riddle which could not be solved without plowing with another heifer than our reason."[12] Baumgarten refused to regard all biblical references to natural events as adequate, but against the advocates of accommodation, whether on the part of Jesus or the biblical authors, asserted that the references merely described natural events with "inauthentic ex-

8. Spinoza, *Theological-Political Treatise*, p. 23.
9. Spinoza, *Theological-Political Treatise*, p. 33.
10. Spinoza, *Theological-Political Treatise*, p. 87.
11. *Johann Georg Hamann, Briefwechsel*, ed. Walther Ziesemer and Arthur Henkel (Frankfurt am Main: Insel-Verlag, 1955), vol. 1, p. 394.
12. Johann Georg Hamann, "Sokratische Denkwürdigkeiten," in Johann Georg Hamann, *Sämtliche Werke*, ed. Josef Nadler (Wien: Im Verlag Herder, 1950), vol. 2, p. 65.

pressions." Semler, on the other hand, maintained the accommodation of the biblical authors to the ideas of their contemporaries. Accordingly, what later came to be called "demythologizing" was in order. That is, all mythological ideas stemming from pre-Christian religions needed abandoning, among them belief in devils, demons, evil spirits, and futurist eschatology since it represented Jesus' accommodation to the hopes of contemporary Judaism. Positively, according to Semler, accommodation eased the acceptance and expansion of Christianity.

But if the Bible came about by way of human instrumentation its authority could not be guaranteed from the outside, say, in a dogma. Luther believed that to treat the Bible in such fashion was no guarantee against the subjectivism of Roman Catholic tradition or enthusiasm. In fact, it was more inhumane than either of those two. From its *scopus,* from its goal, Luther argued, the Bible derived its authority. Calvin denied the Bible any external authority, construing its authority as inward. But, he wrote, the authority that the biblical writings should enjoy among believers demanded the belief that they came from heaven as directly as if God had been heard to utter them. It was a view that would later assume hardened form, but it was not Calvin's. If, according to Müntzer, whoever relied on the mere letter had been abandoned by God, authority could scarcely be assigned to the letter. From the clarity and intelligibility of a Bible available to all Locke concluded that no authority existed beyond the Bible's own designation of the fundamental articles of faith. Locke could give specificity to his argument by describing biblical authority as dependent on the authority of Jesus' teaching. If for Wolff neither the Bible nor the Spirit immediately wakens in us the connection between the text and the idea it intends to convey, authority must lie elsewhere — in reason, in understanding, albeit of the regenerate. For Hamann the Bible was his "a priori." On his view, both Testaments formed the irreversible condition for understanding the world and the self, but, as he contended, within the fellowship of justified sinners. Thus, "insofar as the Bible forms the a priori, thoroughly accidental, but a posteriori necessary condition for understanding self and world, one can speak of it as a historical a priori,"[13] but only within the context cited above. Schleiermacher did not hesitate to speak of "the authority of Holy Scripture," though acknowledgment of it assumed a prior faith. As he wrote:

13. See Oswald Bayer, *A Contemporary in Dissent: Johann Georg Hamann as a Radical Enlightener,* trans. Roy A. Harrisville and Mark C. Mattes (Grand Rapids: Eerdmans, 2012), p. 65.

So it follows that just as the apostles already had faith before they arrived at a condition, other than faith itself, in which they were able to
share in producing these books, so also with us faith must precede,
before, in reading these writings, we are led to accept such [special]
condition in which these books were written and any [peculiar] character founded on it, and that such a doctrine will able to be made
acceptable only to believers.[14]

Stuart was clear: everything about the manner of the Bible was human.
The matter of the Bible, however, was of divine authority.

Again, if a certain humanity attached to the Bible, then its reading
was a matter of human industry, and its status could not be superior to
that of any other human expression. The chorus was loud and long. From
the moment specific attention was given the etiquette required for reading and interpreting texts, from Baumgarten[15] to Edelmann to Semler to
Schleiermacher to Stuart to Bultmann to the Chicago School to Harvard,
Yale, Union, and Princeton, the Bible was denied treatment different from
that given any other book.

One after another, the noble army of interpreters proceeded to the
method of Bible exposition. Luther was clear: since the texts of the Bible
did not circulate within a system, but created space, allowing freedom for
the reader-hearer, interpretation involved putting all the books to the test
to see whether or not they reflected the *scopus.* This meant distinguishing
whatever reflected demand, represented by the law, and whatever reflected
promise and gift, Jesus Christ "in the flesh." According to Calvin, getting at
the mind of the author was the paramount task, and clear brevity was the
way by which to do it. In this Calvin had scores of followers. According to
Bengel, it was the special office of every interpretation to exhibit the force
and significance of the words in order to express everything the author
intended. This meant paying due regard to the biblical writer's feeling.
Wolff described the goal of interpretation as determining the author's intent since it was by way of authorial intent that the consonance of words
and ideas occurred. Thus the interpreter could not offer any idea not joined
to the word by the author's intention. Baumgarten likewise wrote that the

14. Schleiermacher, *Der christliche Glaube,* p. 19.
15. Baumgarten argued that the general art of exposition was indispensable, but added
that a special hermeneutics was needed by which the scriptures, derived from divine inspiration, could be explained.

interpreter needed to comprehend the meaning intended by the author. For Semler, attention to the literal sense was the interpreter's first requirement. Early on, Schleiermacher defined the divinatory aspect of technical interpretation as inquiry into the author's perspective, and later, as entry into his frame of mind, into the world of his experience and feeling. In either case the goal was to understand the author, though in the end to understand the author better than he understood himself. Wolff had already written that where a text was unclear, it was legitimate to deviate from the rule that authorial intent comprised the sole and exclusive goal. In such an instance the interpreter was to replace the unclear with a clear concept, rendering the author clearer than he himself had done. Ewald wrote that explanation had to do with investigating and establishing the author's original meaning. Edwards accented pursuit of the historical meaning of the text by way of philology, that "mental matter." For Stuart the question before the interpreter was, which idea did the author mean to convey? Though he may later have spoofed the critical method with his query respecting "historical-critical" and the meaning of the hyphen between the two, Barth's statement in his second preface to the *Römerbrief* regarding "intelligent comment" as allowing the biblical author to speak in his name and he in his, obviously had something of authorial intent in mind. If for Bultmann existential interpretation began with inquiry into the matter of which the text speaks, and if genuine understanding presupposed a life-relation of the interpreter to the matter created by the text, what or who lay behind that speaking or that matter created by the text if not its author? For Shailer Mathews the shift of biblical authority as text to the men who wrote, and Case's insistence on the social context of the text, had to mean some kind of concentration on authorship, though neither stated by what means. Cadbury wrote of the task of interpretation as consisting in a thorough acclimatization into the temper and mentality of the ancient world, writing, for example, that Paul's personality revealed traits that were more psychological than religious or literary. Piper viewed the interpreter's task as locating each idea in its specific place within the author's total view of life and reality, or, reproducing as far as possible the mental process that went on in the author's mind.

Of all the scholars reviewed, those sanguine enough to believe that sheer exercise of the critical faculties sufficed for interpretation were precious few. From Paul and Augustine Luther had learned that the letter of scripture was dead until made alive by the Spirit. In his debate with Erasmus over the bound will *(De servo arbitrio)* Luther enunciated his thesis of the dual clarity (or obscurity) of scripture. "No one on earth," he wrote, "will understand even the least that is in scripture without the Holy Spirit."[16] On this point Erasmus agreed. The point of contention was whether or not the language of the Bible facilitated understanding of the gospel to the point where the preacher or teacher could point to scripture as a criterion for faith and by way of the external word lead to spiritual understanding. Here Erasmus was skeptical, but Luther vehement in defense of the Bible's external clarity, its perspicuity. Finally, if the letter's coming alive was an event come about by the Spirit and apprehended in faith, that event spelled reversal of the roles of text and interpreter. Now it was the text that assumed the role of interpreter, the text that exegeted the exegete. Calvin agreed with Luther. Taking up the Wittenberger's hermeneutical impulse, he developed the doctrine of the "testimonium Sancti Spiritus internum (arcanum)," and in his *Institutes* of 1559 wrote that just as God in his Word is the only authoritative witness to himself, so also this Word would find no faith in the human heart until it had been sealed by the "inward testimony" of the Spirit.[17] On 1 Corinthians 1:20, the Geneva Reformer wrote, "apart from the heavenly science of Christ . . . man with all his shrewdness is as stupid about understanding by himself the mysteries of God as an ass is incapable of understanding musical harmony."[18] To the text, wrote Calvin, the Spirit added testimony. Müntzer agreed with Luther respecting the activity of the Spirit as giving sense to and deriving sense from the Bible, but had no taste for the external word; whoever relied on it had been abandoned by God. For Flacius biblical knowledge required integration in personal life, and it was Bengel who first phrased what once appeared in every German introduction to the Nestle Greek New Testament: "te totum applica ad textum, rem totum applica ad te" ("Apply your whole self to the text, apply the whole matter to yourself"). Locke seemed to require something more than mere intellectual assent for salvation, if not for Bible interpretation. For all his insistence that the Spirit does not immediately waken the connection between word and idea, that such must be perceived by reason, Wolff stated that it was the regenerated person's

16. *WA* 18, 609, 11f.

17. John Calvin, *Institutes of the Christian Religion,* trans. Ford Lewis Battles, Library of Christian Classics, vol. 20 (Philadelphia: Westminster, 1960), I, 7, 4, p. 79.

18. John Calvin, *The First Epistle of Paul the Apostle to the Corinthians,* trans. John W. Fraser, Calvin's Commentaries (Grand Rapids: Eerdmans, 1960), p. 38. For the relevant passages, I am indebted to Peter Stuhlmacher's essay, "Zur hermeneutischen Bedeutung von I Kor 2, 6-16," to date unpublished.

understanding that led to knowledge of the truth. Further, the central position that "fairness" or "charitable" interpretation enjoyed in Wolff's hermeneutic indicates his advocacy of a supplement to scientific criticism. According to Baumgarten, the interpreter must rouse a strong desire for right understanding, set aside all prejudices so as to encounter the meaning furnished by the text itself. All one's powers, Baumgarten wrote, needed exerting toward this end, and again, as with Wolff, it all spelled "fairness." Hamann wrote that the Bible demanded a reading in the spirit of that "theist who died a shameful, voluntary, and meritorious death." To hear the Word of God more than the text of the Bible was needed; humility of heart was indispensable. Semler's relativizing the results of his research by emphasizing the abiding value of the New Testament message of salvation had to be in the service of a supplement. Early or late, Schleiermacher's notion of "divination" as an "art" that assumed a humanity shared by author and interpreter, thus a "life-relation," was nothing if not a blow aimed at interpretation as a mere cerebral function. Without a religious interest, he argued, occupation with the New Testament could only be directed against it and at best pursued as an alien interest. Ewald could write:

> There is only one who is holy, God. But his words to you . . . should be next to him the holiest. . . . Let yourself . . . be seized by the Spirit who moved all that is here and who will likewise move you.[19]

Edwards declared the "mental matter" to be without redemptive value; a spiritual sense was required, a sense he could describe as "mystical," even "allegorical." At any rate, interpretation involved more than the discovery of objective truth. It involved the molding of the interpreting self by the truth discovered. When combined with historical method, wrote Stuart, "feeling and sympathy" would result in true understanding. For all his apparent reduction of faith to intellectual assent to an infallible document, Hodge still insisted that faith was needed for a genuine interpretation. Barth's description of "intelligent comment" as erasing the distance between author and reader was nothing if not a call for supplement in the face of the dry as dust, "objective" criticism he had learned in the university. Over against those five perils Bultmann had listed, he argued for an interpretation that began with *Sachkritik,* with "content criticism," with inquiry into the matter of which the text speaks, and into its meaning for the inter-

19. Ewald, "Über die Heiligkeit der Bibel," pp. 81-82.

preter. Any "neutral exegesis" was an impossibility. As Hofmann had written years before, biblical hermeneutics was not a science consisting simply in the application of its method to the Bible. It presupposed a "relation" to the biblical content, a *tua res agitur*, "the matter has to do with you." Again, neutrality required abandoning. The results of interpretation could not be guaranteed or controlled as the methodologists assumed. On one's own no one was in control of existence to the point of being able to ignore the question of existence and its possibilities raised by the text. Such was available only to faith. Proper inquiry came by way of faith, grounded in obedience to the authority of scripture. With all this, "historical-critical" and "objectivity" took on new definition. Scholars at Chicago, Harvard, Yale, and Union gave modest space to the supplement. Harper never addressed the problem of scriptural authority on internal grounds, but Foster avowed that certainty in historical science could not effect religious certainty. Lake stated that spiritual experience could throw light on the meaning of events historically vouched for by other means, and Cadbury wrote that "motive criticism," understanding the mind of the author, needed supplementing in a strong religious prepossession. According to Porter, a true life of faith solved the problem of the relation between the historical and religious uses of the Bible. Grant of Union wrote of the interpreter's need to take seriously what the earliest Christians took seriously, thus of a supplement as a matter of faith and insight. However axiomatic use of the historical approach was for Terrien, it required supplementation in the form of the interpreter's "enlistment." Of all the Americans, Piper gave most space to the supplement, in a variety of ways accenting interpretation as involving the dual process of exegesis and appropriation.

The conclusions to which the scholars came were as multifaceted as the persons themselves. According to Luther, arriving at the *scopus,* distinguishing between demand and gift, could mean opposing the literal meaning of a word to preserve its uniqueness. For this reason he argued that the insertion of the word *solum* into Romans 3:21-22a was needed to convey the sense of the text. As he said, "it yields the meaning of the text."[20] Elsewhere he wrote, "where the manner requires it, I have kept to the letters."[21] But where the apostle was dealing with the main point of Christian doctrine,

---

20. Martin Luther, "Sendbrief von Dolmetschen," in *Dr. Martin Luthers Werke* (Weimar: Hermann Böhlaus Nachfolger, 1909), vol. 30, part II, p. 636: "die meynung des text ynn sich hat."

21. Luther, "Sendbrief von Dolmetschen," p. 640.

whoever would speak plainly would have to say, "faith alone, not works, makes us righteous. . . . The thing itself along with the nature of speech demands it."[22] Nor, he added, was he first to make the point; Ambrose, Augustine, and many others had already done so. In connection with Genesis 6:6, "the Lord was sorry that he had made humankind on the earth," Wolff wrote that if we interpret "sorry" in terms of a sadness sprung from something we have badly done, we contradict both natural theology and the clear words of Holy Scripture. According to natural theology, from eternity God saw the evil done of men, nor could he have been ignorant of it when he made man. According to scripture, regret is repugnant to God. Thus, an interpretation after the human fashion departs from the meaning of scripture, conformable to the canon that things said of God in human fashion are to be understood by what reason dictates becomes him.[23]

Ewald countered the Strauss-Baur School with his reference to the three levels of clarity in the Bible, the first represented by passages encountering us as truths but which have taken on hardening from an earlier time; the second by passages where the great truths lie; and the third by those containing the darker secrets. Accordingly, there is nothing in the Bible of what is correctly called myth and is of a heathen spirit. Among the Americans, Edwards was fascinated by typology, and to a degree affirmed accommodation. Respecting the "Genesis narrative" Stuart allowed the contradiction between contemporary evolutionary theory and the biblical narrative to remain. More significantly, he reflected loyalty to the grammatico-historical method in the insistence that slavery was not an evil in itself *(malum in se),* but an institution liable to prohibition *(malum prohibitam),* and thus his defense of the gradual emancipation of the slave. The demythologizing program, or better, the existential interpretation initiated by Bultmann in his address to the clergy at Alpirsbach in 1941 included the three-storied universe, heaven in the traditional sense of the word, good and evil spirits, and the return of the Son of Man on the clouds of heaven. Harper was confident that once higher criticism had its "erosive effect" on the human element in scripture, a "residuum of the divine" would remain, but left it to others to locate the residuum. Lake, advocate of application of the imaginative faculties in analysis, regarded references to the empty

22. Luther, "Sendbrief von Dolmetschen," p. 640: "allein der glaube, und nicht die werck machen uns gerecht, das zwinget die sache selbs neben der sprachen art."

23. Christian Wolff, *Philosophia Rationalis sive Logica,* part III, chapter VII, *De Interpretatione Scripturae Sacrae,* para. 976, in *Gesammelte Werke,* ed. and rev. J. Ecole (Hildesheim: Georg Olms Verlagsbuchhandlung, 1983), p. 700.

tomb and the "third day" as "improper inferences" drawn from the "fact" of the resurrection, thus "demythologized" earliest Christian tradition in face of a hesitant generation. Cadbury's distaste for the biblical theology movement, members of which, as he put it, claimed that only insofar as we share the New Testament belief can we understand it, appeared to allow exemption from whatever of the New Testament belief a twentieth-century reader could not share. Porter was unable to believe in the intervention of supernatural powers, and interpreted the visions and auditions of the Old Testament prophets as mental or emotional experiences. Jesus' consciousness of messiahship, he continued, consisted of a "radical inwardness." Like Semler, Bultmann, and Lake, Porter had aversion to the apocalyptic element. More important, he asserted that the value a biblical record possesses and which is due to the power the facts once had over the biblical author may be taken as valid evidence in favor of the actuality of those events. Later, Piper would ask:

> Will not the historian test the reliability of a document by inquiring whether effects of an alleged event can be found when its historicity cannot be apprehended directly?[24]

Grant had no aversion to apocalyptic, that is, as nuanced in favor of progressive revelation. "Objective scholarship," he wrote, enabled one to regard revelation as progressive, thus to understand the Bible's inspiration as occasional, not constant, and in this way facilitated the understanding of apocalyptic. According to Knox, the way of escape from fundamentalism was to apprehend the event in its original character and impact, which meant discerning the way in which fact and interpretation interacted. More, Knox regarded creation, incarnation, and atonement as belonging to one all-inclusive myth or story, and faulted Bultmann for not having devoted more clarity to the existence of that for which the myth is the expression, that is, the existence of the church. Similarly, Terrien described the Bible as a "time-myth," related to a dynamic view of history that moves from creation to re-creation through incarnation, incarnation serving as key to understanding the Bible.

With some of the interpreters reviewed, a change or alteration in method occurred. Luther broke with the Quadriga, or fourfold sense, in

---

24. Otto A. Piper, "The Virgin Birth: The Meaning of the Gospel Accounts," *Interpretation*, no. 2 (1964): 142.

1517, which, however, had nothing to do with his relation to allegorical interpretation. Only from 1524 on did allegory begin to fall away, and that of itself, without polemic or fanfare. Exposition of the pericopes from the same period tells a different story. Here, allegorical interpretation came to a sudden halt, but without total abandonment of allegorical interpretation. Exposition of the miracle stories, especially of the healing narratives, luxuriated in allegory. Five years later, in 1529, allegory had all but disappeared from Luther's exposition of the pericopes. Yet again, in the postils, those annotations or commentaries made for use in the home or for uneducated clergy, allegory lived on. Clearly, Luther regarded allegory appropriate to the postil, if not to the sermon or pericope. In light of the absence of polemic in Luther's attitude, as well as of his continued use of allegory in the postils, thus blurring the boundaries between the historical-"mystical" or "spiritual" and the historical plumbed for its use or fruit, as he put it, it was a given text or a given situation that determined whether or not the method was to be used or surrendered. In other words, Luther's surrender of allegory was far less a fundamental than an actual, contextual surrender. In the end, however, his practice had the effect of abandoning allegory among his students.[25]

According to Semler, "truth" came by way of the historical-critical task, "truth" as a sufficient correspondence between the event and its description to meet the requirement of their agreement. "Truth" was thus "agreement with reality." At first, this definition rested on Semler's assumption of the unequivocal relation between word and the event it expressed, and as reflected in his phrase "veritas est unica," "truth is one."[26] With a sufficiently careful and conscientious interpretation the "hermeneutical truth" could be established. Later, Semler began to doubt the correctness of his thesis, conceding that more than one single idea could be connected with a word or an utterance. "Veritas est unica" thus did not denote one single truth.[27] Since direct access to historical events was often impossible, the agreement of event or statement with reality could not be tested. Verifi-

---

25. See Gerhard Ebeling, *Evangelische Evangelienauslegung, Eine Untersuchung zu Luthers Hermeneutik* (Darmstadt: Wissenschaftliche Buchgesellschaft, 1962), pp. 48-89.

26. Wolff had made the same assumption, stating that to imagine a multiplicity of ideas as attached to a given word would be to cut off the divine words in enthusiasm; see *Philosophia Rationalis,* para. 970, p. 694.

27. See Gottfried Hornig, "Wahrheit und Historisierung in Semlers kritischer Theologie," *Theologische Literaturzeitung* 116, no. 10 (October 1991): 725. See the progression of Semler's thought in Hornig, "Über Semlers Theologische Hermeneutik," in *Unzeitgemässe Hermeneutik,* ed. Axel Bühler (Frankfurt am Main: Vittorio Klostermann, 1994), pp. 216-19.

cation came down to evaluating the credibility of the witness or witnesses. Knowledge of the truth could perforce be only limited, particular, never grasped in its totality.[28] For this reason Semler could write of his work on the canon: "I know right well that one (commonly) judges quite differently. . . . I am far from despising or reproaching these well-intentioned efforts . . . I only offer my own ideas."[29] Or in the brief analysis of the interpreter's role in his *Vorbereitung zur theologischen Hermeneutik* he could write that since interpretation depended on the intellectual capacities and external circumstances of the exegete, no interpretation could be judged as normative or binding.[30]

According to the popular view, Schleiermacher's "art" meant construing a text or speech entirely from the world of experience and feeling of its author or speaker. This may have been the goal of leaders of the "Storm and Stress" *(Sturm und Drang)* movement, a reaction to Enlightenment rationalism in eighteenth-century German literature, but it was not Schleiermacher's goal, at least not in his early period. The popular view reflects inattention to the difference between Schleiermacher's early view and the view he later adopted. If, according to that early view, the author was at the heart of "technical interpretation," that interpretation had to combine the inner "life element" with a text. Or again, in describing the relation between the grammatical and technical approaches as between the objective and subjective, Schleiermacher insisted that the two could not be strictly contrasted. Just as there is nothing purely objective about speech, that is, since speech always reflects the viewpoint of the speaker, and thus has something subjective about it, so there is nothing purely subjective about speech since it always relies on an object that evokes it, "chooses" it.[31] The extent to which Schleiermacher assigned such "a priori" status to language is reflected in his aphorisms of 1805 and 1809. There, for example, he describes Christianity as "creating" language, as language's "potentiating spirit," for which reason it could not connect with Hellenic truth.[32] It

28. Hornig, "Wahrheit und Historisierung in Semlers kritischer Theologie," p. 725.

29. Johann Salomo Semler, *Von freier Untersuchung des Canons,* ed. Heinz Scheible (Gütersloh: Mohn, 1967), p. 53.

30. Cited in F. Andreas Lüder, *Historie und Dogmatik: Ein Beitrag zur Genese und Entfaltung von Johann Salomo Semlers Verständnis des Alten Testaments* (Berlin: Walter de Gruyter, 1995), p. 86.

31. Kurt Nowak, *Schleiermacher* (Göttingen: Vandenhoeck & Ruprecht, 2001), p. 202.

32. Friedrich Schleiermacher, *Hermeneutik* (Heidelberg: Carl Winter Universitätsverlag, 1959), p. 38.

was in language, Schleiermacher contended, that one's understanding of self and the world was given.

According to Schleiermacher's interpreters, evidence for the change had already appeared in his introductions to Plato and in his development of the discipline of New Testament introduction, but the clearest clue to the change lay in an exchange of the term "psychological" for what he had earlier termed the "technical" approach.[33] It was still necessary to go through language, though language was no longer conceived as the equivalent of thought. The earlier view as expressed in the period between 1810 and 1819, that "essentially and internally the idea and expression are entirely the same," now gave way to the idea as expressed in the compendium-like exposition of 1819 that the object of interpretation consisted first of inner thought, then of external speech.[34] Now, the axiom that the interpreter's goal was the subjective experience of the speaker or author, but never loosed from the text as "choosing" or giving rise to it, was radically altered to the point where the goal was to "understand the author better than himself."[35] Now the divinatory method presupposed a kind of "congeniality," the possibility of the interpreter's identifying with the author or speaker on the basis of their sharing a common humanity. The limits of individuality could thus be crossed by way of feeling, the difference between the interpreter and the author-speaker erased. It would take more than one hundred years to discover that the detachment of language from thought hailed by Dilthey in Schleiermacher and pursued to Dilthey's own ends had not always been made by Schleiermacher.

Heinrich Ewald's change had more to do with external occasion than with questions of method. Following his dismissal from the University of Göttingen in 1838, his elevation to knighthood in 1841, allowing him use of the "von" ahead of his name, at the urging of Ferdinand Christian Baur, he was invited to join the theological faculty of Tübingen University. A supporter of the historical-critical method, he was regarded as Baur's friend and disciple, and of whom Baur wrote, "Ewald is a quiet nature, above all suspicion of demagoguery."[36] In Ewald's first period in Tübingen the two were

33. Nowak, *Schleiermacher,* p. 203; Richard E. Palmer, *Hermeneutics: Interpretation Theory in Schleiermacher, Dilthey, Heidegger, and Gadamer* (Evanston, Ill.: Northwestern University Press, 1969), pp. 88, 93; Schleiermacher, *Hermeneutik,* p. 22.

34. Schleiermacher, *Hermeneutik,* p. 21.

35. Schleiermacher, *Hermeneutik und Kritik* (Frankfurt am Main: Suhrkamp, 1977), pp. 94, 104.

36. Michael Haasler, "Heinrich Ewald und seine Auseinandersetzung mit Ernst Meier und Ferdinand Christian Baur" (M.A. thesis, University of Tübingen, 1996), p. 39.

regarded as joined in the struggle against orthodoxy and pietism. When, for example, Friedrich Theodor Vischer, newly appointed professor of aesthetics and German literature, was given a two-year suspension for announcing in his inaugural lecture an "undivided enmity" and "open and hearty hatred" for pietism, Ewald sided with Baur in registering opposition by way of a *Sondervotum,* or separate vote. The breach with Baur did not occur until 1845 and had a dual occasion. The first lay in Ewald's suspicion that a former student, a certain Ernst Meier, lecturer on the Old Testament, had deliberately engaged in competition with him. Ewald promptly opposed Meier's seating on the faculty. In response, Meier appealed to Baur and Vischer for their support. Ewald was livid. The second, more substantial occasion for the breach occurred with Baur's publications on John and Paul in 1844 and 1845. Recognizing the direction Baur was taking, Ewald was horrified by its results, a direction he dubbed as "Hegelei." All throughout Ewald's attacks on his Tübingen colleagues, in this period he made no mention of Baur, solely of the "Strauss-Vischer-Zeller" method, the latter a one-time pupil of Baur. Not until 1848 did Ewald attack what he called the "Strauss-Baur'ischen Wesen," an "entity" *(Wesen)* which to his mind reflected blindness toward genuine Christianity, genuine truth, and morality; brought confusion of historical research through historical method; and elevated the Hegelian system to an idol. Even as late as 1846, Ewald would refer only to the "Strauss-Vischer affair." In an essay of the same year he wrote,

> The entire Strauss-Vischer method of engaging in science . . . is a purely school matter, not of the church and still less of Christianity. The church should stand too high than that it should fear such error. . . . The true church can only silence foolishness by calm teaching and a better example, not by feverish clamoring and appealing to the authority of the state.[37]

But by this time, named or not, it was clear that Baur belonged to that "affair."

The change with Barth had to do with what Bultmann would have called his "preliminary anticipation of the subject matter" *(Vorverständnis),* that is, his idealism, Hegelianism. In his first edition of the *Römerbrief* he had written of a "secret tendency for good" inherent in all that occurs

---

37. Heinrich Ewald, *Über einige wissenschaftliche Erscheinungen neuester Zeit auf der Universität Tübingen* (Stuttgart: Krabbe, 1846), p. 22.

and is to be, so that it must "cooperate . . . toward restoring the life of the world and men in the peace of God," of an "organic growth-like way of change," of the divine in our existence appearing as "nature, gift, and growth,"[38] of salvation as "process."[39] Hegel-like he wrote that whoever has moved with God from an earlier to a new stage of his activity knows best that "the entire movement must one day again be of benefit to the elements now left behind."[40] In the second edition that synthesis of revelation and history, identified with nature, with its innumerable references to growth and process, was abandoned for their antithesis, with its reference to origin, decision, and crisis. But if the divine, if the kingdom of God, was not nature, growth, and process, then the notion of reality derived from nature, then the idea of the real as sprung from the perceptible had to give way to an idea of reality as linked to the unseen and imperceptible. Then whatever occurs in the world can never be a "divine beginning or seed or kernel," but only a signpost, a parable of the divine. The first edition would never contain this statement:

> [There is] no concrete thing which does not point beyond itself, no observable reality which is not itself a parable. . . . All human doing or not-doing is simply an occasion or opportunity of pointing to that which alone is worthy of being called "action," namely, the action of God.[41]

And if what occurs here exists only as parable, then there is no direct point of contact between here and there, now and then, time and eternity, history-nature and revelation, humanity and deity. In the first edition Barth had written,

> God can be searched out and known to those who seek him. There is, of course, that impenetrability, immeasurability, and inexhaustibility with which he reveals in ever new freshness and freedom a new wealth of his power, a new wisdom of his intentions, a new knowledge of his ways and means to those who seek him day by day and hour by hour.[42]

38. Karl Barth, *Der Römerbrief* (Zürich: EVZ-Verlag, 1963), p. 218.
39. Barth, *Der Römerbrief,* p. 255.
40. Barth, *Der Römerbrief,* p. 318.
41. Karl Barth, *The Epistle to the Romans,* trans. Edwyn C. Hoskyns (Oxford: Oxford University Press, 1933), pp. 275, 432.
42. Barth, *Der Römerbrief,* pp. 344f.

But in the second,

> "The depth of the riches and the wisdom and the knowledge of God"
> is — correcting here what was written in the first edition of this book
> — unfathomable. The Epistle moves round the theme . . . that in Christ
> Jesus the Deus absconditus is as such the Deus revelatus.[43]

Finally, election and rejection, Isaac and Ishmael, Jacob and Esau, could
no longer be "the momentary expression of a movement, like a bird in
flight,"[44] no longer part of an organic process in which the one or other
was merely a stage and never the process itself. But then, whatever else
Isaac and Ishmael, Jacob and Esau, election and reprobation, might
be, they express the unfathomable mystery of the sovereign freedom
of God:

> The God of Esau is known to be the God of Jacob. There is no road to
> the knowledge of God which does not run along the precipitous edge
> of this contradiction.[45]

In his preface to the second edition, Barth described its connection
with the first as the extension of the first edition's position to points further
ahead.[46] This reference to continuity between the two editions needs correcting. The second edition is an entirely new book, and whatever connection exists between the two is purely formal. Both are concerned with the
same object — the Epistle to the Romans, and both with the same subject
matter — the kerygma of Paul.[47]

If it did not denote further change in Barth, it certainly reflected
greater clarity in thought regarding the criteria for evaluating theological
comment. Earlier he had emphasized the provisional, hence vulnerable
character of theological comment, due to the inadequacy of its language.
For this reason, whatever human approval such comment might enjoy,

43. Barth, *The Epistle to the Romans*, p. 422.
44. Barth, *Der Römerbrief*, p. 286.
45. Barth, *The Epistle to the Romans*, p. 350.
46. "Die damals gewonnene Stellung wurde auf weiter vorwärts liegende Punkte
verlegt. . . ." Karl Barth, *Der Römerbrief, Erste Fassung* (1919), ed. Hermann Schmidt, in Karl
Barth, *Gesamtausgabe* (Zürich: Theologischer Verlag, 1985), II, p. vi.
47. Cf. Nico T. Bakker, *In der Krisis der Offenbarung: Karl Barths Hermeneutik* (Neukirchen: Neukirchener Verlag, 1974), p. 72.

there was no appealing to a final criterion in its favor. Later, in *Fides Quaerens Intellectum* he wrote of the "one criterion" that determined whether or not such comment was admissible. "This criterion," he wrote, "is the text of Holy Scripture," then cited Anselm's rule:

> If a proposition accords with the actual wording of the Bible or with the direct inferences from it, then naturally it is valid with absolute certainty, but just because of this agreement it is not strictly a theological proposition. If, on the other hand, it is a strictly theological proposition, that is to say a proposition formed independently of the actual wording of Scripture, then the fact that it does not contradict the biblical text, determines its validity. But if it did contradict the Bible, however attractive it might be on other grounds, it would be rendered invalid.[48]

In his 1926 lectures on theological encyclopedia, Bultmann stated that theology needs a mode suitable to its object, the mode we call faith. Theology, he said, could not be carried on "out of curiosity or to earn a living, but as a work, a venture, in which we ourselves are at risk." He continued, "if God is the object of faith and accessible only to faith, then a science apart from faith or alongside it can see neither God nor faith, which is what it is only by means of its object."[49]

To the question, how exegesis was to be done on the basis of faith, Bultmann replied that the problem raised by the question could not be solved "in principle," that is, by ignoring the concrete situation of the exegete. He wrote that "exegesis of the New Testament becomes the task for whoever stands in the tradition of the church of the Word."[50] No particular method or approach could be justified "in principle." Proper inquiry into the text could only be that of faith, faith based on obedience to the authority of the scripture. "The fact of this obedience," Bultmann continued, "is the presupposition for exegesis, and over this fact I have no control, since it is a free act, not left to any position I may take toward it, but actual only

---

48. Karl Barth, *Anselm: Fides Quaerens Intellectum,* trans. Ian W. Robertson (Richmond: John Knox, 1960), p. 33.

49. Rudolf Bultmann, *What Is Theology?* trans. Roy A. Harrisville (Minneapolis: Fortress, 1997), pp. 35, 37.

50. Rudolf Bultmann, "Das Problem einer theologischen Exegese des Neuen Testaments" (1925), in *Neues Testament und christliche Existenz,* ed. Andreas Lindemann (Tübingen: Mohr Siebeck, 2002), pp. 66f.

in being carried out."[51] Thus, a theological exegesis that has faith as its presupposition can only be ventured; it cannot be reasoned out or legitimated since we are not in control of the presupposition.

At this point Bultmann's readers saw a dilemma: by insisting that proper inquiry into the text occurred only by faith, and by faith alone, he appeared to presuppose what could not be presupposed. After all, he himself had insisted that no particular method or approach could be justified "in principle," that there was no special method of a "theological," to say nothing of a "pneumatic" exegesis.[52] In investigating the subject matter of a text *(Sachkritik)* he was intent on showing "that the idea of revelation does not become an exegetical presupposition over which we have control."[53] But if, as he so often insisted, in encounter with the reality of which the text speaks it is "the word," the kerygma, and not scripture as such that is authoritative, and further, if that encounter is not at our disposal, how to reconcile this presupposition with the other that inquiry into the text must be one of faith, carried on by whoever "stands in the tradition of the church of the Word"?

In the same essay in which Bultmann enunciated the one presupposition, he enunciated the other that would come to replace the earlier, a replacement signaled in his abandonment of the concept of theological exegesis.

> It should be emphasized that the separation of historical and theological exegesis is an untenable position for both, and that one cannot legitimately attach theological commentary to the historical-philological ones. In the actual process of exegesis the historical and theological exegesis enjoy a connection that cannot be analyzed because appropriate historical exegesis rests on the existential encounter with history, thus coincides with the theological, if elsewhere the right to it rests on precisely the same fact. And that existential encounter is not something that could be performed as an undertaking and as such would retain its place in or behind the methodological, philological-historical exposition.[54]

51. Bultmann, "Das Problem einer theologischen Exegese des Neuen Testaments," p. 67.

52. Bultmann, "Das Problem einer theologischen Exegese des Neuen Testaments," p. 71.

53. Bultmann, "Das Problem einer theologischen Exegese des Neuen Testaments," p. 71.

54. Bultmann, "Das Problem einer theologischen Exegese des Neuen Testaments," p. 72.

In other words, the faith by which inquiry into the text was to be undertaken had to occur in the midst of that inquiry, or not at all. It could not be presupposed or be required to exist ahead of or prior to that inquiry. Whether or not it was Karl Barth who first gave Bultmann that concept of "theological exegesis,"[55] now, as part and parcel of a requirement that needed fulfilling prior to encounter with the text, resulting in the call to an interpretive activity separated from the historical-critical, it had to be abandoned.

Finally, since Spinoza, commitment to the historical-critical method on the part of the majority referenced was firm, with some iron-clad. As is well known, Barth furnishes the exception. But so also does Chicago's Shailer Mathews, at the opposite end of the theological spectrum. Mathews had urged that the New Testament student should abandon the techniques of traditional scholarship for the sake of focusing on the "social process" attaching to the evolutionary understanding of Christianity. It was a focus that meant death to philological expertise, and the rejection of the older forms of scholarship, including the literary-critical. It could have been an omen of things to come.

---

55. See Theodor Lorenzmeier, *Exegese und Hermeneutik* (Hamburg: Furche Verlag, 1968), p. 48. From this volume was gleaned the "clue" to the change in Bultmann's position.

CHAPTER NINE

The Malaise

The Attacks

In the last half of the twentieth century, the historical-critical method began to suffer a malaise, or, more appropriately, a steep decline. Scholars began to reflect on the conflicting and at times absurd results to which biblical criticism had led, thus over the total absence of consensus in even the least arguable matters. There was resistance to the method's absolutizing, its expropriation of all the data of text and context for its own exclusive use. There was reference, veiled or not, to the arrogance of the critic. "A whole literature," wrote the British literary critic Frank Kermode (1919-2010),

> produced over many centuries and forming the basis of a highly developed religion and culture, is now said to have value only insofar as it complies with the fore-understanding of later interpreters.[1]

Notorious for "uneasily existing on the axis between the academic and the religious,"[2] the exegetical sciences now came to be described as "hypertrophic," alienating the Bible from the people and delivering them over to the lordship of the specialist.[3]

One by one the charges mounted up. Pursuit of the layered, spatial, dia-

---

1. Frank Kermode, *The Genesis of Secrecy* (Cambridge, Mass.: Harvard University Press, 1979), p. 18.

2. David Jobling, "Writing the Wrongs of the World: The Deconstruction of the Biblical Text in the Context of Liberation Theologies," *Semeia* 51 (1990): 93.

3. Kristlieb Adloff, "Neuen Aspekte der Exegese nach Bultmann," in *Schrift und Auslegung*, ed. Heinrich Kraft (Erlangen: Martin Luther Verlag, 1987), p. 95.

chronic, synthetic, mimetic, representational, referential, traditional method of interpretation was said to have led to frustration and exasperation. The Tübingen scholar Peter Stuhlmacher (1932-) voiced the general opinion:

> For colleagues in the discipline, for pastors performing their office, and for students, historical criticism is the agent of a repeated and growing rupture of vital contact between biblical tradition and our own time.[4]

Stuhlmacher referred to what he called the diastasis between historical criticism and theological interpretation, a diastasis that resulted from the autonomy enjoyed by the method. The underside of the method's emancipating biblical study from dogmatic tutelage was the split between study of the Bible and theological reflection. In fact, historical-critical interpretation bids fair to be not merely a substitute for, but identical to theological interpretation. The consequences of this diastasis, as Stuhlmacher saw it, was the pitting of the Old Testament against the New, a chaotic heaping up of hypotheses, the unraveling of the New Testament tradition into a multiplicity of disjointed communications, situations-in-life, and theologies. Reaction to the diastasis was twofold. On the one hand lay the suspicion of pietism and fundamentalism. For example, the 1977 convention resolutions of one of the most fundamentalist Lutheran bodies in the United States read:

> Resolved, That the Synod reject and repudiate as opposed to sound Lutheran theology and injurious to the Gospel any view of the Bible and method of interpreting it which relates history to the production of the sacred writings in such a way as to diminish their "not of this world" character and to deprive them of their divine authority.[5]

On the other hand, a thousand and one voices were calling to jettison a method whose emancipation from the dogmatic and doctrinaire had grown stale in favor of an equal number of political, socio-critical, feminist, structuralist, post-structuralist, and deconstructionist perspectives.[6] If the task had been to connect "the most radical historical-critical inheritance of the 19th century with biblically earnest speech about

---

4. Peter Stuhlmacher, *Historical Criticism and Theological Interpretation of Scripture*, trans. Roy A. Harrisville (Minneapolis: Augsburg Fortress, 1977), p. 65.

5. Roy A. Harrisville, "Requiem for Biblical Authority," *Dialog* 20 (Autumn 1981): 219.

6. See Stuhlmacher, *Historical Criticism and Theological Interpretation of Scripture*, pp. 20-21.

God,"[7] wherever the New Testament was dealt with in a lively way, the discipline of exegesis was scarcely involved.[8]

When treating the causes of the method's decline, a majority dealt in particulars, but a few advanced to what they believed to be its fundamental faults. In his work on the Pauline and Johannine writings, the Roman Catholic theologian Roman Guardini (1885-1968) pointed to the rationalist concept of knowledge underlying the method's use. According to this concept all data, however different in essence and value, are in respect of their knowability everywhere the same, and hence can be absorbed in quantitative relationships of form and number. Reality, however, consists of *qualitatively* definable things and events incapable of being transferred into quantities. "Knowledge," wrote Guardini,

> is not borne by an apparatus which indicates only numbers and mass but by an organ which comprehends what is peculiar: things, events, relations, essences, values. . . . The knowing organ . . . is actuated before what is living other than before what is lifeless, before what is human-spiritual other than before what is biological, before what is personal other than before what is merely sensuous.[9]

Rooted in this problematic notion of science, preoccupied with what is common, the method lacked preparedness for what was different, lacked awareness of its responsibility for the peculiarity of the existent. It reduced the data, the text, to the single, to the quantitative, to what was everywhere the same. Another critic noted the "obligatory nature" of the historical-critical method, according to which history is a unity uninterrupted by the invasion of supernatural, otherworldly powers, a unity characterized by the continuum of cause and effect. "Of course," writes our critic,

> this causal connection does not exclude the human's free decision, but even this free decision has its cause and effect. Thus, in principle, the continuum of cause and effect cannot be relieved.[10]

---

7. Adloff, "Neuen Aspekte der Exegese nach Bultmann," p. 88.

8. Dieter Nestle, "Über die Häresie und Langeweile in der Auslegung des Neuen Testaments," *Deutsches Pfarrerblatt* 80, no. 10 (1980): 490.

9. Roman Guardini, *Das Christusbild der paulinischen und johanneischen Schriften* (Würzburg: Werkbund-Verlag, 1961), p. 7.

10. Theodor Lorenzmeier, *Exegese und Hermeneutik* (Hamburg: Furche Verlag, 1968), p. 15.

It would be "a genuine miracle," wrote another, if we could salvage from the New Testament what had been handed over to the ash heap of history as archaic primitivity.[11] It was only left to apply the epithet "lower" to historical or analytic criticism, reserving the term "higher" for an entirely different activity.[12] If Schleiermacher had expressed horror over the knots of history loosening to the point where Christianity and barbarism made up one strand and science and unbelief the other, now "theological science" appeared knotted up with a scientifically draped unbelief.[13] But if one party mourned the lazy peace between theology and scientific-technical reason and the resultant faults adhering to the historical-critical method, the other fought to keep awake at the recital of whatever strengths or weaknesses had belonged to it:

> For a student of theology today, struggle with yawning may be all that is left of the heated battles that held students of the fifties in suspense.[14]

Form criticism came in for the lion's share of objections to the historical-critical method. In fact, the flurry of attacks from every conceivable quarter attests to its dominance. In an essay entitled "Fern-seed and Elephants," the British apologist from Belfast C. S. Lewis (1898-1963) registered his "first bleat" over the form critics' call to faith in their ability to read between the lines of the old texts. "They claim to see fern-seed," he wrote, "and can't see an elephant ten yards away in broad daylight." His "second bleat" was over the critics' claim that the real behavior, purpose, and teaching of Christ came rapidly to be misunderstood and misrepresented, but was now recovered or exhumed by modern scholars. "Bleat" number three occurred over the principle that the miraculous does not occur, and the fourth, the "loudest and longest," that the vaunted reconstruction of the history of a text involved "sailing by dead reckoning," its results unable to be checked by fact.[15] In similar vein Roland Mushat Frye

---

11. Adloff, "Neuen Aspekte der Exegese nach Bultmann," p. 104.

12. Northrop Frye, *Anatomy of Criticism* (Princeton, N.J.: Princeton University Press, 1971), p. 315.

13. See Friedrich Daniel Ernst Schleiermacher, "Zweites Sendschreiben an Lücke," in *Neuzeit,* part I *(Kirchen- und Theologiegeschichte in Quellen),* IV/1 (Neukirchen-Vluyn, 1979), p. 170.

14. Adloff, "Neuen Aspekte der Exegese nach Bultmann," p. 108.

15. C. S. Lewis, "Fern-seed and Elephants," in *Fern-seed and Elephants* (Glasgow: William Collins Son, 1977), pp. 111-13, 116.

(1921-2005) of the University of Pennsylvania contrasted an earlier day when interpretation running counter to established doctrine was outlawed and the current "equal and opposite reaction" that denied anything conceivably supportive of belief, then went on to state that the various critical analyses offered highly rationalized suppositions, built layer upon layer into intriguing structures of marvelous intricacy, but that when one looked for evidence, rarely anything could be regarded as convincing.[16]

When the dissidents wrote of the origins of the form-critical method they referred to the History of Religions School *(Religionsgeschichtliche Schule)* and its programmatic according to which the model of evolution was to be applied to the analysis of biblical texts. Application of the model assumed discontinuity between the text's supposed origin and its ultimately taking on fixed form. Discontinuity, the "loathsome ditch" between origin and final form, was thus the starting point of form-critical research, and negotiation of the "ditch" its aim and goal. The *terminus a quo,* as one scholar put it, was conceived to be "an anonymous Jesus and a few early Christians in the inaccessible darkness of the time."[17] At any rate, the pure and original form of the text, whatever "life" it enjoyed before being written down, needed getting at, together with whatever had happened to the text in its assuming final form. Distilling this pure form would enable the historian to describe the history and development of the biblical saying or narrative. The move thus involved a retracing of steps from the current, written text to its pure, original form, to whatever supplied the link in the development from the one to the other. That link had to be the Christian community; who or what else would have transmitted the tradition? The creative, anonymous community as agent in the development of biblical tradition became axiomatic. According to the form critic, just as popular folklore originated with and was handed on by the lower, non-individual layers of society, so the Gospel tradition, itself a kind of *Volk-* or *Klein-literatur,* owed its development and transmission to the anonymous community.

A chorus of objections was raised to the notion that a method actually existed for "layering," for separating the original, pure form from accretions taken on in the development toward fixed, written form. Frye

16. Roland Mushat Frye, "A Literary Perspective for the Criticism of the Gospels," in *Jesus and Man's Hope,* ed. Donald Miller and Dikran Hadidian (Pittsburgh Theological Seminary, 1971), vol. 2, pp. 197, 213.

17. Rainer Blank, "Analyse und Kritik der formgeschichtlichen Arbeiten von Martin Dibelius und Rudolf Bultmann" (Ph.D. diss., University of Basel, 1981), pp. 184-85.

wrote that few if any leading literary historians in secular fields would be comfortable with the widespread assumption among New Testament critics that it is possible to move backward in time from passages in the extant Gospel texts in such a way as to identify previous stages or forms through which the tradition supposedly passed.[18] As for the singularity of that pure or original form, where was the justification for assuming that the original storyteller told the story in only one form? There was grave danger in assuming a single prototype for a literary form and assuming that variations from it were due to editorial manipulation. More, from whence the "romantic" notion of a creative, anonymous community? As noted above,[19] Otto Piper had written that the New Testament documents confirmed the findings of sociology and anthropology to the effect that collectivities are receptive, not creative.

> Any agreement that is found among groups living at different localities, has been brought about by individuals. It is unthinkable that all the early Christian congregations together should have created the "Christ myth." There is no historical analogy that would show that groups with so different cultural, national, and religious backgrounds and different needs were ever able to reach such amazing agreement as found in the gospel pattern of the primitive church.[20]

Construing the development of the Gospel tradition as analogous to the development of popular folklore ran aground on definitions of folklore minus the notion of anonymous creativity. According to one Swiss folklorist, Eduard Hoffmann-Krayer (1864-1936), folklore is simply anything current that has penetrated to wide strata of society and been appropriated by them, consciously or not.[21] Or again, who had decreed that the Gospel tradition, or any other for that matter, developed from the simple to the complex, that spiritual or historical processes followed the rule of zoological genealogies? In so-called lower or text criticism, the rule *difficilior lectio potior* (the more difficult reading is to be preferred) was to be applied in the attempt to arrive at the *autographa* or *idiocheira,* at

18. Roland Mushat Frye, "Literary Criticism and Gospel Criticism," *Theology Today* (July 1979): 207.

19. Page 249 above.

20. Otto A. Piper, "The Origin of the Gospel Pattern," *Journal of Biblical Literature* 78, no. 2 (1959): 123.

21. Cited in Blank, "Analyse und Kritik der formgeschichtlichen Arbeiten," p. 201.

the original text. The assumption that the Gospel tradition had developed in a ladder-like move from the simple to the complex had led to the hypothesizing of a single prototype, thus to the denial that any speech, discourse, parable, or aphorism could have been uttered more than once or in more than one form.

The idea of the Gospel tradition as a move from the simple to the complex was not the form critic's invention. The great folklorist and philologist of the nineteenth century Jacob Grimm (1788-1863) of Göttingen held that research into the oral tradition of his people would disclose unbroken continuity with an ancient past.[22] That continuity involved the move from the simple to the complex, from the poetry of nature, say, to that of art, from the unity of poetry and life to its division in the modern period. Further, literary witnesses from the past and oral traditions yet in use would reveal the persistence of an "original" and "true" myth.[23] As for language, it too had to develop by way of the same move, from the simple to the complex.

Back of this idea of development lay an assumption held by scholars and thinkers of the eighteenth century, the theological nature of which could scarcely be missed. Whether straddling the space between the Enlightenment and romanticism with Gotthold Ephraim Lessing, or reflecting the romanticism of the Storm and Stress *(Sturm und Drang)* period as did Johann Gottfried Herder, they denied that humanity could have been given language through a miracle, thus obviating the need to invent it, or that humans could have learned it through condescension of the Creator. Contrariwise, the invention of language had to occur over centuries, and the Creator's goodness would not have allowed him to keep language from the creature for so long. In a lecture delivered in 1851 at the Prussian Academy of Sciences at which, among others, the philosopher F. W. J. Schelling (1775-1854), the historian Leopold von Ranke (1795-1886), and the naturalist Alexander von Humboldt (1769-1859) were in attendance, Jacob Grimm argued that due to its original imperfection, language could not have originated with the Creator, who reserves his imprimatur for perfection.[24] He wrote,

22. Jacob Grimm, "Volkskunde," in *Religion in Geschichte und Gegenwart,* 4th ed. (Tübingen: J. C. B. Mohr, 1998-2007), vol. 8, p. 1187.
23. "Grimm," in *Religion in Geschichte und Gegenwart,* 4th ed., vol. 3, p. 1296; see also *Religion in Geschichte und Gegenwart,* 3rd ed., vol. 3 (Tübingen: J. C. B. Mohr, 1958), p. 1877.
24. Jacob Grimm, *Über den Ursprung der Sprache* (Frankfurt: Insel-Verlag, 1968), p. 32.

It would contradict the divine wisdom in advance to bring about by force what a free human race ought to possess, just as it would be against his righteousness to allow a divine language given the first humans to sink from its summit for their posterity.[25]

Believing that it was possible to get beyond the "abyss of the millennia" and land on the shore of the origin of language. Grimm went on to trace its development throughout three periods, the first artless, simple, sensuous, a period of coming into existence, of growing and sending out shoots, the second marked by the emergence of inflection, and the third by the impulse toward ideas — all of it a move from the simple to the complex.[26]

It would take a special study to prove the form critic's dependence on the researches of Jacob Grimm in particular, but the application to biblical studies of the idea of continuity embracing the move from the simple to the complex as per the (supposed) development of tradition and language originated with eighteenth- and nineteenth-century folklore and philology.

There was more: form criticism did not concede the existence of a coherent oral stage at any point in the development of the Gospel tradition. The concession would have demanded the abandonment of an axiom the form critic took to be non-negotiable, that is, that the development of the Gospel tradition occurred on Hellenistic soil. Allowing for a coherent, oral stage would have meant drastically reducing the time for the development of the tradition, thus reducing the axiom to the absurd.[27] In his *Memory and Manuscript,* first appearing in 1961, the Swedish scholar Birger Gerhardsson (1926-) argued that many of the characteristics of Jesus' ministry could be traced to his teaching. Further, Jesus' teaching reflected similarity with Jewish (and Hellenistic) transmission of tradition according to which sayings were learned by heart. This tradition, Gerhardsson continued, was perpetuated in the early church, stamped on the memories of disciples still in existence, a "collegium" that handed on the sayings of Jesus analogous to Judaism's transmission of "the word of God" *(Dabar Jahve)* and the oral Torah. Consequently, if the disciples were involved in editing Jesus' teaching, they did so on the basis of a fixed, distinct tradition. To imagine that forgetfulness and the exercise of pious imagination had a hand in

---

25. Grimm, *Über den Ursprung der Sprache,* pp. 39-40.
26. See Grimm, *Über den Ursprung der Sprache,* pp. 38-41.
27. See Blank, "Analyse und Kritik der formgeschichtlichen Arbeiten," p. 209.

transforming those memories in the course of a few short decades would be unrealistic in the extreme.[28] In a later essay, Gerhardsson wrote that taking seriously the altering of traditional material and assuming that early Christianity created the Jesus traditions as the need arose were two vastly different things.

> In brief, one could say that the form critics — in any case Bultmann and his pupils — regard the Synoptic tradition in principle as a creation of the early church after Easter. My opinion, on the other hand, is that we must proceed from the fact that the Synoptic material in principle harks back to the earthly Jesus and his disciples who accompanied him during his ministry, though full credit is due the argument that this memorized material was colored by the understanding and inter-pretations at which earliest Christianity's teachers gradually arrived.[29]

In his 1981 dissertation, Reiner Blank argued that in denying the Jew-ish character of the biblical sources Bultmann was following his teacher Wilhelm Bousset (1865-1920), co-founder of the History of Religions School, and thus was forced to render earliest Christianity dependent on Hellenistic models and perspectives.[30] He rejected the form critic's assumption that institutionalization and with it a conscious process of transmission of tradition could only have occurred within the context of a late-arriving eschatological consciousness. Since, he wrote, it could be demonstrated that apocalyptic ideas and a future-eschatological con-sciousness cohered with strict organization, the argument for the late phase of the development of earliest Christianity and its tradition fell of its own weight.[31] Heatedly, Kristlieb Adloff of Wolfenbüttel wrote that the exclusion of Judaism in scripture exposition corresponded exactly to the appeal to "cheap grace" attacked by Dietrich Bonhoeffer.[32]

The attacks seemed endless. Bultmann was faulted for his inconsis-tency. Initially, he had treated "Q" merely as material held in common by Matthew and Luke and absent from Mark. Later, when none of the existing

---

28. Birger Gerhardsson, "The Origins and Transmission of the Gospel Tradition," in *Memory and Manuscript* (Grand Rapids: Eerdmans, 1998), pp. 324-35.

29. Birger Gerhardsson, *Die Anfänge der Evangelientradition* (Wuppertal: R. Brock-haus, 1977), pp. 62-63.

30. Blank, "Analyse und Kritik der formgeschichtlichen Arbeiten," p. 186.

31. Blank, "Analyse und Kritik der formgeschichtlichen Arbeiten," p. 198.

32. Adloff, "Neuen Aspekte der Exegese nach Bultmann," p. 92.

texts appeared to yield the "pure" form, he appealed to "Q" as source.[33] This transfer of the method of source criticism to a nonexistent text ran athwart the original intent of form-critical method, namely, to research the history of the transmission in the pre-literary stage.[34]

Finally, challenge was hurled at the form critics' assumption that by arriving at the "life" of a given saying or narrative prior to its being written down one could penetrate to the situation-in-life *(Sitz-im-Leben)* that such a piece in its pre-literary form reflected. Joseph Fitzmeyer (1920-), onetime professor of biblical studies at the Catholic University of America, wrote that in its reaction to the multiplicity of senses native to medieval exegesis, historical-critical interpretation had adopted the thesis of a single meaning. "All the effort of historical-critical exegesis," he wrote, "goes into defining 'the' precise sense of this or that biblical text seen within the circumstances in which it was produced." This thesis, Fitzmeyer, continued, had now run aground on the conclusions of language theory and philosophical hermeneutics, both of which affirm that written texts have a plurality of meaning.[35] To this position, the vice-dean of the Prague Catholic faculty added his assent.[36] Twenty years earlier, C. S. Lewis had his eye on the fault:

> The superiority in judgement and diligence which you are going to attribute to the Biblical critics will have to be almost superhuman if it is to offset the fact that they are everywhere faced with customs, language, race-characteristics, class-characteristics, a religious background, habits of composition, and basic assumptions, which no scholarship will ever enable any man now alive to know as surely and intimately and instinctively as the reviewer can know mine.[37]

Ultimately, the form critic's substitution of the creativity of an anonymous community for genuine, identifiable authorship was countered by the argument that the biblical text revealed the existence of a flesh and

---

33. Cf. Blank, "Analyse und Kritik der formgeschichtlichen Arbeiten," p. 205.

34. Blank, "Analyse und Kritik der formgeschichtlichen Arbeiten," p. 207.

35. Joseph A. Fitzmeyer, "The Meaning of Inspired Scripture," in *The Biblical Commission's Document "The Interpretation of the Bible in the Church"* (Rome: Editrice Pontificio Istituto Biblico, 1995), pp. 117-18.

36. Jaroslav Brož, "From Allegory to the Four Senses of Scripture," in *Philosophical Hermeneutics and Biblical Exegesis,* ed. Petr Pokorný and Jan Roskovec (Tübingen: Mohr Siebeck, 2002), p. 301.

37. Lewis, "Fern-seed and Elephants," p. 117.

blood author who pursued a distinct purpose or goal with his work. Redaction criticism, as this perspective was called, was spared the quantity of criticism leveled at form criticism for the reason that its principal vulnerability involved the so-called authorial fallacy.

In *Truth and Method,* Gadamer wrote that understanding is never a subjective relation to an object but to the history of its effects. He thus dismissed authorial intention, writing that when we try to understand a text, "we do not get ourselves into the author's psychic state," adding that in understanding what is written "we are moving in a dimension of meaning that is intelligible as such, and as such yields no motive for harking back to the subjectivity of the other."[38] In an essay on philosophical and theological hermeneutics, the French thinker Paul Ricoeur (1913-2005) wrote that "writing provides a text with a certain autonomy in relation to the intention of the author." For this reason, he stated, "what the text means may no longer coincide with what the author meant."[39]

The severest attack on the "authorial fallacy" may have been made by the French semiologist Roland Barthes (1915-80). In a chapter on "The Death of the Author," contained in his *Image, Music, Text,* Barthes wrote of the author as a "modern figure," a product "emerging from the Middle Ages with English empiricism, French rationalism and the personal faith of the Reformation."[40] As a result, a piece of literature has always been explained in terms of the person who produced it, "as if it were always in the end . . . the voice of a single person, the author 'confiding' in us."[41] Some, Barthes wrote, tried to loosen this authorial tyranny. Stéphane Mallarmé (1842-98), for example, saw that "it is language which speaks, not the author; to write is, through a prerequisite impersonality . . . to reach that point where only language acts, 'performs,' and not 'me.' "[42] The image of the author, Barthes continued, had now been "desacralized," to the point where the author is never more than the "instance" writing, never more than a "scriptor."[43] According to Barthes, this removal of the author has utterly transformed

38. Hans-Georg Gadamer, *Wahrheit und Methode* (Tübingen: J. C. B. Mohr [Paul Siebeck], 1975), p. 276.

39. Paul Ricoeur, "Philosophical Hermeneutics and Theological Hermeneutics," *Studies in Religion* 5, no. 1 (1975-76): 18.

40. Roland Barthes, "The Death of the Author," in *Image, Music, Text,* trans. Stephen Heath (London: Fontana, 1977), pp. 142-43.

41. Barthes, "The Death of the Author," p. 143.

42. Barthes, "The Death of the Author," p. 143.

43. Barthes, "The Death of the Author," p. 145.

the modern text. For one thing, it renders the claim to decipher a text, by which the critic shares the author's "reign," a futile enterprise. Of course, the structure of the text may be researched, but there is nothing beneath the text, only an incessant positing of meaning giving way to an incessant evaporation. Barthes wrote,

> In precisely this way literature . . . by refusing to assign a "secret," an ultimate meaning, to the text (and to the world as text), liberates what may be called an anti-theological activity, an activity that is truly revolutionary since to refuse to fix meaning is, in the end, to refuse God and his hypostases — reason, science, law.[44]

Earlier in the volume, Barthes wrote of the introduction of the personal "instance," the "I" of the author, as an invasion on the part of a "psychological person" unrelated to the "linguistic" person, a person defined only by its place in the discourse.[45] Later in the volume Barthes wrote of the text as able to be "broken," able to be read without the guarantee of its "father." Should the author ever "come back" to the text, he would do so as a "guest," "no longer privileged, paternal, aletheological."[46] "He becomes, as it were, a paper-author: his life is no longer the origin of his work but a fiction contributing to his work."[47]

To what impulses or situations the origin of the decline of the historical-critical method is to be traced is a matter for debate. The Jesuit scholar Michael C. Legaspi (1941-2001), instructor in philosophy and religious studies at Philips Academy in Andover, Massachusetts, traces the "death of scripture (its demise as self-evident inheritance guiding the faithful) and the rise of biblical studies" (its resurgence as an object whose meaning and authority are established from elsewhere) to social, moral, and political factors. Focusing on eighteenth-century Georg-August-University at Göttingen, Legaspi traces the dying and rising to attempts on the part of the university's greats to assign the Bible a status equal to that of the remaining university disciplines, thus to its contribution to a productive life within the state, and by way of recovering its aesthetic superiority. The attempt, Legaspi contends, inevitably led to a separation between two

44. Barthes, "The Death of the Author," p. 147.
45. Barthes, "The Death of the Author," pp. 112, 114.
46. Presumably, a term coined from merging the transliterated Greek term *aletheia* (truth) with the adjective "theological."
47. Barthes, "The Death of the Author," p. 161.

rival communities, the church and the university, a separation persisting to this day. At the book's beginning Legaspi writes:

> In order to maintain the critical distance necessary for objective understanding, scholars of religion created ways of studying their subjects that insulated them from the thing that gives religion power: its claim on the loyalties of the individual.[48]

At its conclusion, he writes:

> I believe that the scriptural Bible and the academic Bible are fundamentally different creations oriented toward rival interpretive communities. Though in some ways homologous, they can and should function independently if each is to retain its integrity.[49]

From the essays of literary theorist W. D. Robertson Jr., if not the origin of the decline, at least the current state of interpretation can be traced to the demand for "romantic and post-romantic emotionalism in everything we read."[50] Blanning writes that for the post-1945 generation grown to maturity in the 1960s, "modernism had become complacent, middle-aged, and — fatal adjective — boring." Accordingly, "youth" threw reason to the side.[51]

Whatever the origins of historical criticism's decline, a great deal may be said for the alternatives brought forward to replace it. In general, the Canadian literary theorist Northrop Frye recommends the new, emergent literary criticism for its view of the Bible, "not as the scrapbook of conceptions, glosses, redactions, insertions, conflations, misplacing, and misunderstandings revealed by the analytic critic," but as the unity they were originally intended to construct. He adds:

> A genuine higher criticism of the Bible, therefore, would be a synthesizing process which would start with the assumption that the Bible is

48. Michael Legaspi, *The Death of Scripture and the Rise of Biblical Studies* (Oxford: Oxford University Press, 2010), p. 7.

49. Legaspi, *The Death of Scripture*, p. 169.

50. D. W. Robertson Jr., "The Historical Setting of Chaucer's *Book of the Duchess*," in *Essays in Medieval Culture* (Princeton, N.J.: Princeton University Press, 1980), pp. 16-17.

51. Timothy C. W. Blanning, *The Romantic Revolution* (London: Weidenfeld and Nicolson, 2011), p. 181.

a definitive myth, a single archetypal structure extending from creation to apocalypse.[52]

In the official journal of the Society of Biblical Literature, another Canadian, David Jobling, refers approvingly to the tension between "exuberant celebration of freedom and methodological plurality" in current literary study of the Bible, and to its aim at furnishing a coherent paradigm able to challenge the prevailing paradigm in biblical studies.[53]

Alternatives

Among the unnumbered paradigms urged in lieu of the traditional historical-critical method, a few stand out by virtue of their influence: rhetorical criticism, structuralism, and deconstruction. The first type interprets the biblical texts in terms of the characteristic products or "players" in classical Greco-Roman rhetorical convention and the devices used. The players include the trained speaker, the politicized audience, and the self-conscious consensus both enjoy.[54] According to George A. Kennedy (1928-), emeritus professor of classics at Chapel Hill, the first to furnish a method for rhetorical criticism of the Gospels and epistles, rhetorical criticism has five interrelated steps. The first has to do with the rhetorical unit; the second with the rhetorical situation; the third with the rhetorical problem and the species of rhetoric, whether judicial, deliberative, or epideictic; the fourth with the arrangement of the various components. (These may include the *exordium,* or introduction; the *captatio,* or attempt to curry favor with the hearer; the *propositio,* or summary of what is to follow; the *narratio,* or statement of facts; the *argumentatio,* or presentation of the rhetor's point of view; and the *peroratio,* or conclusion, designed to glean the hearer's consent through an appeal to reason and emotion.) The fifth component involves evaluation of the rhetorical effectiveness of the rhetorical unit in meeting the situation. Concentration on these steps and their components characterizes rhetorical criticism in contrast to the traditional hermeneutic with its pursuit of the trained critic, the readership as dissenting or dominating, and the text as reusable

---

52. Frye, *Anatomy of Criticism,* p. 188.
53. Jobling, "Writing the Wrongs of the World," p. 106.
54. See Ian Henderson, "Rhetorical Determinacy and the Text," *Semeia* 71 (1995): 162.

weapon. As is clear, by this method determinacy resides in the social contexts of training and performance as reflected in the rhetorical approach rather than in the text itself. Pursuit of the model, however, furnishes a corrective to the neglect of plot structure or sequence in the traditional, synthetic approach with its unilinear, step by step categorization by text, source, form, and redaction. After all, narrative framework and narrated speeches in literate Hellenistic texts such as the New Testament can be expected to reflect or deflect Hellenistic rhetorical conventions.[55] At any rate, attention to rhetorical devices in texts calculated to "carry their readers along" enhances interpretation.

Just as rhetorical criticism, so structuralism is concerned with the synchronic, the coincident as opposed to the diachronic or sequential. Its advocates use the term "structure" in two senses: in the one sense it denotes the hidden structures that unconsciously inform the various aspects of a society, and in the other the organization that gives a text its intelligibility. A child of linguistics, structuralism, or structuralist method in this smaller sense, is occupied with the logic of an entire narrative rather than of a given sentence. It holds that a text, a story, or a myth has structures that are latent or "deep" in nature, by which the narrative is given coherence and meaning. It thus follows the lead of the French cultural anthropologist Claude Lévi-Strauss (1908-2009), who developed the axiom that myths reflect the general structure of the human mind, which is the same in all cultures. These myths, according to Lévi-Strauss, consist of binary oppositions, such as animate/inanimate, masculine/feminine, pure/impure, and the like. Following the lead of Lévi-Strauss and others, particularly the French semiologist A. J. Greimas (1917-92), biblical scholars have been at pains to uncover the laws or "deep structures" that govern and give coherence to biblical narrative. Greimas uncovered two types of laws or deep structures, the best known of which is his "actantial model," which breaks an action down into six "actants": a sender (1) transfers an object (2) to a receiver (3) through the agency of a subject (4) whom other agents may help (5) or hinder (6). Consequently, beginning, not from the static idea of "structure," but from the idea and concept of "differences," as reflected in the binary scheme, structuralism aims to facilitate understanding of the "narrativity" of the story and render it accessible to interpretation.

According to the hermeneutics of suspicion characteristic of current

---

55. Henderson, "Rhetorical Determinacy and the Text," p. 170.

biblical scholarship, interpretation, intent on bridging the gap between the actual and the apparent meaning of a text, is always suspect due to the prejudgments inevitably attaching to it and threatening to inhibit or silence the text. "Deconstruction," a term applied to the "method" of the French thinker Jacques Derrida (1930-2004), may be the most radical type of this hermeneutic. At the same time, the shape it has assumed in this country is in sharp contrast to the politically charged French version, rooted in "destruction" of the Western metaphysical tradition, and hand in hand with Marxism, radical feminism, and psychoanalysis. In the interpretation of texts, deconstruction has two sides. The one accents the text's total lack of support in whatever force, value, logic, referents, and the like outside themselves its words may be presumed to have. Thus, a word has no equivalence with the object it purports to describe. In Derrida's language, it has no "presence." Again, to cite Derrida, there are thus no "signifieds," no referents beyond themselves to which the words may point; there are only "signifiers," the words themselves. Every text comprises a "signifier" without a "signified." The other side of deconstruction accents the endless process of interpretation resulting from the text's lack of support. But this means that "reading has lost its status as a passive consumption of a product to become a performance."[56] It also means that there are as many possible interpretations as there are possible readers, hence the accent on the infinity of the interpretive process. In his primer on deconstruction Paul Strathern (1940-), the British writer and academic, concludes:

> The words on the page — ambiguous in themselves — are merely a sounding board for the reader's interpretation. Derrida carries this analysis to its extreme. Difference without "positive terms" of identity means that language at this underlying level of meaning is almost completely fluid.[57]

Since discourse involves force or power, whether by way of appeal to a system, value, logic, or referent, deconstruction may be negatively described as the subversion of any claim to power inherent in discourse. On the other hand, it may be described positively as including whatever elements a sys-

---

56. The "anti-foundationalist" Stanley E. Fish (1938-), quoted in Fred W. Burnett, "Postmodern Biblical Exegesis," *Semeia* 51 (1990): 55.

57. Paul Strathern, *Derrida in 90 Minutes* (Chicago: Ivan R. Dee, 2000), p. 38.

tem, value, logic, or referent is calculated to exclude from reading and interpretation. In this respect, it is theorized that deconstruction revisits the old "Hebrew versus Greek" distinction, "Hebrew" denoting the side of "free play" reflected, for example, in cabbalistic and rabbinic interpretation.[58] Christian theology may learn from deconstructionist method to revisit an unaccented part of its tradition. For New Testament authors such as Paul, Mark, and John, the desire and longing for life is not conceived as centered on "presence and power" but on love for the other and the self's waiver of rights. In fine, as one Heidelberg scholar writes, "every dyadic conception of signs proceeds in reductionist fashion. The relation belonging to description is genuinely triadic. . . . With this idea the elements of truth in deconstruction can be taken up."[59]

The Current Situation

The return of Bible interpretation to a pre-critical stage is out of the question, but so is a commonly agreed on alternative. For the present, at least, contemporary biblical interpretation yields no unity. In place of a method universally, albeit qualifiedly, recognized and applied for more than a century, now appears a congeries of methods, none of which could elude enlistment as supplement rather than enjoying independence. And, in fact, with its subversion of method as such, deconstruction by definition offers no alternative to traditional method.

A series of problems attaches to current methods that challenges their claims to status as genuine alternatives. To begin with, most tend to emphasize interpretation as "performance" rather than as "passive consumption." That is, the text as independent of interpretation is replaced by the text as the result of the interpreter's activity. One of the twentieth century's most significant thinkers wrote these words:

> There is never a reader before whose eyes the great book of world history simply lies open. But there is also never a reader who, with his text before his eyes, simply reads what is there. Rather, in all reading application takes place, so that whoever reads a text is him-

---

58. Jobling, "Writing the Wrongs of the World," pp. 107-8.

59. Martin Pöttner, "Dekonstruktion," in *Religion in Geschichte und Gegenwart,* 4th ed., vol. 2, p. 639.

self included in the sense he has grasped. He belongs to the text he understands.[60]

In his introduction to a series of essays on interpretation, the reader-response theorist Stanley Fish described his earlier position respecting the reader or text as source of meaning in these words:

> When someone would characterize my position as the most recent turn of the new-critical screw, I would reply by saying that in my model the reader was freed from the tyranny of the text and given the central role in the production of meaning.[61]

The position is carried to its extreme when, as with Derrida, the words on the page function merely as a sounding board for the reader's interpretation. On this view, language is almost completely fluid, thus eluding clarity and whatever "presence" our thought may impose on it.[62]

The view bears striking similarity to a perspective shared by historians and other interpreters of texts more than a century ago. For example, in his *Outline of the Principles of History,* the Berlin historian Johann Gustav Droysen (1808-84) wrote that past events had no existence or duration except in and through the mind.[63] The result of criticism, he continued, is not the "actual historical fact" but a readying of the data to facilitate a relatively reliable point of view.[64] Or again, "for us the complex of ideas illumined by interpretation within a sequence of events is the truth of this sequence. For us, this sequence is the truth, the phenomenal form of this idea."[65] In his exposition of what he termed "narrative description" *(erzählende Darstellung)* Droysen wrote that it is only apparent that "facts" speak for themselves. "They would be dumb," he insisted, "without the narrator who allows them to speak."[66] There is nothing to suggest a dependence on Droysen among the Fishes and Derridas and their counterparts

---

60. Gadamer, *Wahrheit und Methode,* p. 323.

61. Stanley Fish, *Is There a Text in This Class?* (Cambridge, Mass.: Harvard University Press, 1980), p. 7.

62. Cf. Strathern, *Derrida in 90 Minutes,* p. 38.

63. Johann Gustav Droysen, *Grundriss der Historik,* ed. Rudolf Hübner, 4th ed. (München: R. Oldenbourg, 1960), sec. 5, p. 327.

64. Droysen, *Grundriss der Historik,* sec. 36, pp. 338-39.

65. Droysen, *Grundriss der Historik,* sec. 44, p. 344.

66. Droysen, *Grundriss der Historik,* sec. 91, p. 361.

in the biblical field, especially not when a traditionalist such as Tübingen's Martin Hengel (1926-) can write that "the art of the historian" is to bring "the dead past to life."[67] In any case, the similarity exists.

In the introduction referred to above, Stanley Fish distances himself from his earlier view:

> A polemic that was mounted in the name of the reader and against the text has ended by the subsuming of both the text and reader under the larger category of interpretation.[68]

Dieter Nestle had little taste for Hengel's axiom. Writing that the matter became even more burdensome in preaching since the hearer was required to perform a resuscitation, to transfer the text into an act, he added: "I cannot forget that preacher's raised index finger and his summons directed to us several times during the sermon: 'Make the transfer! Make the transfer!'"[69]

A further problem emerges with current emphasis on the synchronic, on the text as "autosematic," and the analysis of its "code" to the possible disparagement of historical context. On this view, no narrative can be transparent to historical fact. The event to which a text could conceivably be related is an invention, an irrational, fictional element. The view of Stanford's Hayden White (1928-) is less violent, though he is persuaded that the various types of historical interpretation originate in some kind of ideological commitment. "Every proper history," he writes,

> presupposes a metahistory which is nothing but the web of commitments which the historian makes in the course of his interpretation on the aesthetic, cognitive, and ethical levels.[70]

According to White, those commitments are not simply flights of fancy. They are rooted in language itself, which furnishes "models of the *direction* that thought itself might take in its effort to provide meaning."[71] At the

---

67. Martin Hengel, *Zur urchristlichen Geschichtsschreibung* (Stuttgart: Calwer Verlag, 1979), p. 52.

68. Fish, *Is There a Text in This Class?* p. 17.

69. Nestle, "Über Häresie und Langeweile in der Auslegung des Neuen Testaments," p. 492.

70. Hayden White, "Interpretation in History," in *Tropics of Discourse: Essays in Cultural Criticism* (Baltimore: Johns Hopkins University Press, 1978), p. 71.

71. White, "Interpretation in History," p. 73.

same time, interpretation requires choice of whatever model or trope language may offer before interpretation takes place. This is clear from White's references to the theories of interpretation proposed by the four great nineteenth-century philosophers of history, Hegel, Droysen, Nietzsche, and Croce.[72]

But if, however immoderately or moderately, emphasis on the synchronic tends to threaten the link between the word and its referent as the event to which it testifies, the results raise serious questions. Can that "extra-linguistic reality" to which a Gospel with its own "narrative worlds" relates really be ignored? If so, is not the idea of unity within the Bible a mere fantasy, thus also that central event in light of which, according to Christian persuasion, the whole movement of history must be seen? Finally, Stanley Fish had to concede a place for the diachronic:

> I am faced with the task of accounting, within the new model, for everything that had been recognized under the old model as being constitutive of the literary institution: texts, authors, periods, genres, canons, standards, agreements, disputes, values, changes, and so on.[73]

The story has been told that on the occasion of Rudolf Bultmann's sixtieth birthday, he was presented with a volume titled "Kerygma," of which every page was blank. If true, it was a mean prank, but aimed at a perceived disconnect of word and event.

While some of the new methods outlaw any interpretation that might mirror a community as "meta-discourse," ignoring the function of the Bible as norm for a community of faith, others concede the existence of communities whose reading strategies precede and influence text and reader. Thus, while for White the referent is a fictive context created by the interpreter and necessarily arbitrary, for Fish the referent is an actual interpretive community. The strategies in question are not the reader's in the sense that would make him an independent agent, but rather proceed from the interpretive community of which he is a member.[74] The difficulty, however, is that a congeries of communities exists without relation to each other. At an annual meeting of the Society of Biblical Literature, one discussion group involved representatives of a welter of unrelated con-

---

72. White, "Interpretation in History," pp. 74-75.
73. Fish, *Is There a Text in This Class?* p. 17.
74. Fish, *Is There a Text in This Class?* p. 14.

texts. The group included a structuralist who exclaimed he could scarcely believe persons still existed for whom words had referents, a feminist who charged that since the group was largely made up of males there could be no common understanding, and a Latino who voiced the same conviction since he was among the oppressed whereas Anglo-American oppressors comprised the remainder. The group was chaired by a logocentrist. As W. D. Robertson has it,

> Our "psychology" as it appears in literary criticism is a . . . product of a society in which the tightly-knit communities of the past have broken down so that the individual is left with a somewhat diminished and fragmented identity as a member of large and loosely organized groups.[75]

If the interpretation of a text is limited only by the number of communities that attempt it, the disappointment that Kermode attaches to interpretation can only be the inevitable result. After running the gamut of the various types of interpretation and the divination each involves, "however intermittently, erroneously, dishonestly, or disappointedly," he concludes,

> whether one thinks that one's purpose is to re-cognize the original meaning, or to fall headlong into a text that is a treacherous network rather than a continuous and systematic sequence, one may be sure of one thing, and that is disappointment.[76]

It may be overreaching to suggest that the accent on synchrony hides a particular philosophical commitment, but the resistance to the idea of a referent, of a word as relating to an object outside itself, the refusal to allow for a "presence" in terms of meaning or truth, at the least suggests a kind of Baconian tabling of religious faith in favor of scientific method. To assert that the word takes the definition of its content solely from its relation to other words in the text, to set aside a correspondence view of truth "in favor of a view of historical representation which leaves it virtually indistinguishable from fiction,"[77] to rid interpretation of that metaphysical

---

75. Robertson, "The Historical Setting of Chaucer's *Book of the Duchess*," p. 7.
76. Kermode, *The Genesis of Secrecy*, p. 126.
77. White, "Interpretation in History," p. 64.

"presence" that has haunted all Western thinking,[78] or simply to identify that presence with the word itself[79] describes a posture irreconcilable with a hermeneutic according to which the destination of words is, as Petr Pokorný (1933-) of the Protestant Faculty at Prague puts it, "The Word himself who interprets the Father."[80]

If, unaccompanied, without complement or supplement, the synchronic method rules out interpretation open to religious faith, it ignores a dimension integral to the reading of a text. Writing from "a semiotic perspective," Daniel Patte states that the "pragmatic dimension" foregrounded in faith-interpretations is an integral part of any reading of biblical texts. From this perspective he recommends applying to Bible interpretation the triadic perspective of the pragmatist Charles Saunders Peirce (1839-1914), according to which a reading is meaningful only when a text as *sign* is read in terms of its relation to an *object* and an *"interpretant."* Patte concludes that the attempt to reduce biblical study to the dyadic, to a description of the interaction between text (sign) and subject-matter (object) alone *"cannot result in a meaningful reading"* (italics his).[81] William James (1842-1910), friend and sponsor of Peirce, put the matter simply:

> To describe the world with all the various feelings of the individual pinch of destiny, all the various spiritual attitudes, left out from the description — they being as describable as anything else — would be something like offering a printed bill of fare as the equivalent for a solid meal.[82]

Writing of deconstruction, Markus Vinzent of King's College, London, refers to its quest for pluralism, its weakening of structures that promise stability, and its rejection of the human's metaphysical orientation as a captivity to ideology. The unity of meaning that belongs to religion is shrunken to a "many-layered aporetic." Differentiating, ever and anon

---

78. Strathern, *Derrida in 90 Minutes*, p. 68.

79. Northrop Frye, *The Great Code: Bible and Literature* (New York: Harcourt Brace Jovanovich, 1981), p. 137.

80. Petr Pokorný, "Christliche Verkündigung als Modell des hermeneutischen Prozesses nach I Kor 14, 23-25," in *Philosophical Hermeneutics and Biblical Exegesis,* p. 236.

81. Daniel Patte, "Critical Biblical Studies from a Semiotic Perspective," *Semeia* 81 (1998): 17.

82. William James, *Varieties of Religious Experience* (New York: Longmans, Green and Co., 1935), p. 490.

reduced to aporia, together with an indeterminate quest free of obligation, allows thought to "swing this way and that." The aporias lead nowhere; they steadily or "unsteadily" withdraw. On the other hand, Vinzent writes that philosophies of religion miss the mark when they refer to the method as a neo-fundamentalism, or when they simplify the vast complexes reaching back to the roots of deconstruction — the religious criticism of Paul Tillich (1886-1965), the "inverse theology" of Theodor Adorno (1903-69), Jacques Lacan's (1901-81) challenge to the notion of subject, the definition of religion in Karl Marx (1818-83) and Michel Foucault (1926-84). But Vinzent concludes with the question as to whether the positing of what is human and the tentative regaining of one's definition can only occur by way of negation through rejection of task, norm, and the like, and whether or not the possibility of inclusivity, even of religions, can be entrusted to this "free play," that is to say, of religions whose sense is "prism-like."[83]

In the history of theology, it has been customary to assume that Friedrich Schleiermacher's definition of faith or religion was calculated to cut it off from the sciences. The Tübingen scholar Karl Heim (1874-1958) wrote of Protestantism's "fateful turn" when in the wake of Schleiermacher it dissolved all connection with philosophy, and believed it could confidently leave everything else to the secular sciences.[84] In *The Christian Faith,* Schleiermacher referred to the "feeling of absolute dependence" that characterized human existence[85] and thus opposed "any possibility of God being in any way given . . . because anything that is outwardly given must be given as an object exposed to our counter-influence, however slight this might be."[86] For decades scholars followed the lead of Karl Barth in interpreting this sentence and others like it in Kantian fashion as excluding the givenness of the divine as such, rather than awareness of

83. Markus Vinzent, "Dekonstruktion/Dekonstruktivismus II," in *Religion in Geschichte und Gegenwart,* 4th ed., vol. 2, pp. 638-39.

84. Karl Heim, *Der Christliche Gottesglaube und die Naturwissenschaft* (Hamburg: Furche Verlag, 1956), pp. 21-22. See also Ratzinger's comment to the effect that Schleiermacher expelled religion from the sphere of reason and gave it what he believed to be a new and secure position within the realm of the sentiments; Joseph Ratzinger and Marcello Pera, *Without Roots* (New York: Basic, 2006), p. 117.

85. The term that Schleiermacher used may be the most elongated and pendulous in theological history: *Schlechthinnigesabhängigkeitsgefühl.*

86. Friedrich Schleiermacher, *The Christian Faith,* English translation of the second German edition (1830/31), ed. H. R. Mackintosh and J. S. Stewart (Edinburgh: T. & T. Clark, 1948), pp. 17-18.

the divine.[87] There is another reading of Schleiermacher, and supported by one of his most notorious contemporaries, David Friedrich Strauss. Reading Schleiermacher from the perspective of the Berliner's lecture on the life of Jesus, Strauss stated that Schleiermacher's passion for the Christ as "personal, historical," reflected the "busy, and one might almost say anxious, activity of his spirit . . . to suit the Christ of faith to thought, and thought to faith."[88]

Current preoccupation with synchrony has produced a like anxiety among many. While conceding that Bible language may be "hieroglyphic" or "radically metaphorical,"[89] they see the absolutizing of the text as a temptation to arbitrariness, as lacking perception of the truth witnessed to in the text, as prey to a loss of history, and in overlooking faith and other "interests" as leading to all nature of "dramatic" excess.[90]

87. See Karl Barth, *The Theology of Schleiermacher,* trans. Geoffrey W. Bromiley (Grand Rapids: Eerdmans, 1982), pp. 61, 66, 76.

88. David Friedrich Strauss, *Der Christus des Glaubens und der Jesus der Geschichte: Eine Kritik des Schleiermacher'schen Lebens Jesu* (Berlin: Drucker, 1865), p. 104. Cf. the discussion in Roy A. Harrisville and Walter Sundberg, *The Bible in Modern Culture: Baruch Spinoza to Brevard Childs* (Grand Rapids: Eerdmans, 2002), pp. 78-82.

89. See Northrop Frye, *The Great Code,* p. 137.

90. Patte, "Critical Biblical Studies from a Semiotic Perspective," p. 22.

CHAPTER TEN

The Historical-Critical Method Down to Size

An alternative to historical criticism does not exist; writing of its "end" is a wish-fulfillment dream. The reasons are myriad. The historical question will not down because an author, real or "implied," is not merely after achieving dramatic results, but after linking them to some independent reality. It will not down because faith or other "interested" interpretations cannot remain aloof from critical testing. Sooner or later the advocate of a referentiality beyond the horizontal or synchronic must allow that referentiality to be challenged. Further, as long as there is the slightest interest in what the biblical texts say of their own time or of their addressees, historical criticism of one stripe or another will be in play. And, if, contrary to what once was supposed, the historical method cannot be equated with historical reality or imagined to restore past reality, it nevertheless serves to make historical constructions intelligible and plausible. Thus, as O. C. Edwards writes, "there is something irretrievably diachronic about Christianity that resists all synchronic reduction."[1]

On Limits

In his introduction to the published works of Ferdinand Christian Baur, Ernst Käsemann refers to the necessity and the limits of the historical-critical method. Baur, he writes, understood history as the process of the revelation of the objective self-realization of the Spirit. Accordingly, every

---

1. O. C. Edwards Jr., "Historical-Critical Method's Failure of Nerve and a Prescription for a Tonic," *Anglican Theological Review* 59 (1977): 134.

datum, every person or event, was construed as a member of a transition within an immanent historical progress toward the Spirit's total self-realization. For Baur, historical-critical work was thus a profoundly religious task; it corresponded in a material way to the historical revelation as address to the one called to faith. Clearly, Käsemann continues, this "total view" did not lead Baur out of "the breezy realm of hypotheses" or postulates into the realm of objectivity. On the other hand, Baur as no other put before us the question as to what the phrase "historical-critical" can possibly mean. Käsemann gives his reply:

> This by no means calls into question the value of historical science and personal responsibility for it. We esteem it highly, do much on its behalf because we simply cannot let it go. The question is rather by what route we are sufficiently aware of historical reality that we fall least prey to deception. Actually, for the first time, Baur disclosed to us the world of primitive Christianity and yet made the path he himself took inaccessible to the generation following. Can we draw any other lesson from this than that methodologically there is no way at all to guarantee access to historical reality? Will not encounter with it always have the character of gift, and is that not true of all reality? Can methodology do more than perform auxiliary service, that is, prepare for this gift by removing cognizable hindrances wherever possible?[2]

At a 2010 scholars retreat called to discuss the "Bultmann School," one of the participants stated that Käsemann's negative criticism of Baur struck as well at his teacher Bultmann who was likewise oriented to the whole.[3]

At any rate, methodology is not derivable from principles, but proves its identity as experiment solely through its usefulness. This leads to a second reflection, writes Käsemann. If anyone at all, then it was Baur who proved that a science free of presuppositions does not exist.

> Within our very methodology we are captive to our dogmatic premises. Not science free of presuppositions but science that inquires in a

---

2. Käsemann, "Einführung," in Ferdinand Christian Baur, *Historisch-kritische Untersuchungen zum Neuen Testament,* vol. 1 of *Ausgewählte Werke in Einzelausgaben,* ed. Klaus Scholder (Stuttgart: Friedrich Frommann Verlag, 1963), pp. xxiii-xxiv.

3. In *Theologie und Wirklichkeit: Diskussionen der Bultmann-Schule,* ed. Martin Bauspees, Christof Landmesser, and Frederike Portenhauser (Neukirchen: Neukirchener Verlag, 2011).

radical way and is ready for continual self-correction is possible. But this means that we give an account of the dogmatic tradition from which we come and in which we are in any given moment.[4]

On Objectivity

Baur's striving after objectivity has nevertheless had a long history and still persists. One hundred years later Harnack would indict his former assistant, Karl Barth, for mixing scientific theology and edifying discourse in his Romans commentary:

> In life, naturally, scientific theology and bearing witness are often enough mixed. But neither the one nor the other can remain healthy when the requirement that they be separated is annulled. . . . Thanks to its object, a scientific-theological exposition can of course ignite and edify. But the scientific theologian who begins with setting aflame and edifying brings strange fire to his altar. Just as there is only one scientific method, so there is also only one scientific task — the pure knowledge of its object.[5]

Lately, in the section entitled "Beads & Boxes: The Jesus Seminar at Work," Fellows of the seminar are described as "critical scholars." "To be a critical scholar," the section reads,

> means to make empirical factual evidence — evidence open to confirmation by independent neutral observers — the controlling factor in historical judgments. . . . Critical scholars adopt the principle of methodological skepticism: accept only what passes the rigorous tests of the rules of evidence.[6]

Such scholarship, the section continues, "is the kind that has come to prevail in all the great universities of the world," and it concludes that "canon-

4. Käsemann, "Einführung," p. xxiv.

5. See Karl Barth, *Der Römerbrief, Erste Fassung* (1919), in *Gesamtausgabe* (Zürich: Theologischer Verlag, 1985), II, p. 643.

6. *The Five Gospels: The Search for the Authentic Words of Jesus,* New Translation and Commentary, by Robert W. Funk, Roy W. Hoover, and The Jesus Seminar (New York: Macmillan, 1993), p. 34.

ical boundaries are irrelevant in critical assessments of the various sources of information about Jesus."[7]

The reduction of research to making "empirical factual evidence the controlling factor," thus, to an objective reading of the data, has had many challengers. In his *Wissenschaft und Weisheit,*[8] the systematician Jürgen Moltmann (1926-) reminds his readers that the Enlightenment's greatest thinker resisted the reduction. In the preface to the second edition of his *Critique of Pure Reason,* Kant wrote that reason was not to be instructed by nature like a pupil who has recited whatever the teacher wants him to say, but like a judge who compels witnesses to answer his questions, adding that

> what reason would not be able to know of itself and has to learn from nature, it has to seek in the latter (though not merely ascribe to it) in accordance with what reason itself puts into nature.[9]

In his *Varieties of Religious Experience* William James stated that "one's conviction that the evidence one goes by is of the real objective brand is only one more subjective opinion added to the lot. For what a contradictory array of opinions have objective evidence and absolute certitude been claimed!"[10] Alluding to the axiom of the Berlin historian Leopold von Ranke (1795-1886), which read that the historian's task was to tell it "like it was" *(wie es eigentlich gewesen),* C. S. Lewis began with a quote from the Aeneid *("Ad nos vix tenuis famae perlabitur aura"* [there scarcely wafts to us a thin breath of their fame]), then added,

> When once we have realized what "the past as it really was" means, we must freely admit that most — that nearly all — history . . . is, and will remain, wholly unknown to us. And if *per impossibile* the whole were known, it would be wholly unmanageable.[11]

---

7. *The Five Gospels,* p. 35.

8. Jürgen Moltmann, *Wissenschaft und Weisheit* (Gütersloh: Gütersloher Verlagshaus, 2002), p. 23.

9. Immanuel Kant, *Critique of Pure Reason,* trans. and ed. Paul Guyer and Allen W. Wood (Cambridge: Cambridge University Press, 1998), p. 109.

10. William James, *Varieties of Religious Experience* (New York: Longmans, Green and Co., 1935), p. 490.

11. C. S. Lewis, "Historicism," in *Christian Reflections,* ed. Walter Hooper (Grand Rapids: Eerdmans, 1967), p. 107.

The political philosopher Eric Voegelin (1901-85), who carried no brief for any religious persuasion, termed the claim to "objective reality" a "narcissistic closure."[12]

On the Neutral Observer

As for the notion of the "neutral observer," it too has been challenged by a long list of those who embraced the principle that the self or "I" of the interpreter belongs to interpretation.

Luther often wrote that the biblical word never reached its goal until it became life and deed. At the end of a Christmas 1522 postil he wrote,

> Here you see from all my palaver how immeasurably unlike every human word the word of God is, how with all his talk none can get at or explain one single word of God. It is an infinite word; it intends to be grasped and examined with a quiet spirit, as Psalm 83 [85:8] reads: I will hear what God himself says to me.[13]

In an 1530 exposition of Psalm 118, the Reformer wrote that Holy Scripture

> does not contain words to be read . . . but words to be lived, plain and simple . . . words that are not put there for speculating or musing over, but for living and doing.[14]

In 1541, he described the Bible after the fashion of Psalm 22:6:

> It is a worm, not a book when matched against other books. It doesn't get the honor . . . other writings do. It is well off if it lies under the pew. Others tear it apart, crucify it, scourge and expose it to all kinds of martyrdom, till finally they . . . do it to death, kill and bury it, to the point where it is shoved off the earth and forgotten.[15]

---

12. Eric Voegelin, *Published Essays 1966-1985*, ed. Ellis Sandoz (Baton Rouge: Louisiana State University Press, 1990), pp. 1-35.

13. *Weimar Ausgabe* (hereafter referred to as *WA*) (Weimar: Hermann Böhlaus Nachfolger, 1883-1993), 10, I/1, 728, 11-15.

14. *WA* 31/I, 67, 9-12.

15. *WA* 48, 31, 8-14.

Thus, according to Luther, to read this book for what it is the self, the "I," simply cannot be excluded.

Calvin was in total agreement. Taking up Luther's point he developed the concept of faith as given through the internal testimony of the Spirit *(testimonium Sancti Spiritus internum),* and in the first book of the *Institutes* wrote:

> For as God alone is a fit witness of himself in his Word, so also the Word will not find acceptance in men's hearts before it is sealed by the inward testimony of the Spirit.[16]

Later, for generations, that inward testimony of the Spirit would be identified with consciousness, faith would be defined in terms of a natural, human capacity, and interpretation would occur without thought for the epistemological consequences of the apostle's word that "no one comprehends what is truly God's except the Spirit of God" (1 Cor. 2:11). It would take a World War to do the idealistic notion to death and bring another to birth. In his second attempt at a commentary on Romans Karl Barth asked,

> Can scientific investigation ever really triumph so long as men . . . are content to engage themselves with amazing energy upon the work of interpretation with the most superficial understanding of what interpretation really is? . . . Do they not perceive that there are documents, such as the books of the New Testament, which compel men to speak at whatever cost, because they find in them that which urgently and finally concerns the very marrow of human civilization?[17]

The new epoch, the new period just begun, would be marked by the conviction that where the biblical text was concerned, there could be no neutral ground, no "objectivity," which, in the words of one of America's historiographers, was the "best substitute for ideas yet invented." The names most attached to this movement were those of Adolf Schlatter, Karl Barth, and Rudolf Bultmann. The differences between them were considerable, but at certain points they converged.

---

16. John Calvin, *Institutes of the Christian Religion,* trans. Ford Lewis Battles, Library of Christian Classics, vol. 20 (Philadelphia: Westminster, 1960), I, 7, 4, p. 79.

17. Karl Barth, *The Epistle to the Romans,* trans. Edwyn C. Hoskyns (Oxford: Oxford University Press, 1933), preface to the second edition, pp. 6, 8-9.

First, all three were struggling to get free of an intellectual tradition, a struggle echoed in Schlatter's word to his students at Tübingen in 1931:

> I admonish every student that he hold fast to evangelical rejection of infallibility in every situation, toward himself and every teacher, every book, every school, every party.[18]

For all three that tradition comprised unequal parts of orthodoxy, rationalism, pietism, of religion construed in terms of "feeling," of positivism and the advocacy of a "religious a priori." Each allegiance came under attack, though Schlatter reserved his bitterest attack for orthodoxy of the Lutheran variety:

> We could not saunter back into the old Tübingen, where everyone had the true, pure faith, and where a violent man sat in the chief official's house, and a thief in the house of the lower city — both, however, indubitably orthodox and Lutheran.[19]

Second, all three were adamant in the conviction that if revelation is a reality within human existence, then the word about that reality, the biblical word, is more than the report of an available fact of world history. Then it is the disclosure of our existence. In a piece entitled "Atheistic Methods in Theology," Schlatter responded to an article by a well-known Freiburg pastor who had urged that theology should work only with the method recognized in the university, which being interpreted meant that God had to be bracketed out of historical study. Only such a method, argued the famous pulpiteer, could be represented as scientific. Theology was thus to be carried on as the science of religion. Schlatter replied that historical research did not put faith in question, but rather uncovered its effectiveness. In other words, the act of thinking followed living, for which reason one's own life-situation had to be incorporated into the historical putting of the question. As far as Schlatter was concerned, that life-situation was given him beforehand, in the context of the effects of the history of Jesus Christ. His historical task, as he saw it, was to understand his existence in that

---

18. Adolf Schlatter, *Zur Theologie des Neuen Testaments und zur Dogmatik,* Theologische Bücherei, vol. 41 (München: Chr. Kaiser Verlag, 1969), p. 259.

19. Schlatter, *Erlebtes* (Berlin: Furche Verlag, 1924), p. 76.

context.[20] Theology, wrote Bultmann, requires a mode appropriate to its object, the mode we call faith. It cannot be carried on "out of curiosity" or for the purpose of earning a living, but as a "venture, in which we ourselves are at risk." He continued: if God is the object of faith and accessible only to it, then a science apart from or merely alongside faith sees neither God nor faith. Theology must be independent of any idea or practice of science that omits or ignores that mode of access appropriate to its object.[21] Years later, Gadamer would write:

> If the text, whether law or message of salvation, is to be properly understood, that is, according to the claim it makes, then in every moment, that is, in every concrete situation, it must be understood in a new and different way.[22]

Or again,

> There is never a reader before whose eyes the great book of world history simply lies open. But there is also never a reader who, with his text before his eyes, simply reads what is there. Rather, in all reading application takes place, so that whoever reads a text is himself included in the sense he has grasped. He belongs to the text he understands.[23]

Later still, another provocative twentieth-century thinker would write:

> There can, as Rudolf Bultmann has shown in his study of the Gospels, be no "presuppositionless readings" of the past. To all past events, as to all present intake, the observer brings a specific mental set . . . there are no non-temporal truths. The articulation now of a supposed past fact involves an elaborate, mainly subconscious network of conventions. . . . None of these conventions is susceptible of final logical analysis.[24]

20. See Luck's introduction to Schlatter, *Zur Theologie des Neuen Testaments und zur Dogmatik*, pp. 13, 17-19, 24-25.

21. Rudolf Bultmann, *Theologische Enzyklopädie*, ed. Eberhard Jüngel and Klaus W. Miller (Tübingen: Mohr, 1984), pp. 20, 22, 84, 102, 155, 160.

22. Hans-Georg Gadamer, *Wahrheit und Methode* (Tübingen: J. C. B. Mohr [Paul Siebeck], 1975), p. 292.

23. Gadamer, *Wahrheit und Methode*, p. 323.

24. George Steiner, *After Babel: Aspects of Language and Translation* (London: Oxford University Press, 1975), pp. 143-44.

Third, as far as Schlatter and Bultmann were concerned, biblical research and faith, that mode appropriate to doing theology, were not at odds. Schlatter wrote:

> For me, faith and criticism never divided into opposites, so that at one time I would have thought in a Bible-believing way, and at another critically. Rather, I thought in critical fashion because I believed in the Bible, and believed in it because I read it critically.[25]

In Württemberg, where Schlatter spent most of his teaching life, theologians had once bludgeoned each other over the question of the degree to which Christians should be occupied with worldly learning and science (the so-called Pietist Controversy of 1840).

In a review of Barth's commentary on Romans, Bultmann wrote:

> When in exegeting Romans I detect tensions and contradictions, places high and low; when I take pains to show how Paul is dependent on Jewish theology or popular Christianity . . . I am not just carrying on historical-philological criticism. I am doing it from the viewpoint of showing where and how the subject matter is expressed, in order to lay hold of the subject matter that is greater even than Paul.[26]

The guild has ignored most if not all of Schlatter's work; has concentrated on Barth's distaste for critical method and on Bultmann's link to phenomenological analysis; and has ignored the passion they shared. For all his commitment to the critical method, Schlatter was damned as a pietist whose faith in the Bible rendered him unfit for scientific work; Barth with his shattering of every religious statement on the idea that God is inaccessibly distant (Schlatter's word) seemed to leave no room for the act of thinking, while Bultmann appeared to do quite the opposite — to reduce the biblical text to one long, elongated, and pendulous disquisition on self-understanding, to the point where he was unable to speak of God in objectifying fashion. "Process theology," with its promise to rectify the error, had its start with those who had fallen out of love with Bultmann or Barth. The logical birthplace was the University of Chicago where, ac-

---

25. Schlatter, *Rückblick auf meine Lebensarbeit* (Stuttgart: Calwer Verlag, 1977), p. 83.

26. Rudolf Bultmann, in *Anfänge der dialektischen Theologie*, ed. Jürgen Moltmann, Theologische Bücherei, vol. 17, part 2 (München: Chr. Kaiser Verlag, 1987), pp. 141-42.

cording to legend, the faculty had once read "Religion in the Making" by Alfred North Whitehead (1861-1947), and invited the process empiricist Henry Nelson Weiman (1884-1975) to the chair in philosophy so that he could explain it.

A truth had been abandoned that historical research itself had established — that the Bible is of such a nature that it requires a decision on its behalf. This may not render it unique, at least not in a formal way. Obviously, in a formal way the Bible is similar to texts that may have absolutely no relation to its subject, texts in philosophy, for example. At any rate, the abandonment was an error historically, for there was no causal connection between the passion those three shared, and the vehicles they used by which to transmit it. Barth was miles from Bultmann, and Schlatter was miles from both. But they had witnessed, experienced, perceived, intuited something quite apart from whatever systems they might later develop: that exegesis, biblical interpretation, apart from a stance toward the text is impossible, apart from what Schleiermacher, largely responsible for all the damage done to theology in the past, had called "sympathy," and what Barth came to call "spiritual exegesis" and Bultmann "decisions-understanding." When, for example, in his *History of the Synoptic Tradition,* Bultmann stated that scarcely a piece of the Jesus-tradition had not undergone alteration prior to its assuming written form, in instances even taking to itself what was alien, this was but the reverse side of the recognition that the gospel must reincarnate itself in its interpreter so as to become a *viva vox,* a living voice. If it took Barth a while to acknowledge that his "inaccessibly distant" God had created a community, and if Bultmann would finally admit that ecclesiology had not stood at the center of his work, their insistence on faith as the mode appropriate to the Bible's interpretation and on revelation as the origin of faith would move Barth to a "Church" and not simply a "Christian Dogmatics," and would move Bultmann to charter membership in the Confessing Church, to remain in Germany and risk his neck in public opposition to the Führer-Prinzip and anti-Semitism.

Of late, many have seconded the assertions of those celebrated three. For example, to the possibility that the new paradigm proposed by Walter Wink (1935-2012) of Auburn Seminary for biblical study[27] restricts the human transformation worked by the Bible to psychotherapy or social action, Edwards responds that "anything that is confined to a closed system of natural cause and effect is less than the human transformation that the Bible

27. Walter Wink, *The Bible in Human Transformation* (Philadelphia: Fortress, 1973).

promises."[28] Daniel Patte writes of the dismissal of faith-interpretations as problematic for the reason that it misconstrues faith-interpretations, ignores an important interpretive process involved in Bible interpretation, and is ethically irresponsible. He goes on to state that the fact that features of a text that are of particular significance for believers may be of no significance for analytical or hermeneutical readings is no reason for branding faith-interpretations as illegitimate.[29]

Before an entire century given to objectivity and neutrality would ignore it, Ferdinand Christian Baur had this to say in an article "wrung" from him by the orthodox Hengstenberg:

> It is only from faith that science learns to cleanse itself of everything alien and impure and give itself wholly and unconditionally to the sacred task of truth. Faith in turn owes it to science that it does not degenerate into slothful ease, but is sustained in fresh, vital movement in order to be ever clearer and more directly conscious of its divine content. As hostile toward faith as science appears to be, continually disturbing it, shaking all its supports, ever after unearthing the soil in which it roots, by this very means it renders it the greatest service. For it is not how much we believe that is at stake, but only what we believe and how we believe, and whether we believe in such fashion that in our faith we also know what is true from what is false, what is certain from the uncertain, what is essential from the less essential. . . . All the doubts raised by the newer criticism are most salutary and fruitful for faith itself, to be seen as a powerful means for educating and forming it.[30]

The faith required for the reading and interpreting of the Bible is not a worldview, or dogmatic principle, an extra-something brought to the task. Nor is it a periodic insight gained in the moment of reading. If it were either, nothing would prevent it from prejudicing the reading, whether by adding, subtracting, qualifying, or revising. The shape or form that the faith needed for interpretation takes is above all, before anything else, to give precedence to the word of the text (cf. Luther's "I will hear what God

28. O. C. Edwards, "Historical-Critical Method's Failure of Nerve and a Prescription for a Tonic," p. 134.

29. Daniel Patte, "Critical Biblical Studies from a Semiotic Perspective," *Semeia* 81 (1998): 16.

30. Ferdinand Christian Baur, "Abgenötigte Erklärung," *Ausgewählte Werke in Einzelausgaben, Historisch-kritische Untersuchungen* (Stuttgart: Bad Canstatt, 1963), I, p. 301.

himself says to me"), which means to go beyond an openness to the claim of transcendence it raises (an openness required of any interpretation within or apart from faith), to the point where the text has the upper hand, where it becomes the interpreter's interpreter, and in this way allows a share in the life of the community of faith. Since such faith is not a capacity given with human nature but a gift to be given and received, it can only occur in yearning and suppliance. Thus, to what is needed for interpretation as well Luther's last words apply: "We are beggars, that's for sure."[31]

On the Community

If, as Käsemann insists, biblical research that makes radical inquiry and is always ready for self-correction must give account of the dogmatic tradition from which it comes, then the historical-critical method cannot do without acknowledging the existence of a community involved in the transmitting of tradition. To a considerable degree, modern biblical interpretation operates on the assumption that knowledge involves only the single level of consciousness, that of the private individual self. But knowing and learning, in this instance the knowing and learning required for an interpretation of biblical texts, has a social character. In his article on "The Doctrine of Chances,"[32] Charles Sanders Peirce wrote that since "logic is rooted in the social principle," to be logical "men should not be selfish." If, for example, the theological students under Rudolf Bultmann's care had never raised questions concerning the Bible's three-storied universe, their teacher would scarcely have been stimulated to such doubt of his theological upbringing, or have been led to such painstaking investigation and provoked to such a frenzy of activity as forced the Western world to use his name to fix a theological era. And, without that continual bombardment from friend and foe, Bultmann would scarcely have revised his original thesis that it is impossible to speak directly about God to read that one may speak directly about God in "analogical" if not in mythological fashion.[33]

---

31. "Wir sind pettler. Hoc est verum," *WA Tischreden,* 5, 318, 2 (Nr. 5677). Thanks are due to Peter Stuhlmacher, whose unpublished article, "Zur hermeneutischen Bedeutung von I Kor 2, 6-16," furnished stimulus for the paragraph above.

32. Charles Sanders Peirce, "Illustrations of the Logic of Science, Third Paper: The Doctrine of Chances," *The Popular Science Monthly,* November 1877, p. 609.

33. Rudolf Bultmann, "Die Rede vom Handeln Gottes," in *Kerygma und Mythos* (Hamburg: Herbert Reich Evangelischer Verlag, 1952), vol. 2, pp. 196ff.

However rigidly he may have held to the theory of the private character of his knowing, in practice he was unable to avoid the existence of a community of seekers and scholars, and hence the public character of knowledge. At the end of his life, to the criticism that the reader would search in vain for any doctrine of the church in his work, he could only reply:

> I concede . . . that I have thought in one-sided fashion — about the individual person and his relationship to the kerygma and not about the community. . . . I confess . . . that ecclesiology has not stood in the midpoint of my work.[34]

Over against Bultmann's reduction of "preliminary understanding" to that of the private interpreter, Gadamer insisted that understanding is never a subjective relation to a given object. To that "object," to the text to be interpreted, belongs the history of its effects (Gadamer called it *Wirkungsgeschichte*). Even the consciousness of the interpreter is historically determined. That is, in the interpreter the "totality of our experience of the world" is always present. Gadamer called it "effective historical consciousness" *(wirkungsgeschichtliches Bewusstsein),* then went on to describe "openness to tradition" as its "highest mode." This consciousness, he wrote,

> authentically corresponds to experience of the Thou. In human behavior, as we saw, what matters is actually to experience the Thou as Thou, that is, not to ignore his claim, and to be allowed to say something about him. To this openness belongs. . . . Without such openness to one another there is no genuine human contact. To belong to one another always and at the same time means to be able to hear one another.[35]

As more than one has acknowledged, in this fashion Gadamer prepared for the role of the church in Bible exposition.

In one way or another a goodly number of current interpreters insists that acknowledgment of the memory and tradition of the Christian community belongs to "triadic" description. Taking a leaf from Schleier-

---

34. *The Theology of Rudolf Bultmann,* ed. Charles W. Kegley (New York: Harper Torchbooks, 1953), p. 278.

35. Gadamer, *Wahrheit und Methode,* p. 343.

macher's *Brief Outline,* without that acknowledgment each tool of inter-pretation, however sharply honed or carefully indexed in its capacities and limits, reverts to those branches of human learning with which it first originated.[36] More important, since the tradition of a Christian community is most often congealed in its confessional statements, interpretation needs to occur within the context of that community's experience as reflected in its confessions. This statement is by no means universally accepted, despite its good sense. For if "the facts and worths of life need many cognizers to take them in," as William James, echoing C. S. Peirce put it,[37] that is, if the interpretive task cannot be executed by any one authority, and if com-munities exist where the biblical word is exposed to the most persistent examination due to its status and function as norm for faith and life, then those communities and that concentration deserve a hearing. They de-serve a hearing, if the guild of scholars is not to be totally irrelevant to the place where the biblical word undergoes greatest concentration and use. Nils Dahl (1911-2001) of Oslo University and later of Yale wrote of the tri-umph within and without the walls of the Christian confessions of critical, philological, and historical methods, which raise the question whether or not exegesis has become a stranger to the sphere where the church actu-ally speaks and acts, and as a result of which the exegetical task has been relinquished to a "supraconfessional guild."

Contemporary biblical scholarship has been characterized as having little or no concern for the Christian community. In fact, some appear to regard the New Testament as an interesting pan-Hellenistic document that deserves investigation and research, but give no attention to its functioning as norm for members of the Christian fellowship; others negotiate transfer from the divinity school to the university "yard," exempting themselves from the preparation of clergy; still others flatly refuse to engage in theo-logical discourse of whatever kind; and others parrot the statement made years ago by a Chicago scholar who allowed he did not "give a damn" what the church thought since John D. Rockefeller paid his salary.

Some believe this lack of concern is of little moment, for the reason that the academic community has seldom exercised any real influence on the general public. From this perspective, biblical research is scarcely cal-

36. See Friedrich Schleiermacher, *Kritische Gesamtausgabe,* I/6: *Universitätsschriften. Herakleitos. Kurze Darstellung des theologischen Studiums,* ed. Hermann Fischer et al. (Berlin: Walter de Gruyter, 1998), para. 6, p. 250.

37. R. B. Perry, *Thought and Character of William James* (New York: Harper and Row, 1964), p. 222.

culated to have any influence on the Christian community. Christians will proceed to an encounter with the living God through the testimony of the scriptures, the fuss and feathers of the academics to the contrary notwithstanding. The thought may be comforting, but it is suspect. Less than thirty years ago occurred the collapse of a regime whose record of cruelty and suffering far exceeded that of Hitler's Germany. At the heart of that regime lay collectivization — a stupid, senseless, and murderous project, in the opinion of one Russologist "so clearly the handiwork of intellectuals; because its ideology appears, like its language, so complex; because it ruled so much of the earth it is difficult to dismiss it as one would, say, a quack medicine."[38]

Again, those communities of faith deserve a hearing if with all their concentration they are not to hold aloof from scholarly research and live in isolation.[39] In the 1970s, following a conversion experience, Eta Linnemann (1926-2009), a distinguished scholar and pupil of Rudolf Bultmann and his successor Ernst Fuchs (1903-83), renounced the historical-critical method. Acknowledging that she had been a "blind leader of the blind," she asked her former students to destroy all her previous publications. In a volume entitled *Wissenschaft oder Meinung?* she wrote of having come to the conviction that the direction of all biblical research had been predetermined, that it all had to pass through a filter consisting of a series of presuppositions, freedom existing only within this restricted space. Even when such presuppositions fell away, Linnemann continued, the idea still lived at the edge of consciousness. She then described the centuries of Western history along with its worldwide influence as the "pathway of sin," and decrying Augustine's description of Christian use of pagan science as analogous to Israel's plundering the Egyptians, warned of the demonic powers lying in wait for all who walked that way, a way that relegated faith to the private sphere and left no room for the living God and his Son in academic thought. Since, she added, the claim to being scientific was an offense against the first commandment, students of theology had best abandon the existing universities.[40] In a later volume, Linnemann wrote that before his death Rudolf Bultmann had "converted and asked forgiveness from his pupils and students." She cited as her "principal witness"

---

38. Brian Moynahan, *The Russian Century* (New York: Random House, 1994), p. 107.

39. See Nils Dahl, "The Lutheran Exegete and the Confessions of His Church," *The Lutheran World* 6 (1959): 3.

40. Eta Linnemann, *Wissenschaft oder Meinung?* (Neuhausen: Hänssler, 1986), pp. 26, 60, 75, 88-89, 97, 110-16.

Ernst Käsemann, "who before his own death said that he, unfortunately, would not follow his teacher in the matter."[41]

Linnemann's solution to the problem of the challenge to the biblical witness on the part of the historical-critical method is as drastic as her earlier commitment to it. And, in fact, if the presuppositions underlying the method are intrinsically inimical to Christian faith, and if, as Linnemann insists, those presuppositions are of such a nature that they absolutely cannot be detached from the method, so that use of the method is restricted absolutely to that of a weapon — an "atheistic method," as Adolf Schlatter called it, but only because he allowed it to table the question of God for a moment — then Christians are obliged to abandon the method, and, in light of the calls for its demise on the part of any and all, may yet maintain a modicum of scholarly integrity. Agreed that the originators of the modern critical method were indifferent toward religious faith; agreed that they used the method under assumptions that reflected that indifference, indeed, that they celebrated the indissoluble connection between the method and those assumptions, thus giving Linnemann and others of her persuasion support for the argument of their indissolubility, what if they were in error? What if the method, despite its advocates and critics, is in fact detachable from presuppositions under which it first set sail? Since the question regarding the relation between method, its presuppositions, and Christian confession is only a piece of the larger question of the relation between revelation and reason, should all the attempts, from Augustine to Jonathan Edwards and beyond, at achieving some sort of entente between them be abandoned for an existence in isolation? It is reported of Kant that he could not endure the academic procession at Königsberg, with theologians in the lead. As soon as the procession arrived at the church door he left the procession and skipped off toward home — his way of protesting the confusion of ecclesiastical with rational faith, of dogma and its need for historical scholarship and religious faith for which reason alone sufficed.

But in the event Linnemann's critique is on the mark, her summons to jettison the method is not. To his earlier remarks Nils Dahl added that neither by recourse to instructions issued by the church nor to the piety of the exegete can exegesis extricate itself from the secular sphere that is a concomitant of modern methodology. The only alternative would be that exegesis forgo its claim to scholarship and thus forgo the gospel's claim to

---

41. Eta Linnemann, *Bibel oder Bibelkritk? Was ist glaubwürdig?* (Nürnberg: VTR, 2007), p. 13.

a public hearing.[42] Even when the academy, Kant-like, assigns moral interpretation to "the God within us," and allows study of the Bible only insofar
as it has to do with that faith for which reason alone suffices, or only insofar
as it deserves examination as an interesting pan-Hellenistic document, in
the end rendering the entire Christian enterprise vulnerable to extinction
through interpretation, attention to the scriptures of Old and New Testament demands a place. It does so because Christian faith cannot surrender
its obligation to make its project public, for such belongs to making defense
"to anyone who demands from you an accounting for the hope that is in
you" (1 Peter 3:15). And as long as a defense is made, someone, somewhere,
will invent a method by which to make it. It is precisely because the Bible
demands a public hearing that it cannot forgo its claim to scholarship,
however clownish at the foot of some royally enthroned academe it might
appear. Christ himself did not fare better before Herod and Pilate.

Of course, multiplying the number of "cognizers" does not guarantee accuracy. Kermode writes that "an institutional tradition . . . does not
inhibit the indefinite multiplication of spiritual readings. One divination
spawns another." He goes on to state with regard to the feeding of the five
thousand that if he says the fishes are one thing it does not prevent someone saying they are another, and just as plausibly; that someone may tell
him "with notable liberality" that he may make them stand for anything he
chooses, "though," he adds, "there will be a family or institutional resemblance between our interpretations."[43] With Kermode, perhaps, that reference to a "family or institutional resemblance" is a mere proviso appended
to the overall theme of secrecy as "the property of all narrative," something
"glimpsed through the meshes of a text," the glimpse of a momentary radiance.[44] But what may serve Kermode as proviso is the heart of the matter.
For to "family or institutional resemblance" belongs the confession of the
Christian community that points the interpreter to the questions that need
asking. "This it does above all," Nils Dahl writes, "by pointing to the center
of Scripture: the gospel of the crucified and risen Lord Jesus Christ and
the salvation offered in his name." Then he adds, "that this gospel constitutes that center will go undisputed at least insofar as one considers that a
forfeiture of its centrality inevitably means a forfeiture of the unity of the

---

42. Dahl, "The Lutheran Exegete and the Confessions of His Church," p. 4.

43. Frank Kermode, *The Genesis of Secrecy* (Cambridge, Mass.: Harvard University
Press, 1979), p. 37.

44. Kermode, *The Genesis of Secrecy*, pp. 144-45.

Bible. Without that center the Bible would dissolve into a kaleidoscope of various literary forms."[45] According to Robert W. Jenson (1930-), lately senior scholar for research at the Center for Theological Inquiry at Princeton, historical-critical reading of scripture has been an affliction for the faith because people have left the church out of their self-understanding. He writes, "some of the pioneers of historical reading did this because they hated the church; many more because German Lutherans (who have been the great practitioners) always tend to leave the church out of their calculations."[46]

No community calling itself Christian does not own the Trinity of the Godhead, and thus the descent of the Son into human flesh for love of the world. No community calling itself Christian assigns that center to a secrecy construed as "the property of all narrative." On the contrary, for such a community there is nothing "momentary" about *that* "radiance," no matter the infinite number of disputes and divisions and conflicts tearing it into denominations and sects. As for the rest, every other interpretation of every other text retains its vulnerability. For the rest, Kermode's axiom applies: "our sole hope and pleasure is in the perception of a momentary radiance, before the door of disappointment is finally shut on us."[47] The old Reformation dogmaticians were careful to assign to the status of *norma normata* whatever doctrines remained once *that* "radiance" was acknowledged, that is, they were assigned to the status of criteria subject to yet another criterion — to scripture, the *norma normans,* where that radiance lay perspicuous and revealed. Bible interpretation, even within the context of the community of faith, is not, and never has been, an exact science. But without that context, or better, without the context of statements of faith reflected in confessions received by the community of faith, there can be only the reader, self-absorbed and alone.

On the Text

First, the observation is irritatingly obvious that the text has a temporal priority. However attractive the notion that the interpreter gives life to

45. Dahl, "The Lutheran Exegete and the Confessions of His Church," p. 9.

46. Robert W. Jenson, "Hermeneutics and the Life of the Church," in *Reclaiming the Bible for the Church,* ed. Carl E. Braaten and Robert W. Jenson (Grand Rapids: Eerdmans, 1995), p. 104.

47. Kermode, *The Genesis of Secrecy,* p. 145.

the text, the text is there, it exists ahead of, prior to, the interpreter. If it were not already there, there would be nothing to interpret. However fascinated by the task of interpretation, without a text there would be no need for it. The entire mass of literature dealing with the art or science of interpretation would never have existed had there not been texts that birthed it, furnished the occasion for it. Since the history of the interpretive enterprise teaches that it is possible for this disturbingly simple fact to escape some who behave as though the text were not there without them, it needs noting. The text enjoys temporal priority.

Second, the text occupies space — another annoyingly simple observation. Whether in the hand, on the desk, or on the table, it occupies a place. If someone should decide to hold it, read it, interpret it, it usurps the place that something else, even another text, might occupy or actually did occupy. In their own way, these two ridiculously simple observations support the autonomy of the text. By the sheer fact of its existing, the text is ahead of anything or anyone taking notice of it, and by virtue of its occupying a position, being placed where it is, resulting in something else being set aside, it enjoys priority, precedence. Priority of time or of place spells power, yields a certain autonomy. When one author writes that the Bible needs to be read as a "focus for fields of force," this can be read as a variation on the theme of the Bible's autonomy. When another writes that if exact theological knowledge is to be possible, then first of all the source must be given the right to speak, this too can be read as a variation on the theme of the Bible's autonomy. When either author adds that the Bible, the "source," must be given the right to speak in a certain way, that is an acknowledgment that the Bible enjoys autonomy beyond chronology or pride of place in terms of the manner, the way in which it exercises its autonomy.

A third, irritatingly simple fact is that unless the interpreter is also the author of the text, a distance exists between text and interpreter. Those who mourn the absence of whatever form the text may have taken prior to being written down regard that distance as a "loathsome ditch," as though being written down were a treachery done the text in its pre-written, perhaps oral, form. The previous chapter indicated the problems attaching to the attempt to determine what "life" a text may have had before being written down, to arrive at the character of the community within which it enjoyed such a life, and thus to determine the authenticity of the text in its written form.[48] All of it is predicated on the assumption that the move from

48. Cf. p. 282 above.

the earlier to the later, from the pre-literary or oral to the written, and the distantiation involved, represented a decline, a deprivation. Deprivation or not, distantiation had to occur at every stage of the Gospel tradition; every stage involved a "text" and its "interpretation." "From its beginning," wrote Paul Ricoeur,

> preaching rested upon witnesses interpreted by the primitive community. Testimony and interpretation of the testimony already contained the element of distantiation which makes writing possible.[49]

To regard the distance between text and interpretation as a deprivation would mean to lament the thing by which the witness was handed down. As regards the Gospel tradition, without the written text the form-critical analysis just described would be an impossibility, for without that text there would be no tradition at all whose alleged antecedents needed investigating. Precisely through its distance the text reaches us. Alienation, distantiation, is thus not merely something to be overcome but the condition for understanding.[50] Romantic reference to a "loathsome ditch" or an abyss misapprehends a fact of human communication for which there is no alternative, certainly not respecting a written tradition.

When in the essay cited above, Paul Ricoeur writes of the originality of the text as linked to its "issue," he is referring to a further fact that gives autonomy to the text. The "issue" of the text, he writes, is its way of referring to a world that is the "world of the text."[51] Writing that if we do not want to reduce interpretation to an analysis of structures, what is left to interpretation is to explicate the kind of being-in-the-world displayed before the text, that is, the "pro-position of a world in which I could dwell."[52] This "issue" or "world of the text," continues Ricoeur, is the central category of hermeneutical theory. All else is based on it or is the preliminary condition for it. For this reason "the first task of hermeneutics is not to proceed immediately to a decision on the part of the reader, but to allow the world or being which is the issue of the biblical text to unfold."[53] Writing that if the Bible can be said to be revealed, the same should be said of

---

49. Paul Ricoeur, "Philosophical Hermeneutics and Theological Hermeneutics," *Studies in Religion* 5, no. 1 (1975-76): 20.

50. Ricoeur, "Philosophical Hermeneutics and Theological Hermeneutics," p. 19.

51. Ricoeur, "Philosophical Hermeneutics and Theological Hermeneutics," p. 20.

52. Ricoeur, "Philosophical Hermeneutics and Theological Hermeneutics," p. 25.

53. Ricoeur, "Philosophical Hermeneutics and Theological Hermeneutics," p. 26.

the issue of which it speaks. Ricoeur defines the issue as "the new being," that is, a "self" received from the text, a "non-egoistic, non-narcissistic, non-imperialistic mode of subjectivity which responds and corresponds to the power of a work to display a world."[54] This "new being" is not to be sought anywhere but in the world of this particular text. What renders it unique, Ricoeur continues, is that the point of intersection for all its parts is a "Name," a Name "bound up with the *meaning-event* preached as Resurrection."[55]

Scripture, the Bible, is a self-effervescing source that does not take its credibility from its interpretation, in or outside the church. Independent, its integrity underived, it is its own interpreter. On its own it yields understanding, for on its own it gives the Spirit through whom it can be understood, and on its own it possesses the quality of certainty that neither feeling nor experience can equal. It was this confession that triggered the debate with the papal legate at Augsburg, brought Cajetan hot and sweaty from Rome in 1518. At Augsburg Luther said:

> *Ego non possum revocare, nisi meliora edoceor, nam a scriptura non possum discedere* ("I cannot recant unless instructed, for I cannot depart from scripture").

For this reason, scripture does not require exposition because it is obscure. The reverse is true: it is most often exposition — whether of the Aristotelian or post-modern variety — which obscures the Bible. More, there is not an exposition that is equal to this self-effervescing source. To paraphrase Luther, our knowledge of scripture resembles a ball on a billiard table, touching the surface at only one spot and moved by the slightest nudge.

What gives scripture this power, this effervescence, this independent and non-derivability is what Ricoeur calls its "issue," its "world," all of whose parts intersect at a Name. In other words, what gives to the biblical text its autonomy is its witness to Jesus Christ. He is its content and rules the method of its understanding. He is the "central category" of the hermeneutical understanding of the Bible.

If by virtue of its priority in time, place, manner, and "issue," the text enjoys autonomy, then obviously the interpreter is not in control. Then, in the midst of his argument that the Gospels fit the genre of dramatic

---

54. Ricoeur, "Philosophical Hermeneutics and Theological Hermeneutics," p. 30.
55. Ricoeur, "Philosophical Hermeneutics and Theological Hermeneutics," pp. 28-29.

history, Roland Mushat Frye writes that recognition of this genre should be coupled with "a primary exegetical respect for the final literary work itself, and a productive concentration upon interpreting that work in its own terms."[56] Then, as Paul Ricoeur writes, "the one to whom a text is addressed is, so to speak, created *as* a reader by the work itself, which paves its own way towards its potential addressee."[57] Then, also, as Oswald Bayer writes, citing Ricoeur, the interpreter's question is not "how shall I interpret the text?" but rather "how does the given biblical text give itself to me to understand it — so that I am understood?"[58]

It may mark the entrée of a radically new and unique type of exposition when, in his thirty-ninth Easter letter, Athanasius, patriarch of Alexandria (A.D. ca. 296-298–373), refers to himself and his community as interpreted by Holy Scripture.[59] Or again, in a reflection on the Psalms in his *Letter to Marcellinus*, who had become bishop of Rome in 296, Athanasius writes,

> But whoever takes up this book, and certainly the prophecies of the Savior, just as with other writings commonly runs through [them] with admiration and adoration, but other Psalms he reads as if the words belong to him; moreover, who has heard [them] *is moved* as if he uttered the very same himself, and *is so affected* by the words of the songs as if they were his.[60]

These sentences move Martin Tetz, patristics scholar emeritus at Ruhr-Universität Bochum (1930-), to ask whether or not the unity of the church is due to such being interpreted by scripture, whether or not the church grows and increases only by being thus interpreted, and whether or not it undertakes to "interpret" only in this sense. Or again, he asks whether the petitioner is to identify himself with the psalmist or the word of the psalm,

56. Roland Mushat Frye, "A Literary Perspective for the Criticism of the Gospels," in *Jesus and Man's Hope*, ed. Donald Miller and Dikran Hadidian (Pittsburgh Theological Seminary, 1971), vol. 2, p. 215.

57. Ricoeur, "Philosophical Hermeneutics and Theological Hermeneutics," p. 29.

58. Oswald Bayer, "Hermeneutical Theology," in *Philosophical Hermeneutics and Biblical Exegesis*, ed. Petr Pokorný and Jan Roskovec (Tübingen: Mohr, 2002), p. 118.

59. Cited in Martin Tetz, "Athanasius und die Einheit der Kirche," *Zeitschrift für Theologie und Kirche* 81 (1980): 207.

60. Athanasius, *Letter to Marcellinus*, in J.-P. Migne, *Patrologia Graeca*, vol. 27, pp. 21-22 (italics mine).

and not rather that he is identified and taken up into the psalmist's prayer. If the biblical saints serve the one Lord and if their various charismata are gifts of the one Spirit, then whoever repeats their prayer in accord with their obedience of faith is drawn into their circle.[61]

On the Author

Virtually every scholar referenced in this volume described the interpreter's task as arriving at the intention of the author. From Augustine to F. C. Grant, authorial intent was taken to be the interpreter's chief concern. According to Calvin it was the interpreter's *sole* concern, and according to Bengel the task involved "everything" the author intended. Christian Wolff insisted that the biblical word "had only one sense, the sense intended by the author," and Schleiermacher assigned the interpreter the task of understanding the author "better than he understood himself." Since Hodge assigned infallibility to the biblical author, divining the author's intent followed as a logical consequence. For Barth, interpretation involved a relationship of trust toward the author, and for Bultmann, existential interpretation sought to understand in what respect the text was "the exposition of the author regarding his understanding of existence." Frank Porter wrote of getting into the "mental atmosphere" of the author, and Grant wrote that as with all other books, the author's intention or purpose was prime. Only two of the authors consulted demurred at the requirement, the "precritical" Luther and the Princetonian Otto Piper.

Since for Luther the way needed clearing for the *scopus,* that is, for whatever the text had to say about Christ, the significance of the author was immaterial:

> Whatever does not teach Christ is not yet apostolic, even though St. Peter or St. Paul does the teaching. Again, whatever preaches Christ would be apostolic, even if Judas, Annas, Pilate, and Herod were doing it.[62]

According to Piper, getting at the "life movement," the "scale of values," or worldview of the author transcended whatever may have been in the

---

61. Tetz, "Athanasius und die Einheit der Kirche," pp. 207-9.

62. *Luther's Works,* ed. Jaroslav Pelikan (St. Louis: Concordia, 1955-86), vol. 35, p. 396.

author's mind. The requirement had particular relevance to prophecy. Whatever was in the prophet's mind at the moment did not exhaust the meaning of his prophecy. It was full of potential beyond any reference to a given historical situation.[63]

The requirement that interpretation concern itself chiefly or exclusively with the author of a text involves arriving at the author's intent. Some years ago, in a recitation of the errors of historical-critical method, Paul Ricoeur gave first place to the attempt to arrive at authorial intent. As he wrote in "Metaphor and the Main Problem of Hermeneutics,"

> My claim is that the hermeneutical circle is not correctly understood when it is presented (1) as a circle between two subjectivities, that of the reader and that of the author, and (2) as the projection of the subjectivity of the reader in the reading itself. . . . The coming to language of the sense and the reference of a text is the coming to language of a world and not the recognition of another person.[64]

Now it has become virtually axiomatic that recovery of the original intent of the author of a biblical text is demonstrably false. It is false since, to quote C. S. Lewis, "an author doesn't necessarily understand the meaning of his own story better than anyone else."[65] It is historically naïve to suppose that the meaning of historical texts can be separated from the complex problem of their reception, or as Piper put it, from whatever "scale of values" or worldview transcended whatever was in an author's mind.[66]

To illustrate, in the prediction of a new covenant in Jeremiah 31:31-34, the character of the covenant conceived by the prophet is legal, juridical. Despite the contrast between the new and the old covenants ("It will not be like the covenant that I made with their ancestors," v. 32), and despite the promise attached to it ("I will be their God, and they shall be my people . . . I will forgive their iniquity, and remember their sin no more," vv. 33, 34), the prophet nevertheless conceives the contrast and the promise within the context of law. "I will put my law within them," the prophecy

---

63. Otto Piper, *New Testament Theology,* part II, unpublished (n.d.), p. 39.

64. Paul Ricoeur, "Metaphor and the Main Problem of Hermeneutics," in *The Philosophy of Paul Ricoeur,* ed. Charles E. Reagan and David Stewart (Boston: Beacon, 1978), p. 145.

65. C. S. Lewis, in *Letters of C. S. Lewis,* ed. W. H. Lewis (New York: Harcourt, Brace and World, 1966), p. 462.

66. Cf. David C. Steinmetz, "The Superiority of Pre-Critical Exegesis," *Theology Today* 37 (1980): 28, 37.

reads, "and I will write it on their hearts." The Jeremiah text is taken up four times by the New Testament writers. In Hebrews 8:8 the text is quoted in its entirety, to prove the obsolescence of the old covenant. Second Corinthians 3:3 contains a reminiscence of the original text in a reference to the epistle's addressees as written with the "Spirit of the living God." In John 6:45 another reminiscence ("it is written in the prophets, 'And they shall all be taught by God'") occurs within Jesus' claim ("no one can come to me unless drawn by the Father who sent me," v. 44). In Romans 11:27 the phrase, "this is my covenant with them, when I take away their sins," is applied by the apostle to Israel's ultimate destiny. In none of the quotations or reminiscences is the legal or juridical context of the prophet's prediction retained. Now, with the advent of Christ and the initiation of the new covenant, whatever of the legal or juridical may have been imagined to attach to it has been removed. Insofar as the prophet saw the arrival of the new and its benefits ("I will be their God . . . I will forgive their iniquity") his prediction deserved to be remembered, but the context within which he viewed that arrival needed abandoning. Here, then, the intent of the author, certainly as regards the context of his vision, could not be the goal of the interpreter. And, in fact, it was not. The use to which the New Testament puts Jeremiah's prophecy is ample proof of that.

On the Right to Criticism

In Christian communities of the Reformation tradition a distinction is drawn between gospel and scripture. That is, the gospel is regarded as exclusively contained or given a home in scripture, but not as identical to it. If it were not seen as exclusively contained there, the scripture would be reduced to merely one of any imaginable aggregation of "witnesses," thus canceling out its normative character. It is this normative character which the so-called exclusive particle *sola scriptura,* or "scripture alone," is designed to express. On the other hand, if the gospel were taken to be identical to or co-terminous with scripture since scripture has more the character of a chain reaction in atomic fission than an unfolding of the Spirit in an ultimately continuous process of development, scripture would lack a core or center from out of which the whole could be understood. It is this core that the so-called exclusive particle, *sola fide* or "faith alone," is designed to express, that is, faith in the redemptive activity of God in Jesus Christ, hence also the "exclusive particle" *solus Christus,* or "Christ alone." While it is not the affair of historical criticism to elucidate or defend the dialectic between gospel and scripture, and thus expose its core, it functions as a handmaid, an auxiliary to that interpretation which is intent on exposing the Bible's core, its principal and chief subject, namely, God's reclamation of the world through the death and resurrection of Jesus Christ. Again, if historical criticism cannot be identified with historical reality, or with the faith from which that dialectical character of gospel and scripture results, nevertheless, because it inquires after historical reality, because it focuses on the historically contingent, on the context of events and happenings within which it is believed God was made manifest, it enjoys not only a methodological but also a theological right to be used.[67]

67. For a lengthier and more developed argument respecting the theological legitimacy of historical-criticism, see Ernst Käsemann, "Vom theologischen Recht historisch-kritischer Exegese," *Zeitschrift für Theologie und Kirche* 64 (1967): 259-81.

CHAPTER ELEVEN

A Last Word

For every student of the Bible concerned with a genuine interpretation the following applies.

First of all, however diverse the critical, analytical study of the biblical text, there is no avoiding presuppositions. To the possible objection that his interpretation of Chaucer's poem had unfairly gone outside it, that one should begin with the text, "without any presuppositions whatsoever," D. W. Robertson replied:

> It is impossible to read anything "without any presuppositions," and what has happened is that most critics of the poem have brought to it a great many post-romantic presuppositions concerning both the subject of the poem and its technique.[1]

The argument is eminently applicable to biblical research. The use of the critical method, however pared down to bare essentials, takes something for granted. It assumes that the Bible is kin to all other literature, that for the sake of its historically conditioned character, its having a home in languages people actually spoke, in places where people actually lived, its authorship by living, breathing human beings, and its destination among living, breathing human beings, the Bible cannot be cut off from the rest of human history and requires the use of the human mind for its exposition. Christians do not regard the Bible as the Muslim does the Qur'an, writ with the finger of Allah, the Blessed and Compassionate, and revealed

---

1. D. W. Robertson Jr., "The Historical Setting of Chaucer's *Book of the Duchess*," in *Essays in Medieval Culture* (Princeton, N.J.: Princeton University Press, 1980), p. 4.

from heaven by the hand of the archangel Gabriel. They regard it as a creation, something become a human work in time, for which reason, initially at least, it requires no other treatment than any other created thing. In fact, many students of the Bible welcome the analysis of its texts by way of the techniques used in the study of other literature. Justification for the existence of biblical research is the church's desire for an appropriate understanding of the Bible. Only the specificity of the task of interpreting the biblical word requires that it embrace and use the techniques available for its own purposes.[2]

If Christian interpretation of the biblical word falls within the broader field of textual interpretation as such, then such research is not confined to Christians. But once the Bible's kinship with the remainder of literature is assumed, it is inevitable that someone like Sportin' Life in Gershwin's *Porgy and Bess* will dismiss it:

It ain't necessarily so.
The things that you're liable
to read in the Bible —
it ain't necessarily so.

For this reason, some still entertain suspicion toward the use of critical tools, as witness Eta Linnemann's demurrer.[3] By contrast, there is evidence of such a method as benefiting the Christian community. If, for example, David Friedrich Strauss had not reduced the New Testament witness to a congeries of "historical" and "pure, philosophical" myths, the quest of the historical Jesus with its attention to the relation between event and interpretation, between history and kerygma or proclamation, might never have occurred. Or, to cite a much earlier example, if the gnostic Marcion had not performed major surgery on the biblical canon, the church would not have wheeled out its armory to explode the barrier between the Testaments.

2. See Kristlieb Adloff, "Neuen Aspekte der Exegese nach Bultmann," in *Schrift und Auslegung,* ed. Heinrich Kraft (Erlangen: Martin Luther Verlag, 1987), p. 94; Roland Mushat Frye, "A Literary Perspective for the Criticism of the Gospels," in *Jesus and Man's Hope,* ed. Donald Miller and Dikran Hadidian (Pittsburgh Theological Seminary, 1971), vol. 2, p. 219; Edvin Larsson, "Notwendigkeit und Grenze der historisch-kritischen Methode," in Kraft, ed., *Schrift und Auslegung,* p. 120; Ricoeur, "Philosophical Hermeneutics and Theological Hermeneutics," *Studies in Religion* 5, no. 1 (1975-76): 17.

3. See pp. 316-18 above.

Next, if Sportin' Life or any other critic should reject the biblical message, it may not be supposed that such a person errs through a certain simplicity of mind. The rejection may arise from a quite proper understanding of the biblical word. If George Steiner (1929-) of Geneva, Oxford, and Harvard, one of the most evocative critics and essayists of the last century, could write that since Bultmann there can be no "presuppositionless readings" of the past, that "to all past events, as to all present intake, the observer brings a specific mental set,"[4] then it can be argued that pre- or non-Christian existence contains "an unknowing knowledge of God," a pre-understanding of the Christian proclamation. "As meaningless as it is to speak of an organ for the divine in man, of a point of contact for the revelation," writes Theodor Lorenzmeier (1927-), emeritus instructor of religion at Bad Salzuflen, "so, on the other hand, it is foolish to contest the presuppositions of faith given in the old existence and its self-understanding."[5] In light of the above, the statement of the Canadian philosopher Jean Grondin (1955-) to the effect that "the existential preunderstanding that Bultmann proposes can only be a Christian one"[6] may reflect a confusion of Bultmann with Barth and the latter's denial of a point of contact between unbelief and faith. More probably, it reflects an earlier criticism made by Ernst Käsemann, to the effect that Bultmann's assigning such universality to existential pre-understanding, and making it so decisive for the understanding of biblical texts, robs the scripture of its "exclusive revelatory claim."[7] Hermeneutics, Käsemann added, enjoys a critical function, but cannot give the exegete his or her object. Faith needs the prior revelation and cannot be reduced to the self-understanding of the exegete.[8]

Because the Christian proclamation involves a witness in writing, that is, makes its advent in a textual witness, whoever attempts biblical research, from whatever corner, of whatever persuasion, is duty bound to acknowledge the claim made by the biblical text. It is precisely the so-called secular approach that is obliged to acknowledge that the Bible's

4. George Steiner, *After Babel: Aspects of Language and Translation* (London: Oxford University Press, 1975), pp. 143-44.

5. Steiner, *After Babel*, pp. 143-44.

6. Jean Grondin, "Gadamer and Bultmann," in *Philosophical Hermeneutics and Biblical Exegesis*, ed. Petr Pokorný and Jan Roskovec (Tübingen: Mohr, 2002), p. 136.

7. Ernst Käsemann, "Probleme neutestamentlicher Arbeit in Deutschland," *Beiträge zur evangelischen Theologie* 15 (1952): 145.

8. Käsemann, "Probleme neutestamentlicher Arbeit in Deutschland," p. 151.

purpose is not to furnish information but to evoke a response that involves an alteration of existence. Any other approach hollows out the aim of the biblical text and cannot lay claim to be critical. Popular courses in "the Bible as literature" are notoriously deficient respecting the issue, and in a number of societies devoted to biblical research the deficiency has all the aspects of a requirement for admission. Analogously, it has long been the habit of persons interested in signal religious figures of history to concentrate on the philosophical, psychological, sociological, and economic results of whatever centrifugal forces were at work in them, rather than on those forces themselves. Augustine, Aquinas, Luther, Kierkegaard, Hamann, have all been the object of unnumbered volumes of research minus attention to whatever it was at the core of them that drove them on. In his attack on the separation of head from heart in Bible interpretation Adolf Schlatter asserted the legitimacy of a "methodological atheism" that in the interest of begetting pure, genuine observation tabled the question of God "for a time" *(nur zeitweilig)*. But to exclude the question of God altogether, he wrote, rendered science a caricature. Theology had a right to be coupled with universal scientific method. As he wrote:

> Now, if we want to exclude religion from the world, then in our research we are logically and from the outset involved in radical contradiction of our object, which does not intend to be excluded from the world, but loudly and tenaciously gives title to the idea of God.[9]

To the question, what shape would pre- or non-Christian understanding of the biblical, Christian witness take, the answer is simple: give ear, listen to the claim to transcendence made by the text! Whether or not one shares the faith that comes to utterance in the object of research, the claim of the revelatory event fixed in that object requires that it be "heard." Such "hearing" involves distantiation, the disassociation of self from the interpretive process. More than one scholar has insisted that *Christian* interpretation involves acknowledging the biblical sources as an a posteriori, admitting that what is to be known through the revelation cannot be known beforehand; that the self lives from the text that offers itself for reflection; that interpretation involves hearing the word as spoken to another, a "contradiction" silenced when one looks away from self

9. Adolf Schlatter, "Atheistische Methoden in der Theologie," *Beiträge zur Forderung der Christlichen Theologie* 9 (1905): 248.

and listens to the text as spoken to another. But distantiation can hardly be a requirement restricted to Christian interpretation. *Any* approach to the biblical text demands that the text be allowed to have its say, that it initiate whatever dialogue ensues with the interpreter, that is to say, "as far as possible," to quote Paul Ricoeur,[10] since the requirement will never be completely met. In this sense, Kermode's dictum applies, to the effect that what is divined in the "meshes" of a text is a "momentary radiance," in the perception of which lies our "sole hope and pleasure."[11] But this word requires a reading that may be athwart Kermode's central thesis, for it is not the text that yields a "momentary radiance." *Our "sole hope and pleasure" lies in the perception of whatever "momentary radiance" may result from interpretation, not from the text.* As regards the prior historical-critical task, the gulf fixed between what is historically ascertainable and what actually occurs, to say nothing of the gulf between computable facts and their theological interpretation, it will eternally be exposed to conflict, incongruence, and contrast, to what among theologians was called *Anfechtung.*

Modern subjectivity, with its identification of text and interpreter, to the point at which the text takes its life from interpretation, or is identified with it, is of a piece with that "post-romantic presupposition" to which D. W. Robertson referred. Unexpectedly, that presupposition makes an early appearance in the second edition of Karl Barth's *Römerbrief:*

> Intelligent comment means that I am driven on till I stand with nothing before me but the enigma of the matter; till the document seems hardly to exist as a document; till I have almost forgotten that I am not its author; till I know the author so well that I allow him to speak in my name and am even able to speak in his name myself.[12]

As robust an opponent of romanticism as Barth professed to be, here, at least, he could be read as whittling down the difference between the biblical text and its reader.[13] At any rate, it belongs to critical research, of

---

10. Paul Ricoeur, "The Canon between the Text and the Community," in Pokorný and Jan Roskovec, eds., *Philosophical Hermeneutics and Biblical Exegesis,* p. 12.

11. Frank Kermode, *The Genesis of Secrecy* (Cambridge, Mass.: Harvard University Press, 1979), pp. 144-45.

12. Karl Barth, *The Epistle to the Romans,* trans. Edwyn C. Hoskyns (Oxford: Oxford University Press, 1933), preface to the second edition, p. 8.

13. See Oswald Bayer, "Hermeneutical Theology," in Pokorný and Jan Roskovec, eds., *Philosophical Hermeneutics and Biblical Exegesis,* p. 116.

whatever persuasion, to acknowledge the priority, the a posteriori character of the text.

Alfred North Whitehead (1861-1947) wrote that the true method of research and discovery was like the flight of an airplane. The method begins from the ground of particular observation, takes flight into the thin air of imaginative generalization, only to land again for renewed observation rendered acute by rational interpretation.[14] While it may not be the task of historical criticism to shatter the docetism that at times may endanger the Christian community, nevertheless, with its focus on the historically contingent, that is, on the context of events and happenings within which it is believed God was made manifest, that is its effect.[15]

The question is not whether we can ever escape this circular character of our knowing, that is, without reducing the drama of life to inert fact on the one hand, or reducing that drama to psychology on the other. The circle is here to stay. The question is rather, how large shall that circle be? Shall it encompass merely the interpreter and the text to be interpreted — the knower and the known against the world? Since, according to Plato, the soul was not only immortal but eternal, and capable of repeated incarnations, its present environment thus temporary and any kind of community without significance, "human affairs [were] unworthy of earnest effort,"[16] and the soul was left to reflect on itself alone. A good deal of modern biblical interpretation operates on the assumption that knowledge involves but one single level of consciousness, that of the private, individual self. But knowing and learning, and in this instance the knowing and learning required for an interpretation of biblical texts, has social character. The reason is simply that the individual consciousness is not sufficient to produce the kind of doubt and inquiry or correction vital to all knowing.

To the circle, then, the Christian community belongs. When, in preparation for the Sunday sermon, the pastor pulls out a commentary from the shelves, obliquely, at least, he or she is confessing faith in the

---

14. Alfred North Whitehead, *Process and Reality* (New York: Harper Torchbooks, 1957), pp. 17 and 7; see *Dialogues of Alfred North Whitehead,* as recorded by Lucien Price (London: Max Reinhardt, 1954), insert no. 2.

15. Ernst Käsemann, "Vom theologischen Recht historisch-kritischer Exegese," *Zeitschrift für Theologie und Kirche* 64 (1967): 281.

16. Plato, *The Laws,* trans. R. G. Bury (Cambridge, Mass.: Harvard University Press, 1961), II, book VII, 803B, p. 53.

"one holy catholic and apostolic church," acknowledging that community as necessary to inquiry, to the correction or confirmation of a view arrived at singly, and thus as the constraint beyond the private self. In this sense, the community becomes the guarantor of the truth discovered. "No prophecy of scripture is a matter of one's own interpretation" (2 Peter 1:20). The interpretation of scripture cannot be undertaken in solitary fashion, but only within the context of common statements of faith reflected in confessions received by the church. It is not merely a matter of the Bible and its interpreter *contra mundum,* but a matter of the consciousness of the effects that the biblical tradition has had on the community for which it serves as norm, effects reflected in common statements of faith.

As noted above, in contrast to Rudolf Bultmann's reductionism, Hans-Georg Gadamer contended that understanding is a relation to the history of effects of a given text (i.e., the *Wirkungsgeschichte*), and that the interpreter's consciousness of that history of effects is always in force (i.e., the *wirkungsgeschichtliches Bewusstsein*). Bultmann's "secret idealism" and Gadamer's insistence on historicality collide. But so also do Bultmann's idealism and Gadamer's idea of tradition, for according to Gadamer the way by which the interpreter is conscious or experiences the history of the effects of a text, or, as he puts it, the way by which "the totality of the interpreter's experience of the world" is always in force, is through remembrance, the remembrance of effects that existed prior to and independently of the interpreter, that is, through that fusion of past and present we call tradition. Ultimately, then, by way of understanding stoked through remembrance the interpreter is made part of tradition.

But inasmuch as the text deserves the priority, to that degree the Christian community and whatever confessional allegiance follows from it cannot be the ultimate guarantor of the interpreter's discovery. Error cannot be avoided by multiplying the number of "cognizers." The power and force of the so-called formal principle of the Reformation *(sola scriptura)* lies in the acknowledgment of the church *under the constraint of scripture* as the guarantor of a genuine interpretation. Hence, though neither Bible nor church can live without the other — the church having given birth to the Bible, and the word of proclamation congealed in the Bible having given birth to the church — the priority of the biblical text is retained, and the church's confessions avoid arrogating to themselves the right to legislate in the matter of exegetical details. For example, in Luther's *Smalcald Articles,* the Reformer makes reference to the mother of Jesus as "ever virgin" *(semper virgine),*[17] and the "Solid Declaration" of the Lutheran *Formula of Concord* refers to Mary's virginity as inviolate *(inviolata).*[18] The reference is an error. Though Jesus was the first to open the womb, the text of the New Testament makes clear that he was not an only child. Mark 3:20 records that Jesus' family went to restrain him in face of the charge that he had lost his mind. The phrase *hoi par' autou* translated "family" in the New Revised Standard Version cannot be restricted to the children of Mary's siblings. It allows a more intimate inference. More specifically, in Mark 6:3 Jesus' audience in the Nazareth synagogue is astounded at his teaching and asks, "Is not this the carpenter, the son of Mary and brother of James and Joses and Judas and Simon, and are not his sisters here with us?" (Mark 6:3). In such an instance, the confession is obliged to concede to the biblical text, an obligation the confession in principle readily assumes:

> We believe, teach, and confess that the sole rule and standard according to which all dogmas together with (all) teachers should be estimated and judged are the prophetic and apostolic Scriptures of the Old and of the New Testament alone. . . . Other writings, however, of ancient or modern teachers, whatever name they bear, must not be regarded as equal to the Holy Scripture, but all of them together be subjected to them.[19]

Such confessions or criteria clearly derive their authority from a source outside themselves. The task of interpretation thus involves a testing of the biblical word against the received confessions, and lest the danger recur of elevating a hereditary and ecclesiastical system of exposition to a dogmatic norm, of testing the received confessions against the biblical word. But in the end, as Dahl writes,

> The hermeneutical task, in the sense of a prolegomenon to translating the message and teaching of the Bible into the present situation of the church, can therefore, in my opinion, not be executed by any one authority — neither by the confessions, nor the exegetes, nor the

17. *Concordia Triglotta: The Symbolical Books of the Ev. Lutheran Church* (St. Louis: Concordia, 1921), p. 460.
18. *Concordia Triglotta,* The Formula of Concord, Thorough Declaration VIII, Of the Person of Christ, para. 24, p. 1022.
19. *Concordia Triglotta,* The Formula of Concord, Of the Summary Content, Rule, and Standard, para. 1, p. 777.

professional dogmaticians, nor the pastors, nor anyone else, be they ever so endowed with charismatic knowledge.[20]

Now the place assumed by faith in interpretation deserves attention. In the 1960s and 1970s a contest arose over biblical research as a primarily historical descriptive task exclusive of theological reflection. In an article on biblical theology in *The Interpreter's Dictionary of the Bible,* Krister Stendahl (1921-2008) of Harvard described the task as follows:

> This descriptive task can be carried out by believer and agnostic alike. The believer has the advantage of automatic empathy with the believers in the text — but his faith constantly threatens to have him modernize the material. . . . The agnostic has the advantage of feeling no such temptations, but his power of empathy must be considerable.[21]

Brevard Childs (1923-2007) of Yale rejected the limitation, and asked:

> Does not theology need normative as well as descriptive categories in order to execute its task? . . . Can the theological task of a commentator be exhausted when he remains on the level of the witness? Is there not a responsibility to penetrate to the substance toward which the text points?[22]

Childs's answer was that the use of the critical method to set up an iron curtain between past and present was an inadequate method for studying the Bible as the church's scripture,[23] and in his commentary on Exodus gave the reason for his answer:

> The rigid separation between the descriptive and constructive elements of exegesis strikes at the roots of the theological task of understanding the Bible.[24]

20. Nils Dahl, "The Lutheran Exegete and the Confessions of His Church," *The Lutheran World* 6 (1959): 7.

21. Krister Stendahl, "Biblical Theology," in *The Interpreter's Dictionary of the Bible* (Nashville: Abingdon, 1962), vol. 1, p. 422; cf. pp. 418 and 425.

22. Brevard Childs, "Interpretation in Faith," *Interpretation* 18 (1964): 433, 436.

23. Brevard Childs, *Biblical Theology in Crisis* (Philadelphia: Westminster, 1970), pp. 141-42.

24. Brevard Childs, *The Book of Exodus* (Philadelphia: Westminster, 1974), p. xiii.

This did not spell mere lip service to the historical task, for which Childs would fault Paul Ricoeur, who he believed construed the Bible as a deposit of metaphors containing inherent powers by which to interpret present experience irrespective of their source, thus displaying little or no interest in the text's historical development.[25] But it was the "subject matter," the "substance" toward which the biblical witnesses pointed, that demanded reflection. "Scripture," wrote Childs, "points beyond itself to the reality of God. The ability to render this reality is to enter the 'strange new world of the Bible.' "[26] To engage this "subject matter" was finally not a matter left to criticism. The hearing, the interpreting of it, required confirmation by the reality it intended to reflect: "Through the Spirit the reality to which the text points . . . is made active in constantly fresh forms of application."[27]

There is nothing novel attaching to the assertion. The history of interpretation, from the early fathers to Augustine and beyond, yields evidence of a persistent emphasis on biblical interpretation as requiring confirmation by the Spirit of God. There are innumerable studies from which can be culled the passages in which Martin Luther rings the changes on this theme.[28] In a postil (homily) for Advent Sunday, 1522, he notes that for the apostles and evangelists only the Old Testament was scripture. As for the New Testament, it was intended to be a living word, for which reason Christ himself wrote nothing.[29] In another he wrote that necessity dictated the writing of the New Testament: "The fact that books had to be written is a great injury and a deficit of the Spirit, something forced by necessity, and not native to the New Testament."[30]

25. Brevard Childs, *Introduction to the Old Testament as Scripture* (Philadelphia: Fortress, 1979), p. 77.

26. Brevard Childs, *Biblical Theology of the Old and New Testaments: Theological Reflection on the Christian Bible* (Minneapolis: Fortress, 1931), p. 721.

27. Childs, *Biblical Theology of the Old and New Testaments,* p. 724. For a fuller discussion of Childs's position, see Roy A. Harrisville, "What I Believe My Old Schoolmate Is Up To," in *Theological Exegesis: Essays in Honor of Brevard S. Childs,* ed. Christopher Seitz and Kathryn Greene-McCreight (Grand Rapids: Eerdmans, 1999), and idem, "Brevard Childs: Biblical Criticism under the Discipline of the Canon," in *The Bible in Modern Culture: Baruch Spinoza to Brevard Childs,* ed. Roy A. Harrisville and Walter Sundberg (Grand Rapids: Eerdmans, 2002).

28. See Walter von Loewenich, *Luther als Ausleger der Synoptiker* (München: Chr. Kaiser, 1954), especially p. 106.

29. *Weimar Ausgabe* (hereafter referred to as *WA*) (Weimar: Hermann Böhlaus Nachfolger, 1883-1993), 10/I.2, 35, 1-2.

30. *WA* 10/I.1, 627, 1.

For this reason, he said, we should not accept what is written as paper *(quam papyrum),* as if paper would save.[31] What is decisive is the reality of Christ announced in the written word. Without it the book avails nothing: "If you do not have scripture in your heart or have searched in it for a bit, the book will be of no help to you."[32] Bible erudition does not lead to Christ:

> The [three] kings sought him through sturdy faith in Balaam's prophecy, while those who are so hostile to scripture they would smash it do not find him. The scribes of the Jews could not find him though they could tell the kings of Micah's prophecy. There is more to it, then, if we are to find him in places of no account, if the star of the Gospel is to arise in us, in a believing heart.[33]

In a sermon for April 7, 1534, Luther states that what belongs to the word *(gehort noch dazu)* is that the Spirit declare it in the heart,[34] and in July 1537 describes the Magnificat as a song, more pleasingly sung or preached, and composed in few words, "but, as is certain, by the Holy Spirit, and without that teacher cannot be understood."[35] Commenting on the preface in Luke's Gospel, Luther states that heretics made Gospel writing necessary, though this could not prevent it from becoming a "book of heresies" *(liber heresium)* or with allegorizing made a "wax nose."[36] For this reason, he argued, the Holy Spirit must direct us just as he directed the Magi to Bethlehem

> since the Holy Spirit always makes himself known in Holy Scripture. But then, where you see the Holy Spirit pointing to scripture, learn that the scriptures are not to be looked down on, for [they] allow the Magi to enter and take from scripture a word so as to be established in faith. If this is what pleases the Holy Spirit, we ought to be humble and give thanks for hearing the scriptures in this way, and allow ourselves to be led to Christ.[37]

31. *WA* 32, 265, 13 (sermon for December 25, 1530).
32. *WA* 36, 318, 22-23 (sermon for September 6, 1532).
33. *WA* 7, 248, 22 (sermon to the Obersten, 1521).
34. *WA* 37, 367, 6.
35. *WA* 45, 105, 5 (sermon for July 2, 1537).
36. *WA* 46, 466, 12 (sermon for July 1, 1538).
37. *WA* 27, 13, 25 (sermon for Epiphany, January 6, 1538).

Calvin was by no means behind Luther in accenting Bible interpretation as requiring confirmation by the Spirit. In the words of David C. Steinmetz (1936-), emeritus professor of the history of Christianity at Duke University, Calvin did not prize "distance from the text as a source of insight, much less alienation from its teaching," adding that "just as a tone-deaf critic should not attempt to interpret the fugues of Bach, so a spiritually deaf commentator should not try to interpret the letters of Paul."[38] In his commentary on 1 Corinthians 1:20, Calvin wrote:

> Knowledge of all the sciences is so much smoke apart from the heavenly science of Christ. . . . [M]an with all his shrewdness is as stupid about understanding by himself the mysteries of God as an ass is incapable of understanding musical harmony.[39]

The first book of the *Institutes of the Christian Religion* is replete with references to the "testimony of the Spirit" in the confirming of scripture. The following gives ample evidence:

> If we desire to provide in the best way for our consciences — that they may not be perpetually beset by the instability of doubt or vacillation, and that they may not also boggle at the smallest quibbles — we ought to seek our conviction in a higher place than human reasons, judgments, or conjectures, that is, in the secret testimony of the Spirit.[40]

> The testimony of the Spirit is more excellent than all reason. For as God alone is a fit witness of himself in his Word, so also the Word will not find acceptance in men's hearts before it is sealed by the inward testimony of the Spirit. The same Spirit, therefore, who has spoken through the mouths of the prophets must penetrate into our hearts to persuade us that they faithfully proclaimed what had been divinely commanded.[41]

38. David C. Steinmetz, "John Calvin as an Interpreter of the Bible," in *Calvin and the Bible,* ed. Donald K. McKim (Cambridge: Cambridge University Press, 2006), p. 285.

39. John Calvin, *The First Epistle of Paul the Apostle to the Corinthians,* trans. John W. Fraser, Calvin's Commentaries (Grand Rapids: Eerdmans, 1960), p. 38.

40. John Calvin, *Institutes of the Christian Religion,* trans. Ford Lewis Battles, Library of Christian Classics, vol. 20 (Philadelphia: Westminster, 1960), I, VII, 4, p. 78.

41. Calvin, *Institutes,* I, VII, 4, p. 79.

Let this point therefore stand: that those whom the Holy Spirit has inwardly taught truly rest upon Scripture, and that Scripture indeed is self-authenticated; hence it is not right to subject it to proof and reasoning. And the certainty it deserves with us, it attains by the testimony of the Spirit. For even if it wins reverence for itself by its own majesty, it seriously affects us only when it is sealed upon our hearts through the Spirit.[42]

In that portion of *The Conflict of the Faculties* dealing with the philosophical versus the theology faculty, Immanuel Kant refers to the various tenets to be observed by the biblical theologian, the last of which reads: "Since there is no human interpreter of the Scriptures authorized by God, he must rather count on a supernatural opening of his understanding by a spirit that guides to all truth."[43] On the surface, the statement appears to support the view expressed above. The difficulty, however, is that Kant would not allow whatever was amenable to rational investigation to be subsumed under the heading of the supernatural. He called the biblical theologian's insistence on "historical content as divine revelation"[44] a "meddling with reason," "leaping over the wall of ecclesiastical faith," and "straying into the free and open fields of private judgment and philosophy."[45] It was apparently such meddling for which Kant faulted Johann David Michaelis, the Göttingen scholar, and his attempt to assign Israel a status equal to that of Greek or Roman civilization.[46]

As for Kant, he missed or dismissed what Luther, Melanchthon, or Calvin had to say of the place of "historical content" in Christian faith. According to Luther, assent to an historical event, even to its supernatural character, was totally without significance if it did not call forth the acknowledgment that it had occurred "for us," "for me." Respecting Christ's birth, for example, everything depended on accepting the *vobis* ("for you") in Luke 2:11 by faith. Or again, the annunciation to Mary was more than a *pulchra historia* ("pretty story") celebrated at church festivals; it was the *donum et thesaurum tibi datum* ("the gift and treasury

---

42. Calvin, *Institutes,* I, VII, 5, p. 80.
43. Immanuel Kant, *The Conflict of the Faculties,* trans. Mary J. Gregor (New York: Abaris, 1979), p. 37.
44. Kant, *The Conflict of the Faculties,* p. 63.
45. Kant, *The Conflict of the Faculties,* p. 37.
46. Kant, *The Conflict of the Faculties,* pp. 15-16.

given to you").[47] In his *Loci Communes,* Melanchthon dubbed such "historical faith" *(fides historica)* mere "vulgar opinion" *(vulgaris opinio).*[48] Calvin wrote that most are deluded when they hear the term "faith," for they understand "nothing deeper than a common assent to the gospel history."[49]

As for Michaelis, whether or not he was first among the "meddlers" to attempt to give biblical research a status equal to that of the other university disciplines, the practice of assigning the "historical content" of the Bible to research apart from its primary, first, and sole intent to evoke faith, perhaps to compensate for a shrinking self-esteem by struggling to legitimize that research among the other, "higher" branches of human learning, has dominated biblical scholarship since the earliest days of the Enlightenment. Whether or not Grondin was correct when he insisted that "the existential pre-understanding that Bultmann proposes can only be a Christian one,"[50] whatever the content of one's pre-understanding, genuine interpretation of the Bible requires a yielding in the faith it intends to evoke. Further, whatever the reason for the chasm between current and contemporary interpretation and the Bible's chief purpose and aim, should a return to acknowledgment of that purpose alienate the "biblical theologian" from the "higher faculties," in Kant's parlance, and thus biblical research be dismissed from the college or university curriculum, such sacrifice might in part atone for the disservice done "The Book" during the last two centuries. The divergent methods and interpretations, from form, redaction, and tradition criticism to structuralism, post-structuralism, and even deconstruction, from presuppositions laced with idealism, existentialism, and pragmatism, if harnessed in service to the text with its peculiar call, all have a rightful place. The obverse side of this statement is that no particular method or interpretation will have the upper hand, all are subordinate to the text and its claim. One writes of the legitimacy in the use of divergent interpretations:

> All these . . . are equally legitimate and equally plausible. They are divergent. . . . [T]heir respective readings of the text are "framed" in

47. See the section "Existentielles Verstehen," in von Loewenich's *Luther als Ausleger der Synoptiker* (München: Chr. Kaiser Verlag, 1954), pp. 83-88.

48. *The Loci Communes of Philipp Melanchthon,* trans. C. L. Hill (Boston: Meador, 1944), p. 185.

49. Calvin, *Institutes,* III, II, 1, p. 543.

50. Jean Grondin, "Gadamer and Bultmann," p. 136.

different ways. . . . Yet, these . . . are equally legitimate insofar as each is appropriately grounded upon actual features of the text.[51]

Another accents the necessity for beginning with a holistic approach:

> Holism, the assumption that the work in front of us is a unity, with all its parts fitting together and relevant to that unity, is the practical working assumption that every act of criticism must begin with.[52]

But whatever the method or interpretation and whatever shape a holistic approach may assume, it is absolutely incumbent on the interpreter at the very outset to inform the hearer-reader of the methodology being used. Critical scholarship demands acknowledging the choice of certain categories among the methods or codes available.

The same holds true of the assumptions and presuppositions underlying one's interpretation. For one reason or another, unconsciously or not, leaving to the hearer-reader the burden of uncovering whatever it is that moves the interpreter to write, an all but universal practice, hardly reflects genuine scholarship. Scores of Bible interpreters have either deliberately hidden or never been at pains to reveal what perspective, commitment, or tenet of faith has moved them to approach and interpret the biblical text. Few have followed the example of Ferdinand Christian Baur and his acknowledged allegiance to Hegel, and in the last century Rudolf Bultmann stood almost alone in revealing the philosophical underpinnings of his Bible interpretation, for which, of course, he paid a heavy price with the ecclesiasts. The question is not of Hegel's or Heidegger's deserving to render such service to theology, but rather of taking public ownership of whatever conceptuality engages one's interest and interpretation, come hell or high water.

Then also, when the interpreter has reached an impasse, honesty requires the acknowledgment of having moved into unknown territory. For example, attempts to interpret Jesus' cursing of the fig tree in Mark 11:12-14, 20-24, result in an impenetrable thicket of opinions.[53] The passage reads:

51. Daniel Patte, "Critical Biblical Studies from a Semiotic Perspective," *Semeia* 81 (1998): 11.

52. Northrop Frye, *Words with Power* (Toronto: University of Toronto Press, 2008), p. 98.

53. See the review of interpretations by Heinz Giesen in *Biblische Zeitschrift* 20 (1976): 96-98.

On the following day, when they came from Bethany, he was hungry. Seeing in the distance a fig tree in leaf, he went to see whether perhaps he would find anything on it. When he came to it, he found nothing but leaves, for it was not the season for figs. He said to it, "May no one ever eat fruit from you again." And his disciples heard it.

One writes of fig trees that give fruit in winter, giving credibility to Jesus' hunger and his curse. Another performs an etiological acrobatic move, writing that the story can be understood only if an actual fig tree stood between Bethany and Jerusalem, and whenever believers approached it they looked for blossoms. A third interprets the curse in terms of the coming judgment on Jerusalem. Still another writes of it as an apocalyptic word originally referring to Jesus' passion, death, and resurrection as the breaking in of the end-time, then later reinterpreted as a curse in view of the end-time's delay. Yet another sets the story within the context of the Feast of Tabernacles, within a season when one might normally expect figs. Still another interprets the story metaphorically: Jesus hungers after the fruit of the fig tree, that is, after Israel's faith, but its *kairos,* the time allotted for its decision, has passed ("it was not the season for figs"). One critic decries such an interpretation as a "massive anti-Jewish exposition,"[54] and yet another sets the scene within the context of Jesus' sayings on faith and prayer.[55] Of the innumerable approaches to the story four take center stage: (1) The story is to be treated symbolically or metaphorically as a judgment on Israel, running the risk of racism; (2) "it was not the season for figs" represents a literalistic reading of what was intended as metaphor, thus running the same risk; (3) "it was not the season for figs" is a later gloss intended to correct an originally apocalyptic prediction due to the delay of the end-time; and (4) Jesus was actually hungry, despite a recent opportunity for having feasted, spied a fig tree whose leaves promised fruit despite the fact that it was not the season for it, and cursed the tree to the point of its withering up.

Even David Friedrich Strauss hastened to spare Jesus inanity, writing that we have before us the same theme in three different shapes: first in concentrated form as gnomon; second, as gnomon expanded to parable; and third, as gnomon realized in an actual event.[56] With this alteration,

54. Peter Dschulnigg, *Das Markusevangelium,* Theologischer Kommentar zum Neuen Testament (Stuttgart: W. Kohlhammer, 2007), p. 300.

55. Douglas R. A. Hare, *Mark* (Louisville: Westminster John Knox, 1996), pp. 144-46.

56. David Friedrich Strauss, *Das Leben Jesu kritisch bearbeitet* (Tübingen: C. F. Osiander, 1893), vol. 2, pp. 266-67.

Strauss continues, the original meaning of the parable was lost, the miraculous was taken to be the nerve of the entire affair, and the speech regarding the power of faith (Mark 11:20-24) was linked to it.[57] But this use of the gnomon for the erroneous interpretation of an allegedly actual event rendered Jesus' behavior morally inexplicable.[58]

From ancient times the story has baffled interpreters, inducing the majority to rush to exculpate Jesus from idiocy. But the story will not bow to the host of exculpators. It stands as irritant to all those anxious heads, like organists aching to take to the keys to fill up the silence. Perhaps Mark saw a connection between this irritatingly puzzling affair and that "secret" threading throughout this Gospel, only this time, aimed at the reader. At any rate, honest acknowledgment that the entire scene defies explanation, rendering all attempts at deciphering it a morass of whimsy, would have sufficed. Let it stand there, thumbing its nose at the would-be interpreter.

Finally, a word or two respecting allegory and accommodation. There is a further challenge to the requirement that interpretation concern itself with authorial intent. It has to do with whether or not the most primitive meaning of the text is its only valid meaning, thus ruling out any "figurative" interpretation. In his *Mimesis*,[59] a work that still retains its impact over the decades, Erich Auerbach (1892-1957), philologist and scholar of comparative literature, first at Marburg, then at Yale, displaced by the Nazis, described what he termed "figurative interpretation," an approach linking two persons or events, in which the one designates not only himself but also the other. Though the two may be temporally separated, both are contained "in the flowing stream which is historical life."[60] This type of interpretation, Auerbach continued, brings an entirely new and alien element to the study of history. It forges a link between two events that cannot be rationally established within the horizontal course of events. Rather, it is established "vertically," that is, "before God's eye." The result is that the "here and now" no longer belongs to an earthly sequence of events, but is something eternal, belonging to every period, "completed in the fragmentary earthly event." It was inevitable, wrote Auerbach, that this conception should collide with the classical view, preoccupied as it was with order, time, and causal connection. Auerbach then noted how

57. Strauss, *Das Leben Jesu*, p. 267.
58. Strauss, *Das Leben Jesu*, p. 261.
59. Erich Auerbach, *Mimesis: Dargestellte Wirklichkeit in der abendländischen Literatur*, 10th ed. (Tübingen: A. Francke Verlag, 2001).
60. Auerbach, *Mimesis*, p. 75.

Augustine struggled to harmonize the two perspectives, though in the end the classical idea proved too fragile; the figural was victorious.[61] Auerbach's interest in figurative interpretation was hardly unconditional; he was aware of and proceeded to list its limitations.[62]

"Alien" or not, this "irrational" interpretation has had its advocates among contemporary interpreters. In an essay on a poem by Chaucer,[63] D. W. Robertson dealt with the objection that his reading unfairly went "outside the poem," that one ought to begin with the text absolutely devoid of presuppositions. In reply Robertson stated that it was impossible to read anything at all without presuppositions, witness the fact that most of the poem's critics had subjected it to post-romantic presuppositions respecting its subject and technique.[64] Small wonder, he added, that a contemporary historian of literature should find Chaucer's poem crude, whereas in the medieval period arriving at the "nucleus" of truth beneath the "cortex" or surface of meaning was "something of the pleasure of a discovery."[65] "Those," he concludes, "who insist on clinging to 'what the poem says literally' are only offering some justification for the usual connotations of the word *academic*."[66]

Northrop Frye (1912-91) offers another example of the appetite for "irrational" interpretation. In his *Anatomy of Criticism,* Frye first acknowledged his debt to William Blake from whom he learned the principles of literary symbolism and biblical typology.[67] Writing that biblical typology is so dead a language that most readers cannot grasp the surface meaning of any poem that uses it, he insisted that the Bible cannot be traced to a time when its material was not shaped into a typological unity.[68] Frye gave further accent to this "figurative unity" in *The Great Code.* There, he defined typology as a mode of thought leading to a theory of historical process, to the assumption that history has meaning and that events will occur to indicate what that meaning is, to the point that they become the antitype

---

61. Auerbach, *Mimesis,* pp. 76-77.

62. Auerbach, *Mimesis,* p. 77.

63. Robertson, "The Historical Setting of Chaucer's *Book of the Duchess,*" p. 4.

64. Robertson, "The Historical Setting of Chaucer's *Book of the Duchess,*" p. 4.

65. D. W. Robertson, "Historical Criticism," in *English Institute Essays,* ed. A. S. Downer (Princeton, N.J.: Princeton University Press, 1950), p. 11.

66. Robertson, "Historical Criticism," p. 12.

67. Northrop Frye, *Anatomy of Criticism* (Princeton, N.J.: Princeton University Press, 1971), p. vii.

68. Frye, *Anatomy of Criticism,* pp. 14, 315.

of what earlier occurred.[69] Then, in language reminiscent of Auerbach, Frye referred to typology as pointing to events that are still to come, so that they contain a "vertical lift,"[70] that is, they point to future events often thought of as transcending time, thus rendering its mythology diachronic.[71] Repeating his earlier comment that typology is the only way to deal with the Bible as the major informing influence on literary symbolism,[72] Frye asserted that this method "is indicated too often and explicitly in the New Testament itself for us to be in any doubt that it is the 'right' way of reading it — 'right' in the only sense that criticism can recognize," that is, conformable to the intentionality of the book itself and the conventions it assumes and requires.[73]

The *Heilsgeschichtler*'s insistence that Bible interpretation must begin with a preliminary understanding that involves appreciation for the Bible's truth as contained in a "process," a "holy" or "salvation history," requires, more, it demands typology for its support and exposition, especially where the Old Testament is concerned. Typology, or "figurative interpretation,"[74] is twin to allegory, the principal difference being that in the latter the persons and events are imagined, invented. Adverting to the boredom evoked by contemporary exposition one critic adds that if he were to pen a catchword over the entire affair, it would have to be over the enmity toward or ignorance of the sacrament characteristic of evangelical exegesis.[75] But if it was actually the sacrament, the liturgy, that gave birth to the portrayal of the biblical events "within a world-historical context by which all members relate to each other and thus are to be viewed as belonging to or above every time,"[76] then, with all their interest in the portrayal of persons and events within a transcendent context, it was a pity that the *Heilsgeschichtler*

---

69. Northrop Frye, *The Great Code: Bible and Literature* (New York: Harcourt Brace Jovanovich, 1981), pp. 80-81.

70. Auerbach, *Mimesis*, p. 75: "*Figuram implere* . . . [to make] a connection which cannot be made in any rational way within the horizontal course of events . . . [but] solely by connecting both events vertically with the divine foreknowledge which in this way alone can plan history and yield the key to its understanding."

71. Frye, *The Great Code*, pp. 82-83.

72. Frye, *Anatomy of Criticism*, pp. 315-16.

73. Frye, *Anatomy of Criticism*, pp. 79-80.

74. "Figuraldeutung," in the original.

75. Dieter Nestle, "Über die Häresie und Langewile in der Auslegung des Neuen Testaments," *Deutsches Pfarrerblatt* 80, no. 10 (1980): 492.

76. Auerbach, *Mimesis*, p. 151; see also Auerbach's recital of "medieval Christian theater" on pp. 151-52.

proceeded to ignore its origin in the community's worship and lodged it with the academics.

Now to accommodation. In 1905 first appeared *The Days of His Flesh,* by David Smith (1866-1932) of Magee College, Londonderry. In his exposition of the "homely metaphors" of the patch and cloak, wine and wineskins (cf. Mark 2:21-22; Matt. 9:16-17; Luke 5:36-38), Smith wrote of the disaster that would follow if the old usages of Judaism were carried into the new life of the kingdom of heaven. "Nevertheless," he added, Jesus had "a generous sympathy with those who clung to their ancient traditions and had difficulty in accommodating themselves to the new order," and concluding with the line from Luke 5:39 that reads, "no one after drinking old wine desires new wine, but says, 'The old is good,'" wrote these words:

> Had the advocates of Christian liberty remembered this large-minded word of Jesus, it would have done much to soften the asperity of that bitter controversy between Judaism and Paulinism which well-nigh rent the Apostolic Church asunder.[77]

Again, at the head of an exposition of Matthew 13:52 according to which every scribe trained for the kingdom of heaven "brings out of his treasure what is new and what is old," Smith stated that Jesus "was always careful to accommodate Himself to the usages of His contemporaries," that "the originality of His teaching lay less in the revelation of new truths than in the disclosure of an undreamed of significance in truths already familiar."[78]

At the time of the printing of Smith's book eyebrows were raised. But it was merely the reiteration of an age-old position, shared by the devout and impious alike. Semler embraced it, no doubt following Sir Isaac Newton (1642-1727), but so also had Augustine and Hilary of Poitiers (ca. 300-368).[79] The principle was key to Calvin's understanding of God's self-revelation.[80] Having flamed up in the seventeenth century, debate over the position reached its zenith in the eighteenth century, condemned by the orthodox and hailed by the rationalists.

77. David Smith, *The Days of His Flesh* (London: Hodder and Stoughton, 1905), pp. 129-30.

78. Smith, *The Days of His Flesh,* p. 183.

79. See Ulrich H. J. Körner, "Akkomodation," in *Religion in Geschichte und Gegenwart* (Tübingen: Mohr, 1998), vol. 1, p. 254.

80. See the various contributors to McKim, ed., *Calvin and the Bible,* pp. 5-6, 29, 45-46, 135, 147, 248-249, 290.

No doubt, Bible interpretation could have been spared the agony over demythologizing and related methodologies if it had not succumbed to the idea of the univocal equivalence between the biblical text and the reality to which it referred. What eventuated was a literalist and fundamentalist biblicism, with calamitous results.[81] On the other hand, when adopted as a kind of epistemological axiom, accommodation led to the text's meaning anything at all. A word or two remembered from Hamann might have put the matter to rest:

> God an author! — The inspiration of this book is as great a humiliation and condescension of God as the creation of the Father and the incarnation of the Son.[82]

> God has adapted himself to the fullest, lowered himself to human inclinations and conceptions, yes, even to their prejudices and weaknesses. This superior mark of his love for mankind, of which all Holy Scripture is full, serves weak heads for scorn.[83]

Certain it is that absent comments on the scriptures in pre-critical times, the method of Bible interpretation as presently employed originated among those intent on undermining its authority. But it has been neither right nor salutary to deny the 150 years of reading the Bible in a fashion that has gained dominance in schools of the Western world. Further, it is possible to separate the method, at least that part of it that still enjoys legitimacy, from the climate of opinion that once gave rise to it. To reject the critical method spells surrender of the church's claim to any scientific basis for its exegesis. Substitution of a "self-evident biblical exposition" for the critical method only repeats a practice that had "come to grief a hundred times in the church's history from Gnosticism to every shade of fanaticism."[84]

More yet, the critical method is able to be harnessed in the service

81. See Roland Mushat Frye, "A Literary Perspective for the Criticism of the Gospels," in Miller and Hadidian, eds., *Jesus and Man's Hope*, vol. 2, p. 204.

82. Hamann, "Über die Auslegung der heiligen Schrift," in *Londoner Schriften*, ed. Oswald Bayer and Bernd Weissenborn (München: C. H. Beck, 1993), p. 59, 1-6.

83. Hamann, "Biblische Betrachtungen eines Christen," in *Londoner Schriften*, p. 68, 33-37.

84. Peter Stuhlmacher, *Historical Criticism and Theological Interpretation*, trans. Roy A. Harrisville (Philadelphia: Fortress, 1977), p. 70.

of gospel proclamation. This is what was learned from the last century's greatest interpreters. For example, Adolf Schlatter of Tübingen, damned by the liberals as a pietist whose faith in the Bible rendered him unfit for scientific work, whom the University of Berne forced to jump through more hoops than any doctoral candidate before or since due to his suspected biblicism, wrote:

> For me, faith and criticism never divided into opposites, so that at one time I would have thought in a Bible-believing way, and at another critically. Rather, I thought in critical fashion because I believed in the Bible, and believed in it because I read it critically.[85]

Somewhere here, a word needs to be said on behalf of the biblical languages. As argued above, there is no reading of scripture, no interpretation or exegesis without presuppositions, and presuppositions that do not require testing and examining to determine whether or not they are legitimate simply do not exist. In the last analysis, the one who stands between this ancient oriental volume on which our lives and sacred fortunes depend and all those in need of its message, that is, the pastor, the priest, the minister, is the last bulwark of freedom against a tyranny of the elite or of the hierarchy. The way of that freedom is through acquaintance with what Luther called the "sheath" of the Word. In face of those too ready to rob the pastor of freedom for scripture reading and interpretation, the summons of the apostle is as relevant as it once was to life under the law: "For freedom Christ has set us free. Stand firm, therefore, and do not submit again to a yoke of slavery!" The church will not live by its professorial elite or hierarchy. Only pastors and congregations can contribute to its life.

"Once more to the breach, dear friends!" — there is no understanding, no interpretation of the Bible apart from faith. Faith alone yields understanding, penetrates behind that poor child in the crib to the Savior of the world. This word will have the heart and soul, and if not, it will work despair. For in the last analysis the Bible is a self-effervescing source that does not take its credibility from anything or anyone. Its integrity is not derived; it is its own interpreter. On its own it yields understanding. On its own it gives the Spirit through whom it is understood. On its own it possesses the quality of certainty that neither feeling nor experience can

85. Adolf Schlatter, *Rückblick auf meine Lebensarbeit* (Stuttgart: Calwer Verlag, 1977), p. 83.

equal. What gives to it this great power, this effervescence, this independence and non-derivability is its witness to Jesus Christ, Lord of heaven and earth. He is its content and rules the method of its understanding.

But just as a sonata takes its revenge on someone without an ear for music, so the scriptures of Old and New Testaments wreak fury on whoever refuses to break with old cognitions, the old moralities, who will not be renewed. The evidence for it mounts higher every day, in all that confused prattle of interpreters. If there is no repentance and belief in the testimony laid down in this book, it will judge one to inconsequence, render the reading of it, the interpretation of it, the preaching of it a comic spectacle to the world to which it believed it had to be adjusted.

But repentance and belief or not, somewhere, in some corner of the world, someone will always take up this book and read. Heinz Cassirer (1903-79), Oxford don, celebrated son of a celebrated father, at the tender age of fifty got himself a Bible that threw in doubt the axiom on which he had built his entire life and career, that is, the axiom birthed by Kant that the capacity to act so as to render one's activity a maxim for universal behavior is given at birth. He read in the prophets who convinced him that such could occur only by way of a miracle, and forcing his way through to the New Testament read that this had in fact occurred with Jesus.[86] Cassirer was baptized, abandoned his university chair, and spent the remainder of his days reading Hebrew and Greek. The Bible will have its way because of the Word of the God it attests.

---

86. See Heinz Cassirer, *Grace and Law: St. Paul, Kant, and the Hebrew Prophets* (Grand Rapids: Eerdmans, 1988).

Index of Names

Frye, Roland Mushat, 281-83, 323, 329, 349
Fuchs, Ernst, 316
Funk, Robert, 198, 213, 304

Gadamer, Hans-Georg, 35, 77, 79-80, 116, 271, 288, 295, 309, 314, 330, 334, 342
Garrison, William Lloyd, 159
Gass, J. C., 113
Gay, Peter, 46-47, 64, 111
Gerhard, Johann, 35
Gerhardsson, Birger, 285-86
Gesenius, Wilhelm, 149, 161
Goethe, J. W. von, 96, 241
Gogarten, Friedrich, 242
Goodspeed, Edgar Johnson, 202, 242
Gottschick, Johannes, 183
Grant, Frederick Clifton, 5, 15, 225-30, 254-56, 258, 266, 268, 324
Green, R. P. H., 9
Green, William Henry, 199
Gregory VII, 42-43
Greimas, A. J., 292
Griesbach, Johann Jakob, 123
Grimm, Jacob, 131, 284-85
Grondin, Jean, 330, 341
Grynaeus, Simon, 33
Guardini, Roman, 280
Gunkel, Hermann, 183, 196

Haikola, Lauri, 37-38
Hamann, Johann Georg, 43, 82-94, 118, 139, 253-54, 256-58, 260-61, 265, 331, 348
Hamor, sons of, 23
Harless, G. C. A. von, 132
Harnack, Adolf von, 174, 180, 183, 251, 304
Harper, William Rainey, 198-200, 202-4, 254, 266-67
Hartknock, Johann Friedrich, 83
Hegel, G. F. W., ix, 85, 88, 112, 126, 130-31, 173, 297, 342
Hegesippus, 27

Heidegger, Martin, 77, 116, 189, 197, 271, 342
Heim, Karl, 300
Heitmüller, Wilhelm, 183
Hengel, Martin, 296
Hengstenberg, E. W., 126-27, 132-33, 137, 152, 161, 312
Henry, Matthew, 138
Herder, Johann Gottfried, 83-85, 190, 284
Hermes, 1-2, 99
Herod, 4, 18, 94, 318, 324
Herrmann, Wilhelm, 174, 176, 183
Hesiod, viii
Hesychius, 43
Hilary of Poitiers, 347
Hillel, 4
Hirsch, Emanuel, 44, 73, 80, 103-4, 123
Hitchcock, Edward, 156
Hitler, Adolf, 182, 238, 316
Hodge, Alexander Archibald, 162, 168
Hodge, Charles, 158, 161-72, 224, 250, 254, 257, 259, 265, 324
Hoffman, Nelly, 174
Hoffmann-Krayer, Eduard, 283
Hofmann, C. K. von, 190, 241, 250
Homer, 1-4, 226
Honecker, Erich, 25
Hug, Johann Leonhard, 122-23
Hugh of St. Victor, 12
Humboldt, Alexander von, 161, 284
Hume, David, 83, 153, 221
Hyperius, Andreas, 37

Inge, William, 250
Irenaeus, 43, 250
Isaac, 178, 274
Ishmael, 178, 274

Jacob, 178-79, 274
Jäger, Johann Wolfgang, 39
James, William, 299, 305, 315, 333-34
Jenkin, Robert, 64
Jenson, Robert W., 319
Jeremiah, 23, 97, 326
Jerome, 34

Index of Scripture References